PRAISE FOR *Chaplaincy and Sp[i]*
Twenty-First Century: An I

"This timely book looks at the evolution of chaplaincy as a profession; the academic and clinical education that prepares chaplains for ministry within interfaith, multicultural contexts; and the diverse identities of today's chaplains. It is an exceptional resource for anyone interested in understanding the unique role chaplains embrace as spiritual leaders."

CHAPLAIN TAHARA AKMAL, clinical pastoral education manager at MedStar Washington Hospital Center and ACPE certified educator

"This wonderful book provides perhaps the clearest picture yet of *what* it means to be a chaplain in the twenty-first century, *how* to be a chaplain, and *why* chaplaincy deserves a central place among the professions of caregiving. It should be essential reading for not only chaplains in training and in practice but any caregiver committed to healing and wholeness."

KENNETH PARGAMENT, author of *Spiritually Integrated Psychotherapy: Understanding and Addressing the Sacred*

"A unique and excellent introduction to the work and training of professional chaplains, this textbook directly addresses contemporary issues, particularly with regard to changing demographics and the increasingly diverse contexts in which chaplains find need for their work in institutions and communities of all kinds. On a broader level, the authors shine a light on the ubiquity and significance of matters pertaining to the spiritual, religious, and meaning-making aspects of human experience."

JOYCE MERCER, associate dean for academic affairs and Horace Bushnell Professor of Practical Theology and Pastoral Care, Yale Divinity School

"We are living in harrowing times. Increasingly, chaplains and spiritual care practitioners serve a first-responder role for those in crisis. This book is a must-read for those invested in understanding the nuances, strengths, and challenges facing this burgeoning ecosystem of care, including the wise, generous people who constitute it."

REV. JENNIFER BAILEY, author of *To My Beloveds: Letters on Faith, Race, Loss and Radical Hope* and founder and executive director of Faith Matters Network

"In identifying and explicating key core competencies shared by chaplains functioning across a variety of settings, this book is an excellent resource for a profession seeking to be responsive to the rapidly changing religious landscape of the twenty-first century and the accompanying shifts to the spiritual care needs of persons they serve."

JASON NIEUWSMA, Duke University School of Medicine and Vanderbilt University Divinity School

"What does a chaplain do? Seems a simple question, but the answer is far from it. Thanks to the careful and diligent work of Wendy Cadge, Shelly Rambo, and the volume contributors, *Chaplaincy and Spiritual Care in the Twenty-First Century* offers long-needed and comprehensive insight into this valuable vocation."

REAR ADMIRAL MARGARET GRUN KIBBEN, chaplain of the U.S. House of Representatives

"Addressing specific cross-context competencies, the history of chaplaincy in the United States, and the importance of a wide variety of trainings for different contexts, this volume breaks down silos between different types of chaplaincy and demonstrates how and why chaplaincy is the future of organized religious and spiritual life in America."

THE REVEREND DONNA S. MOTE, PH.D., Episcopal priest and chaplain, St. Paul's Episcopal Church, Key West, Florida

Chaplaincy and Spiritual Care in the Twenty-First Century

CHAPLAINCY *and* SPIRITUAL CARE

in the Twenty-First Century

AN INTRODUCTION

Edited by WENDY CADGE *and* SHELLY RAMBO

THE UNIVERSITY OF NORTH CAROLINA PRESS

Chapel Hill

*Publication of this book was assisted in part by a generous
subvention from the Henry Luce Foundation.*

© 2022 The University of North Carolina Press

Designed by Jamison Cockerham
Set in Scala
by Kristina Kachele Design, llc

Cover photograph courtesy of Randall Armor.

Manufactured in the United States of America

The University of North Carolina Press has been a
member of the Green Press Initiative since 2003.

LIBRARY OF CONGRESS CATALOGING-IN-PUBLICATION DATA
Names: Cadge, Wendy, editor. | Rambo, Shelly, editor.
Title: Chaplaincy and spiritual care in the twenty-first century :
an introduction / edited by Wendy Cadge and Shelly Rambo.
Description: Chapel Hill : The University of North Carolina Press,
[2022] | Includes bibliographical references and index.
Identifiers: LCCN 2021052603 | ISBN 9781469667591 (cloth) |
ISBN 9781469667607 (paperback) | ISBN 9781469667614 (ebook)
Subjects: LCSH: Pastoral care. | Psychology, Religious. | Clergy. | Chaplains.
Classification: LCC BV4011.3 .C425 2022 | DDC 253—dc23/eng/20211130
LC record available at https://lccn.loc.gov/2021052603

CONTENTS

FIGURES & TABLES

Chaplaincy and Spiritual Care in the Twenty-First Century

An Introduction

WENDY CADGE *and* SHELLY RAMBO

Debra, a middle-aged white chaplain who serves the homeless outside a major American city, may appear at first glance to have little in common with chaplains in healthcare, the military, prisons, and other more traditional places chaplains work. She did research about homeless women as an undergraduate, raised children who are now adults, and started volunteering with the pastoral care department at a local hospital at the same time she joined a Unitarian Universalist congregation. "One time I just came from this amazing visit with somebody [at the hospital]," she explained in an interview, "and I said to the chaplain, 'Is there a place that you can learn more about this?'" The chaplain sent Debra to her mentor, and a few months later Debra was enrolled in theological school. She took every pastoral care class the school offered and did field education along the way at the small nonprofit where she now works. The organization hired her part-time while she was finishing her degree, and she is now its director. Debra is not a "formal chaplain," in her words, "because I don't have four units of clinical pastoral education," or CPE (an acronym used throughout this book). Her time is spent doing "spiritual companioning and accompaniment" while walking the streets, visiting local homeless shelters and soup kitchens, talking with careseekers, going with people to appointments, offering meditation or Bible study or a spiritual arts program, and otherwise being of support to the unhoused in her city.

Debra's work—and her path to it—is quite different from that of Mark, an African American National Guard chaplain, who works just a few miles away. He was serving a local parish when he received a letter in the mail saying the Guard was looking for chaplains. Family connections in the military led him to explore the idea and eventually to join the Guard as a chaplain on a part-time basis. He moved into leadership and today oversees all Guard chaplains in the state—work he carries out in addition to his weekly church responsibilities. "I will be doing an Ash Wednesday service here in a few days," he explained in an interview. "Sometimes I meet with individuals or couples, and I provide pastoral care and support to the chaplains. . . . I also set the training plans for how the chaplains and chaplain assistants will continue to be trained. . . . And I help explain the chaplaincy to senior leadership." This explanation is based in the First Amendment to the U.S. Constitution. In his words, "The chaplaincy is tied to the First Amendment and the free exercise of religion, which is complicated. . . . People might be spiritual and not religious, which would be most senior leaders that I'm talking to . . . so I have to explain what chaplaincy is—that it is inextricably connected to religion, although we're there for people regardless of whether they're religious or not." Much of his work, he says, is "being a cheerleader for them [chaplains], to the senior leadership, so that they can continue to grasp what it is that we continue to bring to the table." Mark completed CPE before being ordained, and he did additional chaplaincy training as part of his professional development in the military.

....

The *Oxford English Dictionary* defines chaplains along very narrow historical lines, calling a chaplain a "clergyman who conducts religious services in the private chapel" of elite leaders or in other private or otherwise constricted spaces and institutions. While some chaplains conduct religious services today, such services are no longer the marker of chaplains' work that this definition implies.

....

Debra and Mark are two of thousands of chaplains from a range of religious and racial and ethnic backgrounds who work in diverse settings across the United States. Their educational paths vary, as do their levels of professionalization. But there is something about their work that is shared: They are trained to meet persons and communities in moments of pain and crisis. They advocate and accompany. They bring a quality of **presence** and care to persons at various life stages and in situations of crisis. While there is no commonly agreed-upon definition of the role or responsibilities of chaplains in the United States and beyond, chaplains themselves offer powerful testimonies to the work that they do. In interviews with chaplaincy educators, they use phrases such as "journey with people in crisis," "bring God into the room," "mediate transcendent experience," "represent the holy," "hold space and work with uncertainty," and "embody compassion." When Amy Greene, director of spiritual care at the Cleveland Clinic, was asked what she thinks people need from chaplains, she responded, "People want someone to see their total pain." Chaplains appeal to a quality of being, rather than simply of doing, that suggests that they tap into currents of life that may surface only in times of need and distress. They develop skills of deep listening, of advocacy, of bridging community, and of navigating conflict that set them apart from other care providers.

This work is often difficult to translate in public spaces. Because of this, it is often invisible and behind the scenes. Even the term "chaplain" can hide the work. In her book *A Ministry of Presence: Chaplaincy, Spiritual Care, and the Law*, religious studies scholar Winnifred Fallers Sullivan calls chaplains and spiritual care providers "secular priests" or "ministers without portfolios," arguing that chaplains are "strangely necessary figure[s] . . . in negotiating the public life of religion today."[1] Chaplaincy has long been guided by rich metaphors rooted in visions of the world drawn from sacred wisdom traditions. This is "home language" in religious settings, but it is often ill-defined or misunderstood in the settings in which chaplains work. Identifying as a "chaplain" can be a stumbling block to the work of care. When one chaplain who interviewed for a project in Boston first approached patients as part of her chaplaincy training, she had to explain the title on her name tag. As a woman raised in a religious tradition that excluded women from formal religious leadership, Julia did not fit the image some had of a chaplain. Caricatures of chaplains (such as Father Mulcahy from the TV show *M*A*S*H*) still hover over the field and no longer reflect the range of people who are chaplains. Recognizing the Christian history of the term "chaplain," some institutions now call chaplains "spiritual care providers" or "spiritual caregivers," which makes definitional questions for some even more confusing.[2] Now a pediatric chaplain, Julia says that part of being a chaplain is reframing the work—both for herself and for those she encounters.

In 2020, the COVID-19 pandemic and renewed attention to racial injustice and inequality in the United States made the work chaplains do more visible. In the *New York Times*, the *Washington Post*, *Newsweek*, and other national media sources, they were profiled running toward the dying rather than away, supporting anxious healthcare providers, and communicating with family members not permitted to be with their loved ones, even in their final moments. These crises brought military chaplains—more accustomed to working with mass causalities—into dialogue with healthcare chaplains quickly adapting to multiple deaths and brought the work of social movement and police chaplains into the national conversations. They shone a light on the common issues of fear, grief, trauma, and uncertainty that chaplains engage in, whether working with people in the streets, in the military, in healthcare organizations, or in protest movements.

Chaplains today work in a range of institutions, including airports, community settings, disaster zones, fire and police departments, higher education, healthcare, the military, prisons, ports, sports teams, the Veterans Administration, and other workplaces. In a 2019 survey, 20 percent of people in the United States reported having contact with a chaplain in the past two years.

The aim of this volume is to feature the work of chaplains and to offer a resource for those exploring and preparing to be chaplains. We do so by naming three broad areas of **competency** important for all chaplains, regardless of sector or level of professionalization. These areas intentionally cut across some of the traditional lines of sector and religious tradition that have historically framed the work of chaplaincy, as well as across chaplaincy education and practice. We understand these three competencies as provisional placeholders that may assist educators in making important—needed—shifts in education to better match the realities of the work on the ground. We intend the volume as a teaching tool to be used in theological schools and clinical settings and invite educators to consider how they are building skills and competencies in these three areas. While there are more detailed competencies in place in many sectors, particularly healthcare and the military, this volume attempts to foster a conversation across sectors for the first time. We encourage these conversations in parallel with conversations about the structural and historical impediments, especially in North America, that have led more white male Protestants than any other group to become chaplains and about the need to support more accessible and equitable paths into the field for all people. We do this work, as editors, from unique vantage points, as neither of us is a chaplain or a clinical educator. Cadge is a sociologist who has conducted research about

The chaplain's office space and a kneeler sit opposite a movable wall at the New England Seafarers Mission in Boston. The wooden partition allows for privacy, as needed, in this shared space. *Photo credit: Randall Armor.*

chaplains in a broad range of settings, and Rambo is a theologian who was motivated to engage more deeply around chaplaincy based on her experiences in the classroom. We come to this work as sympathetic and invested outsiders who have been engaged in years-long conversations with chaplains and those who educate them.

To facilitate a shift from conversations about what chaplains are to what they do and to best prepare people from diverse backgrounds for that work, we invite conversation about the following three competencies we believe are central for all chaplains. First, chaplains need to be able to facilitate practices of meaning making and to navigate worldviews in public settings. This entails being able to interpret situations and experiences by appealing to systems of meaning that align with spiritual and religious traditions. They must bring different angles of vision when they assess questions of meaning and purpose. Steeped in traditions that articulate the value of the human person, they are often engaged in dignifying work, so they need to be conversant in texts and practices that bring meaning and value to the human lives they touch. They should possess basic skills in **religious literacy** and be

Chaplain Ylisse Bess is the interfaith chaplain at Beth Israel Deaconess Medical Center, Boston. *Photo credit: Austin B. Washington.*

A Hallway Encounter

On my way to a patient visit, I am pulled aside by a self-identified Puerto Rican/Afro-Latina nurse for what our spiritual care department calls "hallway encounter" visits (while visits that are counted as any patient or family visit are recorded on the patient's chart, "hallway encounters" are often with staff and thus not formally documented). The nurse wants to discuss the COVID vaccine, her anxieties about it, and her awareness of how Puerto Rican people in particular, and Black and Latinx folks in general, have experienced medical racism, and she is worried about whether she can trust the institution she works for to resist medical racism when it comes to distributing, administering, and monitoring the vaccine. "What if I get sick from the vaccine? I don't know that I can even trust my colleagues to take care of me if I'm admitted." We have this encounter in the busy hallway but find a corner that offers the most privacy we can hope for amid her full day. The nurse discloses xenophobic and racist comments she's heard from her colleagues just this week. I listen. I give eye contact. I shift my body language to indicate I have the time and energy to listen. I believe her. And I normalize her experience and further articulate how much sense it makes to distrust a medical system that has killed so many Black and Latinx people. She expresses gratitude for being heard and believed, because "they [her white colleagues and hospital administration] don't get it." She goes on to say, "I'm going to get it [the vaccine]. It's like, the nurse part of me says, 'Of course!' but the Afro-Latina part is a little skeptical." We laugh, she thanks me for listening, we discuss the vaccine more, and we talk about the opportunities to learn more about it and opportunities for us [people of color] to have this conversation amongst ourselves.

In healthcare chaplaincy, so much focus is on patients and families or on moral distress in nurses regarding challenging cases. I find there is a gap in care to the staff of color who experience the same stressors as their white counterparts, but in the words of one Black nurse, "I have the same stress as the white people, but mine is doubled because of racism from patients, team members, and the institution." By being accessible, listening, affirming, and carving out space during a busy day in a busy hallway, I become a more trustworthy chaplain colleague, a colleague who recognizes how racial trauma manifests in distrust of racist medical systems that fail to take responsibility for racial disparities created by systemic racism that the institution upholds. By listening, I contribute to creating space to acknowledge the weight of the myth of white supremacy on the spirit.

• •

versed in interfaith practices as they work with caregivers and in workplace institutions. They must be adept in identifying aspects of religion and culture and interpreting how persons and communities articulate their values and sources of meaning. This also requires the ability to translate between sacred and secular discourses with the end goal of providing effective care.

Second, chaplains need a set of **interpersonal competencies** and skills in their work. Drawing from theories of human development from the psychological and social sciences, chaplains meet people in crisis situations and need to be aware of the range of human experiences, often related to loss, grief, and trauma. While a "ministry of presence" has become shorthand for the work of chaplains, we emphasize the significance of spiritual integration as an ongoing set of practices that enable chaplains to show up fully, to listen, and to respond to the needs of others without imposition. Because chaplains are often required to make immediate and intimate connections with those seeking care, they need to be able to build trust, embody **empathy**, and differentiate between self and other quickly.

Third, chaplains need skills to navigate systems and organizations. As spiritual caregivers, chaplains work within complex organizations that have reporting systems, bureaucratic processes, structures, and ways of knowing that are reflective of the mission of the organization. Knowing the home

A sign in the Massachusetts Correctional Institution in Norfolk showing symbols of Islam, Judaism, and Christianity as it points toward the "Religious Corridor" of the prison. *Photo credit: Randall Armor.*

languages, policies, and practices of an organization will give chaplains a clear sense of how to move and be effective within it and how to support those in different positions within it. Studies of chaplains show that, almost without exception, they serve not only careseekers but also the staff of the organizations where they work. Understanding the positionality of these different people is crucial for chaplains to be present and supporting them as individuals embedded in a common system. Chaplains also need organizational skills of team building and partnership, including the skills of negotiation, conflict mediation, and ethical reasoning and practices of restorative justice.

As representatives of religion in public settings, chaplains are called upon by authorities within their institutions, such as military commanders or ethics committees, to provide counsel on moral matters. Although some, such as community chaplains, work in less structured settings, all need to discern their authority to speak to current situations and to advocate for persons and communities. As designated leaders, they create public spaces to hold pain, to alter perspectives, and to infuse meaning and purpose into the ordinary and the everyday. This requires the ability to create and lead

rituals, both formal and improvisational. Neither this work nor educational preparation for it is new.

A BRIEF HISTORY OF TRAINING CHAPLAINS AND RECENT GROWTH

Theological institutions, historically and at present, are the primary degree-granting institutions for clergy and professional chaplains. Historically, the master of divinity (MDiv) degree was considered the gold standard for religious professionals and was required for entrance into ordained Christian ministry. Most theological schools trained clergy for leadership within their specific religious traditions.[3] Chaplains were trained much like local clergy. Few theological schools had a separate curriculum—or even classes—aimed at students interested in becoming chaplains. All students pursuing the MDiv were historically required to take core courses in pastoral care, which trained graduates to provide religiously informed care and counsel to parishioners. Most theological schools had a pastoral theologian on the faculty, and some developed counseling programs to train clinically competent clergy.[4] Chaplains then went through processes of endorsement by their religious organizations for specialized ministry. In most settings, they were understood to represent their traditions, even outside of tradition-specific institutions.[5]

Clinical pastoral education—a form of supervised training now completed by many chaplains in addition to their coursework in theological schools—emerged in the 1920s and today exists alongside theological education with a largely healthcare focus. Protestant theological educators in the 1920s started the CPE movement in response to growing ideas about psychology, personal development, and pastoral care in the broader culture. Formal training programs that followed this approach were developed in the 1930s and 1940s.[6]

CPE programs are presently located within clinical settings, most often hospitals, and provide on-site education and experience in spiritual care. One-unit and longer residency programs offer participants opportunities to practice skills of ministry and gain experience in the field of chaplaincy. Participants are immersed in individual and group processes of reflection that are supervised by professional educators. In most sectors of chaplaincy, at least one unit of CPE training (twelve weeks) is required. In Level 1, participants learn the fundamentals of spiritual care. Those pursuing healthcare chaplaincy continue to Level 2 to build upon the fundamentals and move

Ritual in the Time of COVID-19

Imam Bilal Ansari is the assistant vice president for Campus Engagement at Williams College, Williamstown, Massachusetts, and codirector of Islamic chaplaincy at Hartford Seminary, Hartford, Connecticut.

As a former Muslim prison chaplain, I am always just one phone call away from pastoral care as a Black shepherd of Black sheep. Though I hadn't seen Jundullah in seventeen years, I was asked to take responsibility for his burial. This request obligated me to oversee his burial rites, to raise the funds for it, and to provide pastoral care to close family members. In a day, we raised the money, arranged a viewing for the family, and finalized the restricted funeral rites.

At the viewing, a white woman, veiled and masked, stood over the body of this Black man who lay wrapped in the Muslim burial shroud—three white sheets I had perfumed and wrapped him in, leaving only his face visible. A formerly incarcerated Hispanic Muslim, Tomás, had helped me prepare his body for burial under COVID restrictions earlier in the morning.[1] Even though he was dead, I could not help but recall this Black man's beautiful, captivating smile. The white woman offered that she was his parole officer as she walked solemnly toward me, removing her veil but keeping her mask on. There was a gold cross at the nape of her neck. As she tucked away her scarf, I wondered about her sad disposition, for this could not be the first time a parolee of hers, who just got home, suddenly passed away. There was genuine remorse and regret in her voice as she shared her brief memories and why this Black life mattered to her. Her eyes questioned, "How could this happen to this Black man? I did not expect this to happen to him," as she asked me, "Are you Jundullah's chaplain? Jundullah loved Islam." I replied, "Yes, I am. And, yes, he did love Islam."

I ignored her real theological question, just as she ignored the structural racism factors.

She had just found him housing and had been excited to tell him. Her frustration over losing someone whom she had hope for was palpable. But housing was not his only challenge. The social and psychological pressure and the invisible knee on the neck of Jundullah had crushed him quickly.[2] As his chaplain, I saw the knee; as his parole officer, she could not. Socially distanced in isolation, Jundullah spent many years in segregation, and it took its toll. I began remembering Jundullah's joy as he proudly shared pictures of his daughter, Christina, when she was entering kindergarten.[3] Christina entered the room, and it brought me peace to proudly serve this Black family unencumbered by theodicy questions but as a calm Black shepherd focusing on Black joy.

1. Jianhui (Jane) Xiong, Nazila Isgandarova, and Amy Elizabeth Panton, "COVID-19 Demands Theological Reflection: Buddhist, Muslim, and Christian Perspectives on the Present Pandemic," *International Journal of Practical Theology* 24, no. 1 (2020): 5–28, doi:10.1515/ijpt-2020–0039.

2. Sasha Mital, Jessica Wolff, and Jennifer J. Carroll, "The Relationship between Incarceration History and Overdose in North America: A Scoping Review of the Evidence," *Drug and Alcohol Dependence* 213 (August 2020), doi: 10.1016 /j.drugalcdep.2020.108088.

3. Pamela Cooper-White, *Shared Wisdom: Use of the Self in Pastoral Care and Counseling* (Minneapolis: Fortress Press, 2003), 126.

• •

toward greater depth of knowledge and experience.[7] After completing four units of CPE, individuals can work through the process of board certification, established and administered by accrediting bodies. To be a board certified chaplain in healthcare, one needs a graduate-level education in theology, four units of CPE, and endorsement from one's religious body.

Theological schools and CPE programs developed alongside one another—in more ongoing conversation in some years than in others. Within theological schools, chaplaincy education also developed and changed in close connection with the fields of pastoral theology and pastoral care and counseling.[8] Pastoral theologians narrate shifts from clerical models of pastor as shepherding the flock, rooted in biblical imagery, to models of the clinically informed minister, equipped with psychological theories of human development and psychodynamic and systems theories. At the turn of the twenty-first century, pastoral theologians turned attention to the "living human web," widening the scope of care to consider the social, political, and global forces impacting individuals and shaping identities.[9] Pastoral theology became a robustly interdisciplinary field, expanding chaplaincy education to focus on various intersections of the individual and the system, the personal and the political.[10]

Theological educators are held to learning outcomes provided by their institutions and degree programs and set by the Association of Theological Schools. Clinical educators follow standards established by the Association for Clinical Pastoral Education (or ACPE, another acronym used throughout this book). Curricular shifts in pastoral theology, pastoral care and counseling, and CPE education have taken place in silos. Avenues of communication between the settings are currently indirect, even nonexistent. Students move from theological degree programs to CPE programs, but it is unclear whether the feedback loops are in place for educators to effectively work together to achieve commonly recognized competencies. Multiple layers of bureaucratic process are also increasingly seen as confusing by students and potential chaplains.

In the midst of this—and of broader declines in enrollments in theological schools—growing numbers of theological schools started degree programs specifically focused on chaplaincy and spiritual care. The oldest specialized chaplaincy program within graduate theological education—as opposed to alongside or subsequent to it—was established in 1988 at Pentecostal Theological Seminary in Cleveland, Tennessee. Since then, the number of these programs has grown, particularly since 2000. Today about a quarter of theological schools have degree programs (mostly MDiv or master of arts degrees) that include specific focus on chaplaincy and spiritual care. Interest in CPE is also growing. Between 2005 and 2015 the number of student units of CPE completed increased by 25 percent.[11] Growing demand motivates the three areas of broad competency that structure this volume, which we hope will encourage a more holistic, less siloed approach to training.

The curriculums of chaplaincy-related degree programs in theological schools are diverse in form and content with no commonly agreed-upon learning objectives, skills, or competencies across the programs. The simplest do little more than introduce students to the profession of chaplaincy and steer them toward existing courses in the curriculum. Newer Muslim and Buddhist programs have tried to rework the MDiv from Muslim and

Buddhist perspectives. About half of the schools require CPE—usually two units. In interviews, the faculty in theological schools who designed these programs emphasized three broad areas they focus on in their teaching: learning to work in a multifaith environment, learning to help students think and reflect theologically and use that perspective to address suffering, and developing an identity and authority of the chaplain. Educators who lead CPE programs—a professional group distinct from theological educators— talk in interviews about helping students learn practical, on-the-ground skills and sometimes wishing the students came from theological schools with better personal and academic preparation. Theological and clinical educators are not, generally, operating from or educating toward a common understanding of what makes chaplains effective, even as they respond to the same changing contextual factors.[12]

The events of 9/11 also clearly impacted chaplaincy education, with literatures in trauma and **moral injury** becoming part of the theological school curriculum.[13] The religious identities of chaplains and care recipients came to the forefront, as did the dominance of—and slow movement away from— Christian models in the education and delivery systems of spiritual care.[14] Demographic changes, including growing numbers of people who are not religiously affiliated or involved in local congregations, also affect both sets of educators and, more importantly, the people they are training chaplains to engage with on a daily basis. One of the most significant shifts is captured in the titular move from "pastoral care" to "spiritual care" and, in some settings, in a renaming of chaplains to "spiritual care providers."

A NEW COLLABORATIVE APPROACH: AN INVITATION

It is in this context that, with our colleagues, we offer this volume as an invitation to think about the work and educational preparation for chaplains across the settings and silos in which they work and are trained. This conversation brings into sustained dialogue theological educators and clinical educators who train chaplains as well as social scientists to lay the groundwork for spiritual care education in the future. It focuses exclusively on chaplaincy education in theological schools and clinical training programs, primarily CPE. Theological institutions are the best prepared to offer this training, we argue, even as they have struggled to keep up with rapid changes in American religious demographics, because they remain the primary educators of religious professionals. That said, many of the training models at theological schools and the cost of such an education are not broadly accessible and do not effectively correspond to the skills that new chaplains need in order to be effective or to the realities of the people they serve. We intend this volume as a map and invitation to educational and institutional change.

In this work, and in our conversations with authors and others in chaplaincy, we are clear that the best approach moving forward is collaborative and multi-sectoral. To most effectively address the spiritual needs of a changing demographic, we need to be in communication with the chaplains doing the work, with the educators preparing them for it, and with the social scientists and historians who can help us see this historical moment more clearly and think creatively about the pipelines, institutions, and delivery systems.

••••••••••••••••••••••••••••••

The Chaplaincy Innovation Lab developed four case studies, available on its website, to further teaching and learning about meaning-making, interpersonal, and organizational competencies for chaplains. Check them out at https://chaplaincyinnovation.org

••••••••••••••••••••••••••••••

We extend this invitation to think about the work and educational preparation for chaplains because we believe *there is a growing role for chaplains in North American religious leadership given shifting religious demographics.* While many people historically sought counsel from leaders in places of worship that reflected shared beliefs, shifts in religious life suggest that this kind of support—if it continues—will be provided differently.[15] Fewer people, including a third of those under the age of thirty, are not affiliated with local religious organizations, and chaplains are positioned to meet them where they are, as they are, in the midst of difficult life events. In a survey conducted in March 2019, 20 percent of the American public reported having contact with a chaplain in the last two years—just over half in healthcare organizations.[16]

As noted above, chaplains have been present historically in such institutions as the military, federal prisons, Veterans Affairs, higher education, healthcare organizations, and many workplaces. They are emerging in new spaces like social movement organizations, community groups, social service organizations, and veterinary clinics and are now deployed with every Red Cross Disaster team. In their important, often overlooked, work—deployed with members of the armed forces, praying with patients before they enter surgery, and counseling those in the criminal justice system—chaplains encounter people in existentially fraught moments and are in unique positions to comfort, support, and console. Many of these people do not have relationships with local religious leaders and do not receive spiritual care outside of these encounters.

To consider how chaplains can be best prepared for their work today, we begin in the first part of this volume by looking historically and contextually. Historian Ronit Y. Stahl offers a history of chaplaincy in the United States, and sociologist Taylor Paige Winfield explores the policy context for the work of chaplains, comparing and contrasting the mandates and current educational preparation for it. The next three parts focus broadly on three competencies—meaning-making, interpersonal, and organizational. The authors in each part are theological and clinical educators. The volume concludes with reflections on demand and next steps.

This simple structure pushes against the real challenges that confront the work of chaplains and spiritual care providers going forward. We know it is difficult to move from sector/silo thinking to cross-sector thinking and to move from tradition-based models of training and education toward a profession-based model. There is no agreement about the key skills and competencies chaplains need to do this work. And there are more than twenty different organizations offering certification in chaplaincy, with little to no agreement among them on what one needs to demonstrate to complete such certification. We do not know enough about what people who work with chaplains expect from them.[17] There are serious race and ethnic disparities in care provision and chaplaincy representation. And the term "chaplain" bears the weight of its Christian history. We join the authors in continuing to name these challenges and in collaborating toward ways of doing the work of chaplaincy and spiritual care that are accessible and ethically appropriate to all. Will you join us?

PART ONE

Background and Context

CHAPTER ONE

Chaplaincy in the United States: A Short History

RONIT Y. STAHL

ABSTRACT *This chapter offers a concise overview of the history of chaplaincy and spiritual care in the United States. I consider this history in light of the American separation of religion and state and of the settings—the military, federal prisons, and the Veterans Administration—where chaplains are required. I also explore places like higher education, healthcare, ports and airports, and community contexts where chaplaincy has been present but optional. I show growing diversity in who serves as chaplains and the settings where they work as well as how the profession remains young and in transition.*

INTRODUCTION

When the COVID-19 pandemic hit the United States in earnest in March 2020, AdventistHealth chaplain Ney Ramirez—like other hospital chaplains across the country—redefined the scope of his work. Rather than stepping into hospital rooms with patients and meeting families face-to-face, he supported patients and hospital staff at a distance.[1] Months later, and only three days into her new job as the chaplain of the U.S. House of Representatives, Retired Rear Admiral Margaret G. Kibben comforted legislators when supporters of then president Donald Trump stormed the Capitol. Drawing on her combat experience, she engaged in a "ministry of walking," circulating among lawmakers to comfort, pray, and reduce stress. Days later, she described how that situation "confirms why there is a chaplain here in the House and why that's so important. It's not related to a particular faith tradition, it's that there is somebody here who comes alongside in this moment."[2]

While the specifics vary, chaplains have long played these roles in settings across the United States. One hundred years ago in Newport News, Virginia, a chaplain was engaged in "waging a noble warfare"—according to a sailors' magazine—against "the vampires of the waterfront," or the crimps who took advantage of sailors by ensnaring them, through liquor, gambling debt, ladies, violence, and even kidnapping.[3] Port chaplains established inns where seafarers could stay in port and fostered community apart from alcohol and gambling. On college campuses in the late nineteenth and early twentieth centuries, university chaplains tried to instill morals in students, often assuaging the concerns of parents that institutions of higher education lacked religion and, without that religion, were devoid of morality.[4]

This chapter offers a short synthetic history of chaplaincy and spiritual care in the United States. Serving in hospitals and prisons, ports and universities, chaplains have long histories—often at the margins of institutions, where they are frequently overlooked. I briefly summarize that history in the context of the American separation of religion and state and in the settings—the military, federal prisons, and the Veterans Administration—where chaplains are required today. I also consider the Christian origin of the concept and ways it has—and has not—been adapted by and for people from other religious backgrounds, including none. Winnifred Fallers Sullivan calls chaplains "ministers without portfolios" who are "strangely necessary . . . religiously and legally speaking, in negotiating the public life of religion today."[5] I explore how clergy came to these roles and offer important historical context for those working and considering working in chaplaincy and spiritual care today.

EARLY YEARS, WELL-ESTABLISHED SETTINGS

"There can be no doubt that the practice of opening legislative sessions with prayer has become part of the fabric of our society," wrote Chief Justice Warren Burger in 1983. "To invoke divine guidance on a public body entrusted with making the laws is not, in these circumstances, a violation of the Establishment Clause; it is simply a tolerable acknowledgment of beliefs widely held among the people of this country."[6] As Burger indicated in this

Rear Admiral Margaret Grun Kibben is the chaplain of the U.S. House of Representatives as of January 3, 2021. *Photo credit: Laura Hatcher Photography.*

The Chaplain Keeps Prayer in the House

Early in our country's establishment, on September 7, 1774, the Continental Congress began with a prayer offered by a local Episcopal rector from Philadelphia. On May 1, 1789, in one of its first acts, the House elected the Reverend William Linn as the official chaplain of the House. Since Reverend Linn's appointment, for over two hundred years the House chaplain has continued the tradition of opening each day's proceedings with a prayer.

This honor is one of several official duties, which can be identified as prayer, presence, and service. In addition to participating at the legislative sessions, the chaplain offers prayers at official congressional functions and many events occurring on and off Capitol Hill. The chaplain is intentionally present and accessible to members and staff for pastoral care and for support in meeting religiously based congressional staff needs and in times of crisis, sickness, or celebration. The chaplain can often be found on the House floor, in committee hearings, and in the hallways, coming alongside members and staff to provide encouragement and counsel, without discrimination based on party, policy, or religious affiliation. The chaplain's office serves members and staff by providing prayer opportunities; assisting in the observation of religious holidays; facilitating memorial services, wedding planning, baptisms, and other significant milestones; offering talks on religious topics; and sharing information on local religious services.

....

Supreme Court decision about legislative prayer, congressional chaplains had existed since the founding of the American republic.

When the Continental Congress opened its sessions in 1774, Rev. Jacob Duché, rector of Christ Episcopal Church in Philadelphia, provided opening prayers. Not all delegates to the First Continental Congress (or all religious leaders in the early United States) supported these prayers. Indeed, a number of deists, Quakers, and evangelicals debated whether legislative prayer represented what Burger characterized as a "tolerable acknowledgment of beliefs widely held."[7] John Jay objected to choosing a minister on the grounds that it would demonstrate preferential treatment for one (Protestant) denomination over others.[8] After the Constitutional Convention and the adoption of the First Amendment, with its provisions to prohibit the establishment of religion but enable free exercise, John Leland, a Baptist minister and strong advocate of religious liberty, fretted about the "unconstitutional . . . and unnecessary . . . paying of the chaplains of the civil and military departments out of the public treasury."[9]

Nevertheless, two kinds of government chaplaincies emerged in the early republic: legislative and military. While congressional chaplains ministered to lawmakers, the chaplains who served in the American Revolution tended to a broader flock—the wide variety of men who took up arms against the British on behalf of the new nation. What united both was the new federal government that hired and employed clergy. Since then, legislative chaplains have almost always been Protestant Christians, though "guest chaplains" have offered invocations and prayers based on other religious traditions.[10] In contrast, the military chaplaincy expanded to include Catholics by the mid-nineteenth century and formally opened to Jewish, Latter-day Saint, Christian Science, and Eastern Orthodox clergy in World War I.

During this period, prior to the U.S. entrance into the Great War, the military chaplaincy professionalized, creating new educational and ordination requirements for chaplains and altering their roles to exclude auxiliary tasks like managing post libraries, operating commissaries, and delivering mail. Instead, chaplains were religious officers who led worship or coordinated services for personnel of other religious traditions, buried the dead, and provided pastoral care, which ranged from counseling and "sexual morality" lectures to leading Bible studies and communicating with families. As the title of one internal military history suggests, military chaplains moved "up from handymen." As educated professionals with graduate degrees, chaplains were, the military perceived, capable of ministering to everyone, from non-English-speaking enlisted men to four-star generals. The efforts of a multi-faith World War I chaplaincy cemented the tri-faith nomenclature of "Protestant, Catholic, Jew" within the military and portended greater religious cooperation—and, also, competition. By World War II, the military chaplaincy encompassed both mainline and evangelical Protestants as well as Catholics and Jews, while Muslim, Hindu, and Buddhist chaplains entered the Chaplain Corps in the late twentieth and twenty-first centuries.[11]

Other kinds of chaplaincies, or proto-chaplaincies, arose in the early republic as well. Two other spaces—the prison and the seaport—drew the attention of religious leaders who were intent on moral and spiritual reform. In developing penitentiaries in the early United States, an array of Protestants, from "strict Calvinists [to] liberal Quakers . . . earnestly debated the meaning of a true Christian and republican penal practice."[12] Whether focused on city jails or state prisons, and whether assessing these new institutions from the vantage point of a government official or a member of clergy, "reformative incarceration" seemed to require religious leadership. Quakers supported and managed some early prisons like Newgate in Greenwich Village, New York. While their pacifist commitments led to clashes with "state officials concerned with prison order and profit," their departure from the premises led to the "hir[ing of] the nation's first prison chaplain in an effort to secure the right sort of religion within prison walls." The new Baptist chaplain articulated a "prison religion of suffering and redemption," which not only justified the reintroduction of corporal punishment but also created a model of prison ministry centered on redemption through conversion.[13]

By the late nineteenth century, religion continued to suffuse carceral institutions, with prison chaplains collaborating with prison wardens in prison operations. In 1870, Reverend E. C. Wines drafted the "Declaration of Principles" for the American Prison Association, declaring "religion is of first importance." About fifteen years later, he helped form the American Correctional Chaplains Association to further cement the role of chaplains within the prison infrastructure.[14] In this period, prison chaplains not only led services, preached sermons, and visited prisoners but also maintained libraries, taught in schools, and wrote reports for state authorities.[15] At the same time and perhaps because of these varied duties, prison chaplains appeared—much like military chaplains operating in the liminal space between service personnel and their commanding officers—to "ostensibly occup[y] a position between offenders and their custodians." Yet by the twentieth century, prison chaplains became "religious representative[s] in a secularized institution of professionals" and, as a result, needed to legitimize their presence by asserting their value to the institution, rather than to the prisoner congregant.[16]

During the same period of antebellum moral reform, numerous Protestants along the Eastern Seaboard attempted to "improve the social and moral condition of Seamen" as part of a broader effort to shield seafarers from alcohol, gambling, sex workers, and other vices prevalent along the docks.[17] These voluntary efforts by religious organizations often relied on preachers and other ministers who, formally or informally, viewed themselves as port chaplains who served a transient population and, perhaps, kept them out of prisons. Organizations like the Young Men's Church and Missionary Society fashioned churches out of barges from which chaplains could regularly preach and provide outreach—often by offering a conglomeration of services that addressed seamen's needs for post offices, banks, storage facilities, lodging, and funeral homes.[18]

In higher education, chaplaincy emerged from the religious origins of some institutions and as an outgrowth of campus religious organizations at others. The first colleges and universities in the United States were religious institutions, with mandatory chapel attendance and religious study often embedded in the daily life and curriculum. As early as 1750, Yale College held an annual day of prayer.[19] Chaplaincy as a distinct mode of campus ministry emerged in the nineteenth century, alongside the growth of public universities. In 1890, University of Michigan president James B. Angell penned a statement to "allay concerns of nervous parents who conceived of public universities and agricultural colleges as 'godless institutions.'"[20]

By the early twentieth century, a variety of Protestant programs, ranging from the nondenominational YMCA to denominational groups like the Baptist Student Union, as well as the Catholic Newman Center and the Jewish Hillel program, began establishing their presence on college campuses. These groups arose in tandem with efforts to secularize American higher education; in the early twentieth century, the Carnegie Foundation provided funding for institutions willing to relinquish their denominational identities in favor of more academic rigor and intellectual freedom, while students clamored to end mandatory chapel requirements.[21] Because the Newman Clubs and Centers framed themselves as the "official presence of the Catholic Church on campus" and Hillel was designed to "allow Jewish students to rejoice in their history and identity," they needed leaders, typically priests and rabbis, respectively. Often these positions were privately funded and existed parallel to campus programming, but by 1948, when the multi-faith National Association of College and University Chaplains was founded, more colleges and universities had begun staffing their institutions with chaplains, thus hiring clergy and supervising campus religious life.[22]

Also in the early twentieth century, chaplaincy as a profession distinct from the work of local clergy began to develop in hospitals and healthcare organizations. A significant number of American hospitals started as religious organizations. In the 1920s—out of efforts to reform Protestant theological education—clinical pastoral education (CPE) emerged as field-based training for local clergy that took place in hospitals. With time, retired or local clergy who made pastoral visits were joined by those trained in CPE. In 1925, physician Richard Cabot, an adjunct lecturer at Harvard Divinity School, suggested that all ministry candidates receive clinical training similar to medical students to prepare them for work with the sick and dying. With Anton Boisen, he developed a flagship CPE program that placed students in supervised contact with patients at mental hospitals.

By the 1940s, some Protestant religious leaders trained in CPE sought to create a distinct profession. At a 1946 meeting of the American Protestant Hospital Association (APHA), hospital chaplain Rev. Russell L. Dicks convened a group that became formalized as the Association of Protestant Hospital Chaplains, and efforts to professionalize hospital chaplaincy—which would grow alongside the boom in American hospitals generated by new federal funding through the 1946 Hill-Burton Construction Act—began in earnest.[23] A few years later, the APHA standardized a two-unit CPE program. Throughout the 1960s, the American Hospital Association and the APHA collaborated to promote chaplaincy as a "necessary part of the hospital's provision for total patient care" and, at the same time, to systematize what that care encompassed.[24]

In 1969, the Joint Commission on the Accreditation of Healthcare Organizations mandated that hospitals address patients' spiritual needs but did not specify who would do that work. Several years later, the American Hospital Association asserted that certified hospital chaplains, rather than an assortment of local clergy, should be responsible for the spiritual and religious needs of patients but never required this directly.[25] Hospitals remain able to hire whomever they wish as chaplains, even as the research basis for the work grows.[26] As medicine went, so did chaplaincy: the push toward evidence-based healthcare in the late twentieth century also lodged itself in an increasingly religiously diverse chaplaincy sector that needed to prove its capacity to address the wide range of needs in hospitals and health care.[27]

By the mid-twentieth century, chaplains were institutionalized in some form across a number of sectors. Whether in health care or the military,

Rev. Mary Davisson (*left*) talks with a crew member of a ship in port in Baltimore, Maryland. *Photo credit: David Rider.*

prisons or ports, Congress or higher education, chaplains had become a regular presence within public and many parallel private institutions. With the incorporation of chaplains into these domains, professional organizations connected chaplains to one another, interdenominational and interfaith work increased, and some standardization (of credentials, of jobs) started to emerge.

POSTWAR: LESS INSTITUTIONAL SETTINGS

Beyond the relatively well-established zones of work, chaplains have found and continue to find footing in new arenas. In the workplace, Protestant ministers long visited mills and factories on behalf of owners to improve morale and minimize conflict. This was voluntary work, often performed in exchange for a donation to a pastor's church. In the twentieth century, however, evangelical distaste for organized labor—supported by progressive Catholics and Jews—led corporate owners to create paid roles for chaplains and to hire ministers to fortify their business enterprises. In the 1930s, industrialist Robert G. LeTourneau started inviting evangelical speakers to shop meetings and paid a minister to visit workers' camps along the Hoover Dam highway project. By 1941, he hired and stationed industrial chaplains in his factories in Peoria, Illinois, and Toccoa, Georgia. These chaplains organized technical and theological training seminars for workers, counseled workers, visited them in the hospital, and officiated at their weddings and funerals.

The National Association of Evangelicals, founded in 1942, quickly created a Commission on Industrial Chaplaincy. Through it, Baptist minister George D. Heaton collaborated with companies across the American South to develop a theological curriculum in industrial chaplaincy that "considered Jesus the model supervisor."[28] A week before V-E Day in spring 1945, a National Association of Evangelicals brochure promoted its industrial chaplaincy program as a mechanism for tempering the "fires of industrial unrest" that had quieted during the war but stood ready to engulf post–World War II corporate interests. A certified evangelical chaplain could not only pacify labor but also bring about a "happy labor force."[29]

Unlike most other chaplaincy sectors, workforce chaplains did not diversify religiously; they remained a predominantly evangelical enterprise. And much like the human resources professionals who emerged in parallel in the twentieth century, these workplace chaplains provided a service to employees but never strayed from serving employers' interests. Beginning in 2008, in the flood of corporate layoffs during the Great Recession, many large businesses still fronted the expense of contracting chaplains to provide moral support to those workers who remained with the company. Led by businesses such as Raleigh-based Corporate Chaplains of America and Dallas-based Marketplace Chaplains, the workplace chaplaincy industry has grown through contract chaplains, though some companies, like Tyson Foods, continue to follow LeTourneau's model and directly employ—in 2007—120 chaplains across seventy-seven production facilities.[30]

Around the same time that industrial chaplaincy took off in the post–World War II era, so too did commercial flight and, with it, the rise of the airport chapel. In 1951, Archbishop Richard J. Cushing built a Catholic chapel, "Our Lady of the Airways," at Boston's Logan International Airport, the first of its kind. Three years later, customs official Bob O'Brien constructed "Our Lady of the Skies" at Idlewild Airport (now John F. Kennedy International). In the 1960s, both of these chapels expanded in square footage and in their embrace of other religions. Indeed, despite these Catholic origins, over time airport chapels across the United States incorporated Protestants and Jews, added Muslims, and then took on the ever-expansive label "multi-faith."[31] Beyond the physical space, whether a basic room or a more decorated chapel, airport chaplains—frequently local clergy who volunteer or are paid by nonprofits—provide comfort to travelers and also

Rev. Lindsay Popperson leads a service at Sherrill House in Jamaica Plain, Massachusetts. *Photo credit: Pattyanne Lyons.*

to airport workers in the midst of chaotic and often confusing, uncertain, or exhausting moments. Unlike other sectors, the airport chaplaincy has remained relatively unique, operating within the rules, regulations, and customs of particular airports.

Airports are not the only contexts in which irregular or more "pop-up" chaplaincy became common. Over the late twentieth century, disaster, crisis, and community chaplaincy represented arenas in which clergy took on new roles responding to current events and contemporary needs. Beginning with Yale College chaplain William Sloane Coffin, who with Rabbi Abraham Joshua Heschel, Rev. John C. Bennett, and others organized the Clergy and Laity Concerned about Vietnam in 1965, protest chaplains have prayed alongside, ministered to, and joined with Americans engaged in activism.[32] Decades later, when the Occupy Wall Street movement built tent communities to protest corporate greed, chaplains appeared too, offering both faith-specific and interfaith Christian, Jewish, and Muslim services in "Faith and Spirituality" tents set up among the protesters.[33]

In the midst of disasters, ranging from catastrophic accidents to floods, tornadoes, and terror attacks, chaplains also became a ministering presence to aid workers, disaster response teams, municipal personnel, families, and others who needed religious, spiritual, psychological, physical, and emotional support. In some cases, chaplains supported local religious clergy, both augmenting their efforts and tending to the needs of overworked religious leaders to try to limit burnout. In others, they supplied extra hands to do whatever work was needed. As several emphasized in interviews after a major flood in 1985, at its core their work means "Get down in the mud."[34]

In 1996, this work was formalized through the creation of the Spiritual Care Aviation Incident Response Team, a subsidiary of the American Red Cross. In response to the TWA crash on Long Island Sound, in which many affected families and workers found themselves "overwhelmed by . . . 'well meaning but untrained helpers,'" the 1996 Aviation Disaster Family Assistance Act provided the mechanism for training teams of chaplains who were on call and could be deployed to disasters across the country. When terrorists struck the World Trade Center on September 11, 2001, Spiritual Care Aviation Incident Response Team–trained chaplains arrived and provided care through the phases of disaster rescue, relief, and recovery.[35] The Ground Zero chaplaincy, like other iterations of disaster chaplaincy, underscored the importance of quick regional mobilization and coordination and both addressed and was challenged by burnout from providing care in extreme conditions. After 9/11, disaster chaplains coordinated with other clergy and chaplains on the ground, including police and fire chaplains.[36]

While the New York Police and Fire Departments had long included chaplains in their organizations, most police and fire departments made the role of chaplains a more standard one in the organization starting in the 1970s. The International Conference of Police Chaplains, which formed in 1973, brought together this scattered—sometimes volunteer, sometimes paid—municipal workforce to collaborate on care, especially stress management for officers and firefighters, and on outreach to victims and families.[37]

CONCLUSION

Chaplaincy has expanded in numerous directions since the earliest years of the American republic, and chaplains—increasingly called "spiritual care providers" to be more inclusive of multiple religious traditions—can be found in a broader set of institutions and environments. Chaplaincy has become more of a standard feature of some institutional spaces while able to pop up and occupy new space in others. From its earliest origins in government and government-adjacent spaces like the military and Congress, chaplaincy extended to prisons, ports, higher education, and healthcare. Over time, it has also grown beyond institutional arenas to dynamic domains like airports, protests, and disaster zones in which the populations served are ever-changing and in flux, often held together by short-term shared experiences of uncertainty, excitement, or trauma. Chaplaincy also entered the private sector, becoming embedded in industry and workforce to—depending on one's perspective—invest in worker welfare or placate workers.

In addition to being present in more settings, chaplains have become more religiously diverse. Theological schools began to more directly train chaplains after 1990 with growing numbers focused on non-Christian chaplains after 2000.[38] Chaplaincy gradually expanded from a predominantly Protestant activity to a tri-faith Protestant-Catholic-Jewish model to a multifaith, all-comers approach. In some cases, such as the military, this shift reflected a shift in the American population and pressure to make the armed forces' religion branch more representative. In other cases, like higher education, the incorporation of Muslim, Hindu, Buddhist, and other chaplains responded to the needs of students, both American and international, attending colleges and universities. There are exceptions to these diversifying trends. Most notably, corporate workforce chaplaincy has retained its evangelical Protestant character. Prison chaplaincies, especially in private prisons or of privately funded chaplains, have become more evangelical, though in some places there has been a growth in Muslim prison chaplains as well. In most spaces, the late 1990s witnessed a strong push for the inclusion of Muslim chaplains and for chaplains representing other religious minorities.

The mid-twentieth century marked a significant turning point in most chaplaincy sectors. Sufficiently rooted in institutions though often still clamoring for legitimacy, chaplaincy organizations centered on developing professional standards along with parallel education and credentialing programs. The push toward standardization varied and often developed in uneven fits and starts, with financial pressures and needs playing a role in pushing or pulling chaplaincy programs into existence. In many sectors, chaplains take on additional social service or social welfare roles that undergird their rationale for existence. One exception to this is the military, in which chaplains' religious work is segmented from the distinct clinical arenas of psychology and psychiatry. In most sectors, however, chaplaincy has become a hub for a variety of religious, spiritual, emotional, psychological, financial, and other services.

Like many aspects of American religious life, chaplaincy and spiritual care remain in development and transition. The work is vague to some and misunderstood by others. Government chaplaincies in the military, federal prisons, and Congress remain under scrutiny and have often become sites of conflict over the legitimacy of state-funded clergy, the relative representative-ness (or lack thereof) of religious traditions, and religious pluralism and religious sectarianism. Outside of federal settings, the financial basis for chaplains' work is often tenuous, and business models to support it as American religious demographics continue to change are in short supply. Whether the category of chaplain is recognizable to an increasingly non-Christian or less religious public is also an open question for both chaplains and those they serve. While chaplains have a long history in American religious life, the future is being written by those writing and reading this book.

REFLECTION QUESTIONS

1. What factors influenced the emergence of chaplaincy in different settings? Compare and contrast military settings with higher education, ports, or healthcare.
2. What are some new places chaplains have been present in during the last fifty years? What led them to be there?
3. Where are chaplains required in the contemporary United States and where are they optional? Why?
4. What factors led the American public to be more and less aware of chaplains over time?
5. If you could select any time period and setting where you could work as a chaplain, what would you select and why? What would you definitely not select and why?

RECOMMENDED READINGS

Cadge, Wendy. *Paging God: Religion in the Halls of Medicine.* Chicago: University of Chicago Press, 2012.

Cadge, Wendy, Laura Olson, and Margaret Clendenen. "Idiosyncratic Prophets: Personal Style in the Prayers of Congressional Chaplains." *Journal of Church and State* 61, no. 4 (2015): 680–701.

Dubler, Joshua. *Down in the Chapel: Religious Life in an American Prison.* New York: Farrar, Straus and Giroux, 2013.

Stahl, Ronit Y. *Enlisting Faith: How the Military Chaplaincy Shaped Religion and State in Modern America.* Cambridge, Mass.: Harvard University Press, 2017.

Sullivan, Winnifred Fallers. *A Ministry of Presence: Chaplaincy, Spiritual Care, and the Law.* Chicago: University of Chicago Press, 2014.

CHAPTER TWO

Chaplaincy Work and Preparation across Sectors

TAYLOR PAIGE WINFIELD

ABSTRACT *This chapter explores the particular demands of chaplaincy work and preparation across sectors in the United States. Whereas chaplains are currently required in federal prisons, Veterans Affairs facilities, and the military, they are optional in most other settings despite long histories in some. I examine chaplaincy workplaces and their legal contexts and then describe the varied educational requirements for chaplains in different settings. This includes a discussion of training for chaplaincy in theological schools and clinical settings, the emergence of a language of competencies in training in recent years, and reflections on issues of race, gender, sexuality, and religious difference that run through these requirements.*

INTRODUCTION

Chaplains in the United States are from diverse religious and ethnic backgrounds and work across multiple sectors. Chaplains can be found within the military, Veterans Affairs facilities, correctional institutions, hospitals, law enforcement agencies, fire departments, disaster relief organizations, airports, seaports, businesses, campuses, and more.[1] The legal and institutional mandates for chaplains across sectors determine their specific roles within each location. This chapter provides an overview of the current state of American chaplaincy across eleven sectors, detailing the work and preparation in each field. There is no standard for training chaplains, as requirements vary by setting, and in some settings there are no requirements at all. The chapter divides sectors between federal government, healthcare, municipal, workplace, and campus chaplaincy.

FEDERAL GOVERNMENT CHAPLAINCY

Federal chaplains have a clear primary mandate: to protect the constitutional right to the free exercise of religion within their institutions. The First Amendment states, "Congress shall make no law respecting an establishment of religion, or prohibiting the free exercise thereof," and one of federal chaplains' duties is to protect the amendment.[2] The Supreme Court determined across several landmark cases how the establishment clause and the free exercise clause should be applied in federal institutions. In *Abington School District v. Schempp*, the Supreme Court held that the government may hire chaplains to meet the religious needs of individuals in order to avoid infringing First Amendment rights.[3] Similarly, *Marsh v. Chambers* found that the federal government could fund chaplains in order to preserve constitutional rights.[4] *Katcoff v. Marsh* adjudicated that federal military chaplains did not violate the establishment clause and are in fact constitutionally required to protect religious rights.[5] Chaplains could also be just as essential to protecting the freedom to desist from religion as they were to protecting the freedom to practice religion. *Theriault v. Silber* extended these rulings to defend correctional chaplaincy.[6] Currently, individuals within the armed forces, federal prisons, and Veterans Affairs facilities are legally required to have access to chaplains.[7]

Federal chaplains protect First Amendment rights by enabling those within their respective institutions to practice their religions and by arranging religious accommodations when necessary. As part of their work, they lead services and rituals for their own faith communities and ensure there are adequate opportunities for individuals across faith traditions. They are asked to foster healthy religiosity across faith traditions and in no circumstances are permitted to evangelize or proselytize. Federal chaplaincy is replete with unique challenges, particularly those of a legal nature, that do not occur in other sectors. Not only are federal chaplains asked to uphold federal law and regulation as public servants, but they also often work to navigate the religious needs and rights of careseekers within the institutional demands of their sector. Their decisions have real legal and institutional implications and thus are often open to debate and challenges. Winnifred Fallers Sullivan has written that chaplains in these spaces are "strangely necessary figure[s] religiously and legally speaking in negotiating the public life of religion today."[8] The specific tensions that exist for federal chaplains in balancing First Amendment rights and institutional order have evolved, and continue to evolve, as the legal climate and religious demographics of their sectors change over time. Policy and on-the-ground practice remain fluid and in flux within each institutional context. The following sections delve into the details of each federal chaplaincy sector.

Military Chaplaincy

Chaplains facilitate religious practice and accommodations within the U.S. Armed Forces in order to maintain service members' First Amendment rights. Under Title 10 of the U.S. Code, chaplains are the staff officers who execute the commanders' religious support programs and ensure that the free exercise of religion (to practice or not to practice) is available to all service members, their families, and civilian staff.[9] As the armed forces have become increasingly religiously diverse, the most salient questions for chaplains, as posed by Kim Philip Hansen, are these: "What counts as coercion? And what counts as religion?"[10] Chaplains work directly with other military personnel and command leadership to ensure that religious accommodation is achieved whenever possible. In *Parker v. Levy*, the Supreme Court held that service members are not exempt from First Amendment protections, but the constraints of military life and mission may lead to different applications of these rights.[11]

Religious beliefs and preferences within the armed forces span the full spectrum of faith in America.[12] The Chaplain Corps does not yet fully reflect the diversity of the overall military, as it remains largely white, male, and Protestant; yet the Department of Defense is pushing to increase the diversity of military chaplains to better meet the religious and spiritual needs of service members. There is disagreement within the armed forces about whether the Chaplain Corps should include humanist chaplains to meet the needs of service members who may not be religious.[13]

Chaplains' job responsibilities include these:

- leading worship services, liturgies, and rites
- procuring religious items, equipment, and food

- advising the command on religious accommodations and religious conflicts
- advocating for the promotion of moral and ethical behavior within a unit
- providing one-on-one spiritual counseling
- training religious lay leaders to meet diverse needs

They work to ensure the "spiritual readiness" and "spiritual resilience" of the corps.[14] According to the Geneva Conventions, military chaplains are noncombatants—they are not trained to handle weapons and do not engage in warfare. Their role is to care for the service members' religious and emotional needs and stay a moral compass for a unit, ensuring that service members adhere to the rules of engagement and answering larger ethical questions. Chaplains make up the only group in the entire military institution whose conversations are subject to absolute confidentiality.[15]

Religion within the military has received significant media and legal attention, particularly with regard to the hiring and promotion practices of chaplains, the allowance of sectarian prayers at nondenominational military events, and the growing evangelical presence.[16] Several court cases have pertained to the military's attempts to grapple with evangelism and proselytization within the ranks.[17] Beyond questions around proselytization, there have been debates about religious accommodations for service members. A Department of Defense directive from 2020 allowed for the individual expressions of "sincerely held beliefs (conscience, moral principles, or religious beliefs), which do not have an adverse impact on military readiness, unit cohesion, good order and discipline, or health and safety."[18] These types of cautiously implemented leniencies in military protocol have become increasingly common in the past fifty years in response to legal action and advocacy. For example, *Goldman v. Weinberger* was a Supreme Court case in which a Jewish air force officer was not allowed to wear his yarmulke (head covering) when in uniform and on base.[19] Although the Supreme Court determined that the Constitution did not grant him the right to wear his yarmulke, the military soon expanded its definition of "neat appearances" to include this type of ritual garb.

More recently, cases have emerged around accommodations for Sikh service members to keep their beards and wear turbans. In 2017, the Department of Defense changed its protocol to allow service members to keep their beards untrimmed and to cover their hair for religious reasons.[20] Additional religious accommodations include dietary restrictions. Military

Lt. Col. Brian Bohlman is a chaplain in the U.S. Air Force and adjunct professor of chaplaincy at the seminary and school of ministry of Columbia International University, Columbia, South Carolina.

Ready on the Ground: A Military Chaplain's Reflection on Wounded Warrior Ministry at Landstuhl Regional Medical Center, Germany

"Like cold water to a weary soul is good news from a distant land."
—Proverbs 25:25 (NIV)

I will always remember the first wounded warrior I welcomed to Landstuhl Regional Medical Center (LRMC) in Germany within hours after reporting for duty on an unseasonably hot afternoon in July 2006. I was tired and worn out from the long flight from Charlotte, North Carolina, but was determined to keep myself awake until the evening so I could get my body used to the time change. While receiving a tour of the hospital from Chaplain Greg Clapper, the chaplain I was replacing, we were notified that a bus of wounded warriors would be arriving at the ER entrance in about thirty minutes. Chaplain Clapper explained that this would be a good time to train me on how each wounded warrior is greeted by a chaplain as they are offloaded from the medical transport bus onto a gurney and wheeled into the hospital.

As two white air force buses pulled up to the front of the ER entrance, I gloved up and stood behind Chaplain Clapper to watch him greet the patients. As he took his position at the end of the bus, an airman from inside the bus shouted, "Are you ready on the ground?" "We're ready," was the reply from the group of eight service members on the ground who would grab the edge of the stretcher and lower it onto the gurney. Before each patient was offloaded from the back of the bus, a sergeant from the medical administrative command would tell the chaplain the patient's first

Background and Context

name (without rank) so the chaplain could welcome that person by name to LRMC.

As I watched Chaplain Clapper greet each wounded warrior, the reality of war settled into my spirit as I saw—for the first time in my life—the devastating blast and burn injuries that resulted from IEDs. The first patients offloaded from the buses were Critical Care Air Transports and were hooked up to life-support equipment weighing hundreds of pounds. After the most serious patients were offloaded, Chaplain Clapper turned to me and said, "Chaplain Bohlman, it's time for you to step in and greet." As I moved in to take his place at the end of the bus, the sergeant next to me said, "Chaplain, the next patient's name is John."

The moment had come, and it was my turn to welcome my first wounded warrior to a safe haven, a place of refuge and healing. As we lowered the stretcher onto the gurney, I looked into the scarred and swollen face of a wounded warrior with severe burns and said the following: "John, I'm Chaplain Bohlman. Welcome to Germany! You're safe now, and we're here to take good care of you. God be with you." At that moment John reached up and grabbed my hands and wouldn't let go, as if I had a divine power to heal him on the spot. I took a moment to remind John that God was with him, and I promised to visit him later. He finally let go of my hands and we continued to offload the rest of the patients. I will never forget John or the over fifteen hundred other wounded warriors whom I would eventually welcome to Germany during my tour of duty.

For over ten years, Air National Guard chaplains and Religious Affairs Airmen have volunteered for duty at LRMC and provided vital ministry to wounded warriors on their journey home. The ministry of presence, care, and hope is the hallmark of the Chaplain Corps; those characteristics represent the tools of the trade in caring for the emotional and spiritual needs of America's wounded warriors. I will never forget the faces of the warriors I greeted at the ER entrance throughout all hours of the day and night. My tour at LRMC was the most challenging—yet rewarding—tour of duty I had in over twenty years of military service.

As a new "greatest generation" of warriors dwell among us today, let us always be "ready on the ground" to support them and their families whenever they need us. These selfless warriors carried the torch of liberty and freedom into the most dangerous places on earth, and we owe them the best our nation can provide and nothing less. Freedom isn't free!

• •

chaplains can arrange kosher and halal Meals Ready to Eat (MREs) as well as, in certain special circumstances, additional pay for service members to buy food off post, particularly around holidays such as Ramadan and Passover. The Armed Forces Chaplain Board works to direct policy on religious accommodations and how to improve the spiritual readiness, resilience, and moral caliber of the armed forces. Its recommendations go up to the secretary of defense.[21]

Veterans Affairs Chaplaincy

The mandate of Veterans Affairs chaplains is to ensure the free exercise of religion within VA institutions, such as medical centers and outpatient clinics. Chaplains' role is to enable veterans to meet their religious, spiritual, moral, and ethical needs. They work to ensure that the diverse needs of patients are accommodated and that all patients are free from proselytization. Their functional statement includes one-on-one spiritual care and coordination of worship, rites, and liturgy. The VA asks chaplains to work closely with hospital staff and administrators and to collaborate with the full healthcare team to assess patients' needs and plan and execute care. Unlike other healthcare settings, volunteer chaplains are not permitted within the VA system.[22]

Within VA chaplaincy, there are fewer legal cases governing contemporary practice, perhaps because of the emphasis on pluralism within the mandates. Indeed, one lawsuit was brought by two chaplaincy students who were expelled from their program at a VA hospital due to concerns that they were proselytizing.[23] The sector also has fewer concerns around security and order, which leads to more flexibility with religious practice and accommodation.

Federal Correctional Chaplaincy

Inmates have the constitutional right to practice their religions within correctional institutions to the extent possible while maintaining institutional security protocols. The Federal Bureau of Prisons states, "Chaplains administer, supervise, and perform work involved in a program of spiritual welfare and religious guidance for inmates in a correctional setting."[24] Chaplains' responsibilities include leading worship services in their own tradition, accommodating "legitimate" religious needs, providing pastoral care and counseling, and supervising institutional religious activities.[25] Chaplains are involved in distributing religious materials, maintaining religious diet lists, arranging for pastoral visits from local religious representatives (particularly for religious minorities), notifying inmates or their families about the death of an inmate or family member, and helping inmates prepare for release and reentry into the community. They may invite faith representatives from the local community to lead services or provide study opportunities for inmates whose religions are not represented among the chaplaincy staff. Chaplains work as the primary conversation partners with administration to determine religious program policies, including practice, religious articles, religious diets, and standards, to allow for the fullest opportunity for religious practice within the institution.[26]

Prior to *Cooper v. Pate* in 1964, the U.S. Supreme Court tried to avoid intervening in correctional facilities.[27] In the case, Thomas Cooper argued that his First Amendment rights were infringed upon when the institution did not allow him to purchase Black Muslim publications and denied him access to the Koran. He cited these practices as discriminatory, given that inmates of other religions were permitted access to their sacred texts and publications. The Supreme Court ruled in favor of Cooper and affirmed that the Bill of Rights was applicable in correctional facilities. Eight years later, in *Cruz v. Beto*, the court upheld *Cooper v. Pate,* writing, "If Cruz was a Buddhist and if he was denied a reasonable opportunity of pursuing his faith comparable to the opportunity afforded fellow prisoners who adhere to conventional religious precepts, then there was palpable discrimination by the State against the Buddhist religion."[28] The onus was on the prison to ensure that worship practices and items were equitable across religious backgrounds to avoid discriminatory treatment.

Questions regarding the free exercise of religion in prison came to the surface again in 1987 in *O'Lone v. Estate of Shabazz* and *Turner v. Safley*. In these cases, the Supreme Court ruled in favor of the prison administrators, stating that policies that restricted inmates' religious practices for security reasons were not an infringement of the First Amendment.[29] This stance was flipped with the Religious Freedom Restoration Act of 1993, which enshrined the protection of religious freedom to the extent that the government shall not "substantially burden a person's exercise of religion even if the burden results from a rule of general applicability."[30] The federal government was responsible for assuming additional burden in order to protect the free exercise clause of the First Amendment. Although the Religious Freedom Restoration Act was overturned in 1997 in *City of Boerne v. Flores* because it went beyond Congress's enforcement power, it continued to guide decisions in federal cases.[31] For example, in *O'Bryan v. Bureau of Prisons* in 2003, the court ruled that the act governs the actions of federal officers and is applied to their internal operations.[32]

In line with these legal rulings, the Federal Bureau of Prisons' policy on religious beliefs and practices states that federal institutions will provide "inmates of all faith groups with reasonable and equitable opportunities to pursue religious beliefs and practices, within the constraints of budgetary limitations and consistent with the security and orderly running of the institution and the Bureau of Prisons."[33] Chaplains are mandated to arrange accommodations for ceremonial clothing, sacraments and sacred rituals, and religious services and access to spiritual leaders from the same faith tradition. However, the warden, after consulting with a chaplain, may limit religious activities or the participation of certain inmates in religious rituals to maintain the security and good order of the institution. If a warden or chaplain finds that current religious practices do not fall within the "the scope of best correctional practice and religious accommodation" as outlined in the *Inmate Religious Beliefs and Practices* technical reference manual, there may be temporary restriction on practice until there is an evaluation of the practice in terms of "government interests and least restrictive alternatives."[34] Religious groups that employ rhetoric or rituals that advocate for violence or terrorism are not authorized to meet in federal institutions.

The Department of Homeland Security requires a chaplain or religious services coordinator in all Immigration and Customs Enforcement facilities, including local, state, and contract detention centers.[35] Although ICE is run through the DHS, chaplains within ICE facilities are not federal employees. They are typically local contract hires. Correctional chaplains who work within non–federal government correctional facilities, including state prisons, city jails, and detention centers, are also not federal employees. Unlike their federal counterparts, they do not have uniform regulations, training requirements, or strict oversight. Although the Religious Land Use and Institutionalized Persons Act in 2000 ruled that inmates in institutions that receive federal funding should not experience a substantial burden on their religious expression, specific protocols to ensure the free exercise of religion vary by location, budget, and governmental priorities. Nonfederal correctional facilities vary widely among institutions and have dissimilar requirements for their facilities in terms of a religious coordinator. Given that state departments of corrections have to fund these positions, there are dissimilar outcomes depending on state budgets as well as on government priorities.[36]

The synagogue of the Massachusetts Correctional Institution in Norfolk holds a Torah in an ark and can seat ten to fifteen people. *Photo credit: Randall Armor.*

Although the American Correctional Association's standards on adult correctional institutions, including county jails, state prisons, federal prisons, and private prisons, set the target of having one professional chaplain per five hundred inmates, this is often not possible due to funding constraints in multiple federal and municipal institutions.[37] As such, federal and nonfederal correctional chaplains rely heavily on contractors and volunteer religious leaders from the community, and in some cases on trained volunteer chaplain's assistants to fill gaps and meet the needs of those whose religious traditions are not reflected in chaplaincy staff. Although there is no demographic information available on federal chaplains, the Pew Research Center reported that nonfederal chaplains remain largely men and white and stem from more conservative Christian traditions.[38] However, there is a long history of Muslim contract chaplains within corrections as correctional institutions have sought support from the local Muslim communities to support inmates' needs, particularly in light of religious freedom lawsuits involving Muslim inmates.[39]

Healthcare settings are where most Americans encounter chaplains.[40] Chaplains are found across medical centers, including emergency rooms, intensive care units, prenatal units, hospice and palliative care settings, nursing homes, long-term care facilities, and psychiatric institutions.[41] The Joint Commission on Accreditation of Healthcare Organizations requires hospitals to meet patients' spiritual needs but does not explicitly require the presence of a chaplain on staff; however, two-thirds of healthcare organizations still choose to employ them.[42] Hospices are required to have pastoral or other counselors to attend to patients' spiritual needs in order to participate in Medicare and Medicaid Services programs.[43] Whether a healthcare institution will employ chaplains depends largely on location, size, funding, and its religious history.[44] Minority faith communities may fund their own clergy to serve community members in healthcare settings. Although professional associations for healthcare chaplains advocate for hospitals to hire those who have CPE training and board certification, there are no universal hiring practices. Over time there has been an increase in CPE-trained healthcare chaplains.[45]

Chaplains work alongside doctors, nurses, social workers, and other medical personnel as part of multidisciplinary teams to care for patients and staff. They conduct spiritual and religious assessments to augment care plans. Typically, they have access to electronic medical records and add their own notes and assessments into the chart. Medical personnel then use chaplains' spiritual and religious assessments to direct care in a more holistic manner. In many locations, chaplains have pagers and are on call for emergencies. Chaplains position their work through the lens of spiritual care as a way to meet the spiritual needs of patients from diverse backgrounds and of growing numbers of Americans who identify as spiritual but not religious.[46] Spiritual care easily bridges into a conversation of holistic health, which includes physical, emotional, mental, and spiritual components. This positioning of chaplains allows them to work as colleagues and collaborators with other medical staff.

Chaplains, along with other healthcare stakeholders, are heavily advocating for spiritual care departments as a worthy investment for medical organizations. They have adopted evidence-based language and a system of competencies that match those of their medical colleagues.[47] Chaplains increasingly discuss charting, assessment, evaluation, accreditation, and research and have urged payers to cover their services.[48] An emphasis on research has led to a plethora of studies quantifying outcomes of chaplains' interactions with patients, families, and staff. Studies demonstrate that those with access to chaplains in healthcare settings are more satisfied with their stay at the hospital and experience less anxiety and depression than counterparts without access to chaplains.[49] The importance of the ability for healthcare chaplains to communicate with the larger medical team and understand research is reflected in their professional associations' mandated competencies.[50]

MUNICIPAL CHAPLAINCY

Unlike federal chaplains, chaplains working with local government institutions do not have uniform regulations, training requirements, or strict oversight. Although all government institutions that receive federal funding must adhere to the Religious Land Use and Institutionalized Persons Act, specific protocols to ensure the free exercise of religion vary by location, budget, and governmental priorities. Local government chaplains largely are divided between paid professional chaplains and volunteers. This section details the roles and responsibilities of chaplains in such state and city institutions as law enforcement agencies, fire departments, disaster relief organizations, and transportation settings.

Law Enforcement Chaplaincy

Law enforcement chaplains often work as first responders, caring directly for the needs of officers and crisis victims in the face of difficult situations. They provide pastoral and spiritual care to law enforcement officers, their families, department staff, and crisis victims. Law enforcement chaplains may be paid employees or volunteers. Some larger law enforcement departments have volunteer programs in addition to full-time chaplaincy staff in order to increase religious diversity and augment support. The chief of police officially approves a chaplain (paid or unpaid) according to departmental criteria. Paid and volunteer law enforcement chaplains are typically considered staff members of the department equivalent to ranking officers and are given full access to the facilities.[51]

The Federal Bureau of Investigation has a team of volunteer chaplains who provide spiritual care to FBI employees related to their work or personal lives. FBI chaplains work alongside mental health professionals to offer psychological first aid to FBI employees in the aftermath of traumatic situations. They are deployed to mass casualty events to provide additional support. All FBI chaplains are unpaid; however, as part of their work they gain security clearance and access to workplace protections.[52]

Fire Department Chaplaincy

Fire chaplains work to meet the spiritual needs of firefighters (active and retired), emergency medical services members, other departmental staff and families, and crisis victims. Chaplains care for firefighters as they face depression, burnout, post-traumatic stress disorder, or addiction in response to their crisis work and aim to be a beacon of morality in the unit. They oversee funerals and other rituals after the death of active or retired firefighters and provide grief counseling. Chaplains make referrals to local mental health professionals when necessary and may work directly with disaster response organizations. Some larger fire departments hire professional chaplains to serve on their staff, while others have local volunteers. Chaplains may be clergy members, lay leaders, or even in some cases firefighters who are active in their religious or spiritual communities. The departments appoint chaplains to their positions.[53]

Disaster Chaplaincy

The term "disaster chaplain" applies to a wide range of individuals, from volunteers with the Southern Baptist Convention's disaster relief efforts or the Billy Graham Rapid Response Team, to those who deploy directly with the Red Cross in the aftermath of disasters.[54] Chaplains respond to local and national disasters that include mass casualty events, natural or weather related disasters, and transportation accidents to provide spiritual care to survivors and victims. Unlike other disaster chaplains who are sent to minister on behalf of evangelical Christian organizations, chaplains with the Red Cross are mandated to take a pluralistic and open approach to spiritual care in order not to conflict with the Red Cross's principles of impartiality and neutrality.[55]

The Red Cross's disaster chaplaincy program developed in response to several aviation disasters, including the crash of Trans World Airlines Flight 800 in 1996. In the aftermath of the event, the families of the victims went to Congress and said that they were missing spiritual and mental health support. To meet that need, Congress enacted the Aviation Disaster Family Assistance Act of 1997, which named the Red Cross as the partner to care for families in the face of aviation disasters. The Red Cross connected with chaplaincy associations as well as existing crisis chaplaincy programs in order to build up its own disaster spiritual care program. It officially launched the program in 2015 in recognition that spiritual care is an integral part of disaster response. Disaster chaplains with the Red Cross work on Integrated Care Condolence Teams, which include mental health and health professionals, chaplains, and caseworkers. When possible, these teams help a community prepare in anticipation of disaster, then move into response and recovery phases of disaster relief. Recovery includes training local clergy to meet the needs of their community members after the Red Cross team returns home. Red Cross chaplains have responded to such events as Hurricane Katrina in 2005, the Boston Marathon bombing in 2013, and the Orlando nightclub shootings in 2016, as well as to a multitude of other disastrous situations.[56]

Transportation Chaplaincy

Transportation chaplains care for the spiritual and emotional needs of those who are traveling and who work in municipal transit settings. Their presence depends on the permission of location leadership. In some cases they are paid employees, while in others they are sent by religious organizations—typically evangelical Christian—to provide care. Their specific roles and responsibilities vary by type of institution and location.[57]

Aviation chaplaincy takes place in the terminals, baggage claim areas, and multi-faith worship centers in airports. Aviation chaplains care for passengers and staff during times of stress, grief, transition, or conflict. They are there to help staff cope with stress after dealing with difficult passengers, counsel them through challenging moments in their own lives, and conduct services if a colleague passes away. Chaplains may help with conflict resolution during industry conflicts or strikes. During emergencies due to aircraft accidents or other crises, chaplains are first responders to help with spiritual first aid and human welfare at emergency centers. Aviation chaplains collaborate heavily with the Forced Marriage Unit, human trafficking and modern slavery organizations, and the Border Force's Safeguarding Team at some larger airports. Across the board, they are called to work with vulnerable people who are currently displaced, often women, children, or refugees.[58]

Port chaplains work with religious organizations or nonprofits or on their own to care for the emotional, spiritual, and material needs of seafarers. They are not employed by the ports but typically have federally issued transportation worker identification credentials that give them access to secure areas and allow them to escort seafarers off port to seafarer centers. When seafarers are not permitted to leave the ship or port because of visa or time restrictions, chaplains will board the ships and provide materials. Chaplains care for seafarers' emotional and spiritual needs through one-on-one conversations and by offering support when a death occurs on board. Although they do not involve themselves directly in labor disputes, they help advocate for the safety of seafarers and collaborate with the International Transport Workers' Federation if a seafarer is not receiving wages. Chaplaincy organizations exist around the world, and locations work with each other to create a global safety net of supporters for seafarers.[59]

Transportation chaplaincy can also take the form of spiritual care for those on the roads, such as truck drivers.[60] These efforts involve religious services and spiritual counseling for those who are away from home for long periods of time and whose schedules do not allow them to regularly make church services. The chaplains are largely made up of evangelical Christian volunteers who feel called to serve those in their moments of need.

WORKPLACE CHAPLAINCY

There is a long history of chaplains in North American industries, with Protestant ministers present in North American factories since the 1600s.[61] The profession has strong roots in evangelical Christianity, and the majority of workplace chaplains continue to be evangelical Christians who are working for Christian organizations, though they may be asked to care for employees from diverse religious backgrounds.[62] Chaplains in these settings may be company employees or contractors from workplace chaplaincy organizations. They typically provide one-on-one emotional and spiritual support, visit sick employees in the hospital, and help with funerals and memorials if an employee passes away. They also emphasize the ways in which their work achieves organizational culture and goals, even those that are not particularly "spiritual" in nature—such as aiding human resources in conflict management, developing anti-discriminatory policies, cultivating ethical decision-making, and helping connect employees with employee assistant programs.[63]

Unlike chaplains working in government institutions or crisis services, chaplains working within corporations and other for-profit organizations must continuously negotiate their access and demonstrate their value to the organizations, particularly if they are paid employees of the companies they serve.[64] If companies sense there is not sufficient demand for chaplaincy services, they are likely to be cut from the budget. Thus, advocates for workplace chaplains present chaplaincy as a worthwhile investment because it improves company culture and helps manage employees' personal problems that interfere with their abilities to do work well and efficiently. They emphasize studies that show that happy employees and those with better coping skills are more productive and more creative and have higher sales and fewer medical costs; conversely, employees who are depressed, anxious, grieving, or having family trouble lose significant work time.[65] Overall, chaplains focus on their role as caretaker for the staff and on creating a family-like culture at work, which may have the added bonus of positive impacts on business.[66]

CAMPUS CHAPLAINCY

Campus chaplains are common at private and public universities and colleges across the United States.[67] Schools often have multiple religious representatives available on and off campus; however, this section will focus on chaplains hired by the school to provide religious support and programming to the entire student body. There are no uniform training or background requirements to be hired as a campus chaplain; as such, campus chaplains' credentials can vary widely across institutions. Some campus chaplains may be local clergy, others work in the religious studies department, and some have board certification.[68]

Campus chaplains fulfill a wide range of roles at schools. They coordinate religious programming, lead multi-faith conversations, organize memorial programming in response to national or campus tragedies, and provide one-on-one spiritual counseling to students as they navigate their own personal crises and transitions. They contend directly with challenges on campus, such as underage drinking, drug use, sexual assault, anxiety and depression, and discrimination due to ethnic, religious, gender, and sexual identities. Campus chaplains are not Title IX mandated reporters for students, staff, and faculty and are thus one of the few staff on campus who can provide full confidentiality regarding these issues. However, they still are required to report disclosures that include imminent danger to self or others or child abuse.[69]

Official campus chaplaincy positions have historically been held by white Protestant clergymen.[70] Many schools, particularly those that are nonsectarian or open religiously affiliated schools, are now working to create more

Buddhist chaplain Harrison Blum (*right*) facilitates conversations with students at Amherst College's Common Table. *Photo credit: Maria Stenzel, Amherst College.*

diverse and multi-faith religious life programs through recruiting chaplains who are women, laypeople, and from minority religions.[71] Chaplains from non-Christian traditions have the positionality to advocate for students from nondominant religious backgrounds and are able to support students who experience religious discrimination.[72] Chaplains who are Black, Indigenous, or people of color are situated to also address the needs of students who are ethnic minorities. Other chaplains navigate the dynamics between conservative religious students and staff and LGBTQ+ students and associations. Campus chaplains work directly with their schools to negotiate policies and problem-solve religious conflicts when they emerge. On many campuses, they are charged to maintain a pluralistic and respectful environment to those from all spiritual backgrounds. At schools that are more traditional and religiously orthodox, diversity in terms of chaplains and their activities is more limited.[73] Recent work aims to determine the outcomes of chaplaincy programs regarding students, staff, and faculty in order to quantify their impact.[74] Such work parallels a path toward evidence-based chaplaincy that is common in healthcare chaplaincy.

REQUIREMENTS AND TRAINING FOR CHAPLAINS

The title "chaplain" is not licensed or regulated in the United States. As such, chaplains across sectors have varying degrees of training and experience.

Background and Context

Federal government chaplains are the only professional chaplains who consistently have to meet certain criteria in order to be hired; yet, those criteria can be waived due to a shortage of qualified candidates. Table 2.1 shows requirements for chaplains across sectors, as well as professional associations' recommendations. Although certain sectors may not demand specific criteria for employment, employers may still adhere to the professional associations' recommendations or hold their own standards in hiring and promotion decisions. However, there are no systems for enforcing the professional associations' recommendations, and the guidelines set by employers and those set by professional associations do not always match. In some cases, the employers themselves may be faith groups rather than organizations in the sector.

Graduate-level theological education is common for chaplains across sectors and is required in federal chaplaincy. For example, 90 percent of university chaplains have a graduate-level education, even though it is not mandatory.[75] Programs include a PhD in chaplaincy, a doctor of ministry degree with chaplaincy specialty, a master of divinity degree with chaplaincy specialization, a master of arts degree in chaplaincy, and certificate programs. Programs range in content and form across universities with no consensus on the skills and competencies necessary for the profession.[76] Ordination or the equivalent is mandatory for military chaplains, and the Federal Bureau of Prisons requires religious credentialing (ordination, commissioning, or licensed) for its chaplains.[77]

CPE is the core clinical training program for chaplains in the United States and is offered through a number of other organizations, including the Association for Clinical Pastoral Education, the Center for Spiritual Care and Pastoral Education, the College of Pastoral Supervision and Psychotherapy Inc., the Institute for Clinical Pastoral Training, the Healthcare Chaplains Ministry Association, and Clinical Pastoral Education International.[78] In the four-hundred-hour CPE units, students engage in an action-reflection model of learning that allows them to solidify their own pastoral identities and reflect on how their positionality may impact a careseeker's interactions through didactics, case studies, and interpersonal relations time.[79] CPE courses are typically multi-faith in order to foster cross-cultural communication and prepare chaplains for pluralistic environments. CPE is not required in sectors other than Veterans Affairs; however, employers may consider it an asset. Chaplains with CPE training may have varying experiences, depending on where they received their training.[80] Traditionally, CPE was dominant in healthcare settings and was designed to prepare chaplains for

Table 2.1. Chaplaincy hiring requirements

Sector	Experience	Ecclesiastical endorsement	CPE	Education
MILITARY	at least 2 years of professional ministry experience	Mandatory	—	BA and MDiv (or equivalent graduate degree of at least 72 semester hours) from an accredited institution
VETERANS AFFAIRS	at least 2,000 hours of experience, as required for board certification	Mandatory	4 units from a Department of Education–accredited CPE program	BA and MDiv (or equivalent graduate theological degree) from an accredited institution
CORRECTIONS (Federal Bureau of Prisons)	at least 2 years of professional ministry experience	Mandatory	—	BA and MDiv (or equivalent graduate theological degree of at least 80 credit hours) from an accredited institution
CORRECTIONS (municipal)	—	Mandatory	—	—
HEALTHCARE	—	—	—	—
LAW ENFORCEMENT	—	—	—	—

Other

Ordained clergyperson or equivalent; officer training; medical and physical standards; age restrictions and other specifications by branch

U.S. citizenship; board certification by the Board of Chaplaincy Certification Inc. (BBCI). Certification from a nationally recognized body that uses BCCI competencies and qualifications or has reciprocity with BCCI is also acceptable.

Religious credentialing (ordination, commissioning, or licensed); ordinarily no more than 37 years old; physical standards; suitability in terms of employment, financial, and criminal history. The American Correctional Association recommends CPE.

American Correctional Association recommends CPE. One unit of CPE (or equivalent) and endorsement is required for Immigration and Customs Enforcement facilities.

No national or local standards. Chaplain jobs increasingly require board certification as a chaplain, which generally entails master's-level academic training, clinical experience in CPE, work experience as a chaplain, and a rigorous peer-review process to confirm competence.

No national or local standards. International Conference of Police Chaplains recommends a background check, religious endorsement, and at least 5 years of experience. Professional associations provide additional training opportunities.

Table 2.1. Chaplaincy hiring requirements

Sector	Experience	Ecclesiastical endorsement	CPE	Education
FIRE DEPARTMENT	—	—	—	—
DISASTER CHAPLAINCY	—	—	—	—
TRANSPORTATION CHAPLAINCY	—	—	—	—
WORKPLACE CHAPLAINCY	—	—	—	—
CAMPUS CHAPLAINCY	—	—	—	—

Sources: The Appointment and Service of Chaplains, Instruction 1304.28, U.S. Department of Defense, May 12, 2021, https://www.esd.whs.mil/Portals/54/Documents/DD/issuances/dodi/130428p.pdf. For specific information on each branch, see the following websites: for the U.S. Army, https://www .goarmy.com/chaplain/become-an-army-chaplain/requirements.html; for the U.S. Navy, https://www .navy.com/careers/navy-chaplain#ft-qualifications-&-requirements; for the U.S. Air Force, https:// www.airforce.com/careers/specialty-careers/chaplain; for the National Guard, https://www .nationalguard.com/chaplain. See also *VA Handbook 5005/135* (Washington, D.C.: Department of Veterans Affairs, 2020); *Chaplains' Employment, Responsibilities, and Endorsements*, Program Statement 3939.07, Federal Bureau of Prisons, U.S. Department of Justice, 2001, https://www .bop.gov/policy/progstat/3939_007.pdf; *Standards for Adult Correctional Institutions*, 4th ed. (Lanham, Md.: American Correctional Association, 2003); "5.5 Religious Practices," *Operations Manual*, U.S. Immigration and Customs Enforcement, 2011, https://www.ice.gov/doclib/detention -standards/2011/5-5.pdf; Wendy Cadge, George Fitchett, Trace Haythorn, Patricia K. Palmer, Shelly

Background and Context

Other

· ·

No national or local standards. Professional associations provide additional training opportunities.

· ·

No national or local standards.
The Red Cross requires disaster spiritual care chaplains to be one of the following: (1) a chaplain from a national volunteer organization active in disaster; (2) a board certified chaplain; (3) a professional chaplain; or (4) an endorsed leader of a local faith community. The Red Cross provides additional training, and other disaster organizations may require Crisis Incident Stress Management training.

· ·

No national or local standards. Professional associations provide additional training opportunities.

· ·

No national or local standards. Professional associations provide additional training opportunities.

· ·

No national or local standards. Professional associations recommend that campus chaplains have professional training, including a graduate-level degree, CPE training, and religious endorsement.

· ·

Rambo, Casey Clevenger, and Irene Elizabeth Stroud, "Training Healthcare Chaplains: Yesterday, Today and Tomorrow," *Journal of Pastoral Care and Counseling* 73, no. 4 (2019): 211–21; International Conference of Police Chaplains website, accessed January 18, 2021, http://www.icpc4cops.org /chaplaincy-intro/chaplains-work.html; Federation of Fire Chaplains, "FFC Training Institute," accessed January 28, 2021, https://ffc.wildapricot.org/Institute; *Disaster Spiritual Care Standards and Procedures*, American Red Cross, November 2015, https://crisisplumbline.files.wordpress .com/2013/02/dsc-standardsandprocedures.pdf; "Disaster Relief Chaplaincy," Baptist Convention of New England, accessed January 19, 2021, https://www.bcne.net/chaplain; "Training Academy," Marketplace Chaplains, accessed January 28, 2021, https://mchapusa.com/training-academy/; "Training and Development," International Association of Civil Aviation Chaplains, accessed January 20, 2021, https://www.iacac.aero/; and "Standards and Guidelines for Chaplaincy," National Association of College and University Chaplains, accessed January 20, 2021, http://web.archive.org /web/20190308033703/https://www.nacuc.net/standards.

work in this sector. Although there are now a handful of CPE programs in other locations, it can still be difficult to translate the skills into other sectors.

Professional associations for chaplains recommend endorsement across many sectors, and endorsement is required for federal chaplaincy. Endorsing agencies are responsible for ensuring that prospective chaplains are in good standing in the faith community and well equipped to meet the religious needs of those within their care.[81] Endorsement demonstrates that chaplains are fully functional within their faith tradition and have a strong pastoral identity. These two elements are critical, particularly for those who will be working in pluralistic environments. Challenges emerge for endorsement along gender lines in traditions in which only men can be clergy or public leaders. Those who are openly LGBTQ+ may also face difficultly finding endorsement in more conservative religious groups.

Chaplains are increasingly advocating for themselves as professionals with specific training and skills.[82] These efforts occur along sector lines, rather than in a unified organization encompassing all chaplains. Professional associations for military, VA, correctional, healthcare, police, fire, and other chaplains offer their own credentialing or certification programs, each with its own standards and competencies.[83] Certifying bodies advocate that chaplains are most suited to perform professional duties after they receive certification and that certification will lead to promotional opportunities. As some sectors establish criteria for board certification, other sectors and individual chaplains eschew the move toward universal standards, especially when requirements may perpetuate exclusion of those from certain ethnic, gender, class, and religious backgrounds and sexual orientations. For example, some individuals cannot afford theological school and CPE due to the financial costs of tuition, the time investment, and the intensity of the programs that preclude the ability to maintain full-time employment.

Attempts to increase the diversity of the chaplaincy corps across sectors to better match the demographics of the American people must contend with the financial aspects of training programs; the historical exclusion of ethnic, religious, sexual, and gender minorities from theological programs; and inequalities in the credentialing process.[84] For example, all-white, mainline Christian peer review boards for board certification can lead to inequitable outcomes for those who are Black, Indigenous, or people of color or religious minorities. Cumulative inequalities and barriers occur for those who hold multiple marginalized identities in these spaces. One step to move away from the Protestant norms in chaplaincy has been to adopt the term "spiritual care provider," a more neutral term for non-Christian chaplains

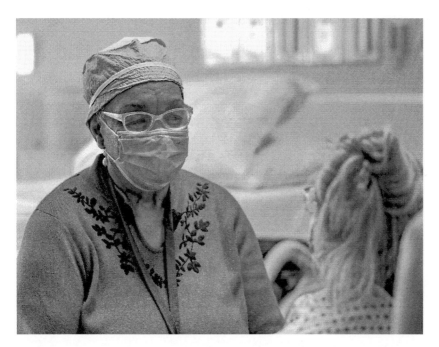

Chaplain Barbara Trawick sits with a patient at Pennsylvania Presbyterian Medical Center, Philadelphia. *Photo credit: John Ehman.*

allowing them to define an authentic practice for themselves and encompassing all of the work they do.

CONCLUSION AND FUTURE DIRECTIONS

Across sectors, professional chaplains have a wide spectrum of workplace roles and responsibilities, ranging from the protection of constitutional rights to improving financial outcomes for corporations. Those working outside of federal chaplaincy have less defined parameters around their training and work, leading to an array of practices within and between settings. Yet, chaplains often share the goal of helping those they care for connect with a sense of meaning, purpose, and belonging through prayer, ritual, and listening. Chaplains are typically placed with people during the most vulnerable, uncertain, and difficult moments of their lives. Hospital chaplains are there for individuals who are dealing with grief or an uncertain prognosis. Disaster and fire chaplains are there for those in the wake of disaster, and law enforcement chaplains comfort families and staff after horrific crimes.

Chaplains are embedded with troops during war and behind the fences of prisons, allowing for institutionalized individuals to gain some sense of normalcy through practicing their religions. Chaplains care for those in transition, whether it is into university, a new job, or a trip through the air or sea. Chaplains encounter those who are grieving and those who are in mental, physical, or spiritual pain and work to heal some of the brokenness in careseekers' lives and in the world.

The power of chaplaincy work has bubbled to the surface of public discourse during the COVID-19 pandemic. Chaplains have served on the front lines and creatively innovated their roles to continue to provide care in unprecedented times, including the development of a tele-chaplaincy. Chaplains are increasingly paying attention to how to lower barriers to spiritual care and advocate for those with marginalized identities. The chapters that follow will detail how chaplains can best fulfill their workplace roles and responsibilities through careful attention to **intersectionality** and power dynamics between the careseeker, the chaplain, and institutions. The skills learned and practiced in this volume will allow chaplains to thrive and promote healing across all sectors and elevate a social justice–informed approach to spiritual care.

REFLECTION QUESTIONS

1. Who can use the title "chaplain"?
2. In which settings do chaplains work? How would you compare chaplains' roles and responsibilities across sectors?
3. What are the training requirements for chaplains? How do they vary among sectors?
4. In which sectors are evangelism and proselytization prohibited? Why might certain sectors prohibit evangelization and proselytization?
5. What are some of the potential benefits of board certification for chaplains? What are some of the potential risks?
6. What sectors would you be interested in working in as a chaplain? Why?

RECOMMENDED READINGS

Cadge, Wendy. "God on the Fly? The Professional Mandates of Airport Chaplains." *Sociology of Religion* 78, no. 4 (2018): 437–55.

———. *Paging God: Religion in the Halls of Medicine.* Chicago: University of Chicago Press, 2012.

Cadge, Wendy, and Michael Skaggs. "Humanizing Agents of Modern Capitalism? The Daily Work of Port Chaplains." *Sociology of Religion* 80, no. 1 (2019): 83–106.

Dubler, Joshua. *Down in the Chapel: Religious Life in an American Prison.* New York: Farrar, Straus and Giroux, 2013.

Hansen, Kim Philip. *Military Chaplains and Religious Diversity.* New York: Palgrave Macmillan, 2012.

Lambert, Lake, III. *Spirituality, Inc.: Religion in the American Workplace* New York: New York University Press, 2009.

Schmalzbauer, John Arnold, and Kathleen A. Mahoney. *The Resilience of Religion in American Higher Education.* Waco, Tex.: Baylor University Press, 2018.

PART TWO

Meaning Making

Introduction to Meaning-Making Competencies

DAGMAR GREFE *and* PAMELA McCARROLL

A unique contribution of chaplains to the well-being of individuals, families, communities, and larger publics revolves around their capacity both to "facilitate practices of meaning making" (see volume introduction) and to interpret values and sources of meaning with people across diverse backgrounds. The chapters that follow include voices of Jewish, Muslim, Buddhist, and Christian chaplains and educators and provide examples of meaning making in pluralistic settings. For chaplains who serve in public institutions, interreligious literacy is growing in importance, enabling them to tap into systems of meaning embedded in the symbols, stories, sacred texts, and rituals of diverse spiritual wisdom traditions. Since chaplains also work with people of no spiritual/religious background, as well as with those who consider themselves "spiritual but not religious," their training increasingly aims at developing competencies in working within secular systems of meaning too. Chaplains listen for the values and beliefs that frame the meaning in careseekers' lives, and when systems of meaning collapse, become stuck, or are in transition, chaplains support careseekers to reframe and reconstruct meaning.

Meaning—the interpretation of life events and actions—is connected to hermeneutics, a term rooted in Jewish Talmudic and other theological scholarship that has been deployed in philosophy and the human sciences.[1] Hermeneutical studies presuppose that the capacities for interpretation and understanding are fundamental to being human.[2] The central focus—how humans interpret meanings—considers the methods and conditions for interpretation through the lens of diverse contexts and meaning-making systems. The hermeneutical component in the study of theology or religion is critical for the preparation of chaplains, for it builds a foundation for their work of meaning making alongside those who seek their care.

Several key themes, central to the meaning-making competency, are embedded within the different chapters of this part. These themes include meaning making in relation to life's transitions and boundary moments; to the givens of existence and suffering; to connecting across cultural and spiritual difference; to the dignifying work of chaplaincy; and to the chaplains' role representing the sacred.

First, even as belonging to religious communities declines in Western Europe and North America, congregational clergy and institutional chaplains are still widely sought out for assistance in facilitating meaning making in the face of **life transitions** and **boundary situations** (see chapter 5). For instance, couples often wish to celebrate their relationship as they move into a shared future with a religious or spiritual ritual, just as parents often celebrate the birth or adoption of a child through dedication rituals. Families burying their loved ones also frequently request spiritual rites. Not only do such rituals mark special and sacred moments, but they also help people manage life's transitions and the shift in meaning as new relationship constellations are formed, as personal identities change, as people's lives are celebrated, and as their loss is mourned. Some of the rituals that chaplains facilitate arise from their institutional and community contexts—when new buildings are opened, for example, or when graduates complete their education, or when members of the community move to a new chapter in their lives. In these transitional moments, when the future is open, chaplains often create sacred spaces and facilitate community, helping people to honor meaning, generate connections, grieve what is past, and reorient to the new.

Chaplains also accompany people in life transitions that mark other boundary situations, as when a patient receives a terminal diagnosis, a soldier is deployed to a conflict zone, an inmate faces loneliness being separated from family, or a couple begins caring for an aging parent. As chaplains walk with people in boundary situations such as these, they assist them in exploring meaning, asking questions, and naming the variety of emotions and struggles that erupt in response to crisis and change.

Second, chaplains work with people when they suffer and are confronted with the givens of existence and suffering. Literature on suffering distinguishes it from pain in one important way: suffering is pain that is uncomprehended—that is, pain that has no perceived meaning.[3] Suffering is commonly conceived as the rupture of meaning, wherein the frames for understanding oneself or one's community in the world are torn apart by traumatic, sudden, or upsetting experiences. In these situations, people ask "why" questions and struggle with the randomness, fragility, and seeming meaninglessness of life. Suffering is also present in the slow grinding down of people whose sense of self, hope, trust, and belonging in the world is destroyed by systems that dehumanize and isolate. Chaplains often enter into spaces of human suffering and bear witness to suffering for what it is while also bearing witness to the possibility for renewed meaning, purpose, and hope.

Chaplains' attention to meaning in the face of suffering is unique to their professional role while also informed by the work of other helping professionals. The Vienna psychiatrist Victor Frankl survived several concentration camps during the Holocaust, but his family, including his pregnant wife, were killed by the Nazis. He developed logo-therapy—meaning-centered psychotherapy—by reflecting on his life experiences. For Frankl, the search for meaning was not a secondary rational process but a primary motivation in life. His search for meaning helped him to survive unimaginable suffering.[4] Existential therapy similarly attends to "persons' conflicts that flow from the individual's confrontation with the givens of existence": existential isolation, death, meaninglessness, and freedom.[5] Both approaches align with chaplaincy practice by insisting that these struggles are not unique to those who seek therapy or mental health support. Rather, they are part of the human condition. The existential and ultimate concerns to which these therapies attest will be familiar to religiously oriented persons, given that so many spiritual traditions, and the sacred texts, stories, symbols, and rituals that they have developed, both attend to human suffering and struggle with the "givens of existence."

Third, chaplains engage in meaning making in a pluralistic society, working across cultural and spiritual difference. Increasingly, introductory courses in spiritual care and CPE prepare chaplains in spiritual/religious literacy, spiritual reflection (see chapter 4), and assessment (see chapter 3) and help them develop the capacity to "translate between sacred and secular discourses" (see volume introduction) in order to support groups and individuals in the search for meaning. Such skills of translation are what sociologists call **code-switching** and **neutralizing**. Code-switching relies on the chaplain's ability to understand and use the practices and language of careseekers from diverse backgrounds. Neutralizing occurs when the chaplain employs broader spiritual language and practices that build upon commonalities rather than differences.[6] For example, in healthcare settings chaplains commonly facilitate public memorials to remember people who have died over a period of time. As they lead such rituals, they bear in mind the variety of spiritual/religious backgrounds represented by the family members, friends, and staff in attendance. Chaplains often consider several strategies in order to create rituals that are inclusive and open to such diversity. For instance, they might invite ritual leaders from other cultural and spiritual backgrounds to participate, or they might include readings from secular and spiritual/religious sources so that words of lament and comfort can be translated across different traditions (code-switching). In their reflections, chaplains might emphasize common spiritual themes (such as gratitude, love, or grief) and make use of shared symbols (such as candles or rocks) as a way to generate meaning based on participants' own associations and experiences (neutralizing).

The reality of each chaplain's own multiple and complex identities underscores the need for training to explore intersectionality, bias, privilege, and the power dynamics inherent in helping relationships. Such training emphasizes cultural humility and prepares chaplains to support spiritual coping and meaning making on the careseekers' own terms. Chaplains working across spiritual, religious, and cultural difference also need to assess the limits of their competence to discern when careseekers might best be served by a representative from their own spiritual tradition.[7] While the capacity to translate and communicate across difference, in our opinion, is important to chaplaincy training, it also continues to be built over time and experience.

Fourth, a central aspect of meaning making in chaplaincy practice involves the dignifying work of chaplaincy—practices that honor the inherent dignity of persons and other sentient beings.[8] Spiritual/religious and secular systems of meaning have many different ways of expressing the dignity and worth inherent in existence. Suffering often undermines people's sense of dignity and worthiness—whether suffering is caused by a sudden and terrible loss or by systems of injustice that perpetuate racism, sexism, ableism, ageism, and all the other "isms" that cause painful ruptures in life. Unjust systems of oppression can distort and marginalize people. In their dignifying work, chaplains raise up and bear witness to the dignity of persons and creatures, especially those most ignored and downtrodden (see case study examples at https://chaplaincyinnovation.org). They commonly seek out the sacred or extraordinary amid the ordinariness of life in public settings, such as prisons, hospitals, the military, and higher education, and on the streets and in homeless shelters. They honor the agency and integrity of persons through empowering and strengths-based models of care. In the chapters that follow, the dignifying work of chaplaincy is visible throughout.

Fifth, an element of the meaning-making competency implicit in all the chapters in part 2 is the chaplain's role of representing the sacred, the spiritual dimensions of life—a role that can itself be deployed in the production of meaning. In private, institutional, and larger public settings, especially in ritual/ceremonial leadership, the chaplain's embodied presence can mediate transcendent meanings and provide a sense that pain is held within a larger wholeness. Consider how chaplains might develop the capacity to embody the authority of this **representative role** in the service of careseekers. Can you think of some examples of in your own life when someone has carried a representative role of the sacred?

While some careseekers may entrust chaplains with this representative role because of their own experiences of spiritual or religious leadership, it is not a given in all situations. Rather, it is a sacred trust that chaplains may earn by walking with people and communities through the highs and lows of life. This capacity is often sought out when questions of ethical or moral integrity arise—for instance, in military, healthcare, or educational institutions—or when existential dimensions are at stake. Chaplains are often at these decision-making tables to represent and in some sense give voice to the sacred or spiritual. As well, they are often called upon because of their understanding of how diverse religious communities might interpret or receive a particular course of action. In this way, chaplains' competence in translating spiritual and religious meanings into secular and public settings can become essential to their representative role.

In exploring meaning making in chaplaincy practice in light of the five themes identified above, each of the chapters that follow in part 2 takes on a distinct perspective. Chapter 3 examines the intersections of meaning making with the arts and skills of **presence**, **spiritual assessment**, and spiritual care **interventions**. Chapter 4 considers how chaplains practice spiritual reflection, especially within contexts of religious/spiritual difference, in ways that bear witness to the search for meaning in human life. Finally, chapter 5 explores how chaplains embody a public role that honors and generates meaning through public rituals.

CHAPTER THREE

Meaning Making in Chaplaincy Practice: Presence, Assessment, and Interventions

DAGMAR GREFE *and* PAMELA McCARROLL,
with BILAL ANSARI

ABSTRACT *During life's transitions and moments of crisis, trauma, and loss, the struggle to make meaning can compound the experience of suffering. Chaplains help careseekers make meaning and reconnect with life in the face of suffering.[1] Meaning making has often been associated with religion. Yet, even as adherence to institutional forms of religion wanes in North America, the need to make meaning persists. Meaning making is intrinsic to being human and constitutes a central focus for the work of spiritual care. This chapter delineates three primary competencies that equip chaplains to assist their careseekers in the holistic process of meaning making:*

1. Presence *is foundational for meaning making in the spiritual care relationship. We introduce three skills that help chaplains communicate presence with careseekers:* **resonance**, *self-awareness, and* **reflective listening**.
2. Spiritual assessment *enables the chaplain to listen for careseekers'*

symbols, narratives, resources, and strengths in order to support their coping and meaning-making processes.

3. Spiritual care interventions *support and build up careseekers' capacities for meaning making through crisis intervention/spiritual first aid, spiritual counseling, advocacy, and group facilitation.*

INTRODUCTION

Throughout this chapter, the following vignette and dialogue provide reference points for multiple aspects of the meaning-making competency offered through the arc of a chaplain's care:[2]

On a university campus in a small town, the incidence of student suicide is increasing. Health and emergency mental health services are overloaded, resulting in limited access. Within the month of November, leading up to exam time, three students throw themselves to their deaths over balconies inside the University Center. Many students witness these tragic deaths. The university community is shaken. While the chaplains support student advocacy efforts and participate in protests demanding better mental health services on campus, they also become the primary means by which care is offered.

Within hours of the third suicide, the chaplains set themselves up at the University Center, offering whatever is needed—a listening ear, crisis intervention, spiritual support, referrals, and opportunities for ritualized and symbolic acts of remembrance and hope. Not only are they present for the students, staff, and faculty, but they also bear witness to the sacred meaning of the lives of those who have died. The sudden suicide of so many students during an already highly stressful time of the semester exacerbates the sense of crisis across campus. Students already struggling with stress and anxiety now feel even more overwhelmed and fearful.

Throughout the week, many students notice the chaplains stationed in the University Center and gesture a grateful nod or smile as they pass by; others stop and light a candle in silence; others share their own struggles with anxiety and suicidal thoughts. Some of the students arrange counseling sessions with a chaplain to work through the struggles that erupt because of the suicides. Other students sign up for one of the groups offered by the interfaith chaplaincy to provide a safe place where they can connect with others and work toward greater resilience.

After a week, the chaplains leave their post in the University Center, but they leave behind the installation of candles to honor those who died and those who are struggling. This installation becomes a site of a growing memorial through the rest of the semester and a centerpiece for a service of remembrance offered by the chaplains a week later.

PRESENCE

When asked what their work is about, chaplains often describe it as a "ministry of presence." Many chaplains associate their ministry—or service—of presence with mindful attention to the presence of "the sacred."[3] Sometimes, the sacred is perceived as a compassionate presence that abides alongside suffering, a sense of "sacred presence in the room." Other times, the sacred is perceived in the details of the careseeker-chaplain encounter when trust builds and connection deepens. Sometimes, the sacred is perceived through the presence of the chaplain offering rituals of meaning and transition; other times, the sacred is perceived within the soul and life of a careseeker—their inherent dignity, glimpsed in real time. However the sacred is perceived, the focus on presence in chaplaincy includes mindfulness to the sacred within the details of life and establishes important ground for the task of meaning making.

An aspect of presence common to many forms of chaplaincy is the expectation that chaplains will "show up" and be present in the midst or aftermath of crises. Unlike therapists and other mental health professionals who usually are sought out by careseekers in counseling offices, chaplains often show up during a crisis or shortly after one unfolds. This is not to suggest that chaplains do not meet with people in offices; many do. However, chaplains are also often present in the settings of careseekers and their communities. Chaplains provide spiritual care on the spot: in emergency rooms and at disaster sites, in waiting rooms and hallways, on street corners and in schools, in military convoys and in prison chapels. Being present amid crisis reflects the spiritual vocation of the chaplain to honor the sacredness, meaning, and dignity of life, especially in those moments when life is undermined and under threat. The work of chaplains moves beyond individual encounters with careseekers and involves active participation in the life of the community. Presence means being awake to the concerns of a community and responding.[4] The vignette above reflects this kind of presence, with chaplains attending to the crisis of several suicides on campus and "showing up" in the University Center.

Both psychology and spiritual wisdom traditions shape the work of chaplaincy and emphasize the importance of presence for healing and vitality.[5] Many sectors of chaplaincy training draw on specific psychological approaches, interpreting them through a spiritual frame. For example, Carl Rogers's person-centered therapy has been highly influential for many sectors of chaplaincy in North America.[6] His concepts of **unconditional positive regard** and empathy—skills that can be learned—provide a basis for presence in chaplaincy practice. Unconditional positive regard communicates the caregiver's stance of acceptance toward the careseeker as a person of worth and value. Empathy is an ability to "feel with" the careseeker and to communicate this "feeling-with" through the therapeutic encounter. While they may not agree with a careseeker's worldview, through such training chaplains learn to pivot away from evaluation and judgment in order to develop an empathic understanding of the careseeker's inner world. Besides building the therapeutic alliance and supporting careseekers' self-expression, empathy and unconditional positive regard communicate the dignifying work of chaplaincy by insisting that careseekers "matter" and that their life has meaning and value.

A focus on presence is also central to the teachings of a wide range of spiritual wisdom traditions. While each has its own particular insights and flavors, they share some common themes regarding the importance of presence. In several traditions, for example, being is foundational for doing, and action is balanced by contemplation. Mindfulness, meditation, and prayer practices in Buddhism and contemplative practices within Christianity, Judaism, and Islam all facilitate awareness of the present moment within a larger horizon of meaning, which some call "the eternal now."

The practice of presence includes a focus on emptiness, or self-emptying, in order to make space to be fully present. The concept of *tsimtsum* within Jewish thought refers to the voluntary withdrawal of G—d to make space for creation.[7] In Buddhism, presence relates to the notion of the emptiness (*śūnyatā*) of the separate, individual self, raising awareness of inter-being, the interconnectedness of everything.[8] Within Christianity, presence is reflected in the symbol of incarnation, God's self-emptying in Christ—fully experiencing the nature and fate of humanity while revealing its divine ground.[9] The concept of *hudur* in Islamic thought is centered on the idea of being present and prepared, settled in oneself, emptied of distractions, and attentive with a self-examining presence of mind.[10]

Spiritual wisdom traditions also understand presence through expressions of compassion, solidarity, and care for fellow beings who suffer. This emphasis is evident in the Jewish practice of *bikur cholim*, visiting the sick;

in the Christian call to care for the stranger, the sick, and the prisoner; in the Buddhist focus on *karuṇā*, being present with suffering and compassion for all sentient beings;[11] and in the Islamic practice of *shubat*—to companion, or keep company with those whose care is entrusted.[12] In such traditions, as well as in chaplaincy practice, the notion of presence as solidarity and compassion in the face of suffering is central to the meaning-making competency. When suffering isolates and disconnects people from life, the presence of another not only signifies that one is not alone but also suggests a horizon of meaning beyond suffering.

Let us take a closer look at the work of one of the chaplains at the aforementioned university campus. Joan is a white cisgender female chaplain who is ordained in the United Methodist Church. She is holding a "wake" where students gather after the suicides to share memories and to honor those who have died. She notices a young Black hijabi gazing at the candles that students have placed to memorialize their fellow students. The young woman's shoulders are turned downward; she looks sad. Joan feels empathy and an internal pull to approach but also is hesitant to intrude on her private space. Joan notices she feels a bit nervous and acknowledges to herself that her nervousness is a natural response to the enormity of the crisis. Her sense of self-compassion helps settle her internally and also enables her to reach out to the young woman. Joan moves gently toward her to introduce herself.

Chaplain 1: Hi, I'm Joan and I am one of the campus chaplains here.

The young woman cautiously looks up.

Student 2: Hi, my name is Fatema. What is it you do?

Joan realizes that Fatema may not be familiar with the role of a campus chaplain.

C3: Oh, I work for the Office of Spiritual Life on campus. We have student groups of different traditions and are here today to offer support.

She notices that Fatema's eyes shift away for a moment, senses a disconnect, and feels clumsy about her introduction.

C4: We are just here today because this has been so shocking and sad for our community and want to offer support.

Fatema smiles and seems relieved.

Meaning Making

S5: It's nice to meet you. I came because I knew one of the students who ended their lives.

Her eyes lower and seem a little moist.

C6: You knew one of the students?

S7: Yes, his name was Jamal. We took one class together, chatted at breaks sometimes. We both studied a lot.

C8: I'm sorry you lost one of your friends. You work pretty hard then.

S9: It's my first semester. I can imagine how overwhelmed he felt with everything. We are both in our first semester.

C10: Starting out here can be overwhelming; there are all the exams and new studies, and then being in college and away from home can be overwhelming, too.

S11: Mmmh . . . yeah, he didn't talk much about it. We mostly talked about the class stuff but I know I feel pretty overwhelmed with everything, especially being away from home.

C12: Sounds like you can really identify with Jamal—the overwhelm and being away from home.

S13: Yeah, *(pause)* it's hard . . . I get how desperate he felt . . . though I won't hurt myself, it goes against what I believe, but I get it. I wish I could have helped him, but I just didn't know.

C14: You didn't know; you couldn't know.

S15: *(pause . . . sense of relief)* I keep thinking through the last time we were together, what he said, what we talked about . . . I just didn't know anything was wrong.

C16: No, you couldn't have known. I hear you though—thinking through last times together following a death, especially an unexpected and tragic death like this, is normal and part of how we humans process the shock of it all and try to make sense of it. Be gentle with yourself. It will take some time. If you feel like talking, my door is always open.

S17: Thanks . . . *(some thoughtful silence)*. I'm from Atlanta, you know. A big change coming here.

C18: That must be a bit of a culture shock coming to this small university town. What has it been like for you to move here to the Northwest?

S19: Yes, at home our family is always together; I have never spent as much time alone.

C20: You must miss your family a lot—and probably friends, too. The first semester can be lonely. Have you met some other students to hang out with?

S21: A few, but not very well, not many students of color on this campus. Quite different from my hometown.

Joan thinks, "As a white chaplain I am aware that my social identity impacts our caregiving relationship. I wonder how best to serve this relationship. I wonder if a Black chaplain or Muslim chaplain may be more helpful in making a connection?"

C22: Since you wear the hijab, I assume you are Muslim, am I right? *(Fatema nods.)* We do have a Muslim student group on campus, and I can get you information when they meet; I think it's one night per week for dinner. *(Joan notices that Fatema's body posture and eyes are low.)* This must be so sad for you, losing a friend and being so new on campus that you don't have a community yet. *(Joan wonders if Fatema would like to light a candle. She does not know if it would be culturally meaningful. She decides to ask.)* How would you feel about lighting a candle together to remember Jamal? Is that a practice that is compatible with your tradition?

Fatema smiles a bit and nods.

S23: Yes, we are careful to not make an idol of anything in the world, but it is fine to remember my colleague Jamal.

They walk toward the candles; Joan gets one for herself and one for Fatema. They light them and place them with the others. They stand in silence for a while, looking at the many candles lighting up the dark space.

C24: Would it be okay if I say a few words? *(Fatema nods. Joan continues.)* Our intentions are with Jamal. We do not know all the emotions he experienced. We know he was one of the friends Fatema made. He studied so hard. We dedicate this moment of silence to Jamal. *(Fatema becomes tearful.)* May this moment of silence and remembrance give comfort to Fatema.

COMMUNICATING PRESENCE: RESONANCE, SELF-AWARENESS, AND REFLECTIVE LISTENING

Presence is communicated through several specific micro-skills, some of which may be considered intuitive or part of the "art of being human." Not all sectors of chaplaincy include micro-skills development in their training. However, for the purposes of this book, we believe delineating key micro-skills invites intentionality, insight, and awareness in a chaplain's capacity to communicate presence.

Resonance describes the relational connection between chaplain and careseekers that occurs when the chaplain is attuned to the body language, voice, and nonverbal communication of the careseekers. Without resonance, Fatema likely would not have engaged in a conversation with Joan or joined her in the ritual. Resonance is foundational for a sense of safety, trust, and **rapport** in the helping relationship; it establishes an important ground for the work of meaning making, highlighting embodied ways of knowing and communicating meaning. Imagine picking the strings of a guitar. The body of the guitar amplifies the sound. Long after you have touched the strings you can feel the vibration, and the sound reverberates. Empty space is needed to create such resonance. Similarly, in order to create relational resonance and connection, some chaplains practice "self-emptying" so as be receptive and open for careseekers and their concerns—emptying the mind of distractions, judgments, the need to fix a perceived problem, and the impulse to direct the conversation.

Humans communicate much through our bodies; resonance includes **attunement** to verbal and nonverbal communication.[13] For psychologist Shari Geller, therapeutic presence involves listening effectively to the whole experience of careseekers.[14] Being attuned means listening to words but also to body language, to content but also to delivery. As chaplains enter new situations, they often consider the body postures, breathing patterns, voice, and pace of speech of their conversation partners. They consider what is being communicated somatically. Is there tension, stress, sorrow, or calm? When you imagine how individuals look when they are stressed or sad, what body language do you expect to see? How do you expect their voice or breathing to sound? While it is always wise to verify one's perceptions, much can be discerned through nonverbal communication.

In our vignette, Joan observes Fatema's "sad posture," which prompts her to approach her with care. The body language of the careseekers can also communicate how the chaplain's words are being received. Chaplains can check their observations and correct the course of the conversation, re-building connection and trust. When Joan notices Fatema's facial expression of "disconnect" (in response to line C3), she adds a clarifying comment that seeks to reestablish connection and a sense of greater comfort for Fatema.

Chaplains also communicate with careseekers through their own body language. In their practice of empathy, they can match their posture or tone of voice to that of the careseekers. For example, if a chaplain responds with an upbeat, energetic tone to a careseeker whose speech is slow and sounds sad, the mismatch in tone and emotional states can undermine trust. Matching is not an imitation of the careseeker; rather, it reflects a way of responding through body and voice that communicates to care-seekers that they are seen and heard. In situations of crisis, however, when careseekers are in shock and overwhelmed by emotions, most chaplains quickly learn to refrain from matching for it only increases the intensity for the careseekers. Instead, they practice **non-anxious presence**,[15] using their voice and posture to communicate a sense of calm—being present with careseekers yet detached from their chaotic emotions. This practice de-escalates the intensity. Emotions are often contagious, and our neurons receive a careseeker's experience on a visceral level.

When chaplains are able to calm their own nervous system through preparatory **grounding** practices, it can communicate a sense of safety and assist others in grounding their nervous system.[16] They develop specific practices to ground themselves in their bodies prior to entering situations of crisis. Such practices may be simple, like being mindful of feeling one's feet making contact with the floor when moving toward a crisis situation. Becoming aware of our own physical sensations can help us move away from thoughts and assumptions and move into our bodies in the present moment. Intentionality,[17] prayer, and various breathing practices can also help chaplains to ground themselves to be more fully present with careseek-ers in crisis and to transition from one careseeker's situation to another. Imagine yourself as a chaplain moving into a crisis situation. What are some grounding practices that might help you?

Developing self-awareness, or reflexivity, has been a strong pillar in the formation of chaplains in clinical pastoral education. Self-awareness is a skill used in the service of careseekers and their process of meaning making. When self-awareness is lacking, it cannot be used in service of careseekers, and a caregiver's own issues and reactivity can undermine care. Through the development of self-awareness, chaplains can learn to manage their own **countertransference**. Countertransference refers to all the unfinished business, triggers, and personal experiences that may arise within caregivers during conversations with people seeking care. Countertransference may include value judgments, reactions, or biases toward the careseekers.[18] For example, if a careseeker starts describing a problem or traumatic experience, a chaplain's own trauma may come into consciousness, internally triggering feelings that have little to do with the careseeker's story. Managing this process and making use of emerging emotions to serve the careseekers are vital for communicating presence.

In our vignette, Joan demonstrates an intentional use of self-awareness to support Fatema. At the beginning of their conversation, Joan is aware of her own tentativeness in approaching; she feels clumsy about her introduction of her role and anxious and inadequate because of her spiritual and cultural differences from Fatema (see also line S21). Attending to her own inner anxiety, Joan is able to shift into a posture of compassion, openness, and curiosity toward Fatema.

Awareness of bodily sensations and emotional responses can help chaplains manage them for their careseekers' benefit. It can be difficult to stay present in the midst of suffering; the sense of helplessness can sometimes lead to impatience and the compulsion to offer solutions or advice. However, awareness of such feelings can deflect from trying to "fix the unfixable" through advice or solutions. Ideally, chaplains can use their own self-awareness (of helplessness, for example) as a bridge to the careseekers (and their sense of helplessness), leading to a yet more empathetic presence. Chaplains' journey of self-awareness is ongoing, no matter how experienced they may be. Just as with all helping professions, it is important for chaplains to create safe spaces where their own emotions, struggles, clinical crises, and perplexities can be processed. As we continue to address our own unfinished business, we become better able to use our emotions and bodily sensations to serve our careseekers. Indeed, in Islam, systematic self-monitoring (*muraqabah*), part of a science called *tassuwuf*, has been developed by spiritual sages as a way to foster the growth of reflexivity in emotional and cognitive presence of mind.[19]

Because chaplains often work with people in the face of death, loss, and crisis, it is especially important that training include self-awareness in relation to the chaplain's own existential vulnerability and mortality. Spiritual wisdom traditions recognize how meaning can be forged through the fire of suffering and existential crises. In order to accompany those who suffer, chaplains often do their own deep inner work through which they face their own vulnerability—and the limits of their own ways of making meaning. By doing such inner work, they may further develop their capacity to be present with others who struggle to make meaning.[20]

In addition to resonance and self-awareness, reflective listening is a primary means by which the chaplain communicates presence with careseekers. It serves the meaning-making competency at both ontological and practical levels. At an ontological level, reflective listening communicates that the careseekers matter—that their experience and life have meaning and are valued in any and all circumstances. At a practical level, the skills of reflective listening can enable chaplains to listen for, draw forth, and reflect back the stories, symbols, and values that frame careseekers' meaning-making processes. The key skills described below, drawn from the work of Herschel Knapp and illustrated in our case vignette, are skills that can be learned.[21] Even so, attentive listening is a discipline: over the course of a conversation, even experienced chaplains must remind themselves, sometimes repeatedly, to put this practice to use.

Reflecting and paraphrasing are skills that communicate to careseekers that the chaplain is present with them, paying attention and understanding what they are expressing. These tools also help chaplains to verify their understanding of what has been shared. When chaplains reflect back or paraphrase what they have heard, careseekers often experience a sense of affirmation and feel understood hearing their own story/thoughts through the words of another. Reflecting can be as simple as repeating words or sentences the careseeker has used, as illustrated by Joan's statement in lines C6 and C12. Paraphrasing makes use of slightly different words or images to verify understanding and to explore nuances of meaning, as in line C8 above.

Another reflective listening skill is summarizing, which helps keep track of the careseeker's story. Summarizing may be done within or at the end of a conversation (or both) to communicate that the careseeker's main concerns have been heard. Joan lets Fatema know that she has heard her concerns in her summarizing statements in lines C16 and C24. On some occasions, incorporating a careseeker's own words and phrases in a prayer practice may serve as a summary, communicating understanding and providing a sense of closure to the conversation. In addition, using the careseeker's own words in prayer or other spiritual practices places the careseeker's concerns within a transcendent horizon of meaning.

Validating and **normalizing** are responses that communicate empathy to careseekers. By validating, the chaplain demonstrates respect for how the careseeker feels without judgment or evaluation. Joan validates Fatema's experience in lines C10, C18, and C20 by empathizing with the stress of her transition to her first semester in a new state.[22] Further, people in crisis or in a highly emotional state can feel alone; at times they may be unsure whether their feelings are extreme. Through normalizing, a chaplain can provide a wider perspective that helps careseekers feel less alone and more connected with others who have also gone through similar experiences. Joan's statements in lines C10 and C16 normalize Fatema's experience by referencing the experience of other students and persons who are struggling with tragic death. Some situations may require a more directive communication. For example, in a crisis, when people are flooded with emotions, chaplains can support and direct careseekers through the initial phases of shock and emotional release.[23]

Typically, encounters in spiritual care are careseeker-centered and careseeker-directed. They make space for experiences and emotions to be heard—honoring careseekers' own processes, making room for pauses and silences, following their lead, and going with the flow of conversation. The skills of presence outlined above express care for those who are suffering and in crisis, help stabilize emotions, and establish a sense of trust and safety. These skills are foundational for the work of meaning making in a therapeutic encounter.

ASSESSMENT

An inductive interpretive process, spiritual assessment involves listening for the ways people construct meaning in their lives through the plotlines, symbols, and themes of their narratives, as well as in practices and words that express their beliefs and values. In healthcare particularly, chaplaincy assessment has been formalized into specific spiritual assessment tools that align with other professional disciplines. In other sectors, however, chaplains often do not use formal assessment tools, and some even reject the term "assessment" altogether, concerned that it distances them from those whom they serve. Our concern in this section is not with specific tools for assessment or with building walls that distance. Rather, we use the term "assessment" here to point to an inductive and interpretive process of deep listening that enables many chaplains to discern the contours of meaning, the "interpretive schemes" (chapter 4), in the stories of people's lives. As interfaith educator Eboo Patel notes, "A narrative identity is not a laundry list of random personal happenings. It is a careful selection and stringing together of the moments and events that matter for a particular purpose. In other words, one's narrative identity is an act of intentional interpretation and meaning making."[24]

Many chaplains have been educated within spiritual/religious wisdom traditions and are familiar with the study of symbols and images in sacred texts. They apply a similar approach to their study of "living human documents"—the "sacred texts," so to speak, of their careseekers' lives.[25] They listen for—and work with—symbols, myths, values, practices, and beliefs central to the spiritual/religious traditions that often underlie the stories people tell. Can you identify some of the key symbols, values, or beliefs central to the way you make meaning?

When tragedy strikes, people suffer when they have no way to make meaning of what has happened to them. Narratives or systems of meaning can become "stuck" or fragmented. **Spiritual distress** (discussed below) often involves a rupture in established systems of meaning commonly formed through spiritual/religious frames. In the immediate aftermath of a traumatic incident, for example, shock can be compounded by the inability to make meaning of what has happened, overwhelming survivors and causing intensifying spiritual distress. Sharing their stories, especially when people are feeling vulnerable, can facilitate a cathartic release of emotion that opens space within; people may begin to reconstruct new meanings as stories are heard and told, reclaiming a sense of agency and identity. Inviting careseekers to share their stories and explore their meanings is a primary means for spiritual assessment; it also can function as a spiritual care intervention that is itself therapeutic.

Many chaplains engage a strengths-based approach that considers careseekers as people who possess resources to address the problems and crises that erupt through the arc of their lives. This approach emphasizes the inherent sacredness and dignity of all persons and their potential for healing, wholeness, and resilience.[26] In the spiritual assessment process, chaplains focus their attention on the spiritual and emotional resources embedded within people's stories, lives, and practices. They explore with the careseekers how their resources can help them to discern new meanings, especially when former ways of meaning making collapse through sudden or traumatic loss. The journey to healing takes its time and involves

Dr. Nisa Muhammad is the assistant dean of religious life at Howard University, Washington, D.C. *Photo credit: Sadrea Muhammad.*

Where Are the Cameras?

During my early days at Howard University as the assistant dean for religious life, a student I knew from *Jummah* prayer service and the Muslim Student Association came into my office looking perturbed. "What's this thing called a *shahadah*?" he said.

I was stunned. The *shahadah* is a pillar of faith in Islam. It's the declaration of faith bearing witness that there is no God but Allah and Muhammad is God's Messenger. It is essential in Islam and something new Muslims say upon conversion. "Have a seat," I said. "Tell me more about your question."

"I was reading this book, and it said something about taking a *shahadah*. I've been a Muslim since freshman year. I pray five times a day, fast during Ramadan, come to *Jummah*, which is the first time I've heard about a *shahadah*. I converted on my own after hearing some excellent lectures. Does this mean Allah has rejected all my prayers? Does this mean I'm not a Muslim? What will my friends say?"

While I was listening, I looked around my office for the cameras. Was I on a Muslim prank show? Where were the cameras? Was he really asking about something so central and foundational to our shared faith? I took a deep breath.

Being a chaplain means guiding students through crises and helping them find meaning in what may seem to be the worst moments of their spiritual lives. Has God rejected me? Will God still love me if I do A, B, or C? What is the ruling or law about X, Y, or Z? Should I drop out of school to maintain my life? We don't give answers; we empower our students to find the answers for themselves. We are a bright light in a dark alley for them to see the way.

....

an integrative process of reconstructing or re-imaging the narratives and meaning-making systems by which we live. It engages the resources of spiritual wisdom traditions and communities as these relate to careseekers' own lives, beliefs, and practices.

At its best, spiritual assessment is practiced with cultural humility and mindful engagement of diverse existential and spiritual beliefs and practices. The term **interpathy** describes a caregiver's capacity to enter into another's narrative, cultural, and symbolic world—their meaning-making system. When engaging in interpathy, chaplains bracket out their own worldview (as much as possible) and move inside that of another, viewing life and circumstances from within.[27] This skill can be developed through religious literacy and through case study or verbatim accounts of therapeutic interactions that are role-played and discussed in group and individual supervision. Interpathy also refers to caregivers' capacity to move between the narrative worlds of careseekers and themselves, recognizing the distinctions and spaces of overlap. In practicing interpathy, chaplains frequently employ cross-cultural techniques that invite careseekers to share their own understandings of practices and beliefs on their own terms. Interpathy often includes code-switching, whereby chaplains use careseekers' spiritual/religious language to move inside their meaning-making systems with them. They also may incorporate broader spiritual language and practices that build upon commonalities across different meaning-making systems, a practice referred to as neutralizing.[28] (See examples in the part introduction.)

We live in contexts with complex intersectional identities and communities that form and shift in relation to the social, institutional, and political realities that press in upon us. Spiritual assessment, at its best, is intersectional, recognizing that individuals, families, and communities are embedded within larger systems of power and privilege. It acknowledges systemic inequities while appreciating and honoring the inherent dignity of each person. For example, certified chaplains in the United States and Canada are trained to understand their own intersectional identities and the many ways these play out in their own narratives and relationships. They are also trained to assess how issues of privilege and power may impinge on careseekers in their given contexts and to acknowledge and manage them in order to serve the careseekers. As part of the spiritual assessment process, chaplains consider the ways systemic inequities and injustices cause and compound suffering in the lives of careseekers, their families, and their communities.

Meaning Making

In our verbatim interaction, for example, Fatema indicates her lack of access to power on campus (line S21) through her feeling of isolation as "a person of color." Chaplain Joan (between lines S21 and C22) wonders how her own power and privilege may be affecting the capacity to join and build rapport with Fatema. Not only does she have privilege because of her race, religion, education, and culture, but she also has institutional power as one paid by the university to serve spiritual needs of students. In the vignette, Joan considers how she may harness her power and privilege to empower and support Fatema and, recognizing the complexity, wonders whether another of the campus chaplains may be more helpful for Fatema.[29] Imagine how intersectionality and power dynamics might operate in other contexts, such as prison ministry or military chaplaincy, for example.

So far, we have presented three key emphases of spiritual assessment distinctive to chaplaincy practice and central to the meaning-making competency: an inductive interpretive process, a strengths-based approach, and intersectionality. We now share several spiritual assessment foci through which chaplains listen for how people make meaning in their lives.

Studies show the role religion plays in how persons cope with crisis and trauma.[30] Even when suffering is unavoidable, we have choices in how we relate to that suffering.[31] When we cope with a crisis, we can play an active role in how we interpret and engage our life stressors. In a primarily theistic context, Kenneth Pargament developed and validated criteria for positive and negative religious/spiritual (R/S) coping. Many are not conscious of their R/S coping mechanisms, which are the result of one's spiritual/religious formation. For example, seeking to connect or cooperate with a transcendent Source (God) and letting go of worry are both constructive ways that spirituality can serve positive R/S coping in a crisis. Interpreting one's crisis as punishment from God or feeling abandoned by one's religious community can add to spiritual distress and amplify suffering by feeding negative R/S coping.[32] Several studies have associated spiritual distress with decreased quality of life, increased depression, and some poorer health outcomes.[33] A chaplain can explore together with a careseeker how the careseeker's spiritual beliefs and values emerge in the crisis and how reframing negative spiritual coping mechanisms can open new constructive approaches to a crisis.

We examine several foci that can shape chaplains' postures when listening deeply to those whom they serve.

    1. Sense of connectedness with the sacred/transcendent/sources

of spirituality: When careseekers tell a story, is there an anchor beyond themselves? Is the sacred present within? For those who believe in God, how is God part of their narrative or not? How is God imaged, and how do these images undermine or support their coping? Do careseekers turn to spiritual communities, practices, specific texts, art, and music regularly or when they are in crisis? How do their sacred texts, stories, and songs speak to them in times of distress and shed light on the meanings in their lives? How have they helped in the past? How might they help now? We invite you to pause and consider these questions in relation to your sense of meaning and the sacred.

In the brief interaction with Fatema, Joan can sense that Fatema holds particular beliefs that ground her values (see line S13) and has an internalized understanding and sense of belonging to Islam (see line S23). Fatema mentions her feeling of "overwhelm" several times. During potential future meetings with Fatema, Joan might explore how sources of her spirituality (practices, community, readings) could support her through this difficult time and how she might begin to build these in her new university environment.

2. Sense of connectedness with family, friends, social world: What are the key relationships of import for the person? What are the communities to which careseekers belong, and how do these communities offer a sense of belonging and meaning for their lives? How do these communities and relationships show up in the narratives of meaning that people share? We invite you to pause and consider these questions in relation to your own sense of meaning and belonging.

Fatema suggests that her family and community connection are important to her (see lines S11 and 19), that she misses a community on campus, and that she has an acute sense of being part of a minority on campus (see line S21).

3. Sense of values and how they provide orientation, determine goodness and trueness in a person's life, and guide choices and actions: What does the person most value? How does the careseeker's life reflect congruence with this? Again, we invite you to pause and consider these questions for yourself.

We hear Fatema note that "hurting herself" goes against what she believes (line S13). Her values and system of meaning and her desire to remain congruent with her values provide grounding for her—a protective factor for her own risk of suicidal ideation.

4. Level of risk of harm to self: As with all helping professions, it is important that chaplains are trained in screening for suicide assessment and other self-harming behaviors. Exploring whether people have harmed or thought of harming themselves, the regularity of these thoughts, and whether the person has a plan and the tools to act on it are key elements of risk assessment. In terms of spiritual assessment in relation to risk, chaplains would listen for the beliefs, relationships, and practices that may increase or reduce risk. Purpose, meaning, and a sense of belonging in life are considered protective factors in assessing for suicide risk.

In the interaction, Joan names the sense of identification Fatema has with Jamal (lines C12–C16) as a summarizing statement of what she has heard. This intervention also furthers the conversation by nondirectly inviting Fatema to clarify how far her identification with Jamal goes. Fatema responds by distinguishing her own beliefs about self-harm and indicating that she wouldn't hurt herself. Joan would assess that Fatema's belief system lowers the risk of suicide and may provide an important resource for healing.

The process of assessment often frames a working **plan of care** and helps to shape the chaplain's interventions (see below). A plan of care is developed in dialogue with the careseekers and works with the careseekers' needs and rhythms. If we consider what we know of Fatema in our brief encounter, a plan for care may include the following:

1. Fatema's sense of isolation as a member of a racial and religious minority and her overwhelm and lack of belonging may be met by connecting her with communities on campus—first through the Muslim student association and perhaps later through other relevant groups and with a Muslim chaplain or African American chaplain.
2. Her sense of loss over the death of her friend is engaged through the candle-lighting ritual action and participating in memorial events. If they meet again, Joan would listen for how the death

of Jamal may be causing Fatema ongoing spiritual distress or emotional pain. In future meetings, the chaplain might explore how Fatema is building community, finding resources and ways to manage, and listening to the stories that support her beliefs. Joan may explore what spiritual practices and beliefs have been important to Fatema in the past and how they are helping her journey through this time.

SPIRITUAL CARE INTERVENTIONS

In this section, after describing some best practices, we outline specific therapeutic interventions that chaplains may provide that serve the work of meaning making. Several of these interventions are addressed in the opening vignette: spiritual first aid, spiritual counseling, advocacy, spiritual/ritual practice, and facilitation of group support.

Chaplaincy interventions often work from an empowerment model that seeks to support careseekers' own healing capacities by engaging their sense of agency, meaning-making systems, spiritual values, and resources. Effective spiritual care interventions are often trauma-informed, recognizing the many ways that traumatic experiences cause protective coping mechanisms to emerge as part of the pathway of survival. Often the trauma histories of people operate beneath the surface, without a person's own awareness. Therefore, it is important that chaplains are mindful of how crises can trigger trauma responses and how to maintain a sense of safety as much as possible. For example, trauma-informed approaches will not pressure careseekers to share stories or information that feels unsafe for a careseeker to share. In the context of unequal power relations between chaplain and careseekers, such pressured sharing can re-traumatize careseekers and undermine their sense of agency and trust. Trauma-informed chaplaincy interventions acknowledge the prevalence of traumatic experience across all populations—on personal and familial levels as well as on the larger societal level in which unjust systems have inflicted racial and social trauma.

During and in the aftermath of crisis, chaplains often offer spiritual first aid and crisis intervention, facilitating space for careseekers to express their shock, grief, and confusion. Spiritual first aid adapts psychological first aid practices with a focus on spirituality and meaning making.[34] In applying spiritual first aid, chaplains accompany people through crisis, making space for "why" questions and the struggles for meaning common during these times. They offer psycho-spiritual education to help normalize careseekers' experiences (see lines C16 and C20) and prepare them for other reactions within the immediate aftermath of a crisis. They help careseekers identify and reach out to their support network and identify local social supports available if distress escalates. Chaplains may offer guidance with end-of-life issues or facilitate ritual practices at the time of death or near death. These practices support careseekers in honoring and marking the meaning of their loss. And finally, using spiritual first aid, chaplains offer referrals and follow-up support as needed. In the case of the university campus, we see the chaplains set up a table in the university center immediately after the third suicide in order to offer spiritual first aid and crisis intervention to students.

Spiritual counseling includes both formal and informal support. Formal counseling is commonly short-term (four to eight sessions) and, depending on context, is often combined with other opportunities for care such as support groups and mental health services.

In both Canada and the United States, certified chaplains are required to demonstrate competence in integrating psychological knowledge into their spiritual care practice. As well, many graduate-level courses in spiritual care provide students with basic knowledge for short-term counseling in grief and loss, bereavement, trauma, communication skills, intercultural care, and spiritual first aid. Certified chaplains, especially those serving in healthcare, employ an integrative approach that brings together several different psychological-psychotherapeutic perspectives within a larger spiritual frame. The perspectives most often integrated into spiritual care practice include self-psychology, person-centered therapy, attachment theory, humanist-existential therapies, narrative therapy, family-systems perspectives, mindfulness, somatic and arts-based modalities, liberation psychology, and social justice therapies.

Depending on the context, spiritual counseling is most often related to supporting people through spiritual distress/struggles—crises of identity, vocation, meaning and purpose, traumatic loss, moral distress and injury, bereavement, and recovery from catastrophic events—and tending to longer-term dying processes or chronic progressive illness. Spiritual counseling draws on empowering practices to support careseekers' growing resilience and trusts the process of healing within. It facilitates expression of careseekers' stories and emotions to address spiritual distress and enhance spiritual resources (see "Assessment" section). It is a collaborative process whereby the effectiveness and initiation of interventions are regularly discussed and negotiated with careseekers. Spiritual counseling uses spiritual/theological reflection drawn from careseekers' own traditions and experiences to explore meanings and coconstruct new meanings congruent with the careseekers' values and beliefs (see chapter 4). Spiritual counseling routinely employs spiritual practices, rituals, prayer, and meditation as interventions promoting resilience and healing (see chapter 5). These interventions may take place in the counseling session, in collective spaces, and through guided spiritual practices offered as "homework" between sessions. All of these interventions function to serve careseekers' capacity to make meaning in the face of life's adversities and challenges.

If Joan and Fatema met for a second or longer visit, Joan might be intentional about going deeper with the conversation. Two tools for deepening an encounter are adding specificity and asking open-ended questions that invite reflection and rich descriptive responses (see, for example, lines C18 and C20). Joan might ask for more detail in response to line S7 to gain a fuller sense of Fatema's loss and its meaning for her. In response to line S19, Joan might ask more about Fatema's family and friends and explore her feelings of loneliness related to social contacts and her sense of being a minority on campus. Adding specificity can help the chaplain to understand the situation of careseekers more fully; more importantly, it can help careseekers to move more deeply into their own inner world, to explore embedded meanings and uncover resources for healing.

In many contexts, advocacy is also an important part of the chaplain's role and can be central in building trust, tending holistically to careseekers, and manifesting a social justice focus for care. In accompanying careseekers through challenging times, chaplains often hear how institutional processes and systemic structures impact and sometimes tear into peoples' lives in ways that cause suffering. Providing advocacy within institutions and empowering careseekers to advocate on their own behalf can be important therapeutic interventions. Depending on the accountability structures in particular institutions, the advocacy function of chaplaincy can sometimes be complicated. Advocacy is nevertheless an essential function, because it seeks to transform public spaces and structures in ways that promote human flourishing. Our vignette on the university campus shows chaplains participating in protests for greater mental health services on campus and supporting student leaders as they strategize and bring their concerns to administrators.

Finally, it is important to note that chaplains often facilitate groups. CPE and courses in theological schools introduce the theory and practice of group process and leadership. Chaplains offer many types of groups to nurture well-being, to respond to and debrief crises, to build resilience, to provide support, to collaborate on justice and ecological initiatives, and to offer spiritual practices. In working with groups, chaplains help mediate the emergence of community and a sense of belonging while also promoting the development of safe spaces and resilience. Indeed, meaning in life is constituted through one's sense of "mattering" to others and of belonging to something greater than one's self. Facilitating groups is an important skill for the meaning-making competency.

Some groups emerge in response to crisis, while others are ongoing. Debriefing groups, for example, arise in response to critical incidents, meeting once or twice following particularly difficult times. In a healthcare setting, staff may meet following a difficult death; in the school system, students and staff may gather following a shooting; in the military, personnel may assemble when members have died or been injured. Debriefing groups allow those gathered to share their experiences with one another, to feel supported through difficult times, and together to begin to articulate and make meaning of what has happened. Chaplains may also make themselves available to individuals beyond the debriefing groups and can assess who may need more supports or referrals.

Ongoing groups, such as support, grief, and spirituality groups, encourage participants to share their thoughts and experiences through facilitated conversations around specific themes common to participants' lives. Justice-based groups encourage discussion, advocacy, and action around specific themes relevant to a given context. For example, an eco-justice group on campus may meet regularly to discuss the ecological crisis, organize educational events, and mobilize to effect change toward eco-friendly practices. Belonging to a group builds resilience and promotes a sense of meaning in life while providing protective factors that serve positive coping and well-being.

Group facilitation skills are therefore foundational in a chaplain's toolbox. In our sample vignette, Fatema was invited to join the Muslim student association; if she and Joan were to meet regularly, she may have also joined another one of the interfaith chaplaincy groups. Can you think of additional groups that chaplains facilitate in healthcare or street chaplaincy, for example?

CONCLUSION

Meaning making is a holistic and relational process central and distinctive to chaplaincy practice. The meaning-making skills and processes described in this chapter affirm the inherent dignity of all people and the sacredness of life. They integrate the knowledge and practice of spiritual wisdom traditions and psychology to tend to the human need to make meaning. Through the skills of presence, chaplains accompany careseekers in the face of crisis and trauma, when life bottoms out and meaning is ruptured or lost. Through the skills of assessment, chaplains work with careseekers to explore and draw forth the sources of meaning and resilience in their lives. Through various therapeutic interventions, chaplains support careseekers through all stages of their journey in imagining and constructing new meanings and in reconnecting them with the sacred in life.

REFLECTION QUESTIONS

1. Presence: Identify, discuss, and role-play three of the skills central to communicating presence in the helping relationship.
2. Assessment: How do you make meaning in life? When bad things happen, how do you interpret why these things happen? Consider the foci for spiritual assessment earlier in this chapter. How would you answer these questions yourself?
3. Can you think of a story, song, or image—religious or secular— that has been helpful to you or another person during a crisis? Describe how it has been helpful to you.
4. Reach out to a person of another cultural or spiritual tradition to find out about a story or symbol that helps them make meaning in the face of suffering. What are similarities to and differences from your own views?
5. Interventions: Review the vignette of the university campus. What interventions do you see referenced here? Imagine you are one of the students who has lost someone by suicide. What would you need from the chaplains in the short term? In the longer term?

Meaning Making

RECOMMENDED READINGS

Friedman, Rabbi Dayle A., ed. *Jewish Pastoral Care: A Practical Handbook from Traditional and Contemporary Sources*. Woodstock, Vt.: Jewish Lights, 2001.

Grefe, Dagmar. *Encounters for Change: Interreligious Cooperation in the Care of Individuals and Communities*. Eugene, Ore.: Wipf and Stock, 2011.

Isgandarova, Nazila. *Muslim Women, Domestic Violence and Psychotherapy: Theological and Clinical Issues*. New York: Routledge, 2019.

Lartey, Emmanuel Yartekwei. *In Living Color: An Intercultural Approach to Pastoral Care and Counseling*. 2nd ed. London: Jessica Kingsley, 2003.

McCarroll, Pamela R. *The End of Hope—the Beginning: Narratives of Hope in the Face of Death and Trauma*. Minneapolis: Fortress Press, 2014.

CHAPTER FOUR

Leading and Facilitating Spiritual Reflection

VICTOR GABRIEL *and* DUANE R. BIDWELL

ABSTRACT *Spiritual reflection helps people order, structure, and create mean-ing from their experiences. It uses any and all sources—religious and nonreli-gious—that give meaning to people's lives. As chaplains provide care, they reflect spiritually on what they see and hear to shape their responses and interventions; they also lead and facilitate spiritual reflection with individuals, families, com-munities, and institutions. The ability of chaplains to identify, access, engage, and evaluate life-giving spiritual resources—stories, songs, symbols, rituals, sa-cred texts, spiritual practices, and more—sets them apart from other helping professionals; in most settings, spiritual reflection is a role and responsibility that belongs uniquely to chaplains. This chapter illustrates how chaplains lead and facilitate spiritual reflection as experts at identifying, exploring, and responding to the spiritual dimensions of experience. Chaplains are not necessarily experts on the content or meaning of people's experiences, especially when caring across religious differences. We advocate for chaplains to develop robust, comparative spiritual understandings; engage personally in reflective, spiritual practices; and cultivate the ability to work across spiritual/religious differences. Key capacities include accessing and engaging ethically with spiritual worldviews, clarifying values, facilitating reflexivity, and helping people construct selves congruent with their spiritual/religious commitments.*

INTRODUCTION

A motorcycle injury left Roger's sixteen-year-old son with a brain injury that required doctors to remove parts of his skull in four surgeries over two days.[1] The hospital chaplain saw the family several times during the surgeries, and Roger seemed upbeat—certain that everything would be fine. In their conversations, Roger said repeatedly, "God will heal my boy."

As they talked, the chaplain used active listening and assessment skills to understand how Roger made sense of his experience. After establishing and strengthening their relationship, the chaplain used prayer, sacred text, and other religious resources to comfort and support him while gently exploring his worldview. Learning that Roger valued personal prayer to God, the chaplain encouraged him to express his feelings and experiences in prayer.

This sharing of feelings erupted suddenly on the third day of the crisis, during his son's fourth surgery, when Roger suddenly sank to his knees, pounded the waiting room floor, and cursed God while his family and others watched.

"You are using my son to punish me!" he screamed. "That's not right, Lord! It's not right! This is not how I was taught God behaves!"

The chaplain stayed present to witness the feelings and attend to Roger as he expressed himself in prayer. Noting how Roger's body responded to the cathartic moment—tensed muscles, sobbing, shallow breathing, pounding veins—the chaplain knew it was too early to talk together. Later that day, after his body calmed, Roger apologized.

"I'm sorry I lost it, chaplain," he said. "I hope you weren't offended."

"Not at all," the chaplain said. "I'm glad you were able to be honest with God and with me. Lots of people have felt the way you do—it's totally normal to 'lose it.' Do you want to talk about what that was like?"

Gently, the chaplain asked Roger about the tension between his interpretation—that God was punishing him—and his image of God as a caring, merciful presence. "How do you think God responded while you were sharing your anger?" the chaplain asked. "What sort of response do you expect?" Using scripture and insight from the Christian tradition, the chaplain influenced Roger's worldview by seeking to enhance his agency and by identifying possibilities, choices, and actions Roger could use to align his behaviors and values.

The following day, a curious peace descended on Roger. "After that major fight with God yesterday," Roger told the chaplain, "I've had a sense of peace like I've never had before. I was trying to keep control of the situation, blaming it all on myself and putting myself at the center, and that's just not the way it is. I know that now. God's in control. I even called the man I blamed for my son's accident and told him there was nothing I needed to forgive him for and that I loved him."

Roger's movement from optimism to anger to peace illustrates how he and his chaplain used spiritual reflection to structure, order, and make meaning of his son's life-threatening injury. First, Roger turned to his untested, embedded assumptions about God and healing ("God will heal my boy"). When those assumptions no longer contained or sufficiently accounted for his pain, Roger decided that God must be punishing him—an interpretation that did not fit his prior experiences or expectations ("This is not how I was taught God behaves") and thus caused confusion, anger, and spiritual crisis. He reflected on this tension with the chaplain, exploring other ways of making sense of God's role in the situation. Finally, Roger received consolation after he cursed God in prayer and decided he was focused on himself rather than on God or on his son ("God's in control").

This chapter illustrates how many chaplains lead and facilitate spiritual reflection with people like Roger. First, it introduces key concepts, issues, and values for spiritual reflection, highlighting necessary practices and capacities. As detailed below, meaning making through spiritual reflection uses a number of a chaplain's skills: intersectional analysis, accessing and influencing worldview, enhancing agency, clarifying values, constructing identity, and aligning behavior and values.

Spiritual reflection draws on a chaplain's interreligious and multireligious literacy but doesn't require expertise in all religious traditions. Chaplains also do not have privileged knowledge about the nature, content, or function of people's spiritualities. Rather, chaplains are experts in the process of helping people identify, explore, and respond to spiritual resources and the spiritual dimensions of experience. This entails engaging how people make meaning and how they understand ultimacy[2] or the basic and fundamental nature of reality. Chaplains lead and facilitate reflection by drawing on a person's spirituality rather than by providing or prescribing specific religious content. Chaplains are careful not to impose their own spiritual/religious traditions and understandings.

Roger's reflection was explicitly religious, but that isn't always the case. Spiritual reflection involves any and all sources—religious, secular, textual, visual, and so forth—that help people make meaning of their lives. It engages core values, identity, and existential choices.[3] Sometimes spiritual reflection is intentional and overt; at other times it is implicit and subconscious. Skillful chaplains are attuned to both dynamics. People in all contexts—prison, hospital, school, military, workplace, and beyond—benefit when chaplains learn to reflect effectively on spiritual experiences. Chaplains acknowledge and value people's spiritualities without dismissing or romanticizing them. They also attend to the assumptions, power, and privilege embedded in their own religious locations.

Chaplains typically reflect spiritually by identifying, accessing, engaging, and evaluating the spiritual thoughts, experiences, and resources at play in caring conversations. They attend carefully to what they see and hear, using those observations to shape responses and interventions. They also lead and facilitate spiritual reflection with individuals, families, communities, and institutions. With Roger, this meant exploring where and how he developed an image of a punishing God at odds with what he had learned through worship and study. A social worker or psychotherapist might have helped Roger express his anger or "process" his grief but probably would not directly engage Roger's spiritual distress. The ability to identify, access, engage, and evaluate life-giving spiritual resources and reflection—stories, songs, rituals, symbols, sacred texts, spiritual practices, and more—sets chaplains apart from other helping professionals. In fact, the responsibility for leading and facilitating spiritual reflection belongs uniquely to chaplains in most settings.

Knowing about and demonstrating these skills is a first step; learning when and how to use them effectively is a process that involves training and practical wisdom gained through experience. Most chaplains, especially those certified by the Board of Chaplaincy Certification, gradually learn to use spiritual reflection to make meaning through a years-long process of formation that can involve clinical training and supervision, peer consultation, and ongoing education.

WHERE WE STAND

All human understanding is partial. It is limited and shaped by social and religious location—not just what people believe or what religions they profess but also the complex ways in which their religious and spiritual bonds relate to race, gender, ethnicities, age, sexualities, geography, and other dimensions of their identities. We begin the chapter, therefore, by highlighting our own social and religious locations. We also briefly identify what we value about spiritual reflection and name some differences between our approaches.

Victor writes:

I grew up in a multiethnic, multireligious, upper-middle-class family in Singapore. I am ordained as a Tibetan Buddhist priest (*ngakpa*), and at the same time I find comfort in Christian, Buddhist, Hindu, Muslim, Taoist, and Vodun services. I had the privilege of studying experientially the interreligious philosophy of Fr. Bede Griffiths and Reb Zalman Schacter Shalomi zt'l. They named their approach "deep ecumenism," which for the purposes of this chapter I would call "qualified perennialism." This approach proposes the nature of spiritual reality is One while acknowledging that due to our unique geographical, historical, and cultural locations there will be diverse and sometimes conflicting interpretive models for meaning making. More simply, this perspective states that spiritual reality is singular because It can only be experienced through the human mind and body, which we all share. However, this singularity may lie beyond our conceptualizations and human language.

Although this is my understanding, I am careful as a chaplain not to impose this on others. What I value in the process of spiritual reflection is that spiritual reflection embodies both our unique connection with that spiritual reality and our similarity as human persons. I think that the differences between Duane and me as authors are a question of emphasis—I have a tendency to highlight the similarities rather than the differences in the process of spiritual reflection.

Duane describes his social and religious locations:

Growing up, my family was nominally Presbyterian (a Protestant Christian denomination made up primarily of educated middle- and upper-middle-class White people) but rarely attended worship or other religious activities. My parents were decidedly blue-collar, but we lived in a diverse university town in the Midwest. From grade school on, my friends were Buddhist, Christian, Hindu, Jewish, Taoist, and Unitarian. I studied Buddhism in college and later with Burmese, Thai, and Vietnamese teachers. Today I am spiritually fluid,[4] both Buddhist and Christian. I am a minister of the Presbyterian Church (USA) and a practitioner in the Theravada Buddhist tradition. By reflecting spiritually, I gain a richer understanding of life. Spiritual reflection also allows me to identify how human experience "talks back" to sacred texts, doctrines, and institutions to

Meaning Making

reduce suffering caused by religion and spirituality. Unlike Victor, I emphasize the differences between spiritual perspectives. I want to honor the ways we are not alike and to acknowledge that different religions lead people to different places and outcomes.

KEY TERMS AND CONCEPTS

Several key terms and concepts are central to how the two of us make sense of meaning making. For us, "meaning making" encompasses an active, creative, social, and reflexive process of making sense of inner and outer experiences. It goes beyond shallow descriptions, such as "Stop signs are red octagons," to create rich, layered, and nuanced accounts: "Today, stop signs in the United States are red octagons, but the country's first stop signs were large, black-and-white squares; the government standardized the shape in the 1920s and changed the color to yellow to help people see them at night. In 1954 stop signs adopted the shape and color we know now: a white outline and white letters on a reflective, red background to match red traffic lights so that there was a universal color that means 'stop.'"

Meaning making looks deeply at experiences to create complex and contextual understanding. It can be seen as one element of spirituality (alongside communion and purpose), helping turn people toward life and the Holy when threatened by death, despair, and nonbeing.[5]

Religions provide participants with a worldview and a direction, helping people understand how they came to be and where they need to go. This aligns with John Thatamanil's definition of religion. He sees religion as "a comprehensive qualitative orientation"[6] that functions as both an interpretive scheme and a normative, therapeutic regimen.[7] Within this worldview, religions and spiritualities diagnose the human condition and propose a pathway to healing; this is the therapeutic aspect of a particular tradition.

As humans, chaplains and careseekers explain and order inner and outer experiences to create a coherent, meaningful structure. This process becomes spiritual reflection when it concerns our relationship with the sacred and our values and when it changes the quality of our awareness or challenges us. The content of spiritual reflection is not necessarily religious; it can include anything in our lives.

A chaplain pays attention to the life-giving or life-denying potentials of spiritual reflection. Sometimes a spiritual framework's misunderstandings and misconceptions create life-denying meanings. They can be transformed toward life, however, as illustrated in the cases of Roger, above, and Cecilia and Amy, below.

MEANING MAKING AND THE VISION, GOALS, AND PURPOSES OF SPIRITUAL REFLECTION

Many years ago, Duane cared with a woman who bruised and scraped herself with a meat cleaver and an ax. "I am not suicidal," Cecilia said.[8] "I just want my body to show some evidence of the pain I feel inside."

Twenty years earlier, Cecilia had been diagnosed with bipolar disorder, a mental health condition that can cause extreme mood swings. Years can pass between episodes. Cecilia had been stable for a long time but had entered an exceptionally severe and disabling depression; at times, she could not feed, clothe, or bathe herself. She never forgot God, however; even at her lowest, Cecilia continued her primary spiritual practice: "making beauty" in the form of exquisite beaded jewelry that she considered an offering to the world. "As long as I can do this," she said, "it means the depression can't swallow me completely. Even in pain, I can add to the impractical beauty of the world." Cecilia understood her jewelry as a reflection of God's wanton generosity and creativity. Yet she and Duane had a hard time reconciling her commitment to beauty and life of prayer with the violence against her body. In the process, Duane asked questions about Cecilia's image of God, understanding of prayer, and sense of how God felt about and responded to her self-injury. He remained curious about her answers and experiences rather than steering her toward a particular interpretation, helping her develop a rich, nuanced description of her suffering before attempting to make meaning of it.

When such difficult and compelling questions arise, spiritual reflection can help people make sense of life in ways congruent with their spiritual and religious commitments. It provides an opportunity to clarify values, explore how people relate to the sacred, and develop stronger and more trusting connections to transcendence. This means engaging moral values and aims, constructing a coherent vision of life, and identifying beliefs about the fundamental nature of reality, such as whether the universe is benevolent.[9] Chaplains who effectively lead and facilitate spiritual reflection embody a "constellation of capacities"[10]—attitudes, understandings, and skills that include self-awareness, authenticity, openness, and tolerance.[11] This chapter assumes these capacities as initial building blocks toward competent spiritual reflection.

In our view, a chaplain who wants to lead and facilitate effective spiritual reflection must be able to recognize and engage spiritual experience and to access and influence a person's worldview without misusing power. In many graduate-level courses in spiritual care and in clinical pastoral education, chaplains are trained to hone these abilities, attending to how a person relates to the sacred and to how transcendence and meaning make themselves known and influence a person's life. Chaplains normally strive to explore a person's spirituality with curiosity and openness, working diligently not to impose norms foreign to the person but to help them identify and clarify the values, commitments, and preferences embedded in—and congruent with—their own ways of relating to the sacred. But most chaplains do not stop there. They also help people respond to their experiences as part of an ongoing conversation with the sacred. Ideally, these responses take place once people make meaning of their experiences. Responses might be formal, involving, for example, prayer and ritual; they might also be informal and include practices such as offering thanks, serving others, creating something, or committing to new actions and understandings.

In our view, effective chaplains bring three values to the process of spiritual reflection. First, they engage in their own spiritual, religious, and theological reflection on a regular basis, working alone or with a psychotherapist, a spiritual guide, or a trusted friend to make meaning of their experiences in light of spiritual and religious understandings. For example, after working with Cecilia, Duane wrote a formal reflection on how he might have contributed to her suffering, using a model proposed by feminist theologian Mary Solberg.[12] This is an example of using religion as an interpretive scheme to make sense of experience. We emphasize chaplains engaging in their own reflective practices because we assume we cannot successfully or ethically lead others in a practice that we do not use ourselves.

Second, chaplains model and facilitate reflexivity, the practice of examining, without defensiveness, these feelings, reactions, assumptions, privileges, and motives to understand how they influence thinking, feeling, and behavior in particular situations. This takes practice. We learn to do it, and to facilitate it among others, in two ways: first, by observing people more skilled at reflexivity than we; second, by consulting with supervisors, mentors, and trusted colleagues to explore the often hidden dimensions of our own ways of being in the world. Analyzing verbatim reports of spiritual-care conversations with peers and supervisors also strengthens reflexivity.

Finally, effective chaplains collaborate with care receivers to construct and live into an identity consistent with and reflecting the best of the person's spiritual/religious commitments. When invited, chaplains might share their perspectives but offer those ideas tentatively, framed as possibilities and not as necessities or absolute truths. It is more important to be curious about the person's own understandings than to shape them toward the values and visions a chaplain adopts. In particular, chaplains honor the therapeutic regimens central to a person's spirituality.

Let's look at concrete examples of how chaplains engage in spiritual reflection themselves and how they facilitate it among others.

THE CHAPLAIN'S OWN REFLECTION PROCESS

Not only do chaplains lead and facilitate spiritual reflection with others, but the capacity to make meaning of what they see and hear is developed through a process of reflection on chaplains' own experiences of caring relationships. A chaplain's reflection serves three purposes: to help the chaplain respond effectively to a particular care receiver; to help the chaplain respond more effectively when faced with similar situations in the future; and to help the chaplain construct new religious, spiritual, or theological understandings.[13]

Early in Duane's career, for example, a Latino colleague asked to talk about suffering—anxiety, sadness, relational strife—resulting from a curse that a bruja, or witch, had placed on him. His statement indicated that the man, a Roman Catholic Christian, was also influenced by *brujería*, an indigenous, Afro-Latinx spirituality common in Latin America and the Caribbean (and increasingly visible in the United States and beyond). The man said the bruja cursed him by slipping his photo into a coffin just before it was sealed and buried. The only way to break the power of the curse, he said, was to remove the photo from the grave. The man's distress focused less on the curse than on the logistics, permissions, and expense involved in retrieving the photo. His suffering was less related to the curse than to his response to it. He kept asking Duane, "What should I do?"

The situation required Duane to reflect spiritually and theologically on his own experience: Did he believe in curses? What would it look like to relieve suffering in this situation, thus honoring one of his vows as a Buddhist practitioner? What would it look like to promote abundant life in this situation, one of his priorities as a Christian pastor? How would God like him to respond to this person?

Duane reflected on these questions by reading the Bible and praying, concluding that to reject the curse would be premature. The man's pain, whatever its cause, was real and amplified by his belief in the curse. Duane decided that to relieve suffering in this situation meant to address its causes: the curse and the man's attachment to its effects. To promote abundant life meant to affirm the man's identity, spirituality, and cultural norms; to liberate him from the fear evoked by the curse; and to identify with him how God might be working to change the situation. Duane used his religious traditions and the traditions of the careseeker to make sense of the man's distress (religion as an interpretive scheme) and to identify how that distress could be relieved (religion as a therapeutic regimen).

After consultation with a colleague and time in prayer, Duane returned to the man and said something like, "I wonder if there's a way that the photo could disappear without digging up the grave? Do you think a funeral home would know how long it takes embalming fluid to leak from a body and destroy paper and photographs?" The man nodded. "I didn't think of that!" he said. "I'll have to check it out."

Later, he called Duane and said that the photograph would be destroyed in a few weeks; this would break the curse. "I just have to be patient and not worry so much," the man said. "Things will get better on their own."

This illustrates one way chaplains might reflect spiritually on their own experiences to benefit careseekers. Duane used journaling, sacred text, prayer, and consultation to find a way to respond that was congruent with Duane's values and reflected the best parts of his religious traditions. He relied on interpersonal skills, self-regulation, and sociocultural competencies[14]—including honesty about what he didn't and couldn't know—to guide his spiritual reflection. He adopted a stance of humility rather than pretended his worldview was more accurate than the careseeker's. Duane did not privilege or indulge the cultures in which he was raised, which rejected curses and witchcraft, but explored where those embedded beliefs came from, why the man trusted them, and what the implications might be if Duane imposed a positivist worldview that centered white, mainline Protestant norms. Can you think of a conversation with another person whose cultural values and viewpoints differed from your own? What did you learn about yourself in such a dialogue?

REFLECTING WITH OTHERS

Amy grew up as the youngest child in an evangelical Christian family. Initially, she did well at school and at church. In fact, she was to become the church's next youth minister. However, Amy gradually became depressed and sullen. Her school work deteriorated. She stormed out of a meeting with her pastor over disagreements about a youth outing. When her parents discovered scars on her hands as the result of self-cutting, they brought her to see Victor, whom they knew.

In the first conversation, Victor acknowledged two sets of careseekers: Amy and her parents. Amy was the "identified careseeker," but the parents' bewilderment, pain, and anxiety needed to be acknowledged. A Buddhist chaplain enters into the caring encounter with the intention to reduce suffering—a manifestation of the Buddhist chaplain's spiritual framework. A Buddhist chaplain's most basic therapeutic regimen is the reduction of suffering. Victor chose to focus on the parents first because their suffering might affect Amy's own healing.

Amy's parents spoke of an ideal vision of their family that was challenged by Amy's incident with the pastor and her self-cutting. Victor explored their spiritual framework about family that was based on hopes and dreams they had developed in their families of origin and from popular media. Amy's parents felt seen and heard by the chaplain. This led them to have faith and hope in the chaplain's subsequent conversations with Amy.

Amy's "presenting issues" were self-cutting and her behavior toward her pastor, but to Victor these were symptoms of her suffering, not the cause. His spiritual framework emphasized the Buddha's Four Noble Truths: first, the truth of suffering—in this case, Amy's self-cutting and behavior toward the pastor; and second, the truth of the suffering's cause. At this point, Victor chose not to determine the cause of the behaviors but to understand how they fit into her spiritual framework. Amy reported that she felt she was "defective" and had failed a test from God. Victor (who in his personal spiritual framework does not believe that the sacred would ever test us) adopted a stance of not knowing, asking Amy to explain the test and how she knew she had failed it.

Amy said that she found herself enjoying time with a girl schoolmate. She was appalled and saddened to discover she was romantically attracted to this friend. This was the test that she believed her God sent her. Amy believed that the sacred sends her tests to see if she continues to be worthy. At a party with this friend, she kissed her friend and her friend kissed her back. This created a crisis in Amy's comprehensive qualitative orientation; her interpretive scheme led her to feel she had failed God's test and, in fact, failed God. Amy believed she should have recognized how wrong this attraction was, within her spiritual framework, and had the strength to resist the friendship.

Victor's spiritual framework does not believe that attraction to a person of the same gender is wrong, but he acknowledged what was true for Amy. A chaplain has genuine, authentic respect for how careseekers have made meaning of their life in a particular spiritual framework and how that framework orders their life. That said, it is important to emphasize that chaplains need to be sensitive when meaning making takes life-denying forms, as discussed below.

After the kiss, Amy avoided all contact with her friend but was still conflicted. This made her sullen and depressed. She also felt she had lost the close emotional tone that previously connected her with her God and her church. She had begun to feel numb; out of that emotional turmoil, she started to cut herself to counteract the numbness by feeling something. Having checked that Amy was safe, that she was not in an emotional place to self-cut, Victor asked how important feeling—"feeling close," "feeling numb"—was to her spiritual framework. Amy said these feelings were significant; this gave Victor insight into Amy's path to healing (the Fourth Noble Truth) toward wholeness (the Third Noble Truth). Somehow, feelings were to play a part in Amy's healing.

Victor asked Amy how she thought she could repair her relationship with her God. Victor wanted to know what therapeutic regimen "fit" Amy's spiritual framework. She said she had prayed, meditated, and asked to be forgiven. She believed she was forgiven but also that she was denied God's grace—which she called "a gift from all-loving God." Victor asked why Amy believed an all-loving God would withhold grace if she was forgiven by her God. Amy's eyes started to tear; soon she was crying, and with that, the emotional burden of failing the test dissolved. It was the consolation she needed.

Victor did not question the interpretive scheme provided by Amy's spiritual framework—that her God would test her to determine her worthiness. Victor identified possible life-giving and life-denying meanings associated with this belief. What he found life-denying was that her God provided her with tests. What he found life-giving was her belief in an all-loving God. He appealed to her belief in an all-loving God to transform her understanding that she had failed a test sent by God.

BECOMING COMPETENT AT SPIRITUAL REFLECTION

Responding effectively to psycho-spiritual distress requires chaplains to prepare to lead and facilitate spiritual reflection by developing the capacities to identify and explore spiritual experience and to facilitate robust responses to the meaning that emerges. This section draws on what we teach in our courses on interreligious care and on chaplaincy to explore each capacity and identify the types of knowledge that inform those capacities. Not all chaplains learn these approaches, of course, but we suggest that chaplains in any context adopt and adapt these capacities for their own work.

Capacities for Spiritual Reflection

Like much preparation for chaplaincy and spiritual care, we think preparing to lead and facilitate spiritual reflection requires more attention to "being" than to "knowing" or "doing." Chaplains prioritize the cultivation of internal and interpersonal capacities that enable them to use their knowledge and skills effectively. Who chaplains are—the environment they create with their being, their capacity to remain non-anxious and nonjudgmental in relationships with careseekers—matters more than what a chaplain knows or does. A number of capacities and resources shape a chaplain's stance toward careseekers.

Three intra- and interpersonal capacities set the stage for spiritual reflection. First, as described in chapter 3, effective chaplaincy embodies intercultural humility and a not-knowing stance, acknowledging that what we don't know can be as important as (or even more important than) what we do know. Humility and not-knowing also mean acknowledging that a chaplain's cultural assumptions about religion and spirituality are not universal or better than the assumptions fostered by other cultures. What chaplains learn about spirituality from their own cultures, training, and experiences might be less helpful than their ability to remain open and curious about how the sacred manifests in a particular person's life and how that person makes sense of those experiences.[15] In our view, a skilled chaplain resists the temptation to "play the expert" and works to reduce the expectation that "expert" is a role a chaplain ought to assume. A chaplain's expertise is limited to the caring relationship and the process of care; careseekers are the experts about their experiences and what they mean. Most chaplains, especially those who have received clinical training, have appropriate, general knowledge about spirituality and the process of care but do not know about a particular person's spirituality or how care can be useful to them. We simply cannot know everything about how the sacred behaves, manifests, or influences others. Therefore, rather than imposing interpretations that grow from the chaplain's perspective, professional chaplains help others clarify their own interpretations of spiritual experience. As in medical ethics, the careseeker's self-determination takes center stage. This process informs spiritual assessment, which can overlap with spiritual reflection and is addressed in chapter 6.

Second, chaplains leading and facilitating spiritual reflection use the resources of their spiritual and religious traditions, as well as secular practices such as psychotherapy, to develop "alterity virtues" like humility, compassion, and gratitude[16] when relating to people whose social and religious locations differ from theirs. These virtues manifest as "a differentiated openness to other perspectives, a tendency to view others as equal to self, and an ability to accept human limitations in knowing . . . [; as] caring for the suffering of others . . . beyond immediate social and kinship networks toward an ever-widening circle of concern for humanity and the cosmos . . . [; and as] intercultural competence and . . . a tendency to appreciate others and their contributions."[17] Many of these attitudes and values are reflected in the Code of Ethics of Professional Chaplains and thereby become a part of chaplains' interpretive schemes, if not also part of the therapeutic regimen advanced by their personal spirituality.[18]

Third, based on these core values of professional chaplaincy, spiritual care providers work to accept difference and recognize the positive, transcendent meanings that emerge across religious, cultural, and social differences. As understood by Steven J. Sandage and his colleagues, this entails remaining open and curious about difference and approaching religious others with respect and compassion.[19] We add that chaplains who recognize the positive, transcendent meanings that emerge from cooperation across difference will strive to see and interpret unfamiliar spiritual/religious traditions as generative and life-giving; religious diversity functions as a gift from which to learn about people, the world, and the sacred, rather than as a problem to solve or a danger from which to protect self and others.

Each of these capacities suggests types of knowledge and practice that effective chaplains continuously strive to embody. In particular, three resources are helpful in preparing to lead and facilitate spiritual/religious reflection: interreligious and multireligious literacy, intersectional analysis, and consultation.

Interreligious and multireligious literacy entails awareness of the basic beliefs, history, ethics, and practices of a variety of spiritual/religious traditions. It also involves an ability to articulate one's own spiritual/religious location[20] and to develop a robust philosophy of religious diversity to make sense of the variety of religions and sometimes conflicting truth claims.[21] We suggest that as chaplains become more skilled, they strive to move beyond basic awareness of multiple traditions toward fluency in a second tradition different from their own. This requires not only "book knowledge" but also practical engagement and apprenticeship—studying, worshiping, serving, and practicing with people and communities who represent the second tradition and know it well. A Buddhist chaplain who wants to become fluent in Islam, for example, might study the Koran and practice Islamic prayer with a Muslim colleague, learn Arabic, or participate in education activities at a local mosque.

Intersectional theory can help chaplains become aware of how different social experiences and identities—such as race, socioeconomic class, gender, ethnicity, sexuality, spirituality and religion, nationality, disability, and others—interact in dynamic, ever-shifting ways to create overlapping and interacting privileges and disadvantages in different settings. For example, speaking English as a first language can create social and economic privilege in the United States but social and economic disadvantages in China or Russia. Considering these overlapping experiences and identities helps us understand the complexity of people's experiences.

It isn't sufficient, of course, to know about intersectional theory; we think chaplains must also be able to use it for intersectional analysis during spiritual reflection. This means accounting for the ways that race, gender, ethnicity, sexuality, nationality, and other categories shape a person's spiritual and religious experiences, qualitative orientation, interpretive schemes, and healing regimens; for their access (or not) to the full resources of a particular religious tradition; and for the way structures of power serve to privilege, disadvantage, highlight, and erase their spirituality. It means considering the chaplain's own intersectionality as a factor that shapes caring relationships and the power dynamic between chaplain and careseeker. (This is one reason, for example, we identified our social and religious locations at the beginning of the chapter.)

Consultation skills help chaplains reach out to religious leaders from other traditions to avoid practicing beyond their expertise. Like other helping professionals, effective chaplains recognize and acknowledge their own limits, accept that they do not know everything, and establish professional relationships with religious leaders in their community and beyond. Having colleagues to consult deepens understanding and enriches spiritual/religious reflection; it is essential for chaplains who want to perform or provide appropriate and effective spiritual care to everyone they meet.[22]

All of these capacities, skills, and knowledges prepare chaplains for identifying and exploring spiritual experience through spiritual/religious reflection. Three additional skills can help chaplains identify and explore the spiritual framework a careseeker uses to make meaning around spiritual, existential, religious, and theological experiences:

- Accessing and influencing worldview. The chaplain is able to ask questions beyond those that get at a clearer picture of the presenting issues. A skillful use of questions can clarify careseekers' spiritual frameworks and their life-giving and life-denying meanings; later, life-denying meanings can be transformed into life-giving meanings.
- Privileging descriptive spiritual knowing over interpretive spiritual knowing. Chaplains listen carefully to careseekers' descriptive spiritual knowing, which often takes the form of engaging the five senses. The chaplain follows up on descriptive knowing without rushing to interpretive spiritual knowing. Careseekers often try to interpret spiritual knowing too soon, but a chaplain needs to direct energy to exploring descriptions of experience, which often lie in a person's senses.
- Facilitating the acceptance of difference and recognition of the positive, sacred meaning of cooperation across difference. A chaplain can offer alternative interpretations that normalize difference for a careseeker. For example, some Jews offer some money to charity, while others offer a chicken to charity during the ritual of *kapparot*. Skilled chaplains acknowledge that we live in a pluralistic society, with as many differences within a religious tradition as across traditions. These chaplains recognize the sacred across difference among traditions and within a tradition to cooperate with others to provide healing to our careseekers.

As a caring conversation moves from identifying and exploring spiritual experience to responding to spiritual experience, a skilled chaplain asks questions to generate awareness of possibilities and choices, including a range of actions in response to the experience.[23] From our perspective, this entails four interventions from the chaplain:

- Clarifying a careseeker's assumptions and values in light of spiritual experience, as in the way Victor highlighted the tension between Amy's belief in an all-loving God and her sense that she had failed a test and therefore did not receive grace.
- Helping careseekers construct a preferred spiritual/religious self,

as in the way Duane helped Cecilia explore whether violent actions toward herself were congruent with her spiritual values.
- Highlighting differences within traditions, such as exploring various understandings of the Jewish ritual of *kapparot*.
- Exploring how careseekers can better align behavior and interpretation with their preferences and values so that their "best self" shines, as when Roger voiced forgiveness of the man he had blamed for his son's injuries.

A chaplain can clarify assumptions and values by asking curious questions about careseekers' experiences and the meanings they attribute to them. "You want to be 'at peace with the universe,'" a chaplain might say, "so you know you're aligned with positive energy. Tell me about a time when you've been aligned with positive energy in the past—how did you know? How did it happen? What did you value about that?" A chaplain might also ask, "What does it say about you as a person when you're able to be at peace with the universe? What does it make possible? How does the universe feel about you when that happens?" Attending to the answers can help a chaplain understand a person's orientation toward the world, the things they value, their preferred way of being, and their assumptions about spirituality and the sacred.

A chaplain's questions can also help a person clarify and construct a preferred identity or sense of self in light of spiritual, existential, religious, and theological commitments. A chaplain might ask, "How do you hope your relationship to the universe shifts in the future? What does it say about you that the positive energy shows up this way in your life? What parts of your life are most aligned with positive energy? Least aligned? What becomes possible for you when you're at peace with the universe that's not possible other times? If you asked the universe what sort of person you should be, what would it say? How and where did you learn that the universe values these things?" These questions invite careseekers to think about the future in light of the spiritual values and commitments that are a part of the interpretive scheme and therapeutic regimen of their spiritualities.

Sometimes, careseekers' thoughts, values, and behaviors seem to conflict with what they were taught (or assume) about the sacred or about being a "spiritual" or "religious" person. Someone might say, for example, "Allah wants me to honor my wife, but her parenting style conflicts with Muslim values. If I support her, I'll let Allah down." When this happens, a chaplain can usefully highlight and normalize the internal diversity of a careseeker's

Meaning Making

religious tradition: "Some Muslims believe that; others believe this. Which seems most congruent with what you know about Allah from your experience and your congregation?" Chaplains can also ask if careseekers' fears are consistent with what they know about or how they experience the sacred: "You are afraid that taking antidepressants will violate your vows as a Buddhist. Is that consistent with what the Buddha taught about reducing suffering? Do you think you benefit from Buddhism as much when you're depressed as when you're not? What would the Buddha say about addressing your suffering?"

Although all religions and spiritualities include a range of beliefs, values, and practices, some careseekers—and some chaplains—remain unaware of the diversity within traditions. This is a reason to cultivate a network of colleagues and religious leaders to consult about traditions less familiar to the chaplain. A basic understanding of multiple traditions helps a chaplain prepare to lead and facilitate spiritual reflection, but there are times when a basic understanding remains insufficient. Seeking consultation helps a chaplain avoid doing harm when caring across religious differences.

Often, a chaplain's primary task is helping people clarify values and make decisions that reflect those values. A chaplain's questions shift from constructing identity to clarifying and encouraging agency by asking questions that help careseekers align their responses to and interpretations of spiritual experience with their key values and preferences. "When you are aligned with the universe's positive energy," a chaplain might say, "how will you respond to this experience in a way that reflects your best self? What action would help you feel at peace with the universe?"

Questions like these invite people to take action that reflects their spirituality, transforming meaning into behavior. Keeping actions congruent with values remains a key to the healing regimens of many spiritual and religious paths. By encouraging an embodied response to experiences of the sacred, chaplains help people enact meaning in the world in ways that others can see and experience. Responding to spiritual, existential, religious, and theological experiences can be a vital dimension of careseekers' relationships to what they consider sacred or most valuable.

CONCLUSION

In most settings, chaplains are the professionals responsible for leading and facilitating spiritual reflection. They help people make meaning of their experiences to inform life-giving actions in the world. Chaplains' ability to identify, access, engage, and evaluate life-giving spiritualities sets them apart from other helpers. Guiding people to order, structure, and create meaning from their experiences carries great responsibility. It draws on all resources, religious and nonreligious, that give meaning to people's lives, requiring chaplains to reflect spiritually on their own experiences as they help lead and facilitate reflection among careseekers. Doing it well requires that chaplains know how to access and engage spiritual worldviews, clarify values, facilitate reflexivity, and help people construct selves that behave in ways congruent with their religious/spiritual commitments.

REFLECTION QUESTIONS

1. How does the spiritual/religious location of the authors shape your response to this chapter? Do their spiritual/religious locations affect their credibility for you? Would someone from a different spiritual/religious location think differently about meaning making through spiritual reflection?

2. The authors argue that religions and spiritualities function as interpretive schemes and healing regimens. How do the interpretive and healing aspects of religion and spirituality influence spiritual reflection and make meaning of life experiences?

3. Describe a time when you engaged in spiritual reflection that created meaning across spiritual/religious differences. What skills or competencies from the chapter can you identify in your experience? What skills or competencies could have made your practices of reflection and meaning making more effective?

4. Look at the section "Becoming Competent at Spiritual Reflection." What capacities would you add or remove from the ones the authors discuss? Why? How would you articulate the capacities there in the language of your own religious/spiritual or cultural traditions? How does your spiritual/religious location affect your response to those capacities?

5. Duane claims "relief of suffering" and "promotion of abundant life" as key commitments and values for his practice of spiritual care. What are some of the key religious/spiritual commitments and values you bring to spiritual care?

RECOMMENDED READINGS

Sanford, Monica. *Kalyāṇamitra: A Model for Buddhist Spiritual Care*. Ottawa: Sumeru Press, 2020.

Snodgrass, Jill, ed. *Navigating Religious Difference in Spiritual Care and Counseling: Essays in Honor of Kathleen J. Greider*. Claremont, Calif.: Claremont Press, 2019.

St. James O'Connor, Thomas, and Elizabeth Meakes. *Theological and Spiritual Reflection*. Waterloo, Ont.: Waterloo Lutheran Seminary, 2011.

Townsend, Loren. "Theological Reflection and the Formation of Pastoral Counselors." In *The Formation of Pastoral Counselors: Challenges and Opportunities*, edited by Duane R. Bidwell and Joretta L. Marshall, 29–46. New York: Routledge, 2007.

CHAPTER FIVE

Meaning Making through Ritual and Public Leadership

ROCHELLE ROBINS *and*
DANIELLE TUMMINIO HANSEN

ABSTRACT *Chaplains respond to individual and communal needs of meaning making through facilitation of rituals. They provide rituals to support careseekers in contexts of liminality, transition, and boundary situations, such as crisis, disaster, and death. Through several examples and two fictional cases, this chapter describes the contexts for rituals as well as the functions they fulfill. The chapter introduces five competencies for the facilitation of rituals: (1) assessing needs, (2) drawing on wisdom traditions for contemporary meaning making, (3) structuring rituals, (4) facilitating connections, and (5) integrating diverse spiritual resources. The ancient Hebrew biblical concept of tzaraat, affliction, is used as an example of how chaplains can use concepts from their own sacred texts to shed light on meaning for contemporary times. The concept describes how the chaplain as a representative of the sacred can facilitate community and give voice to personal, communal, and systemic afflictions. Rituals can provide stability, mark sacred time and space, remember and reveal, nurture resiliency, and empower and inspire new visions of freedom from affliction.*

Maura is a chaplain at a boarding school for high school students in the northeastern part of the United States called the Robsen School. As a chaplain, Maura's job is to teach religious studies courses to students, offer spiritual care to students and faculty, and lead daily interfaith worship. Maura considers the final of these three tasks to be the most important part of her job. Her facilitation of the daily service is a highly visible form of public leadership and is the only regular opportunity for the entire school community to share a collective experience.

In early January, news breaks that a sexual assault has occurred at Robsen's rival boarding school nearby. Many of the girls at Robsen are upset about the sexual assault because it reminds them of the many ways they feel vulnerable at Robsen, which historically had been a boys' school.[1] A group of female students come to speak with Maura and express that they are upset about the incident and feel marginalized at the school because of their gender. Maura suggests it might be helpful for the girls to find a way to speak about their experience during their daily interfaith gathering. The students say they do not feel comfortable speaking publicly because they are afraid of judgment from their peers and teachers—a reality that only reenforces for Maura concerns about embedded gender biases of the school.

Maura discerns an opportunity to provide leadership through ritual in a way that can contribute to changing the culture at the school by acknowledging the young women's experiences and empowering them to speak their truth while also honoring their desire to remain anonymous. With the students' permission, Maura creates an interfaith ritual for International Women's Day[2] that is designed to name the experiences of women and girls in the school. Weeks before the ritual, Maura invites women-identifying faculty and students to write about their experiences and dreams and to submit these anonymously in a box outside the office. She collates the submissions and gathers volunteers among the student body to read them as part of the interfaith ritual. She prepares a program ahead of time to be given out when the community begins to gather. Included with the program is a pen and Post-it note to be used as part of the service. She readies the space, placing large colorful posters cut in the shape of persons on the wall. Near the entrance is a table with refreshments prepared for informal gathering after the service. The ritual opens with Maura welcoming everyone to the space, identifying the purpose of the gathering, and acknowledging the range of emotions and experiences present in the room. She begins with these words:

> We are here today to mark International Women's Day. In marking this day, we join with people across the world who are committed to working toward gender justice and parity. We gather to remember and honor those women and girls whose lives have been marred by prejudice, violence. We gather also to learn and to recommit ourselves personally and collectively to a world where all may flourish, no matter gender, creed, or color. It is not an easy day to mark, as we live in a world in which gender-based violence continues to destroy lives and communities. The recent highly publicized sexual assault in our neighboring school reminds us of how close it is. It also reminds us that we have work to do in our own community as well. The hope today is that we can begin this work by listening to the voices of the women in our community. As we hear their stories and their wisdom, we can begin to learn and grow together in our commitment to be a community where all experience welcome and inclusion.

A group of young women musicians from the school are invited forward to perform "Singing for Our Lives" by Holly Near. Then Chaplain Maura continues:

> Even as we are aware of challenges facing women in broader society, today is also a time to acknowledge challenges that face women within our community as well. It is not easy to hear this, as we seek to have a community where everyone is welcome and able to flourish to their fullness. Part of our journey as we continue to build a community that is inclusive is to have the courage to speak and to listen to each other. Over the next few minutes the words of members of our community will be shared. Some of them include upsetting thoughts and feelings; some of them reflect dreams for our life together. I invite you to hear these sentiments with an open heart.

She then asks the students, staff, and faculty representatives who had volunteered to read the anonymous submissions to begin. The readers include all genders. Some recite messages that may upset listeners, statements like, "I feel uncomfortable walking past groups of students who call out and make comments about my appearance"; "I worry about photos of private times being posted online without my consent"; "I feel anxious about walking on my own at night, and wish I could have the freedom to move freely like my male friends have."

Other messages are about hopes and dreams for justice and inclusion, such as, "I dream of seeing pictures of a female headmaster next to all the men on the wall"; "I dream of having a dorm named after one of our distinguished women alumnae"; "I hope that my education will help me have the same job opportunities that my male classmates do, that people won't just think I went to college to find a husband"; "I yearn for a world where all people can live without fear because of their gender and race"; "I dream of seeing the kind of reality we hear about in chapel—a world where everyone can flourish because we are each made in the image of God."

The sharing continues for several minutes with reflective pauses between each reading. Maura then guides the community to be aware of their feelings and thoughts and to sit together in silent reflection, prayer, or meditation with one another in order to consider the opportunities for learning and transformation that are before them. The ritual closes with a symbolic action. Maura invites all gathered to take their Post-it notes and write one thing they feel inspired to express or commit to, following what has been shared. She then asks people to come forward and place their notes on the cut-out figures around the room. Gradually the figures become covered with notes of apology, of commitment, of gratitude, of sadness, of resolve, of hope. They are transformed from empty outlines to a tangible symbol of the community's desire to change.

After the service, several students come up to Maura, including some of the initial group of young women who had approached her back in January, to say that this was the first time they felt that their experiences were heard and respected by the larger community. They were hopeful. Several faculty members also said that they learned about how the culture at Robsen was affecting the confidence and identities of the girls at the school, not just intellectually but also physically and spiritually.

This case illustrates how bias and belittling enabled by systemic forms of oppression like sexism can create feelings of isolation that have a dimension of spiritual suffering. They might be said to have a plague-like impact in the lives of individuals and in the systemic life of a community. This isolation can exist even in a community where numerous others are impacted by the harm because individuals feel they are not believed or given a safe space to share their experiences. In such times, a chaplain has the opportunity to use public rituals to make space for voices to be heard and to invite transformative change. These rituals can also become a locus of tension when they present uncomfortable truths that the community might not wish to acknowledge, an important step in and of itself. Maura seemed to understand her community well enough to know that a ritual could provide both of these things—and that both of these things were needed to help change the culture of the school. In this way, Maura exercised public leadership by believing the students at the school and by creating a service to amplify their voices so that they might become an impetus for change.

THE CONTEXTS OF RITUALS

Among the different interventions with which helping professionals support persons in crisis or need, the facilitation of rituals is often unique to chaplains. Many rituals have been developed throughout history in spiritual communities, and, depending on the needs and spiritual/religious identity of the careseeker, chaplains frequently rely on these traditional forms of comfort and support. As the role of religion changes and familiarity with traditional rituals becomes less common, chaplains may also modify traditional rituals or create new ones (as we see in the case study above) to help careseekers express their feelings, facilitate community, invite transformation, and provide stability and grounding. Chaplains often meet careseekers in "high stakes" moments, in life-and-death and boundary situations, or in times of transition. Liminality or **liminal spaces** are terms that capture the "in-betweenness" of these moments. Liminal spaces are points on the map of life that are in between normalcy as we have known it and what life will become. Sometimes liminal spaces are physical spaces—like a hospital room—and sometimes they are spaces of time, as in the case of the time between the death of a loved one and the funeral.[3] Either way, they can lead to transition, changing boundaries, and new thresholds and meanings. They have the potential to allow us to acknowledge circumstances from which might emerge new possibilities that can simultaneously feel promising and out of our control.

Trauma often instantiates liminal experiences, as do times of public and private grief and loss, career or educational transitions, moving from one home to another, and joy. When people experience any of these events, they may feel as if they are in an in-between state of existence that can call forth a not-knowing, a lack of orientation, and a sense of being caught between longing for what life used to be and the possibilities of hope for the future. Experiences of liminality can be especially challenging when we do not desire or request to enter them. When trauma, illness, dying, death, displacement, or isolation are forced into our experience—especially but not exclusively when it is unexpected—then individuals may find not only that they are in a liminal space or a liminal time but that they inhabit a liminal self that seems mystified and foreign.[4] Nothing is as it once was, including the individual.[5]

While individuals can perceive themselves to be in a liminal state, societies can also exist in that same state of in-betweenness. This may be particularly apparent during times when the culture is experiencing trauma and systemic difficulties and when it feels as if the stability that might have been culturally assumed in the past is no longer present.[6] In such times, individuals often experience the effects of systemic liminality. Systemic liminality can be particularly challenging to navigate, as it means that people cannot rely upon society as a source of stability. For instance, the events of September 11, 2001, created a public crisis that caused the United States to enter as a country into a collective liminal space. Many chaplains volunteered at Ground Zero in the aftermath of September 11, providing care to first responders.[7] As the magnitude and death toll of the tragedy mounted, chaplains initiated rituals of public mourning and supported public symbols memorializing those who had died. Another example of chaplains offering their skills during a time of collective liminality would be those who provided spiritual care—including end-of-life rituals—to patients, families, and medical health professionals during the COVID-19 crisis.[8]

These examples show how rituals are an important resource that chaplains can draw upon in response to larger-scale societal upheavals caused by human beings and natural disaster.[9] In such cases, it becomes important for the chaplain to acknowledge that individuals are navigating personal experiences of liminality—of suffering and affliction—in the midst of a society that is also trying to navigate the disorientation of liminality. Circumstances of systemic liminality can make it more difficult for a person to cope with the event because the culture at large is also in that place. Rituals, in response, can offer a safe way to process a liminal event, even societal ones.

As noted, chaplains are regularly called to offer spiritual care during times when an individual, an institution, or the wider culture is in a liminal state. They may be asked to engage in acts of public leadership during times when the culture at large is experiencing in-betweenness in ways that affect individual lives. For instance, following the school shooting in Newtown, Connecticut, a number of institutional chaplains and congregational clergy facilitated a multi-faith service designed to help the public name and grieve what had been lost. Many also led vigils in the days following the shootings.

Because these rituals occurred in the immediate aftermath of the shootings, family members of the deceased as well as the public were in a liminal state in which many were suffering and struggling to understand what had happened.

Yet times of cultural suffering and affliction can also be moments of radical spiritual transformation. Liminal moments offer society an opportunity to lament and to protest the affliction. Those who are directly and indirectly impacted by an event can experience equality and a level ground of connectedness, even if only for a moment. The chaplain's vision can assist the community in responding both to the aftermath of the violation and to the reality of interhuman betrayal that emerges as a result of systemic forms of oppression. One way the chaplain can help do this is by naming this dual reality for the community within the context of ritual. For example, the ritual led by Chaplain Maura in the case study above named, lamented, and mourned systemic injustice and oppression, even as it offered hope to the community to forge a new way forward.[10]

Additionally, chaplains have the opportunity to name the complexity of interhuman suffering within the context of ritual. Through the lens of emotional and spiritual suffering caused or severely exacerbated by others, the sufferer not only asks why did God or nature bring about the traumatic event but is also compelled to ask questions about senseless ill will, evil, and pathology within and among human beings. It is one trial to live with a pandemic and quarantine; it is an entire other level of suffering to live with social chaos and ill will at the center of it. The chaplain's willingness to speak about these hard truths within a sacred space can potentially transform the meaning of the experience for careseekers.

WHAT RITUALS DO

Rituals function in a variety of ways. In the immediacy of a crisis, they help stabilize and support those who are in shock or overwhelmed. Following a devastating loss, they make space for communities to remember and to mourn, and—as in our case example of the Robsen school—they help people to begin to imagine a way forward. In institutional settings, rituals or ceremonies also mark important moments in an organization's life, such as the beginning of a school or fiscal year. Likewise, rituals provide ways to honor meaning and can facilitate sacred turning points for communities following difficult experiences or devastating loss. It is important to remember that this kind of ritual work is unique to the chaplain. Chaplains are often the only individuals in their respective organizations who make use of ritual in their workplaces. It is therefore through the facilitation of rituals that chaplains enact one of their most distinctive leadership functions.

Rituals open spaces not only for thought but also for emotions and sensations, especially when people are heartbroken and confused because they are navigating liminal experiences. They engage the whole person: their bodies, spirits, and minds. In a ritual, participants might stand and sit. They might sing. They might hold hands with the person next to them. These embodied experiences—even if done virtually by holding one's hands out to others through the camera—can create a sense of physical safety and relational connection, especially when the ritual is familiar and consistent. These experiences can also impart a sense that the careseeker belongs to and is supported by a larger community.[11] Chaplains can therefore use rituals to create safe, communal experiences that offer support and to begin to envision hope that emerges from lament and sorrow.[12]

Finally, rituals often function to remember and to reveal. They not only meet the needs of a careseeker in the moment but also offer a glimpse of hope for what the future will be. This capacity to hold space both for the past, honoring what has been lost, and for the future, pointing toward hope, can be transformative for careseekers. Hence, when individuals and communities need help to live in between experiences of liminality, rituals support, stabilize, and help people through transitions.[13]

DEVELOPING RITUALS

How does a chaplain go about developing an appropriate ritual? We outline competencies for the facilitation of rituals:

1. Assessing needs
2. Drawing on spiritual and wisdom traditions for contemporary meaning making
3. Utilizing a structure
4. Facilitating connection
5. Integrating diverse spiritual resources

First, it is important to assess the spiritual needs of the people, given that chaplains are oriented toward the need of their communities. Once the chaplain can name the particular need at hand, the pragmatics of the situation can be considered: What symbols are important to this community? What songs are meaningful? What space is appropriate? Who should be involved in crafting the ritual? What resources are available, and are any additional resources needed? Answering these questions will help guide chaplains as they craft meaningful rituals for their communities. The chaplain thus makes a careful assessment of the needs of the individuals or communities involved and the context of the ritual.

While rituals are often helpful for supporting careseekers through times of transition, times of in-betweenness (or liminality) often call for rituals that foster stability and support. For example, when a family is waiting for news during a health crisis, the chaplain may facilitate a ritual that is familiar and grounding because hearing familiar words and participating in familiar actions can connect those present to their own tradition and provide a sense of comfort. For a Roman Catholic family, the chaplain may gather the household together to pray and recite the Lord's Prayer. For a family who practices the Jewish faith, the chaplain may use a prayer for healing called the *mi sheberach*. For a family that does not identify with a particular faith, the chaplain can ask what kind of ritual would feel meaningful to them and craft something appropriate with their needs in mind. What these examples share in common is that the chaplain actively listens to the needs of the careseekers. Starting from this place of intentional listening fosters empathy in the chaplain and helps the chaplain absorb not only the text but also the subtext of the careseekers' concerns so that it becomes possible to effectively shape meaningful rituals that support the needs of the family, group, or individual.

In circumstances of the imminent death of an individual and other urgent crises that impact families and small groups, chaplains are asked to fulfill requests for immediate prayer and ritual. Deathbed rituals often include opportunities for loved ones to gather together and to touch, hold, kiss, and say what they need to say to the one who is dying or has died. They may include a reading, a prayer, or a time of silence to honor and hold compassion for the one who has died. When people are struggling, they frequently seek ways to connect with sources of transcendent meaning. Prayer, reflective reading of sacred stories, and guided meditation are common ways chaplains incorporate ritual into care practices. When a careseeker desires prayer, the chaplain may inquire what the careseeker would like to be spoken in the prayer or may consider if the careseeker comes from a tradition where standardized prayers are common. Careseekers may wish to express concerns and feelings in their own words. In gathering careseekers in prayer, the chaplain will first have assessed their needs and their comfort level with prayer and tailor her or his words to meet their context as much as possible.

Second, when chaplains facilitate rituals, they regularly draw on spiritual wisdom traditions, connecting careseekers with their particular lineage in their process of meaning making for the current situation. Chaplains have the opportunity to integrate frameworks available from careseekers' own traditions to interpret and respond to experiences of liminality and suffering. We illustrate this by utilizing the biblical concept of *tzaraat* to explore experiences of liminality in human life and how chaplains engage in practices of care through liminal times and spaces. The Hebrew Bible offers one way of thinking about liminality that may be helpful for chaplains as they develop a framework for considering their identity and the needs of careseekers in liminal times. *Tzaraat*, a Hebrew word, is often translated as "dis-ease" or "affliction." The definitions and conditions of *tzaraat* in the Hebrew text are more expansive than a one-word definition in English. They include the condition of "*tzaraat*, skin affliction, which is frequently and inaccurately translated as leprosy."[14] In biblical times, the *metzora*—the human being living with *tzaraat*—would have been diagnosed by a priest and then placed under quarantine outside of the encampment of the larger society. *Tzaraat* can also refer to a non-desired state in the quality or the health of fabrics or building structures. This might refer to matters like mold or mildew. Unhealthy exposures—as *tzaraat*—are discussed in the biblical text. Experiences of *tzaraat* often draw people into liminal spaces. It can be argued that in contemporary times, these experiences can be medically based—as in the case of COVID-19—or they can also manifest as racism, sexism, classism, and other forms of systemic oppression.

Ancient, medieval, and contemporary interpretations of the affliction of *tzaraat* and the state of the *metzora* are varied and wide—beginning with literal elucidations of the illness, to questions about what causes it and how one may recover from it. What is relevant here is that *tzaraat* possesses a liminal dimension. As Samson Raphael Hirsch writes, "*Tzaraat* wasn't a physical ailment at all. Rather, it was a spiritual ailment and a call of distress for priestly intervention and assistance."[15] While Hirsch is right that there is a spiritual dimension to *tzaraat*, we would venture to say that the experience also incorporates the physical, psychological, and intellectual dimensions of being. Therefore, we use the word "affliction" or the phrase "that which causes suffering" in relation to *tzaraat*, highlighting the physical, emotional, and spiritual afflictions and sufferings that occur on both personal and societal levels. Other religious traditions or worldviews may use a different term for this concept. The Islamic Hadiths, Japanese Buddhist Endishiki writings, and the Vedic scriptures of Hinduism and Indian religions all possess texts that contain words and concepts that address connections between physical, emotional, and spiritual sufferings. What is important to illustrate here is how chaplains are equipped to draw from ancient spiritual wisdom traditions as resources for their practice today.

Individuals who exist in liminal states, in spaces of *tzaraat*, often feel separated, isolated, or different from others. That sense of isolation functions as a kind of spiritual affliction that chaplains are uniquely able to address because, unlike doctors or psychologists, spirituality is their area of expertise. People who lived in ancient times recognized that suffering had a spiritual dimension that religious leaders were uniquely equipped to address. This is why a priest would anoint the *metzora*, to facilitate that person's return from the liminal state. Posited here is the notion that moving from a crisis back into a non-liminal state is very much modeled in the biblical tradition, and thereto in contemporary chaplaincy practices. The modern chaplain—like the ancient biblical priest—has an opportunity to create rituals for those who are in liminal states to help them transition from one state of being to another. The *metzora* and the condition of *tzaraat* therefore indicate an ancient reference point to the relevance of liminality in healing. This example also suggests that chaplains have a unique set of skills that they can offer at the most crucial individual and societal moments of upheaval or affliction and that rituals can build resilience as people emerge from crises. When the individual or community is disoriented after a liminal event, the spiritual care provider draws upon old and new resources to help individuals discover that they can move beyond the liminal state and into a new state of being. As Yael Danieli and Kathleen Nader summarize, "Rituals are group methods that serve to maintain a culture's social structure and its norms, strengthen the bonds of individuals to their communities, assist adaptation (to change or crisis), manage fear and anxiety, and ward off threats."[16]

Third, chaplains often utilize an existing structure or scaffolding for the design of a ritual. Some rituals are highly formalized. In military chaplaincy, for example, when a soldier is killed in a war zone, the chaplain is responsible to conduct a ramp ceremony at the airfield. All military personnel are in attendance, the deceased is remembered, prayers are offered, and a flag is draped over the coffin. Led by the chaplain, military colleagues accompany the coffin to the airplane for the final return home. Other examples of formalized rituals that draw on specific religious practices include a Roman Catholic priest offering "the anointing of the sick" with a practicing Catholic, or a Buddhist chaplain offering specific chants for a Buddhist who is dying. Even when careseekers do not practice a particular religious tradition and

Meaning Making

chaplains improvise to create a ritual, such as a memorial service, chaplains may still rely on elements of traditional rituals with opening words, readings, symbolic actions, and blessing-like closure. At times, it is important for chaplains to bring in spiritual leaders of religious traditions to lead and guide specific ritual practices. This may occur when the chaplain is not qualified to lead the practice, such as when a hospital patient asks a Hindu chaplain to perform a Christian anointing ritual. It may also occur when the chaplain is not familiar enough with the ritual practice that a careseeker needs—even the most skilled chaplains do not have expertise in every kind of ritual practice.

Fourth, when designing rituals, chaplains engage participation and facilitate connection. Rituals can respond to careseekers' needs for agency and voice, even as vulnerability and liminality remain at the center of the spiritual care response.[17] In the case study about Chaplain Maura, the chaplain asked students and faculty to write their experiences as girls and women on Post-it notes and to participate in the service through reading and symbolic action. This activity offered an opportunity for the entire community to participate and for members to build stronger connections.

Relatedly, rituals are most often communal events with the potential to facilitate connection and belonging. For example, when hearing the shofar during the High Holy Days, many Jewish people will be touched deeply and feel connected both to the Jewish community they currently participate in, to Jews around the world, and to the Jewish communities of the past that also engaged in this ritual. "You're supposed to hear the blast of the shofar 100 times in a single day. By the time you get to the 100th one, a really long blast, you're so overwhelmed with emotion, because the sound is vibrating in your chest. I cry when I hear it."[18] What this quotation shows is that many people feel connected to something larger than themselves and often feel grounded and held by a transcendent power when hearing familiar prayers and chants. Words and symbolic actions that have been performed repeatedly over the years create connections to one's community in the present as well as to the past. In this way, rituals can facilitate a sense of social belonging.

Finally, when facilitating rituals, chaplains often integrate diverse spiritual resources. While chaplains try to connect careseekers with religious leaders of the careseekers' tradition when desired, an interfaith chaplain in a crisis situation often does not have access to local resources and may instead offer prayers or readings from the tradition of the careseeker. Chaplains benefit from developing a literacy and resources in diverse spiritual traditions in order to meet the needs of the people they serve. In some situations, they ask the careseekers to participate and contribute from their own tradition. The following case illustrates how chaplains can be responsive to diverse spiritual needs of their community.

CASE 2

A Christian school situated in an urban part of the United States gained a reputation for being the most intellectually rigorous school in the city. Admission to the school became competitive, and many parents sought a placement for their children not because of the school's religious identity but because they believed it would give their children a better education and chance at college acceptance than other schools in the city.

Traditionally, the school had required students to participate in "chapel" services led by the school's Christian chaplain. As the school's reputation increased, a significant number of Jewish and Hindu students enrolled. The school chaplain felt a need to respond to the increasing diversity of spiritual identities within the student body. She organized a gathering of parents and students of Christian and non-Christian traditions to discuss how spiritual/religious ritual needs could be addressed. At the gathering, the participants decided to form an extracurricular student-led group with support from the chaplain and some parents in order to decide on how to make the required chapel space into one that truly exhibited spiritual belonging. First, the group decided to change the name of the school's worship time from "chapel" to "spiritual reflection services." Second, the group developed a calendar of religious holidays that included the major holidays of the Jewish, Christian, Muslim, Hindu, and Buddhist traditions. The plan was to acknowledge and celebrate these holidays in school services. The chaplain connected with Jewish, Hindu, Muslim, and Buddhist local religious leaders for guidance and participation in these services. Third, the students advocated for inclusion of spiritual reflection services that would involve students who did not identify with any particular religion.

The chaplain met with the school's board to advocate for these changes. Some board members expressed concern that the school would give up its identity as a Christian school. Other members welcomed the new concept as a tool for intercultural education in an increasingly pluralistic and diverse society. The chaplain pointed out that she had been encouraged by the increased student engagement to conceptualize the "spiritual reflection services" and welcomed the energy of the students and non-Christian parents. She also shared that Christian holidays and themes would continue to be part of the services of celebration. The school's board decided to pilot the new form of "spiritual reflection services," the first of which would commemorate the Hindu holiday of Diwali.

The chaplain and the newly formed student group met with Hindu students and parents to plan a ritual. One student suggested that the school community assemble a *rangoli*—an elaborate and intricate design usually created on the floor of a space during festivals—inside the chapel. Another said they could make it out of flowers. A third suggested that maybe some of the older students could design the *rangoli* themselves, and a fourth added the idea of having the Hindu students begin the ritual by reading a children's book about Diwali out loud to explain what the festival was. The chaplain agreed that all of this sounded like a great idea, and she partnered with the students and families to help arrange the ritual. In the weeks leading up to it, she sent a newsletter to the school community that explained what Diwali was and how they would be celebrating it. The ritual became one of the most beloved events of the year and eventually became a tradition at the school.

In this example, the chaplain started by assessing the needs of those entrusted to her care by actively listening and empathizing with their spiritual needs. She recognized her own limitations and the need for all members of the community to feel included. She fostered inclusivity and empowered the community members' agency to create rituals. In this way, the chaplain led by handing leadership over to those who were best equipped to do the ritual work. The chaplain's work here involved exercising leadership in a specific way. Rather than functioning as a counselor or spiritual director, the chaplain was called to envision a way to bring a community together for the purpose of inclusion and belonging.

The chaplain at the Christian school therefore served all students, faculty, and staff and wanted to generate a sense of belonging for all, not just those who were of the Christian faith. This commitment led to some concrete changes in ritual practice: the chaplain changed the name of the worship services from "chapel" to "spiritual reflection services" because the former title had Christian connotations that did not meet the needs of this new intercultural school community. This change allowed for more participation during school-wide rituals, as services began to be more inclusive and reflective of the cultural and spiritual traditions that were represented in the community.

The chaplain also generated a sense of community by engaging the students in the new project of "spiritual reflection" at the school. She realized her own limitations as a Christian chaplain and invited students, parents, and local religious leaders from other traditions to participate and cocreate the diverse services fostering intercultural connection and learning.

She also made space for students to develop their own reflections and rituals, including those who did not identify with any particular tradition. Thus, she sought to include the increasing number of youth and young adults who do not belong to a religious tradition while at the same time they are exposed to different expressions of faith and spirituality.

While many rituals have been celebrated over centuries and connect participants with a long tradition, rituals can be cocreated and emerge suddenly. For example, after mass shootings many people gather spontaneously to light candles and hold vigils. Rituals can present spaces to manage shock, grief, and uncertainty through creative connections and in community with others.

CONCLUSION

Chaotic societal and personal experiences of affliction and suffering, as well as joyful places of positive transformation, are areas that the chaplain enters to honor human experience. These often call out for expression in ritual. As a member of multidisciplinary teams in healthcare organizations, jails, prisons, social service agencies, and corporations, the chaplain is often the only person in an organization who cares for the spiritual well-being of careseekers, including their ritual needs. Rituals become embodied enactments of human suffering, liminality, and visionary hope for the future. They are often critical for healing and become pivot points in the memory of individuals who sought a chaplain's care. In this way, the creation of rituals becomes one of the most important tasks that falls to a chaplain, a task that is sacred and timeless.

In closing, this chapter used the lens of liminality to explore the place of rituals in chaplaincy practice. It suggested that public leadership can take place—and hopefully will take place—in a variety of settings, including ritual settings. It also explored how the chaplain can work within a system or with an individual to help transform embedded beliefs and assist with the process of bringing awareness and voice to needs that may otherwise go unnoticed, thus increasing the well-being of individuals and communities. It showed, in short, that ritual is pivotal to the meaning-making work of the chaplain.

REFLECTION QUESTIONS

1. How did the chaplains in these case studies demonstrate spiritual leadership?
2. How did the chaplains demonstrate empathy?
3. What do you imagine might be challenging when preparing a ritual?
4. What resources do you have from your spiritual life that might help you in preparing a ritual?
5. How does your spiritual tradition conceptualize liminality?

RECOMMENDED READINGS

Cutter, William, ed. *Healing and the Jewish Imagination: Spiritual and Practical Perspectives on Judaism and Health*. Woodstock, Vt.: Jewish Lights, 2007.

Ramshaw, Elaine. *Ritual and Pastoral Care*. Minneapolis: Fortress Press, 1987.

Roberts, Stephen B., ed. *Professional Spiritual and Pastoral Care: A Practical Clergy and Chaplain's Handbook*. Woodstock, Vt.: SkyLight Paths, 2012.

PART THREE

Interpersonal Competencies

Introduction to Interpersonal Competencies

CARRIE DOEHRING *and* ALLISON KESTENBAUM

THE NEED FOR INTERRELIGIOUS, SOCIALLY JUST SPIRITUAL CARE

Research on how therapy helps people change demonstrates that the relationship formed between therapist and client is important in the change process. Therapeutic alliances are mediators of change for those in therapy: the stronger the alliance between therapist and client, the more likely treatment will have positive outcomes, a finding consistent across a range of psychotherapeutic approaches.[1] While there is no research on how an alliance helps people change through spiritual care, similarities between spiritual care and behavioral healthcare suggest that alliances are equally important in spiritual care. What makes spiritual care alliances different from therapeutic alliances? Spiritual care alliances have the added dimension of spiritual interconnectedness: the sense of being held within trustworthy relational webs beyond oneself. Spiritual care, then, helps people experience spiritual trust that goes beyond the caregiving relationship to include spiritual dimensions of relationality (see chapter 4 for a description of how a mindful attention to the presence of "the sacred" is part of spiritual care).

Spiritual trust is named in many ways: for example, as an immanent ground of being and a transcendent oneness with creation. What is common across diverse ways of experiencing and describing spiritual trust is a felt sense of spiritual interconnectedness beyond oneself. Spiritual trust helps people collaborate with community faith leaders, chaplains, and spiritual mentors in searching for values and beliefs (a distinctive aspect of spiritual care described in the chapters of part 2). Chaplaincy has been called a "ministry of presence,"[2] as noted in chapter 3, suggesting that the chaplain's religious/spiritual vocation is what makes spiritual care different from other helping professionals. In our chapters we focus on the role of spiritual trust—the spiritual aspects of the relationship between chaplain and careseeker—as a mediator of change. When spiritual care relationships help people experience spiritual trust, those people will be more likely to experience spiritual care as helpful.

What makes chaplains spiritually trustworthy? Within secular contexts like healthcare, hospice, long-term care, the military, and educational and prison contexts,[3] people are more likely to trust chaplains who demonstrate respect for their particular practices, values, and beliefs. While all people working in these contexts are expected to respect cultural differences, what makes chaplains unique is their respect for religious, spiritual, and moral differences that integrates their graduate studies, especially comparative studies of religion, with formation and clinical training. At their best, these academic and clinical qualifications help chaplains learn and practice interreligious care. As we note in chapter 6, while the term "interreligious" highlights a specialized intercultural humility, it could appear to exclude spiritual care to those with humanist, agnostic, or atheist orientations, as well as those who reject the term "spiritual" in describing their traditions and communities (for example, Buddhist, Confucian, Hindu, or American Indian persons). We use the term "interreligious" to include all of these diverse practices, values, beliefs, communities, and traditions.

Interreligious spiritual care fulfills ethical mandates of spiritual care professionals described in the *CASC/ACSS Policy and Procedure Manual*:

> When Spiritual Care Professionals behave in a manner congruent with the [following] values of this code of ethics, they bring greater justice, compassion and healing to our world. . . .
>
> • affirm the dignity and value of each individual;

- respect the right of each faith group to hold to its values and traditions;
- advocate for professional accountability that protects the public and advances the profession; and
- respect the cultural, ethnic, gender, racial, sexual-orientation, and religious diversity of other professionals and those served and strive to eliminate discrimination.[4]

Religious beliefs and practices have tragically been used to justify discrimination, prejudice, and even violence. Systemic racism and, indeed, overarching colonialist systems of power have been supported by religious abuses of power. Spiritual care may inadvertently or advertently reinforce religious, racist, sexist, and other kinds of prejudice that support systemic oppression. Indeed, all spiritual care relationships are embedded in cultural systems of oppression. For these reasons, chaplains must practice interreligious spiritual care that is also socially just. We use the term "socially just spiritual care" to describe the need for chaplains to understand how systems of social privilege and disadvantages interact in their own lives, in the lives of careseekers, and within the organizational contexts where they practice spiritual care. How can chaplains integrate knowledge gained through academic studies and possible clinical training with interpersonal competencies for socially just interreligious spiritual care in the practice of care? The chapters in part 3 answer that question.

CHAPTER OUTLINES

Chapter 6 defines, describes, and illustrates three interpersonal competencies that are specific to the practice of interreligious, socially just spiritual care: spiritual **self-differentiation**, spiritual empathy, and spiritual reflexivity. Learning these competencies requires chaplains to first experience spiritual trust for themselves through spiritual self-care. When chaplains are grounded in experiences of trustworthy spiritual interconnectedness, they will be able to use spiritual practices to monitor how their responses to stress make them more likely to blur differences between their religious/spiritual moral orientations and those of others. Using calming spiritual practices will help them maintain healthy spiritual boundaries and not use their power in spiritually coercive or neglectful ways. Spiritual self-differentiation helps chaplains become spiritually and socially empathic—more able to imagine how the other's stress/suffering generates coping practices, values, and beliefs shaped by intersecting social advantages and disadvantages. The final competency of spiritual reflexivity is the capacity to work across and among these differences in a process of cocreating meanings.

Chapter 7 describes how chaplains practice these competencies in spiritual care with those experiencing suicidal despair, addictions, trauma, and moral injury. This chapter builds upon chapter 6 by using a model—the Helping Styles Inventory—that describes four different interpersonal styles that chaplains might use to help those receiving care: celebrant, consultant, manager, and guide. How do chaplains use these different helping styles of spiritual care when people struggle with despair and thoughts of ending their lives or with addictions or when they have experiences of trauma and moral injury? This chapter integrates research-based knowledge with interpersonal competencies in response to these forms of suffering, using an extended case study of a chaplain intern providing spiritual care to a veteran in a Veterans Affairs medical center.

Chapter 8 describes the central role of social justice in spiritual care, bringing into view the ways social injustice plays a part implicitly or explicitly within the organizations where chaplains work. Competency in socially just spiritual care requires specialized knowledge about power, **social location**, patriarchy, and systemic racism—knowledge necessary for understanding the power dynamics and systemic disparities across organizational levels within contexts that include spiritual care. This chapter examines the near history of spiritual care based on a therapeutic approach, which was expanded to include a communal contextual approach and now includes a socially just approach. Richard Coble and Mychal Springer open with a case study first introduced in chapter 6. They compellingly illustrate how chaplains may need to intervene when the spiritual well-being of a care receiver is undermined—even threatened—by an interdisciplinary team member's prejudice. A closing case study illustrates how interreligious care is combined with socially just care.

Throughout these chapters, we use the term "competency" as a shorthand way to reference essential qualities distinct to spiritual care relationships. The word "competency" may be a misnomer, implying a skill set acquired by an individual at a stage of learning that remains forever the same throughout that person's professional career. We more often use the phrase "practicing spiritual care" to describe how chaplains are always learning through practice within relationships of collaborative accountability with peers and educators in classrooms, clinical training, and professional consultations. Interreligious, socially just spiritual care is profoundly challenging and always unfinished. It cannot be done alone. Learning how to practice spiritual care is a lifelong integrative process. We hope that chaplains introduced to the interpersonal competencies described in these chapters will be able to develop goals for learning them from the outset of their education and, when needed, clinical training—in their first role-plays in academic courses or maybe their first spiritual care interactions in clinical training. We hope that they, like the authors of these chapters, will feel compelled to continue this lifelong learning process within peer supervision and consultation.

CHAPTER SIX

Interpersonal Competencies for Cultivating Spiritual Trust

CARRIE DOEHRING *and* ALLISON KESTENBAUM

ABSTRACT *This chapter describes three interpersonal spiritual care competencies building upon each other to cultivate spiritual trust: spiritual self-differentiation, spiritual empathy, and spiritual reflexivity. In the lifelong process of learning these competencies, chaplains need to practice spiritual self-care that helps them self-differentiate by maintaining healthy boundaries within the power dynamics of caregiving. Chaplains practice spiritual differentiation by drawing upon their religious, theological, and clinical education to focus on differences between their own and another person's beliefs, values, and spiritual practices. Spiritual differentiation is at the heart of interreligious care, which makes chaplains more spiritually trustworthy. Building upon spiritual differentiation, spiritual and social empathy helps chaplains imagine how another person's suffering generates contextual values, beliefs, and coping practices that may be shaped by systemic abuses of power. People are more likely to trust chaplains who are spiritually differentiated and empathic. Such trust makes people want to search for meanings with chaplains, a process described in previous chapters. Chaplains become spiritually trustworthy when they are spiritually reflexive about how values and beliefs are contextually shaped by aspects of one's social, religious, or spiritual identities. A case study illustrates how chaplains use communication skills in practicing spiritual care that is spiritually differentiated, empathic, and reflexive.*

SPIRITUAL TRUST: THE RELATIONAL FOUNDATION FOR LEARNING AND PRACTICING SPIRITUAL CARE

In this chapter we describe three interpersonal competencies—spiritual self-differentiation, spiritual empathy, and spiritual reflexivity—that help chaplains establish spiritual trust, which is the relational foundation unique to spiritual care. Spiritual care, as we define it, is an integrative process that begins with exploring calming spiritual practices that help people to experience spiritual trust. We use the term "spiritual" as a simple way to describe complex and diverse relational experiences of transcendence. Many people experience and name transcendence through sacred texts, music, symbols, and rituals from religious or spiritual traditions. When spiritual practices help people feel held within compassionate and trustworthy relationships, they will be ready to explore what their suffering means (an essential function of spiritual care described in the chapters on meaning making).[1] When they feel overwhelmed by suffering, they can rest in practices that instill trust. In this chapter we build upon the description in chapter 3 of how chaplains listen for the ways that people may experience a sense of connectedness with the sacred/transcendent/sources of spirituality.

Chaplains become spiritually trustworthy when they convey respect for the unique ways people experience and name incarnational or transcendent aspects of their lives that mediate a deep sense of mystery, awe, beauty, goodness, holiness, or the sacred. Chaplains may be especially helpful when people experience religious and spiritual struggles that disrupt practices previously connecting them to transcendence.[2] Chaplains may invite people to collaboratively explore any sorts of calming practices that help them feel self-compassion when physiological, emotional, and moral stress overwhelms them. Calming practices help people reexperience that deep sense of connection that instills a sense of trust. In a parallel fashion, chaplains trust the process of learning spiritual care when they use spiritual practices that center and calm them when they feel overwhelmed by suffering (see chapter 3 for a description of chaplains developing specific practices to ground themselves in their bodies). We illustrate the importance of spiritual self-care in the following case study[3] used throughout our chapter.

Case Study, Part 1: Practicing Spiritual Self-Care

Our chapter's case study describes Angie, a twenty-five-year-old single African American woman with advanced Hodgkin's lymphoma, who is expected to die during this hospitalization. She is unresponsive, and medical examinations suggest that the systems of her body are shutting down in a way that is typical at the end of life. The chaplains on the floor have been making brief daily visits. She receives no other visitors. The walls are bare of cards, and there are no flowers in the room. You know from the prior visits by chaplains on this floor and the chart notes that Angie is alienated from her family and distances herself from people she said were "bad influences" before her cancer diagnosis and earlier recovery from addiction. She credited a return to the Pentecostalism of her youth as the reason she has remained clean and sober.

Angie has been unresponsive for more than a week. You are a student chaplain new to the oncology unit today. You had spoken with other chaplains about Angie. The nurses tell you today that Angie has had moments where she is more alert. One nurse, who is very experienced with end-of-life care, tells you that it is common for patients who are dying to experience perceptions or sensations that are comforting to them. Sometimes there is no clear medical explanation for these experiences. You were anticipating that she would still be unresponsive and you would simply need to offer a silent prayer. Before going into Angie's room, you take a deep breath and realize how anxious you are. If she has a conversation with you, you will have to chart your visit and report back to your chaplaincy colleagues and summarize your visit at rounds with the medical team.

When you enter her room, you find that Angie is indeed awake and eager to tell you about an "amazing experience with God" when she was unresponsive. Her voice is low and quiet. She invites you to sit close to her so you can hear what she says. "It was just me and God dancing together up there in the corner. I had on a red dress. The prettiest red dress. I've never worn anything like it. We danced and danced. You know, people always say, 'God is this' or, 'God is that.' God isn't anything we know about, even if he is a darned good dancer. It's just, 'God is.'" She pauses. There are tears in her eyes. "Not even, 'God is.' Just, 'is.'"

Angie goes on to tell you that she received a blessing and a healing and that even though she will die with the cancer, she has been made whole.

Trusting the Process of Learning Spiritual Care

What helps chaplains instill spiritual trust in those facing the void of death, like Angie in our case study? Chaplains serve as a liaison between participants in the care recipient context (for example, in healthcare, between patients and their medical caregivers). At the same time, chaplains enable careseekers like Angie to trust the process of spiritually integrating their suffering when chaplains are on their own journeys of spiritual integration. Spiritual integration is a collaborative and relational process of using calming spiritual practices that help people explore life-giving beliefs about suffering and hope. Spiritual integration is "the extent to which spiritual beliefs, practices, and experiences are organized into a coherent whole."[4] What helps chaplains on the parallel course of spiritual self-care/integration while caring for others?

Like the process of spiritual care, spiritual integration begins with exploring and using calming practices for coping with stress. If you were the student chaplain in our case study, you might feel overwhelmed by the challenge of offering spiritual care to this young African American woman dying of cancer who has been unresponsive for a week and is now periodically stirring and more responsive. It is easy to imagine your stress response. Your breathing becomes shallow. Your heart beats faster. Your shoulder and facial muscles tighten. You feel momentarily overwhelmed by the complexities of interdisciplinary spiritual care to dying patients who experience sensations or perceptions that are comforting. You want to empathize with this patient's emotional and spiritual experience while placing it in an interdisciplinary clinical context that honors her dying process. You want to align your body language with the compassion of your heart and your interdisciplinary understanding of her spiritual experiences of dying.

Imagine taking several slow, deep breaths while you focus for a moment on something with spiritual meanings, such as a sacred text, or a place or image with sacred meanings. Calming practices like slow, deep breathing can be incorporated into regular spiritual practices like prayer, devotional reading of sacred texts, participating in liturgies, mindfulness meditation, and yoga, as well as any sort of practice that instills a sense of beauty, awe, or goodness through the arts and nature. Calming spiritual practices ground chaplains in their own religious or spiritual heritage, identity, and communities in ways that enhance spiritual differentiation, empathy, and reflexivity—three core interpersonal competencies for socially just and interreligious spiritual care that build upon a spiritually integrative learning process. As we noted in the introduction to part 3, we use the term "socially just spiritual care" to describe the need for chaplains to understand how systems of social privilege and disadvantages interact in their own lives, in the lives of careseekers, and within the organizational contexts where they practice spiritual care. Developing interpersonal competencies is a lifelong learning process within relationships of collaborative accountability with peers and clinical pastoral educators, as we illustrate in the following descriptions of spiritual self-differentiation, spiritual empathy, and spiritual reflexivity.

SPIRITUAL SELF-DIFFERENTIATION

Self-differentiation helps chaplains maintain healthy relational boundaries within the power dynamics of spiritual care, so that chaplains do not become emotionally/spiritually fused with careseekers and their families or with colleagues. The importance of managing relational boundaries in the emotional intensity of intimacy and family relationships was first defined and described in Murray Bowen's family theory and therapy exploring intergenerational family patterns of relational boundaries.[5] Self-differentiation in intimate/high-investment relationships is both an interpersonal process of managing relational boundaries and a psychological process of managing emotions, thoughts, and behaviors. "In Bowen's approach," David Schnarch and Susan Regas tell us, "differentiation of self is the most critical to mature development and attainment of psychological health."[6]

The emotional intensity of spiritual care can cause chaplains to lose their "emotional balance" and blur the boundaries between self and other. Emotional contagion infuses chaplains with another's emotional struggles. Chaplains may feel overwhelmed by another's overt emotional distress. They may feel swept off their feet by the hidden currents of another's sadness, anger, or shame. They may reexperience memories of life threats, magnifying their moral responsibility to protect others from harm. Chaplains may cope with fusion using emotional disengagement or cutoff, which, as Schnarch and Regas emphasize, is not the opposite of fusion but an attempt to regulate one's emotions and sense of self.[7]

Conflicts involving power dynamics and relational boundaries are an inevitable part of couples' and family relationships, or any relationship in which people have an emotional investment. Schnarch and Regas's "crucible therapy" promotes "anxiety tolerance rather than . . . reduction" during "the natural emergence of emotional gridlock as a result of healthy differentiation."[8] Their crucible approach views "gridlock as normal and inevitable, and conflict as healthy and necessary for personal growth. . . . The ability to maintain good cognitive functioning and emotional self-regulation during stressful situations develops through high-anxiety, high-meaning encounters, which emerge during the course of marriage, love relationships, family, school, and work life." They define four points of balance necessary to navigate gridlock:

1. A solid, flexible self that is not dependent on "a positive reflected sense of self from others, allowing you to maintain your own psychological shape when other people pressure you to conform. Likewise, it reflects the ability to change and adapt, accept influence from others as good judgment dictates, and heed good advice without losing sight of your goals and values."
2. A quiet mind and calm heart, using soothing and calming practices for managing conflict without "dominating or accommodating others, or by becoming emotionally distant or intrusive."
3. Grounded responding, using "the ability to make modulated proportionate responses to provocations and difficult circumstances . . . [by] not locking into arguments or over-reacting, while also staying emotionally invested and not avoiding difficult people or situations that need to be handled."
4. Meaningful endurance, using "the ability to get out of your 'comfort zone,' tolerate discomfort for growth, and persevere through disappointment and hardship to accomplish your goals."

Those in professional helping relationships learn how to psychologically self-differentiate in order to maintain healthy boundaries. The added dimension of spiritual self-differentiation is what makes chaplains competent in interreligious spiritual care (see chapter 4 for the importance of interreligious care—unique to spiritual care—in the search for meanings). We use the term "interreligious" to describe a specialized kind of intercultural humility that integrates

- knowledge of the socially constructed nature of religious beliefs, values, and rituals;[9]
- attitudes of intercultural humility toward cultural, religious, moral, and spiritual differences and the ineffable mystery of the other;
- capacities in spiritual differentiation, enabling chaplains to distinguish among particular religious, spiritual, and moral orientations of others; and
- skills in spiritual self-care for coping with the anxieties or losses of letting go of absolute meaning or value systems that avoid, polarize, or minimize religious and spiritual differences.[10]

Chaplains learn interreligious care through graduate studies, especially comparative studies of religion, and clinical training that enhances spiritual self-differentiation in religiously diverse contexts. We recognize the limitations of the term "interreligious" for describing spiritual care to those with humanist, agnostic, or atheist orientations, as well as those who reject the term "spiritual" in describing their traditions and communities (for example, Buddhist, Confucian, Hindu, or American Indian persons).

Spiritual care combines psychological and interpersonal growth through self-differentiation with an interreligious radical respect for differences in the narrative "truth" of one's own and another's spiritual/moral orientation to stress or suffering. How can chaplains develop a solid flexible spiritual self (using Schnarch and Regas's first point of balance for self-differentiation)—sometimes called spiritual or pastoral authority? First, chaplains need graduate education in comparative studies of religion that helps them pay attention to how Christianity is used in normative and hierarchical ways to interpret and "rank" other religious traditions through Christian categories and beliefs. In describing spiritual empathy and reflexivity, we will elaborate how a social constructionist comparative approach is combined with a de-colonialist understanding of the fusion between colonialism and Christianity. Spiritual self-differentiation within religiously diverse contexts must truly respect religious differences by not enacting a caste system of religious/spiritual traditions and practices, with some more superior or truthful than others.

This cognitive dimension of a solid flexible spiritual self is challenging to practice within religious traditions that have not developed beliefs, values, and practices supporting radical respect for religious differences. Chaplains practicing spiritual care in religiously diverse contexts often struggle with becoming spiritually differentiated when their religious "family"—the community or organization that may ordain them and endorse their vocations of spiritual care—requires them to affirm the absolute truth of that community's religious doctrines and to practice spiritual care that "saves souls" through adherence to doctrine. Chaplains often cope with these doctrinal demands by adopting an inclusive orientation to religious differences that searches for commonalities and assumes that all religions of the worlds share common beliefs.[11] While inclusivism may alleviate religious conflicts between bi-vocations as chaplains and faith community leaders, inclusivism minimizes and ignores vast differences across religions of the world, especially historical trajectories and cultural contexts. When inclusivist spiritual caregivers assume there is "one God"[12] at the heart of each person's

Interpersonal Competencies

experience, they risk spiritual coercion by overlaying their experience of God onto another's unique experiences, values, and beliefs.

When chaplains are able to practice interreligious spiritual care using cognitive capacities for respecting a careseeker's narrative truth, they will be able to trust the cocreative process of spiritual care—the intermingling of their and a careseeker's stories, practices, values, and beliefs. Chaplains practice spiritual self-differentiation by combining a solid spiritual self that is grounded in their ongoing process of spiritual integration with a flexible spiritual self that trusts the spiritually intersubjective process of searching for contextually meaningful practices, values, and beliefs.

In our case study, Angie's description of her experience of God could easily overwhelm chaplains, especially within the drama of her emerging from a week of being unresponsive. They could be tempted to foreclose meanings cognitively through skepticism that questions Angie's sense of "reality"—her conviction that God was "speaking" to her. Skepticism could be a way of coping with emotional/spiritual fusion through disengagement. Such skepticism could be justified within progressive religious traditions that question "direct revelations" of God. Skeptical chaplains could easily become anxious about how those in their "religious home" would question any endorsement of such revelations. Alternately, chaplains within religious traditions that believe in direct revelations and miracles could become emotionally and spiritually fused with Angie in proclaiming this as a miracle. In either scenario, spiritual and emotional fusion will be more likely when chaplains do not understand what happens medically when people are intermittently responsive and then unresponsive due to the shutting down of their organs and body processes.[13] Collaboration with medical providers helps chaplains to be aware of medical reasons for a patient's unusual perceptions or unresponsiveness. Is the patient unresponsive due to a medical episode that can be treated and may or may not end their life? Or, as in Angie's case, are patients in their final days or weeks of life and not responsive because this is the body's way of minimizing suffering at the end of life?

By using calming spiritual practices in a spiritually integrative learning process (Schnarch and Regas's second point of balance for self-differentiation), chaplains can recognize when stress makes them cope with jarring experiences of religious differences by minimizing, polarizing, or using inclusion as a way of "recentering" themselves in familiar or habitual orientations that blur differences, which are shaped by childhood and culture. By grounding themselves using spiritual practices, such as deep, slow breathing that shifts chaplains out of a stress response into calmness, chaplains can reconnect with a felt sense of trust in the collaborative, cocreative process of spiritual care. With trusted others, they can explore what jarred them—what emotions were part of feeling overpowered and what values and beliefs about religious differences were generated by their stress responses. Spiritual practices that ground them in self- and other-compassion can help them use critical thinking skills in theological and religious studies to search for values and beliefs complex enough to bear the weight of suffering and offer realistic hope for healing and social justice.[14]

In our case study, chaplains could use calming spiritual practices when jarred by Angie's description of her experience with God in order to become more emotionally and cognitively able to cocreate meanings with her, especially about how she has "received a blessing and a healing"—that even though she will die with the cancer, she has been made whole. Our case study illustrates how chaplains can remain spiritually balanced and self-differentiated when they have developed a *solid flexible spiritual self* and *a quiet mind and calm heart* using calming spiritual practices. These cognitive and spiritual capacities of self-differentiation could help them use *grounded responding* as they cocreate contextual meanings arising from Angie's experience. They will be able to "surf" the anxiety of hearing about and responding to Angie's amazing experience of God by being able to *get out of their cognitive/theological "comfort zone,"* tolerating discomfort for spiritual growth. In order to understand what spiritual self-differentiation looks like in practice, we need to understand differences between agential and receptive power.

The Role of Agential or Receptive Power in Spiritual Self-Differentiation

A key aspect of spiritual differentiation is paying attention to how one uses agential or receptive power from one moment to the next. Agential power "influences, guides, and shapes, while receptive power receives and takes in."[15] Agential power is grounded in chaplains' specialized knowledge of and training in spiritual care and in their organizational role, which often includes interdisciplinary teamwork within health, hospice, and long-term care as well as within educational, prison, military, and nonprofit organizations. Receptive power is grounded in spiritual self-differentiation that opens chaplains to the mystery of the other. Agential and receptive power use different styles of communication, ranging from following to guiding and directing, and different communication skills of listening, asking, and informing.[16] Agential power typically uses directing and guiding styles, along with informing and asking skills. Receptive power uses a following style along with listening skills. How do agential and receptive power and their related communication styles and skills play out in a spiritual care conversation?

Chaplains usually begin by introducing themselves in ways that help others "locate" the chaplain's agential power within the organization's purpose/mission—in our case study, holistic healthcare with possibilities for hospice care. Chaplains often then shift from agential power to receptive power, using a following style and listening skills to receive the other's response—especially communicated through a person's body language. If the other seems hesitant to interact, chaplains might shift into agential power by using a guiding style and asking skills to gently seek permission to either say more about their role or find out more about the other's hesitation. For example, questions about the chaplain's religious affiliations may arise from another's desire to find commonalities or from religious or spiritual struggles that make that person suspicious of those with religious/spiritual authority. When chaplains use "in the moment" calming practices like slow, deep breathing, they can differentiate their own need to help from the other's hesitancy over or refusal of spiritual care. They will then be able to receive and respect the other's response.

Let's imagine how a chaplain might use agential and receptive power and related communication styles and skills in an opening conversation with Angie.

Case Study, Part 2: Practicing Spiritual Self-Differentiation

Our chapter's case study continues with Angie, who is expected to die during this hospitalization. Her chart indicates that she has no family support and that returning to her childhood Pentecostal faith has help her recover from addiction. Angie has been unresponsive for a week due to the shutting down of her bodily systems at the end of her life. The chaplain is visiting her on a day when she is having intermittent periods where she is somewhat responsive.

> Chaplain: Hello, Angie. I am [name], a chaplain in the Spiritual Care Department of this hospital. (Chaplain uses agential power, a directing style, and informing skills to clarify professional/organizational role.)

> Angie: Chaplain, I am so glad to see you. I had an amazing experience with God. I tried to tell the nurse and doctor but they were

too busy assessing my health and doing tests. (Angie conveys a sense of immediate trust and desire for spiritual care.)

Chaplain: I'd like to hear about your "amazing experience with God." (Chaplain shifts into receptive power, using a following style that respects Angie's unique experiences by using her words.)

Angie: It was just me and God dancing together up there in the corner. I had on a red dress. The prettiest red dress. I've never worn anything like it. We danced and danced. You know, people always say, "God is this" or, "God is that." God isn't anything we know about, even if he is a darned good dancer. It's just, "God is." [She pauses. There are tears in her eyes.] Not even, "God is." Just, "is."

Angie goes on to tell the chaplain that she received a blessing and a healing, and that even though she will die with the cancer, she has been made whole.

Angie's chaplain draws upon receptive power, using a following style and listening skills to echo Angie's words without adding interpretations. The chaplain minimizes asking questions, which would put the chaplain in the "driver's seat" by directing the conversation. Spiritual self-differentiation supported by calming spiritual practices helps this chaplain recognize and set aside any immediate need to "fill in the puzzle" of Angie's story by asking for narrative, emotional, or spiritual details that would "make sense" of the mystery of her experience. The chaplain can make a mental note to speak with the bedside nurse or attending physician to further understand the medical and psychological aspects of Angie's experience. Spiritual trust will deepen when the chaplain follows Angie's searching for meanings, assuming the role of a respectful guest who has been invited into the mystery of Angie's "amazing experience with God." Spiritual self-differentiation helps this chaplain honor the narrative and contextual "truth" of Angie's experience of God. Her chaplain might be tempted to use agential power to negatively judge Angie's experience by using stereotypes of Pentecostalism. Conversely, her chaplain might become "stuck" in receptive power that conflates Angie's experience with the chaplain's own intense religious experiences, absolutizing both in ways that blur religious differences.

This case study raises the question, how are the chaplain's reactions to Angie shaped by his or her perception of interacting aspects of Angie's identity (such as gender identity, religious/spiritual identity, racial identity, and other salient aspects of identity)? Religious and spiritual identity is always contextually experienced as intertwined with other aspects of identity.

In this conversation, the chaplain's immediate impressions are shaped by his or her perceptions of Angie's gender, age, race, health status, and other perceptions of her identity. How do chaplains begin to imagine what it is like to be Angie? How do they build upon spiritual differentiation by using spiritual and social empathy to imagine Angie's spiritual world at this moment?

SPIRITUAL AND SOCIAL EMPATHY

Spiritual empathy helps chaplains imagine how another's stress-based emotions generate contextual spiritual/moral orientations to stress and suffering—"lived" values, beliefs, and coping practices—that "make sense" given family and cultural contexts, especially intersecting social advantages and disadvantages generated by systemic racism, sexism, heterosexism, ableism, and other forms of social oppression. Psychologists using brain imaging technology have mapped the neural circuits active during empathy,[17] demonstrating how "affective empathy describes the physiological aspects of vicariously feeling what another person is feeling; while cognitive empathy involves the mental processing of another's feelings, thoughts and intentions."[18] Affective empathy occurs in part at an unconscious, physiological level. Chaplains need self-differentiation in order to manage affective empathy so that, as we noted earlier, boundaries between self and other are not blurred. The cognitive component of empathy uses perspective-taking to imagine what it is like to stand in the other's shoes. Spiritual empathy uses spiritual perspective-taking. Chaplains imagine others' emotional responses to stress and suffering and how their emotions generate a moral/spiritual orientation to their stress or suffering.[19]

Chaplains draw upon specialized knowledge from their theological and religious studies to combine psychological perspective-taking with spiritual perspective-taking that pays attention to religious, spiritual, and moral differences and particularity. As we noted earlier, chaplains need to listen for and echo back the particular words others use to speak of themselves spiritually. Do they use words like "God"? What is particular to the way they use this term? If they describe pain and suffering, what words do they use? How do their words and bodies convey emotions that might empower or overwhelm them? How do these emotions seem to influence their relational boundaries from one moment to the next? Do their boundaries blur in their rush to disclose or in a projection that blurs the chaplain's identity with another's? Does the careseeker seem to experience an emotional and spiritual disengagement in order to protect what is vulnerable and precious?

In answering such questions, chaplains draw upon their emotional and spiritual attunement to careseekers while using spiritual perspective-taking at several levels. They are using spiritual empathy to gain a perspective on the careseeker's experience of overwhelming stress or suffering—in Angie's case, an amazing experience of God. They are also paying attention to how the careseeker understands this spiritual care conversation and are considering how to be a liaison with medical providers so that the patient can receive holistic, culturally responsive care. Medical providers are trained to assign diagnostic categories to patient experiences, and a chaplain will be in a position to also provide spiritual care to staff who may be distressed about encountering a situation that may have no clear medical explanation. Just as chaplains enact their values and beliefs about spiritual care in this conversation, as much through body language as through words, so, too, careseekers put into practice their beliefs and values about spiritual care in their body language and the ways they respond to the chaplain. When chaplains are experienced as trustworthy, they will be invited into a careseeker's spiritual home with its immediate experiences of pain and suffering, lament, mystery, and hope. Perspective-taking entails imagining that any and all aspects of this careseeker's spiritual home may be sacred or memorials of desecration.

Social empathy builds upon spiritual empathy by considering the macro systems of intersecting social privileges or disadvantages within a careseeker's current contexts. Perspective-taking of another's intersecting social systems of privilege and disadvantage is enhanced by knowledge about social oppressions, especially oppression justified through religious dogma. Intersectionality is a theory and strategic practice of identifying which systems of social oppression interact contextually to benefit or harm persons in distress. Black feminist scholars[20] and womanist pastoral theologians[21] help chaplains develop spiritual social empathy that pays attention to how religious and spiritual identities intersect in helpful and harmful ways in careseekers' struggles. For example, womanist perspectives could be used to explore how racism might interact with sexism in our chapter's case study.[22] Social and spiritual empathy fosters an appreciation for the alterity or mystery of another whose spiritual orientation or social location is radically different from one's own.

In order to understand the interrelationships among systems of oppression such as racism, classism, heterosexism, and sexism, chaplains need an overarching orientation of "post/decolonialism"[23] to name the ways that colonialism exercises power over all aspects of ecological, transnational, political, and economic life. As practical theologian Kristina Lizardy-Hajbi argues, "These collective systems and dynamics are part of the larger construction of the U.S. as a modern colonial empire; therefore, post/decolonial leadership frameworks that seek justice, transformation, and the re-existence of marginalized peoples and ways of being-thinking-acting are necessary for the collective liberation of all people of faith."[24] Colonial systems of power can be likened to gravity. They are an interconnected and ever-present force, irreversibly harming this earth's ecology, decimating Indigenous peoples and their lands and cultures, perpetuating poverty, and locking in economic disparities. All of us who benefit from colonialist power systems traverse our daily lives with the power/gravity of colonialism holding our privileges together in invisible ways. These privileges are often misnamed as accomplishments that open doors and keep us safe from harm.

Bringing post- and de-colonial orientations to understanding spiritual care interactions makes chaplains realize the impossibility of "doing no harm" in a world organized by colonialism. For example, the places where we live and work are built on Indigenous lands stolen in settler colonialism and on the genocide of Indigenous peoples.[25] Lizardy-Hajbi states, "The actions of resistance, subversion, and reclamation by those harmed and abused by colonialism constitute the beginnings of postcolonial and decolonial practice."[26]

Socially just spiritual care that does no harm is enormously challenging and always unfinished. When chaplains use calming spiritual practices, they may be able to feel in their bodies and their very bones their interconnectedness with a suffering humanity and creation. Social empathy often evokes lament, especially for racial violence, which may be shared within spiritual and religious rituals of repentance and social rituals of protest (see chapter 5 for descriptions of rituals that mourn and lament systemic abuses of power). Pastoral theologian Larry Graham describes how lament may be a process of "sharing anguish, interrogating causes, and reinvesting hope" with God as "our co-creative partner in healing, sustaining, and guiding the shaken, shattered, exploded, bombed, bulleted, and drowning human community."[27] Spiritual and social empathy develops in a collaborative learning process grounded in spiritual and communal accountability.[28] The profound shame, guilt, grief, fear, and moral distress of such learning can be supported only through personal and communal practices of lament.[29]

Case Study, Part 3: Practicing Spiritual Reflexivity

The next morning, you report your conversation with Angie at interdisciplinary rounds just before the treatment team enters Angie's room. You preface your report by asking the medical providers for a summary of her medical condition. You use her words to describe her experience of God when she was unresponsive and relate how she feels as though she has received "a blessing and a healing"—that even though she will die of cancer, she has been "made whole." The chief oncologist, a white male agnostic, turns to the students and says, "And here we have a prime example of drug-induced delirium. People experience all sorts of things because of the medications we give them for pain management."

SPIRITUAL SELF-REFLEXIVITY

Once chaplains have begun to develop spiritual differentiation and empathy, they will be ready to learn spiritual self-reflexivity. Self-reflexivity has been described by pastoral theologian Kathleen Greider as "disciplined, accountable practices to decrease our unconsciousness and increase in depth our understanding of our life narrative, sense of self, participation in relationships, and social-historical location."[30] (Chapters 4 and 5 describe the role of meaning-making in spiritual care). Spiritual reflexivity goes beyond theological reflection to understand how a chaplain's and a careseeker's social and religious/spiritual identities interact in the process of exploring contextual values and beliefs about suffering. Reflexivity begins with identifying one's own stress-generated beliefs and values (for example, about Angie's suffering and her experience of God) and then intentional values and beliefs that emerge from using calming spiritual practices. Spiritual self-reflexivity is then used to identify how one's stress-oriented and intentional beliefs and values are shaped by one's own intersecting social privileges and disadvantages.

The next step is to use spiritual and social empathy to imagine the other's stress-generated values and beliefs and how these are shaped by that individual's social location. We have described how a chaplain would begin that process in a spiritual care conversation with Angie that searches for and cocreates meanings about how she experiences God as blessing and healing her and making her whole as she faces death.

The case study now presents chaplains with the opportunity and challenge of using spiritual differentiation and empathy to imagine this oncologist's beliefs and values about Angie's experience and how these might be shaped by his social identity and medical training. Spiritual reflexivity includes understanding possible interactions among the chaplain's beliefs and values about Angie's experience, role as her chaplain, and social location; Angie's beliefs and values about her experience, her role as a patient, and her social location and medical condition; and the oncologist's beliefs and values about Angie's experience, his role as her doctor, and his social location. This multilayered process of searching for meanings is explored more fully in part 2. In this chapter on interpersonal competencies, we describe how spiritual self-reflexivity is an interpersonal competency that makes chaplains accountable for tracking how their own beliefs and values influence the search for meanings in spiritual care encounters and for understanding how another's social location shapes that person's values and beliefs. Chaplains become relationally self-reflexive[31] by using educational and supervisory relationships to understand the complex interactions among their and another's beliefs and values. A collaborative search for meanings in spiritual care is like a jazz improvisation. Chaplains are playing in the ensemble while using spiritual reflexivity to listen for and understand each player's unique contribution.

How might chaplains respond to the oncologist? Chaplains using calming spiritual practices during grand rounds will be more able to draw upon their competencies in spiritual self-differentiation, empathy, and reflexivity. They will likely realize that an immediate response is called for, given the ways that this oncologist's beliefs about Angie's religious experience could cause medical harm if he is not familiar with research on experiences of "God's benevolence" that have positive outcomes.[32] This oncologist's judgment could make Angie question her spiritual experience and her need for a process of integrating this experience of cancer as she faces death. If she does not trust her medical team, she may hold back important subjective medical details that could be red flags about suffering or could improve her quality of life. She may well experience internalized racist and sexist shame associated with sacred aspects of who she is. How might you as chaplain advocate for Angie who, like many persons of color, might have experienced health disparities and have justified mistrust of medical providers?

Spiritual self-differentiation helps chaplains rely upon a solid flexible spiritual self and a quiet mind and calm heart using spiritual self-care practices. These cognitive and spiritual capacities of self-differentiation could help the chaplain in the case study to use grounded responding with the oncologist, as the chaplain "surfs" the anxiety of responding to the doctor's interpretation of Angie's experience. Here is an example of how a chaplain might reply: "Doctor, as you may know, research demonstrates that experiences of God's benevolence have many benefits for patients. Knowing about the variety of experiences patients have at the end of life, can we, as a team, embrace Angie's experiences and support her in her search for wholeness as she faces death?" After using his or her agential power to guide and inform this oncologist and the team, the chaplain could use receptive power to listen for this oncologist's beliefs and values about holistic healthcare and for his possible distress about facing a situation that does not have a clear medical explanation. The chaplain could follow up in a later conversation, inviting the oncologist to say more about his beliefs and values.

This extended case study illustrates the complexities, challenges, and benefits of socially just, interreligious, evidence-based spiritual care that draws upon competencies in spiritual differentiation, empathy, and reflexivity. Chaplains learn these competencies and practice them within clinical learning communities. They are not solo virtuosos. For example, the chaplain in our case study's grand rounds conversation may or may not be able to practice interpersonal competencies to the best of his or her abilities. The chaplain can take this experience back to his or her learning community so that they can all learn together and strategize next steps in advocating for Angie and engaging her treatment team in further conversations.

LEARNING TO USE INTERPERSONAL COMPETENCIES IN ASSESSMENT

Interpersonal competencies in spiritual differentiation, empathy, and reflexivity are practiced in spiritual assessments that go beyond simple assessments (like questions about religious identity or how important religion or spirituality is) often asked during initial conversations (see chapter 3 for a description of spiritual assessment as an interpretive process in meaning making in chaplaincy practice). Being research-literate is yet another learning outcome, beyond the scope of this chapter, that integrates knowledge (in this instance, psychological research on when aspects of religion and spirituality help or harm) seamlessly with spiritual and social empathy and reflexivity in person-centered spiritual care. In other words, knowledge is always integrated into the flow of a spiritual care interaction that gives primary attention to the needs of those seeking care.

We now describe how to integrate spiritual assessment into the early phases of getting to know those seeking spiritual care. The **Spiritual**

Assessment and Intervention Model (Spiritual AIM) provides a conceptual framework for the chaplain to

1. focus on an individual's primary unmet spiritual need—through observing the patient's words and behavior in relationship with the chaplain, as well as through the chaplain's self-awareness of the interpersonal dynamic with careseekers;
2. devise and implement strategies for addressing this need through embodiment/relationship; and
3. articulate and evaluate the desired and actual outcomes of a focused conversation.[33]

Spiritual AIM is best understood through illustrating how it is used in spiritual care. Along with generalized forms of assessment, assessments of specific stressors have been developed, such as the PC-7, which measures unmet spiritual concerns of palliative care patients near the end of life.[34] While we illustrate AIM by continuing our case study, this assessment approach can be used in any kind of spiritual care setting (like a faith community, an educational context, the military, or a correctional/prison context) or in disaster relief.

Case Study, Part 4: Assessing Spiritual Needs

Spiritual assessments explore how people's beliefs, values, and spiritual/coping practices function for them. In this case, Angie feels that her faith has been a crucial force in helping her to stay sober and is a great source of support. In the course of the chaplain's pastoral conversation with Angie, Spiritual AIM serves as a road map for utilizing the relationship to facilitate spiritual healing. The chaplain sets out to make an assessment and diagnosis about the prominent spiritual dimension where Angie is most in need of healing. AIM helps the chaplain and Angie identify one primary spiritual need. Having this focus will help to avoid a meandering encounter, which is of the utmost importance, especially given the tension with the medical team and the fact that her life is coming to an end. The chaplain observes Angie's actions and reflects on what he or she knows about Angie's history. The chaplain listens to her lovingly recount her spiritual experience of dancing with God and uses this information to make an assessment and craft spiritual interventions, which will inform how the chaplain interacts with the patient but also how he or she advocates for her with the medical team. The chaplain will know that the assessment is "correct" if Angie demonstrates some of the Spiritual AIM outcomes. If she does not, the chaplain can assess a different spiritual need and try those corresponding interventions.

Angie's history of broken relationships and addiction indicate a spiritual need of reconciliation/to love and be loved. Angie tells the chaplain that she does not trust her medical providers and can sense their judgments and dismissive attitudes, especially about her spiritual experience. The chaplain's interventions focus on empowerment. He or she identifies the ways in which Angie is feeling powerless and reminds her what is still in her power. This includes allowing her strong and loving relationship to wash over her whenever she is feeling alienated from others, articulating her needs and wishes, and choosing which medical providers she feels she can trust. The chaplain act as her partner in prayer, a practice that connects her with God.

Spiritual AIM emphasizes the importance of the relationship, prompting the chaplain to look inward and recognize his or her reactions to Angie. Part of the reason why using any spiritual assessment model is helpful is because it balances emotions that arise in the caregiver, activating the analysis required of making an assessment. This process results in a relationally based yet somewhat more objective assessment. In embodying a truth-teller and prophetic voice to Angie, the chaplain acknowledges the systemic and explicit prejudice she is facing. But the chaplain also offers compassion for her feelings of powerlessness while reminding her of the influence that is impossible to be taken from her. Angie is able to state her truth and her wishes to her medical team and to continue to trust God.

CONCLUSION

This chapter describes and illustrates the lifelong learning process of integrating specialized knowledge with interpersonal competencies that fine-tune communication skills for particular spiritual care encounters. Developing interpersonal competencies in spiritual care is a deeply relational process grounded in a felt sense of spiritual trust experienced in one's body through calming spiritual practices. This grounding in a relational web that includes transcendent dimensions enables chaplains to trust the process of spiritual care, especially when care of self or others elicits religious and spiritual struggles and interpersonal challenges.

REFLECTION QUESTIONS

1. Describe a spiritual care encounter with someone whose spiritual orientation or social location is radically different from your own. How might you combine a solid spiritual self that is grounded in your ongoing process of spiritual integration with a flexible spiritual self that trusts the spiritually intersubjective process of searching for contextually meaningful practices, values, and beliefs?

2. Reflecting on the same spiritual care encounter, how might you draw upon spiritual self-differentiation to make a grounded response to a "jarring" difference between their practices, beliefs, and values and yours?

3. In spiritual care with those whose suffering is compounded by intersecting social oppressions that are religiously justified (for example, a gay or lesbian person whose community or family justified prejudice with religious beliefs), how would you respond to their suspicions about your religious/spiritual beliefs that make them hesitant to trust you?

4. What aspects of education, spiritual formation, clinical training, or religious/spiritual tradition/community help or hinder you from demonstrating radical respect for differences? Which of these aspects help or hinder you from counteracting cultural and religious abuses of power that judge others' beliefs, values, and practices as less true or meaningful than your own?

5. Socially just spiritual care is enormously challenging and always unfinished. The profound shame, guilt, grief, fear, and moral distress of such learning can be supported only through personal and communal practices of lament. What helps you remain committed to a collaborative learning process grounded in spiritual and communal accountability?

RECOMMENDED READINGS

Doehring, Carrie. *The Practice of Pastoral Care: A Postmodern Approach*. Rev. and exp. ed. Louisville: Westminster John Knox Press, 2015.

Graham, Larry Kent. *Moral Injury: Restoring Wounded Souls*. Nashville: Abingdon, 2017.

Lartey, Emmanuel Y., and Hellena Moon, eds. *Postcolonial Images of Spiritual Care: Challenges of Care in a Neoliberal Age.* Eugene, Ore.: Wipf and Stock, 2020.

Snodgrass, Jill, ed. *Navigating Religious Difference in Spiritual Care and Counseling: Essays in Honor of Kathleen J. Greider.* Claremont, Calif.: Claremont Press, 2019.

CHAPTER SEVEN

Interpersonal Competencies in Spiritual Care

THOMAS ST. JAMES O'CONNOR
and MICHELLE KIRBY

ABSTRACT *Chaplains and community religious leaders may be first responders when people struggle with four kinds of suffering: suicide and despair, addictions, trauma, and moral injury. How can they offer immediate and ongoing evidence-based spiritual care? What interpersonal competencies do they need in order to build trust when people struggle with suicide, addictions, post-traumatic symptoms, and moral injury? In this chapter, we use the Helping Styles Inventory[1] along with an extended case study to illustrate how chaplains integrate research-based knowledge with interpersonal competencies in response to these forms of suffering.*

COMPETENCIES FOR BUILDING
INTERPERSONAL SPIRITUAL TRUST

Interpersonal competencies consist of three elements.[2] First, there is knowledge and research for assessing and treating spiritual suffering, such as suicide, addictions, trauma, and moral injury. Second are the interpersonal skills a careseeker needs to utilize the relevant research. Third are the sound clinical judgments or the wisdom of chaplains, which includes their capacities for spiritual and social empathy and self-reflexivity. Those receiving care also bring their wisdom in dealing with these issues and discerning the trustworthiness of those offering spiritual care.[3] Knowledge can be learned in academic courses, in workshops, in CPE units, and through reading. Skills are usually acquired through observation and practice, participating in role-plays, and doing clinical work under supervision. Skills in listening and responding are crucial to interpersonal competencies.[4] Clinical judgment and wisdom reflect the ability to make wise responses and choices using empathy and self-reflexivity for understanding the unique ways others experience suffering and hope. This reflexivity utilizes feedback from supervisors, peers, and others.[5] Knowledge of intersectionality and systemic racism highlights the need for assessing the ways that systemic racism and enduring colonialism compound suffering.[6] Chaplains and community religious leaders need interpersonal competencies to build the relational foundation of spiritual trust described in chapter 6. In an evidence-based approach to spiritual care, clinical wisdom and judgment draw upon knowledge of the relevant research to understand the distinctive needs of the spiritual care receiver.[7]

As a chaplain or spiritual care provider approaches a patient or care receiver for the first time, a basic competency is understanding and utilizing a model to guide that person's care. One example of a model is the Helping Styles Inventory (HSI), developed by Peter VanKatwyk. This model describes four areas of interpersonal competency that a beginning chaplain needs for working with spiritual care receivers.[8] The tool consists of four quadrants reflecting interpersonal styles: celebrant, consultant, manager, and guide. Each style describes a different helping role and interpersonal competencies that spiritual caregivers can utilize to help spiritual careseekers.[9]

In conjunction with a universal assessment model, spiritual caregivers also need skills for addressing the forms of suffering they are likely to encounter in the clinical environment or community they serve. In this chapter, we will explore four aspects of suffering through a composite case study of a chaplain resident, "Joe," providing care to a military veteran, "Alex," in a Veterans Affairs medical center.[10] The purpose of the case study is to demonstrate how the chaplain approaches the aspects of suffering in a single case as it develops over time. We recognize that chaplains in many settings may have only one opportunity to visit a patient, while some spiritual caregivers may develop short to long-term relationships with those they serve. This case study is meant to be illustrative rather than prescriptive.

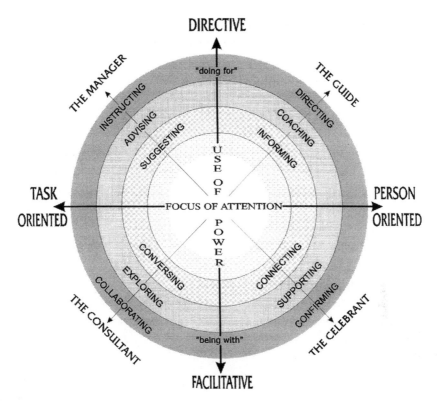

DIRECTIVE

"doing for"

THE MANAGER

INSTRUCTING

ADVISING

SUGGESTING

THE GUIDE

DIRECTING

COACHING

INFORMING

USE OF

TASK
ORIENTED

FOCUS OF ATTENTION

PERSON
ORIENTED

POWER

CONVERSING

EXPLORING

COLLABORATING

THE CONSULTANT

CONNECTING

SUPPORTING

CONFIRMING

THE CELEBRANT

"being with"

FACILITATIVE

The Helping Styles Inventory Map, developed by Peter VanKatwyk. *Reprinted with permission from Wilfrid Laurier University Press.*

CASE STUDY: MILITARY VETERAN ALEX, CHAPLAIN JOE, AND SPIRITUAL CARE OF SUICIDE RISK

We introduce our case with the basic information Joe presented to his peers for his first consultation on this case:

Chaplain: Joe
Veteran: Alex[11]
Visit #1
Age: 42
Faith tradition: Catholic
Location: Acute Psychiatric Unit
Branch: Army
Ethnicity: Latino

Diagnosis/pertinent medical history: 72-hour suicidal ideation hold, acute alcoholism

Reason for visit: Sunday spirituality group

Topic: Guided Imagery Meditation using Psalm 23

Background/observations: After group, Veteran requested a Bible. Patient stated that he was not active in his faith. He was looking down, as if ashamed. He had been quiet during group.

Plan: Bring veteran a Bible, establish rapport with patient, and if possible, explore shame. Explore faith practices that may help him cope with hospitalization.

Chaplain residents serving in hospitals with acute psychiatric or behavioral health units often lead spirituality groups, requiring them to have a basic understanding of group facilitation.[12] Most chaplain residents enter CPE with worship and small group leadership experience, such as heading Bible studies or youth groups. Leading a spirituality group in a secular institution such as the VA requires chaplains to facilitate engagement with patients of many faiths and with no faith. It also requires a basic knowledge of mental health.[13]

Knowing that Alex was receiving treatment for suicidal risk, Joe was ready to pick up on any cues that Alex's struggles with despair and suicidal thoughts were intensifying. All chaplains should be familiar with a suicidal risk assessment, such as the Columbia-Suicide Severity Rating Scale protocol for asking questions about suicide.[14] When Joe returned with the Bible, he planned to follow up on Alex's statement that he was no longer active in his faith. Drawing on the HSI, he approached Alex with "facilitative" skills. Alex thanked Joe for the Bible, saying, "I need to get back to my faith" while looking down at the floor. Hearing that Alex was ready to connect, Joe invited Alex to say more. Alex replied, "My family is very religious. I need to go to treatment. I wasn't ready before. I wanted to run around and party. I thought I was too young to be sober, but I'm over forty now. It's time for me to grow up. It was stupid of me to take all those pills, I know. I was just so mad when my sister said I couldn't sleep on her couch anymore. Everyone in my family is sick of me." Embodying the celebrant, Joe responded, "I'm glad you're here getting help. Tell me how having this Bible might help in the next couple of days." Joe found himself wondering how the Bible was going to help Alex. He feared that if Alex read passages portraying a judgmental God, it might cause him more distress.

Alex looked down as his hands tightened around the Bible. He did not initially respond. Then he said in a low voice, "I'm not sure. What you said in group about God being the good shepherd made me feel safe. I thought maybe I should read the Bible, but I have no idea where to start."

Knowing that his time with Alex was brief and there was a clear risk of Alex experiencing religious struggles with God that could intensify his shame, Joe decided to risk shifting into a guiding style by asking for permission to help Alex use the Bible and Psalm 23 in a calming, breath-centered practice.[15] "Alex, would you be okay with trying a way to feel like God is the good shepherd right now?" Alex said, "You mean, like saying a prayer?" Joe responded, "It's sort of like praying. Do you want to try that spiritual practice I talked about in chapel today? [Alex nodded.] We get a sense of our feet touching the ground [Joe gently bounced his feet on the floor] and we sit up straight, with our backs feeling supported by the chair. [Joe adjusted his posture and Alex followed suit.] Next, we are going to take some slow, deep breaths together. We are going to breathe in slowly, counting to four. [Joe modeled this and Alex followed his lead.] Now we are going to hold to the count of four. [Joe paused to do this.] Now we breathe out slowly through our mouths." Joe guided Alex in taking another slow, deep breath, noticing that Alex looked down while he did this. Joe led him in several more deep breaths, inviting Alex to feel the weight and warmth of the Bible in his hands.

A few moments of silence followed. Joe saw that Alex's shoulders had relaxed and his hands around the Bible were no longer clenched. When Alex looked up, the muscles around his eyes had relaxed. Alex sighed, saying, "That was good." Joe suggested that Alex might try taking some slow, deep breaths while holding the Bible over the next couple of days. Then, if he wanted to, he could open it to Psalm 23, where Joe had put a card with his name. Alex could try reading the psalm and pausing to breathe deeply, especially when he felt pulled back into troubling memories.[16] Alex said he'd like to try this. Joe arranged to check back with him in a few days.

SUICIDE AND DESPAIR

This initial visit reflects a myriad of skills and competencies demonstrated by Joe. For the purposes of this chapter, the immediate presenting issues are suicide and despair. Suicide and despair are closely linked to depression, hopelessness, and "psychache."[17] Psychache is "intense, unrelenting psychological pain" that can lead to suicide.[18] Suicide is present in most cultures. In 2019 the United States recorded 47,000 suicides;[19] in Canada there were 4,000 deaths by suicide.[20] High rates of suicide and suicidal ideation in the U.S. military and among veterans are well documented.[21]

Research demonstrates that spirituality is a mediating force in protecting against suicide attempts.[22] Renne Bazley and Kenneth Packenham argue that "perfect listening" on the part of the chaplain is the most healing tool in dealing with the despair of attempted suicide.[23] This case study also demonstrates the use of a mindfulness strategy, which has well-documented evidence in the literature. Despair can lead to suicide when a person regards every attempt at living a meaningful and productive life as futile. Paul Tillich asserted that such meaninglessness is one of the fundamental anxieties of human experience.[24] This branch of philosophy known as existentialism became contextually meaningful in the twentieth century in response to genocides such as the Holocaust. Existentialism asks, Is there any meaning to life, or is life just the survival of the fittest? Where was the divine in all these atrocities? Feminist theologian Susan Nelson describes how moral and redemptive ways of finding meaning are often inadequate for those in despair, who often need, instead, a "paradigm of radical suffering [that] stands in this place of suffering and incoherence, recognizes everything such evil threatens, realizes that this evil cannot be justified but must be resisted, and asks in the face of such evil, 'Where is God?' or 'What kind of God . . . ?' or 'Is there a God at all?'"[25] Nelson describes how, for those in despair, hope may be experienced in the present, and not just the future, in practices of care: "Prisoners at Auschwitz practiced acts of resistance to the evil of that place. . . . Others resisted evil by practicing simple acts of justice and kindness that bore witness to a world order far beyond the terror and cruelty imposed by the Nazis."[26]

Spiritual care helps those in despair experience their interconnectedness within life-giving webs often experienced as transcendent or sacred. This sense of spiritual trust enables them to search for meanings without being overwhelmed by despair. In the aftermath of trauma, even the horrors of genocide, survivors grounded in a sense of interconnectedness with the inherent goodness of humanity may be able to look back on their suffering and search for life-giving meanings. Viktor Frankl, a Jewish psychiatrist who was imprisoned in a concentration camp in World War II, developed a form of therapy that describes how, once a therapeutic alliance is established, people can enter into a process of searching for meanings in the aftermath of profound suffering.[27]

Returning to our case study, we can see how Alex sought the chaplain for guidance in finding meaning in his life, through his request for a Bible. Often a spiritual guide, what John O'Donohue calls a "soul friend," who journeys with the person in the darkness can be beneficial.[28] Helping a person identify a source of hope is an important element for those who survive a suicide event. Pam McCarroll and Helen Cheung did an extensive review of the literature on hope using healthcare, theological, and pastoral literature.[29] The despair and hopelessness that sometimes gives rise to suicide is exacerbated by substance use. In our case study, how did Joe foster hope within Alex, who has attempted suicide and struggles with addiction? Returning to the HSI, Joe served as a consultant by helping Alex identify sources of hope that could motivate him to address his addiction, which exacerbates suicide ideation and despair. The chaplain can carry the hope for the spiritual care receiver for a time through belief in the systems that can offer help.[30]

A significant interpersonal competency needed for chaplains is the ability to assess despair, suicidal thoughts, and impulses. Chaplains need to be able to draw upon knowledge about suicide risk and use interpersonal and communication skills to go through a suicide assessment. The consultant role in the HSI allows the chaplain to ask questions in a nonjudgmental way, conveying support and empathy. Chaplains need skills to manage their anxiety about suicide and not let it get in the way of their assessment and care plan.

CONTINUED SPIRITUAL CARE OF ALEX

As promised, Joe followed up with Alex in a few days. By this time, he was admitted to the hospital's twenty-eight-day Substance Abuse Recovery Program. Joe made the following note about his second visit:

Veteran: Alex
Faith tradition: Raised Catholic
Reason for visit: Spiritual intake
Observations: Veteran shared story of military discharge due to
    excessive drinking/drug use, which spiraled recently as a way of
    coping with an injury at work. He linked his excessive drinking
    and drug abuse to a history of failed romantic relationships
    and broken family relationships. Veteran connected this story
    to childhood sexual abuse and military sexual trauma. Veteran

denies reporting abuse and stated: "I didn't want people thinking I was gay."

Assessment: Veteran self-rated low (1–2) in 12/15 items on Moral Injury Symptom Scale.[31] He acknowledges his part in broken relationships and seems eager to engage in the work of recovery.[32] Veteran is motivated to reconcile with his family and conflates his faith/relationship with Higher Power with his relationship to family.

Interventions: Empathetic listening, reviewed intake assessment, and explored faith, family resources.

Outcome: Veteran requested ongoing support from chaplain. Reported using Psalm 23 and "breath prayer" to stay grounded.

This second visit again demonstrates several competencies, including the use of an evidence-based assessment tool. In addition, Joe drew on Alan Wolfelt's theory that post-traumatic stress disorder is a form of complicated grief.[33] This theory is not meant to reduce PTSD to grief but rather to identify grief work as part of the healing process for PTSD. Wolfelt's theory was transformative for Joe because he felt comfortable with facilitating grief as a chaplain. Approaching Alex's PTSD as a form of grief helped him focus on the ways that spiritual care is different from therapy. In addition, Joe developed a more thorough understanding of the role of guilt, shame, and anger—the primary emotions woven through Alex's story.[34]

One competency described in the previous chapter is knowing when to seek supervision. Joe came to supervision, after this visit, with a sense of anxiety and urgency. Over the next couple of weeks, while Alex completed the substance abuse recovery program, Joe "unpacked" his conversations with Alex in supervision. While he knew that providing spiritual care to persons of diverse backgrounds, including diverse sexual orientations and gender identities, was a competency needed by spiritual caregivers, Joe had never previously faced a care receiver questioning his sexual orientation. Joe initially found it hard to reconcile a psychological understanding of sexuality and mental illness with his fundamentalist theological heritage, which attributed both to the devil and sin. Due to the significance of sexuality in most people's lives, it is vital that chaplains develop skills in approaching patients' intimate feelings about the subject. In supervision, Joe disclosed unresolved guilt about previously espousing fundamentalist beliefs against LGBTQ+ people, as well as his ignorance about sexuality outside of heterosexual marriage. He also voiced a fear of judgment from his lesbian-identified educator.

In these disclosures, Joe demonstrated the vulnerability that helped him courageously consult about sexuality with his peers and supervisor.

In parallel with his spiritually integrative learning, Joe's relationship with Alex continued to deepen, through spirituality groups and individual meetings. Like Joe, Alex had struggled with a God he perceived to be punishing. Since he was molested as a child, Alex believed he was "damned" and began drinking at a young age as a way to cope. His abuser, an uncle, had died when Alex was on a deployment many years ago. Alex felt a mixture of relief and guilt for never confronting his uncle. He buried these complex feelings in alcohol and recreational drugs. His experience of military sexual trauma began with getting special privileges from a senior officer, which led to the assault. Alex again buried the experience in drugs and alcohol. Alex said, "I saw a lot of stuff over there, but none of that bothers me." Joe understood this to mean that while Alex had combat-related triggers for PTSD, his experience of military sexual trauma was what haunted him the most.[35]

At times, Joe felt overwhelmed by Alex's story. However, he took solace in knowing he was part of Alex's treatment team. Through serving in the substance abuse recovery program, Joe developed a working understanding of the twelve-step addiction program and helped Alex articulate what he believed about God.[36] Alex participated in weekly spirituality groups focused on topics of moral injury, including forgiveness, betrayal/trust, guilt, and shame. The concept of military moral injury emerged from therapy with veterans whose post-traumatic stress included lasting moral conflicts about harm caused by themselves, fellow service members, or those in authority. Alex worked in therapy to comprehend how he carried a profound sense of betrayal from his experience of assault. His story helped Joe understand moral injury and recognize a degree of moral injury in himself.[37] To heal his feelings of moral injury, Joe processed feelings of guilt for perpetuating harm against LGBTQ+ and mentally ill people at the behest of former church leaders. As Joe worked on reconciling his moral injury, he helped Alex grieve his past, acknowledge his loss of innocence, and develop trust in using the Alcoholics Anonymous program.[38] Alex also had unresolved grief about leaving the army and even about missing his uncle's funeral. When he finished the substance abuse program, Alex acknowledged that he was not yet ready to forgive his abusers but was working on forgiving himself for the part he played in compounding his trauma. He left the VA for a transitional care home and expressed his commitment to rebuilding the relationship with his family. Alex's involvement in the twenty-eight-day addiction program began to address his addiction to alcohol and drugs.

However, Alex was not "fixed" in twenty-eight days; he will be on a lifelong healing journey. This program brought out his underlying experiences of trauma, post-traumatic stress, and moral injury, which fueled his addictions. Spiritual care providers need a basic working understanding of these spiritual struggles in order to journey with those in their care. What follows is an attempt to introduce the reader to these areas of study and to encourage further exploration.

SPIRITUAL CARE AND ADDICTION

Treatment for addiction has different approaches. Michelle Cleary and Sandra Thomas in a review of the literature summarize six:

1. Spiritual means
2. Medical interventions
3. Individual therapy
4. Group therapy
5. Twelve-step programs
6. Family therapy[39]

These different aspects of treatment follow two major pathways. One is abstinence from alcohol, drugs, and addictive behaviors; the other is harm reduction of the drug or behavior. The abstinence approach is usually associated with the twelve-step program of AA for alcohol and of Narcotics Anonymous for addictive drugs. Both programs emphasize a desire for complete abstinence from the drug and behavior of choice, even if this takes some time to achieve. Daily, weekly, and monthly peer-led meetings are widely available online and in person. In these groups, persons with addictions tell their stories and struggles with the addictive substance and receive support and wisdom from other persons in recovery from addiction.[40] Individuals are expected to engage in an intensive process of self-reflection with the help of an active sober member, called a sponsor, using the twelve steps:[41]

1. We admitted we were powerless over alcohol—that our lives had become unmanageable.
2. Came to believe that a Power greater than ourselves could restore us to sanity.
3. Made a decision to turn over our will and our lives over to the care of God *as we understood Him.*
4. Made a searching and fearless moral inventory of ourselves.

Interpersonal Competencies

5. Admitted to God, to ourselves, and to another human being the exact nature of our wrongs.
6. Were entirely ready to have God remove all these defects of character.
7. Humbly asked Him to remove our shortcomings.
8. Made a list of all persons we have harmed, and became willing to make amends to them all.
9. Made direct amends to such people wherever possible, except when to do so would injure them or others.
10. Continued to take personal inventory and when we were wrong promptly admitted it.
11. Sought through prayer and meditation to improve our conscious contact with God *as we understood Him,* praying only for knowledge of His will for us and the power to carry that out.
12. Having had a spiritual awakening as the result of these steps, we tried to carry this message to alcoholics, and to practice these principles in all our affairs.

The twelve steps are highly spiritual, having originally arisen from Protestant Christianity. However, one can be an atheist or agnostic and live the AA program. The higher power can be anything that person envisions as greater than self and that offers help, such as faith in the treatment team or twelve-step group or a belief in Love. Chaplains can support people in twelve-step-based programs by helping them articulate their understanding of their higher power and develop their practices of prayer and meditation. Spiritual care providers can also help by supporting patients' journeys with the twelve steps, for example, in celebrating milestones of recovery.[42]

Other evidence-based interventions include self-forgiveness and forgiveness of others, noted in step 9. Harm reduction refers to the reduction in use of the drug or behavior of choice. Harm reduction became more known as an evidence-based approach when the World Health Organization, the United States National Association for Public Health Policy, and the Canadian Drug Strategy "endorsed the principles of harm reduction in key documents."[43] Harm reduction may be helpful for patients who feel unable or unwilling to cease certain behaviors entirely. Again, the chaplain may support people in harm reduction programs through celebrating victories and bolstering their commitment to healthy behaviors. All chaplains need the competency to support patients' values rather than impose their own upon patients. Thus, while a chaplain is not expected to support behavior that they find immoral, they are expected to support the values of a person, such as a reduction in their dependence on an addictive behavior.

How else does spiritual care help persons such as Alex with addictions? Gabor Mate maintains that compassion, empathy, and listening are important to those struggling with intractable addictions.[44] Like suicide and despair, a spiritual care relationship built on positive regard, empathy, and congruence can be healing for Alex. He needs to work with Chaplain Joe as an integral part of the whole treatment team.

Besides the spiritual care relationship, other spiritual care practices can be beneficial. Mindfulness and meditation are often used to help slow the impulsivity and compulsion that lead to addiction. Joe used the guiding style earlier, when he showed Alex how to use the phrase "The Lord is my shepherd" from Psalm 23. A spiritual care provider may also suggest passages from a sacred text or twelve-step literature or rituals/practices for practicing forgiveness for self and others. These practices may augment work being done in therapy and recovery, such as the process of making amends in step 9. Chaplains need to use their skills of assessment to determine when the manager and guiding styles (from HSI) are most helpful and to offer or teach skills when careseekers are interested.

Joe developed trust with Alex as he journeyed with him through the twenty-eight-day program. Fortunately, Joe quickly realized that he was out of his depth with Alex's story and brought those conversations to his supervisor to discuss. This led him on his own journey of healing and discovery, apart from his work with Alex. In CPE, Joe unpacked his initial reactions to Alex's comment associating sexual abuse with being gay. In consultation with his supervisor, he realized that he had moved past his childhood church's stance on homosexuality and that he needed to develop his own theology of sexuality. Another competency of a skilled practitioner is identifying ongoing learning goals. Joe identified ongoing learning goals about understanding human sexuality, trauma, and moral injury.

TRAUMA AND POST-TRAUMATIC STRESS DISORDER

Trauma is an area of suffering that spiritual care providers face in their work. Alex experienced trauma in childhood sexual abuse and adult sexual assault in his military career. For Alex, both events were by authority figures whom he trusted: an uncle and a military officer. These traumas were factors in Alex's addiction and attempted suicide.[45] What knowledge, skills, and clinical judgment does Joe need as Alex discloses his experiences of trauma?

Interpersonal Competencies

Trauma has many definitions. Patricia Berendsen defines trauma as "an experience of being so overwhelmed that one's capacity to cope is compromised."[46] Trauma is a threat to one's physical, emotional, and spiritual health.[47] The result of trauma can be post-traumatic stress disorder, which affects the body, mind, emotions, and spirit of the person.[48] Trauma is stored in the body and psyche.[49] Flashbacks and dreams can replay the trauma in the person who has experienced PTSD. Somatic therapy and spiritual practices focusing on the emotional, mental, and physical aspects of trauma can be helpful.[50]

For a spiritual care provider, Carl Rogers's core aspects of spiritual care are crucial to help a person with PTSD: unconditional positive regard, congruence, and empathy.[51] Compassion for the traumatized person is key to healing.[52] The chaplain should be able to listen, summarize, and work from the celebrant and consultant approaches of the Helping Styles Inventory. Further, the chaplain needs to be a non-anxious presence, especially if the traumatized person describes the traumatic event.[53] Berendsen says that it is essential to create a safe place for the spiritual careseeker.[54] The victim did not feel safe in the experience of the trauma. One must move slowly, be supportive, and let the spiritual careseeker set the agenda and pace. The spiritual care provider needs to be careful around probing questions, especially when the person shows resistance. One does not want to re-traumatize the victim.[55] The key is to do no harm.[56] In listening to the trauma event, a caregiver begins by asking what strengths the person has to survive the event.[57] These strengths need to be affirmed especially in the person who felt powerless in the experience. The fact that the survivor physically got through the event indicates strength.

Research indicates that trauma victims do best with a spiritual care provider who is trauma-informed—that is, the spiritual care provider has had some experience of working with trauma victims under supervision and has some knowledge and skill in the area.[58] This means having the basic skills to assess PTSD and knowing when and where to refer to someone more trained. Usually, a beginning chaplain needs to work under a trauma-informed supervisor to know how to be helpful to the victim. A spiritual care provider can experience vicarious trauma by listening to the story of trauma from a spiritual careseeker. Supervision and possibly therapy for the spiritual care provider are highly recommended in vicarious trauma.

In our case study, Joe recognized that Alex avoided the pain and shame of his traumatic experiences through the compulsive use of alcohol and drugs. Addiction then became a source of moral failure, which further complicated his life. Once Alex began to abstain from drugs and alcohol, he began to address his underlying attachment issues—namely the sexual abuse he suffered as a child, which led him to abusive, unhealthy relationships as an adult.

What should clinical chaplains know about moral injury, and what interpersonal competencies do they need in order to address this issue in spiritual careseekers? First, it is important to have a working definition. Defined in the literature, moral injury is about breaking one's own ethical code,[59] which leads to moral stress. Carrie Doehring sees moral injury as the extreme end of a continuum on moral stress.[60] Moral injury and moral stress occur when a person experiences danger, life threat, and suffering that compromise core values that give purpose to that person's life, vocation, and roles. Doehring argues that "moral stress is inherently spiritual and religious requiring both psychological and theological approaches to care."[61]

Most people have an ethical code that guides their behavior. Situations may occur where people break their own moral code. These could also be called acts of commission. In the military and law enforcement, people are trained to use lethal force. In retrospect, they might realize that an action, such as taking a life, broke their own code. There are also moments when the code is broken by omission, such as when one sees wrongdoing and does nothing about it. Moral injury may also result from being part of an organization or system in which people feel betrayed by those in authority. All forms of moral injury can result in guilt and shame. Sometimes moral injury includes a situation where the victim feels responsible for the transgression of another. Victims of sexual assault often report unresolved guilt and shame, often due to engaging in substance use and being assaulted while under the influence. Military sexual trauma can be exacerbated by the explicit moral codes to protect each other at all cost. Since military units can function for service members as replacement family, the implicit sense of betrayal is more akin to sexual abuse by a parent—a person duty-bound to protect them. The guilt and shame resulting from traumatic events such as these, compounded by addiction and other comorbidities, may lead to a downward spiral of despair, resulting in attempted suicide. For Alex, moral injury was exacerbated by a view of the divine that was harsh, judgmental, unforgiving, and punishing. Having an unprocessed adverse childhood trauma is also a risk factor.

According to Doehring, chaplains can help the spiritual careseeker in three ways:

1. Connect with God/a sense of transcendent goodness/ benevolence through compassion based spiritual care.
2. Identify embedded beliefs and values shaped by family and culture that cause moral stress and injury.
3. Cocreate life-giving beliefs and values with trusted others that are flexible and integrated, are capable of complex meanings, and support life-giving relationships.[62]

Resolving moral injury and moral stress requires a commitment of both the spiritual caregiver and the careseeker.

CONCLUSION

We have examined the interpersonal competencies needed by spiritual care providers to help a person who has attempted suicide and experienced addiction, trauma, and moral injury. We have illustrated these competencies through the case study of a veteran, Alex, seeking care from Chaplain Joe and through what Joe learns from the case in supervision. The Helping Styles Inventory has served as a guide, showing the diversity of approaches, skills, and interpersonal competencies needed by spiritual care providers. But the HSI is only one map/tool to guide these interpersonal competencies. We have also drawn on relevant theory and research in an evidence-based approach.

REFLECTION QUESTIONS

1. Carl Rogers stresses the interpersonal competencies and skills of unconditional positive regard, congruence, and empathy as crucial in spiritual care. In the case scenario, how would you rate Joe on these interpersonal competencies on a scale of 1–10 with 10 being high and 1 being low? How would you rate yourself in your clinical work? Are there any patients in your practice where you would rate yourself low on Rogers's three core conditions of helping? Why?

2. The research indicates that spirituality is a factor in healing shame and guilt that arise from attempted suicide and addiction. Do you see that in your spiritual care work?
3. What are your personal and professional barriers in discussing suicide ideation with a spiritual careseeker? What strengths do you bring to this conversation?
4. After reading the sections on trauma and moral injury, do you feel you have enough knowledge, skill, and clinical experience with these issues to deal with them? What was helpful to Joe in working with Alex's trauma and moral injury?
5. Peter VanKatwyk describes four styles in the Helping Styles Inventory: celebrant, consultant, manager, and guide. Which of these styles do you use the most in your spiritual care practice? For which ones do you need more training?

RECOMMENDED READINGS

O'Connor, Thomas St. James, Kristine Lund, and Patricia Berendsen, eds. *Psychotherapy: Cure of the Soul*. Waterloo, Ont.: Waterloo Lutheran Seminary, 2014.

Ramsay, Nancy, and Carrie Doehring, eds. *Military Moral Injury and Spiritual Care: Resources for Religious and Professional Leaders*. Nashville: Chalice Press, 2019.

VanKatwyk, Peter. *Spiritual Care and Therapy: Integrative Perspectives*. Waterloo, Ont.: WLU Press, 2003.

Waters, Sonia. *Addiction and Pastoral Care*. Grand Rapids, Mich.: Eerdmans, 2019.

Wolfelt, Alan D. *Reframing PTSD as Traumatic Grief: How Caregivers Can Companion Traumatized Grievers through Catch-Up Mourning*. Fort Collins, Colo.: Companion Press, 2014.

CHAPTER EIGHT

Interpersonal Competence in Contextualizing Power Dynamics in Socially Just Spiritual Care

RICHARD COBLE *and* MYCHAL SPRINGER

ABSTRACT *Social justice is a core facet of spiritual care because contextual power dynamics and systemic disparities within the institutions where chaplains work impact the well-being of their careseekers. In order to gain competency in socially just spiritual care, chaplains must grasp the basic vocabulary, trends, and history of these dynamics. While the meaning and specifics of power dynamics and systemic disparities will change depending on each chaplain's context, this chapter serves as an introduction to the knowledge and skills necessary for competence in socially just spiritual care. The chapter introduces core terms—power, social location, patriarchy, and systemic racism—in their relation to chaplaincy and then provides an overview of the history of the communal contextual shift in spiritual caregiving. Finally, through two case studies, the chapter illustrates how chaplains can employ this competency toward immediate care for their careseekers as well as shift systemic dynamics within their home institutions toward greater well-being and justice.*

For chaplains, systemic justice and spiritual caregiving are linked because they do not meet their care receivers in a vacuum, without context or power dynamics. Rather, by definition, their work is institutional. Chaplains work for and are a part of organizations such as hospitals, prisons, the military, long-term care facilities, and college campuses. Even chaplains who work on the street with populations experiencing homelessness nonetheless maintain close ties to nonprofits or denominations or faith communities. Likewise, the care receiver is generally under the care or authority of the same institution that employs the chaplain but as a patient, inmate, soldier, resident, student, or staff member. Inherent in each of these settings and designations is a complex network of relationships, procedures, boundaries, and possibilities that chaplains must understand and navigate in order to provide care. Moreover, intertwined with these institutional systems is a broader, even more abstract network of social systems that transcend but also have direct bearing on all chaplaincy settings. These involve differing experiences and social outcomes linked to identity, including but not limited to one's race, gender, class, sexuality, ability, and religion. Chaplains must have interpersonal competency in navigating these wider social systems and the differing power dynamics that come with them, because these layers of systems have direct influence on the overall wellness of their care receivers.

The interconnection between systemic justice and spiritual caregiving is encoded in both chaplaincy training and certification. For example, the Association for Clinical Pastoral Education mandates competency in "initiat[ing] helping relationships within and across diverse populations" in its Level I curriculum.[1] With relationships across diverse populations, of course, come the power dynamics between the differing social locations of the careseeker and chaplain that the caregiver must understand and account for in order for the relationship to be, in fact, helpful. This curricular focus on just relations and systems is more explicit and detailed for Level II CPE, where the student demonstrates competency in "provid[ing] pastoral ministry with diverse people, taking into consideration multiple elements of cultural and ethnic differences, social conditions, systems, justice and applied clinical ethics issues without imposing one's own perspectives."[2] The focus here thus expands to the wider institutional and social systems in which the caregiving relationship takes place. The Board of Chaplaincy Certification's standards found in "Common Qualifications and Competencies for Professional Chaplains" then echo the connection between care and justice, or rather the reality that justice is an integral part of care.[3]

This chapter serves as an introduction to the basic vocabulary, frameworks, and quandaries that a chaplain must know and consider in order to provide competent, socially just spiritual caregiving. Throughout, we ground our overviews of these competencies with caregiving case studies in order to show the contextual nature of just caregiving. We begin with a return to Angie, a case study covered by Carrie Doehring and Allison Kestenbaum in chapter 6.

Angie's case is illustrative of how power imbalances and systemic oppression can function in the hospital setting and of what chaplains may do in response. Angie is a twenty-five-year-old single African American woman with advanced Hodgkin's lymphoma who is expected to die during her current hospitalization. She is also a recovering addict and a practicing Pentecostal Christian. Angie has had episodes of being unresponsive, likely because the systems of her body are shutting down as she nears the end of her life. During a visit with her chaplain, Angie relates an experience of the presence of God that she had during one of these episodes, where God was dancing with Angie and making her whole in the midst of her fatal cancer prognosis. After this conversation, the chaplain consults with a nurse with expertise on how dying patients may have perceptions or sensations that are comforting in ways similar to Angie's description. When the chaplain speaks with the care team, an agnostic white male physician dismisses Angie's religious experience and sense of wholeness as a drug-induced delirium that should be disregarded. As Doehring and Kestenbaum point out, this dismissal endangers Angie, because it rejects her religious-positive coping, an empirically proven aid for enhancing physical, emotional, and spiritual well-being.

What is the chaplain to do? In order to navigate this situation competently, there are a number of core issues that the chaplain must be familiar with prior to the encounter. However, competency here is not simply a cognitive understanding of a group of terms and trends. Chaplains must not only comprehend the terms outlined below but also employ this knowledge to contextualize each individual spiritual care situation within wider sociopolitical trends and dynamics in order to fully grasp what is happening and to access what interventions to take. In the case of Angie, the chaplain must set the physician's dismissal within wider issues and trends of power, social location, patriarchy, and racism in order to determine the most life-giving intervention as the patient's spiritual caregiver.

First is the issue of power. In relationships, power is simply the ability to determine what happens to oneself and the ability to influence others. There is nothing inherently wrong or bad about power. It is a morally neutral term. In fact, everyone has a certain amount of power in any given relationship. In the context of spiritual caregiving, however, there is necessarily a complex imbalance of power. Simply by being part of the organizational structure of the institution in which they work, chaplains have a higher degree of power than the care receiver. As Doehring helpfully explains, "Equal relationship of mutual give-and-take can occur among those who are peers, such as friends, marital partners, peer colleagues, and siblings. When one person in a relationship is in the role of minister, rabbi, imam, or teacher there is a difference in power. . . . Caregivers are responsible for monitoring power dynamics, which can easily slip and slide between life-giving and life-limiting power dynamics."[4] As Doehring points out, the imbalance of power between spiritual caregiver and care receiver does not necessarily turn into domination, though there is a possibility for such a life-limiting abuse of power when it is used improperly.

There is a clear misuse of power in the case of Angie. The physician, as a leader of the care team, uses his power to silence Angie's spiritual experience, saying that it does not pertain to the work of patient care. The chaplain, however, also has power in this situation. Because of the natural imbalance of power between the chaplain, as a member of the institutional care team, and Angie, as a patient in the hospital, the chaplain has the opportunity—and, in fact, the obligation—to empower the patient by reiterating the importance of her spiritual health and experience.

However, the case becomes more complex when we examine the social location of those involved. Institutional affiliation, where one person in a relationship is designated the spiritual caregiver or chaplain and the other the care receiver (or patient, soldier, inmate, or the like), is only one of several identity markers that make up an individual's social location. These markers also include one's race, gender identity, class, ability, sexuality, and religion. Each designation within these categories has a level of power adhering to it based on the general way it is recognized and treated in a given context. Moreover, the identity categories that make up a person's social location interact and intersect with one another. Critical race theorist Kimberlé Crenshaw was the first to use the term "intersectionality" to denote how these varying markers interact together in terms of social power. In

Crenshaw's words, "Intersectionality is a lens through which you can see where power comes and collides, where it interlocks and intersects. It's not simply that there's a race problem here, a gender problem here, and a class or LBGTQ problem there."[5] Rather, these issues intersect because we each stand in multiple identity categories, and these markers hold varying levels of power based on the context in which we find ourselves, as Doehring and Kestenbaum explore in their discussion of spiritual reflexivity in chapter 6.

The differing social locations of the physician and the patient in this case increase the power differential already in place due to their institutional locations. In order to unpack this imbalance, we must explore two further terms. First, "patriarchy" is defined as the dominance of men over women.[6] This power imbalance remains today. For example, according to the Pew Research Center, women earned only about 85 percent of the wages that men made when doing the exact same job in 2018.[7] Moreover, though women earn more undergraduate and graduate degrees and account for nearly half of the American labor force, they are disproportionately underrepresented in positions of power. For example, women make up 40 percent of physicians and surgeons but only 16 percent of medical school deans. Likewise, they earned the majority of doctorates for eight successive years but make up only 32 percent of full professors.[8] These numbers show the persistence today of the wide-ranging structural advantage of men over women known as patriarchy.

In our case study, the chaplain must put the male physician's dismissal of Angie's spiritual experience within the wider context and trends of patriarchy. Such trends are operative in healthcare, where, following patriarchal norms of masculine stoicism and individualism, men have higher death rates than women, spend less time with their healthcare providers, receive less advice, and are asked less often by their doctors to change their behavior.[9] The dismissal of Angie's experience is in line with wider trends within healthcare that prioritize men's agency. In contrast, in the hospital, women are told what to do rather than heard. Angie's case is a stark example of such dismissal of women's experience.

However, as we saw in the definition of social location above, we cannot look at gendered power dynamics simply in the binary of men over women. Such a narrow focus excludes intersectional power differentials such as race and class. Therefore, black feminist scholars such as bell hooks have critiqued employing the term "patriarchy" alone to name oppression while excluding other intersectional factors. In hooks's words, "Since all forms of oppression are linked in our society because they are supported by similar institutional and social structures, one system cannot be eradicated while others remain intact. Challenging sexist oppression is a crucial step in the struggle to eliminate all forms of oppression."[10] Patriarchy is thus a critical label but not the sole name for systemically imbalanced power dynamics.

In addition, the chaplain must examine how systemic racism plays into Angie's case. Often, racism is associated with individual or group prejudice based on skin color, such as with fringe radical groups such as the Ku Klux Klan who espouse the superiority of the white race over other races. However, when thinking systematically about the institutions in which chaplains operate, such associations and definitions hide the much more widespread, systemic advantage that white-identifying people and the cultural customs associated with them hold in Western society.[11] Systemic racism is a complex set of biases, norms, laws, and trends that foster differing social outcomes based on racial identity.[12] In the hospital system, one way that systemic racism shows up is in the persistence of racist understandings of physical differences between the races among medical professionals. Journalist Linda Villarosa recently reported on this topic in the *New York Times*:

> A 2016 survey of 222 white medical students and residents published in *The Proceedings of the National Academy of Sciences* showed that half of them endorsed at least one myth about physiological differences between black people and white people, including that black people's nerve endings are less sensitive than white people's nerve endings. When asked to imagine how much pain white or black patients experienced in hypothetical situations, the medical students and residents insisted that black people felt less pain. This made the providers less likely to recommend appropriate treatment. A third of these doctors to be also still believed . . . that black skin is thicker than white skin.[13]

Such widespread racist beliefs even among well-educated medical students and physicians play an integral part in divergent healthcare outcomes between African Americans and their white counterparts. Black men have a 26 percent higher death rate than white men and black women a 19 percent higher rate than white women.[14] These disparities are lessened but nonetheless persist when controlling for other systemic disparities in education level and income rates. The physician's dismissal of Angie, then, is in line with wider medical trends that dismiss African American patients' experiences in general.

Set in this wider context, the case study is not simply about isolated behavior; the physician's dismissal is a microcosm, rather, of wider power dynamics and inequalities. The competency necessary for socially just care in this situation is the ability to contextualize individual actions within such a wider social frame. In doing so, the chaplain may now access what action is needed. In this case, it is not enough for the chaplain to say they are not personally sexist or racist (or ableist, classist, and so on). As a clear example of the persistent inequalities examined above, Angie's case calls for more overt action if the chaplain is truly going to offer effective care. A chaplain with competency in socially just care would be ready to set the physician's remark within the oppressive context in which it takes place and therefore involve the medical team in a more thorough discussion about the positive health outcomes of spiritual experiences. This would include engaging the physician himself to understand more of the motivations, blind spots, and possible stressors that led to his dismissive remark. In doing so, the chaplain would be employing their own power as a part of the hospital and a member of the care team to resist these structural inequalities. The chaplain would, in fact, be working to change the power dynamics of the institution itself, making it a more just place.

The chaplain's ability to contextualize these power dynamics while also employing active listening in order to understand the actions of the care team is an illustration of the dynamic interplay between individual care and broader systemic awareness at the root of competent, socially just spiritual care. This dynamic interplay between individual care and broader systemic awareness and change actually has its roots in the historic development of the discipline of spiritual caregiving. In order to understand the roots of this competency, we turn now to this history.

BETWEEN TWO PARADIGMS

The understanding of spiritual care as taking place within a wider network of power relationships that the caregiver must understand and navigate along with the care receiver is a relatively recent innovation in the field of spiritual care and counseling. It is a move from what scholars in the field term the "therapeutic paradigm" to the "communal contextual paradigm."[15] In the early days of CPE and the teaching of care and counseling in theological schools in the first half of the twentieth century, spiritual care held a narrower focus on the individual relationship between caregiver and care receiver. An early champion and educator in the CPE movement was a Presbyterian minister named Anton Boisen (1876–1965), who himself had suffered from what was then diagnosed as reoccurring catatonic schizophrenia. After finding a dearth of spiritual care in his own hospitalizations, Boisen went on to promote spiritual caregiving in clinical settings. Moreover, he saw such work as a necessity for training in religious leadership. As he said in one of his memoirs, "In a time when students of religion were making little use of methods of science, and scientists were failing to carry their inquiries to the level of the religious, we were seeking to make empirical studies of living human documents."[16] Boisen's term "living human documents" became central to the early CPE movement and to what became known as the therapeutic paradigm. It meant that spiritual caregivers and seminary students could learn about the human condition and the divine by studying human experience in the caregiving relationship.

As the therapeutic paradigm evolved in the early decades of the discipline, its specialized focus on the caregiving relationship often excluded wider attention to the social context in which it took place. Pastoral theologians Rodney Hunter and John Patton record this omission in their overview of the paradigm's characteristics. Among others, they highlight the following characteristics:

- Priority of What Human Beings Have in Common over Ways in Which They Differ from One Another . . . The pastoral field and its related therapeutic psychologies accented the idea of the "common core" of experience, and assumed that psychological and pastoral knowledge is equally applicable to either gender and to all races and classes of persons.
- Priority of Personal Needs over Institutional Needs . . . The secular institutional setting in which most pastoral care and counseling has occurred has enabled it to focus almost exclusively on matters of personhood and relationship through its singular attention on the one role function of ministry (pastoral care) with relatively little attention to those functions that more directly represent collective, institutional claims and agendas.[17]

This emphasis on the caregiving relationship itself was a reaction against earlier trends in theological education that focused more squarely on systematic theology and biblical scholarship to the omission of interpersonal relationships and caregiving.[18] The therapeutic paradigm's omission of wider contextual and systemic issues, recorded by Hunter and Patton, was

Interpersonal Competencies

the result of a push toward the interpersonal nature of care and the employment of empathy, to ensure that care receivers can feel heard and understood, experiencing the healing that is possible in attuned relationships. These primary values of the therapeutic paradigm continue into chaplaincy practice today and are central to the competencies of the profession.[19]

However, while not eschewing the centrality of empathy, the field expanded its understanding of the scope of caregiving starting in the 1980s and 1990s as it became more influenced by movements in feminism and critical race theory. Pastoral theologian Bonnie Miller-McLemore's article "The Living Human Web," which itself drew on the earlier work of scholars Archie Smith and Catherine Keller, among others, was a key early work tracing this shift. Miller-McLemore expanded Boisen's early image of the "living human document" to the image of the web in order to illuminate the growing attention to context and power dynamics within caregiving relationships.[20] In another article, one of this chapter's authors, Richard Coble, outlines Miller-McLemore's contribution in this way:

> Miller-McLemore's innovation then is in employing the web of selfhood to critique and modify the practices of care that Boisen's image inaugurated. In proposing the living human web, she draws together past scholarship critiquing the individualism of Boisen's generation while also pushing towards a more overt political agenda for care: "In the past decade, several feminist pastoral theologians have modified the individualistic leaning of Anton Boisen's metaphor by turning to an alternative, related image of the living web . . . It simply means that the individual is understood in inextricable relationship to the broader context." By challenging Boisen's sense of individuality and objectivity, Miller-McLemore critiques the ideal of decontextualized empathy that is assumed by the image of the living human document, lest care unknowingly omit and reinforce wider structural inequalities and oppressive forces.[21]

Throughout the last three to four decades, caregivers coming from social locations beyond that of white heterosexual men, who made up the vast majority of the scholarship of the therapeutic paradigm, have likewise stressed the need for education about the particular experiences, needs, and outcomes of care receivers based on their social location in order for caregivers to provide competent, socially just care. One of the central images from Miller-McLemore's early article is that of a male caregiver offering "too much indiscriminate empathy" to a female survivor of sexual assault.

Miller-McLemore demonstrates that if such a caregiver downplays the power differential and differing experiences rooted in gender, then such caregiving might actually only "foster further damage and violence" as he further disempowers the assault survivor by refusing to hear or acknowledge her particular experiences.[22]

The current communal contextual paradigm thus teaches us that competency in spiritual caregiving today includes ongoing education about the unique experiences of care receivers, especially those coming from social locations different from one's own. In addition to reading the ever-expanding scholarship about the particularities of care for varying social groups, much of this knowledge can also be gained by a close, listening ear. However, in reverse of the therapeutic paradigm's practice to prioritize commonalities over differences, chaplains must, in fact, listen for differences. As intercultural pastoral theologian Emmanuel Lartey puts it, caregivers must be attuned to the way that "every human person is in certain respects 1. Like all others 2. Like some others 3. Like no other."[23] This means that while there are basic similarities that connect us all and allow for the possibility of empathy, caregivers must also pay close attention to social group and individual differences. Beyond indiscriminate empathy that assumes only similarity, this attention to context calls for a deeper listening, gaining trust by seeking out the unique experiences of our care receivers.

Thus, it would be a mistake to characterize the shift to the communal contextual paradigm as a way of forgetting the original concerns of the therapeutic. Of course, the central work of the chaplain is precisely in the caregiving relationship that is still marked by the use of empathy and active listening techniques to ensure care receivers feel heard and that their experience is appreciated. As pastoral theologian Edward Wimberly names in his introduction to *African American Pastoral Care*, "Story-listening involves empathically hearing the story of the person involved in life struggles."[24] Given the growing awareness of systemic power dynamics within spiritual caregiving, in order truly to understand such struggles and thus have access to the empathy Wimberly names, spiritual caregivers must extend interpersonal capacities for empathy and psychological self-reflection to include social empathy and self-reflexivity. These interpersonal capacities integrate knowledge of social location and contextual power disparities into whether and how spiritual trust is possible, given the ways all caregiving relationships are entangled in systems of social injustice.

The necessity of such competency is illuminated by the case study with Angie. Womanist practical theologian Evelyn Parker describes the unique needs and contributions of Black women in the fields of spiritual care: "How must we care for the body and soul of a black woman? How is she God's unique gift to herself, her community, and the global society? What is the nature of care and counseling that gives her life in abundance? What are her experiences and how are her stories fundamental to life-giving pastoral care practices? These are questions womanist pastoral theologians seek to answer as scholars in ministry with black women."[25] Spiritual caregivers of all social locations must then learn about such particularities of social location and care needs through scholarship coming from differing communities, employing these lessons as a means of connection with our careseekers, while also listening for the unique ways these experiences are lived out by careseekers such as Angie. In this way, the more recent communal contextual paradigm is an expansion and deepening of the original emphasis on interpersonal relations by the field's founders such as Boisen.

RETURN TO CASE STUDY I: ANGIE'S CASE STUDY

Returning to the case study with Angie, the communal contextual paradigm thus brings our attention to the particular spiritual experiences of African American women. Womanist pastoral theological literature offers a repeated critique of the silencing of Black women's voices both as care receivers and also in basic understandings of the role and outcome of caregiving. In one of the first book-length works of Womanist pastoral theology, Carroll Watkins Ali writes that "theological reflection for the African American context . . . acknowledges that the people indigenous to the context are the subjects of their own stories rather than the objects of projections and/or perspectives formed by other worldviews."[26] In Angie's case, this means that the value of her spiritual experience should be determined from her own standpoint rather than dismissed from another's. Indeed, in a more recent article, CPE educator and Womanist pastoral theologian Teresa Snorton writes about the constant dismissal of Black women's experience in chaplaincy care and training, explaining, "I am convinced that black women and their liberation are dependent upon the freedom to give voice to the pain of their individual and collective lives."[27] This point is echoed by another Womanist CPE educator, Jacqueline Kelley: "From a womanist theological perspective, women must learn to value their personal story enough to use it as a tool to measure and evaluate their personal experience."[28] These Womanist authors point to the positive contribution of Black women's spiritual experience in their own healing and wholeness.

In light of this literature, contextualizing Angie's experience means seeing it in both negative and positive valence. First, the chaplain must put the physician's dismissal within much broader oppressive trends in which Black women's perspectives in general are denied and unheard within healthcare. However, the chaplain must also see the positive, which is that within the experience itself, Angie is expressing her spiritual movement toward wholeness, not from an outside, putatively objective measure of health but rather from a subjective encounter of the divine, holding and dancing with her in her final days. The chaplain competent in socially just care must also set Angie's comment in a Womanist spiritual frame that sees the positive individual experiences of Black women as expressions of their movement toward healing in an otherwise oppressive environment. Knowing this, the chaplain can not only inquire into the reasons behind the care team's dismissal but also help them see purpose and the positive work of Angie's experience in a fuller understanding of health and wholeness.

DIALOGUE WITH PHYSICIAN FROM THE CASE STUDY

Physician: This dream is a drug-induced hallucination.

Chaplain: Doctor, I think about this differently.

Physician: You do?

Chaplain: Yes, this experience Angie has had of the presence of God dancing with her, making her whole, is a powerful spiritual event in her life. Whatever the possible scientific explanations for the dream, we need to understand the dream in the context of Angie's identity as an African American Pentecostal Christian. This dream is an important gift to Angie as she copes with dying and finds comfort in the arms of the divine.

Physician: Hmm.

Chaplain: I'd be happy to share some resources about African American and Pentecostal spirituality with you, if you like.

Physician: Thanks. That would be great.

CASE STUDY 2: RELIGIOUS NEEDS AT THE END
OF LIFE AND COVID-19 SAFETY PRECAUTIONS

Having examined Angie's case study from a contextual and historical point of view, we turn now to a longer case study in order to examine the complexity of socially just care in the midst of the opportunities and limitations of the hospital system. The following study outlines how systemic power dynamics, boundaries, and safety precautions within the hospital system can be in tension with the religious needs of a patient and family and how the chaplain can employ power in ways that expand the empathy and possibilities of the careseekers, the care team, and the very system itself.

During COVID-19, when visitation in hospitals was suspended, many chaplains received frantic phone calls from family members asking for help (see the volume introduction, chapters 1, 2, and 5, and the conclusion for further discussion of spiritual care during COVID-19). Many Jewish families sought out rabbis in various hospitals. One type of request was particularly fraught, as rabbis needed to negotiate complex dynamics between families and staff. The following composite case study illustrates power struggles when organizational policies make it challenging for members of minority religious groups to practice their religion.

A Jewish son contacts the chaplain with this urgent request: "Help! My mother is dying, and the hospital said we cannot come for an end-of-life visit. But we know that end-of-life visits are allowed by the Department of Health. We have a legal right! The doctor called this morning and told me she is dying. I must be able to come and say viddui [the final confession] for my mother.[29] Can you please help!"

The hospital-based rabbi, like all chaplains, lives between the world of the hospital and the world of communal religious practice. The family member who calls—in this case, a son—trusts that the rabbi is an insider in the hospital and also has shared faith-based values that will propel the rabbi to advocate on the patient's and family's behalf. Despite never having met in person, family members hope and expect that the rabbi will do everything possible to enable practices of faith—in this instance, an end-of-life visit. The family may be prevented from entering the hospital, but the reality that the rabbi has the power of institutional position and proximity may allay their fears and may help families feel that they will be heard and understood both in the caregiving relationship and in the wider institution. Being heard and understood builds spiritual trust, as this and previous chapters illustrate.

While people from many backgrounds feel a deep need to be heard and understood, people from minority populations may have a particularly acute need, especially if their practices and approaches to care differ from the institutional norm. Research has shown that minority populations are significantly less likely to engage in advance care planning and to consent to a "do not resuscitate" request, based on issues that include "distrust of the health care system, health care disparities, cultural perspectives on death and suffering, and family dynamics such as parent-child relationships."[30] In this case study the son is a Hasidic Jew, someone who lives in an insular religious world that intentionally keeps its distance from mainstream American society. But in a time of great physical vulnerability, he has brought his mother to the hospital to save her life, in keeping with his religious teachings and practices. Yet, he searches for a way to influence the hospital in order to practice faith traditions and follow commandments that accord with his and his mother's deepest values. The rabbi is a bridge. It is likely that the rabbi is not a Hasid from the son's community, so this initial encounter is already a negotiation of difference. While Jewish communities can remain siloed in much of ordinary life, the hospital is one place where rabbis who would not be considered authoritative in a patient's communal context are suddenly key allies.

In this case study, the rabbi is a woman, whose rabbinic status is not recognized in most of the Orthodox Jewish world, and certainly not in the Hasidic world. In order to navigate the complex intersections of patriarchy and religious minority status, the rabbi needs to draw upon her capacities for spiritual empathy and self-reflexivity (described in chapter 3), which will help her identify and reflect upon any ambivalence she may feel about holding insider-outsider status in relation to the care receiver so that she can lean into her power most appropriately. Without such self-reflexivity, she could unintentionally neglect this patient and her family or wield her power in a less-than-conscious effort to assert her religious authority.

The rabbi hears the son in his distress, responds with empathy, and agrees to help in whatever ways are possible, aware of the strict restrictions on visiting. The rabbi holds the identity of the patient as she has been described by her son: a nurturing mother of nine, a *tzadekes* (righteous woman) who is quick to perform *mitzvoth* (commandments) and has always welcomed strangers to her Shabbos table, an *eshes chayil* (a woman of valor). The rabbi goes to talk to the nursing administrator, who is the gatekeeper on the patient unit, the one who decides whether a visitor is allowed. As the rabbi opens the conversation with the nursing administrator, the rabbi will once again be aware of dynamics of difference. Is the nursing administrator Jewish? Secular? Religious and of a different faith? What kind of experiences might this nursing administrator have had with Orthodox Jews, especially in end-of-life care? As ethicists Ezra Gabbay and Joseph Fins have explored, Orthodox Jews have a reputation for religious struggles in hospitals at the end of life.[31]

The rabbi discovers that the nursing administrator has several objections to allowing the son to pay an imminent death visit. One of them is that if this son comes, then others will know about it and will also advocate to be able to come, which will be disruptive on the unit. The nursing administrator wants to be fair, to keep order, to treat everyone the same. The nursing administrator may well feel a profound obligation to minimize harm in a devastating pandemic by keeping out visitors who can spread the virus and are themselves vulnerable to contracting a life-threatening disease. But what about the obligation to accommodate an imminent death visit, in accordance with the New York State Department of Health "Health Advisory: COVID-19 Guidance for Hospital Operators Regarding Visitation"? That document states, "To prevent the introduction of COVID-19 into hospitals: Effective immediately, suspend all visitation except when medically necessary (i.e., visitor is essential to the care of the patient) or for family members or legal representatives of patients in imminent end of life situations."[32] Here the nursing administrator could argue that the patient is not in a category of imminent end of life, because she has the status of a full code, which means that she will receive all possible medical interventions to revive her if her heart stops. And would the patient ever qualify for an imminent end-of-life visit when her medical team is ethically required to revive her? The nursing administrator could say no; there is no such thing as imminent death when patients have not completed advance directives that include "do not resuscitate" instructions when death is imminent. But this Hasidic woman will receive all possible medical interventions when her death is imminent because of her religious conviction that life is precious and cannot be given up on, even if it is the tiniest drop of life that remains at the end. And so, the culture of the hospital and the belief system of this woman are in an irreconcilable conflict. What is a rabbi to do?

The rabbi, trained in translation and rabbinic logic, can draw on multiple cultures to arrive at a compromise.[33] She asks the nursing administrator how long the patient is expected to live, even with the team's resuscitation efforts. The nursing administrator assesses twenty-four hours, perhaps forty-eight. The updated "Health Advisories" specify that "the Department defines imminent end-of-life situations as a patient who is actively dying, where death is anticipated within less than 24 hours."[34] Using rabbinic logic, the rabbi finds some wiggle room for satisfying both the family's and the hospital staff's needs. She postulates that twenty-four to forty-eight hours are not so different from twenty-four hours. What if the son has his imminent death visit now, with the understanding that the family will not get another visit later, should the mother live beyond twenty-four hours? It is crucial for the family that this visit happens while the patient is alive, so that she can have the proper prayers to escort her to her death. If they are not allowed to come until the patient has died, it will be too late. In this composite case study, the nursing administrator is willing to allow one family member, the son, to stay for fifteen minutes, outside the room. Both the nurse and the rabbi need to anticipate that the son may refuse to leave. They agree that the unit will call security if that happens. The son comes for an imminent end-of-life visit, escorted by the rabbi. He prays outside the room. He is profoundly grateful that he can accompany his mother with the proper prayers at this moment. And he leaves peacefully at the end of his fifteen minutes.

In this case study, hospital staff members are upset when they witness this family visit. They are aware that this son is part of a community where COVID-19 has hit the hardest. Perhaps they are further exposed to COVID-19 risk by his presence. To them, this exposure is unnecessary. They are already upset that the patient has a full code status, because this means that she will need to have aerosolizing procedures, which are the ones that put the staff most at risk for becoming sick from COVID-19. Staff members have already become sick. Some have become hospitalized and put on ventilators. Some have even died. They question whether it is right to perform "futile" treatments on patients—treatments that will not prevent a patient from dying, even if those treatments might prolong the dying process for a little while—when they put staff at risk. How much risk is it okay to expose staff members to for the sake of care that fulfills religious obligations when someone is dying?[35] Imagine the added complexities if a staff member is African American and is living with heightened fears of vulnerability to COVID-19.[36] Imagine if frontline healthcare workers live in extended family households with vulnerable family members. Here, the differences of race and ethnicity come into play in particularly painful ways. As a chaplain who works in the hospital, the rabbi cares for patients, families, and staff. While needing to advocate for the patient, the rabbi must also offer care to staff members who are wrestling with moral stress about core values in conflict.

They want to provide the best possible healthcare they can while not harming themselves or their family and community members. The rabbi needs to hear the anguish of staff members who are afraid for their lives and offer spiritual support to them.

The hospital's ethics committee might be wrestling with the same questions about the limits of treatment at end of life. As a member of the ethics committee, the rabbi has a voice in helping to shape the conversation about futile treatment, maintaining safeguards for different religious beliefs, and the need to pursue treatment at the end of life. It is possible that the rabbi might hold that Jewish wisdom allows people at the end of life "to peacefully and comfortably pass rather than employ disproportionate aggressive medical interventions with little or no prospects of meaningful benefit."[37] But as a rabbi for Jews of all backgrounds, within the context of the hospital, the chaplain needs to extend her religious imagination to the spiritual commitments of others who do not share her views. And while there are many voices for the staff, there are far fewer voices for the minority religious groups whose views and practices trouble the waters.

What if the patient does not die within twenty-four hours? Perhaps she lingers for another day or two, or even three. The family may now feel more at peace with her imminent death and with the regulations that they cannot visit again. They may also place their spiritual trust in the rabbi, who regularly returns to the patient and stands outside her room, praying. They are comforted when she lets them know that she has seen their mother, who is comfortable and being well cared for. The rabbi's spiritual care may prompt conversations with this patient's medical care team, who confer with her about how to involve the family in end-of-life interventions. The rabbi and the doctor initiate a call to the family, in which the doctor explains that the mother is in a full medical code, receiving the maximum amount of medication, which is still not preventing their mother from dying, so she does not have much time left. The doctor suggests that it might be in keeping with their beliefs to allow for the full medical code to be sufficient intervention, without the chest compressions that are a violent way to come to the end of life and will cause her considerable pain. Will the son agree that the doctor can make that determination when the time comes and not request that the team perform chest compressions if they will be futile at that point? In this instance, the son says yes, and the team breathes more easily. If the son were to say no because he believes he must say no, then the team would have to be resigned to initiate chest compressions.[38] Either way, the patient dies. Questions about how her wishes have been honored and how her life has been held as sacred can give rise to moral distress when the team disagrees with family decisions in which spiritual and religious values do not align with team members' beliefs about what makes a death "good." On the other hand, when patients and their families are fully involved in facing together the "void of death," they may be able to negotiate profoundly meaningful and comforting end-of-life care that honors the mystery of life and death.

As this case study illustrates, a chaplain must have knowledge of the pathways, gatekeepers, and boundaries of the hospital system, as well as of wider systemic issues such as differing needs and outcomes of patients, family members, and care team professionals based on varying intersectional social locations. But even beyond this base knowledge, the chaplain must first have a listening ear for the differing, often conflicting needs of the various human beings involved, in this case, a Hasidic family with certain boundaries on end-of-life healthcare designations and religious practices and a care team seeking the safest possible protocols in the midst of the COVID-19 pandemic.

These then are the competencies of socially just spiritual care: the ability to contextualize individual care situations within wider trends and dynamics that create differing institutional outcomes based on social location; the humility to watch for and learn from difference rather than assume similarity across difference; and finally, the willingness to employ one's own institutional power to empower one's colleagues, careseekers, and the system itself to be more empathic, more just, and more willing to learn from and grow with one another. This chapter serves as a basic introduction to these competencies, but, as the case studies of this chapter illustrate, socially just care requires ongoing practice and improvisation. The institutions in which chaplains operate can always be more just and thus more caring. It is within chaplains' scope of practice that their care strives toward this ever-expanding goal.

REFLECTION QUESTIONS

1. What does the chapter's opening sentence mean when it states that chaplains do not meet their care receivers in a vacuum, without context or power dynamics?
2. What power does a chaplain hold? What is proper use of that power, and how can it be abused?
3. What does it mean to contextualize isolated events in caregiving

within wider trends and power dynamics? How might this contextualization aid your own caregiving?

4. How does the history of the progression from the therapeutic paradigm to the communal contextual paradigm of spiritual care impact your understanding of chaplaincy?

5. How do you see the core terms defined in the chapter (power, social location, patriarchy, systemic racism) at work in the second case study presented in the chapter?

RECOMMENDED READINGS

Bishop, Jeffrey. *The Anticipatory Corpse: Medicine, Power, and the Care of the Dying.* Notre Dame: University of Notre Dame Press, 2011.

Coble, Richard. *The Chaplain's Presence and Medical Power: Rethinking Loss in the Hospital System.* Lanham, Md.: Lexington Books, 2018.

Kujawa-Holbrook, Sheryl A., and Karen B. Montagno, eds. *Injustice and the Care of Souls: Taking Oppression Seriously in Pastoral Care.* Minneapolis: Fortress Press, 2011.

Stevenson-Moessner, Jeanne, and Teresa Snorton, eds. *Women Out of Order: Risking Change and Creating Care in a Multicultural World.* Minneapolis: Fortress Press, 2010.

Sullivan, Winnifred Fallers. *A Ministry of Presence: Chaplaincy, Spiritual Care, and the Law.* Chicago: University of Chicago Press, 2014.

PART FOUR

Organizational Competencies

Introduction to
Organizational Competencies

BARBARA McCLURE *and* MARY MARTHA THIEL

Chaplains are in a unique position in the organizations they serve. Having organizational competencies allows chaplains to analyze how organizations actually work and then to leverage their role within them to help move those organizations in the direction of greater human and global flourishing. Chaplains are moral leaders, holding forth for an organization a vision of just and sustainable communal thriving rooted in their religious/spiritual/ existential traditions.[1] They are also change agents. This part of the volume represents its authors' conviction that chaplains, in whatever sector they serve, are called to dismantle white supremacy and its component isms, including racism, sexism, and classism, and to contribute to the cultivation of organizations that are life-giving for *all their members* as well as for those whom they seek to serve.

Chaplains are inextricably linked to organizations. Organizations are inescapable in human life. They are fallible, capable of great good as well as great harm. The authors of part 4 share the belief that organizations can also be changed. Chaplains with organizational competencies can work toward a more just vision for an organization. They can also be coopted by it if they do not hold on to the vision of a more just world they received from their religious/spiritual formation. Effective chaplains work deliberately with the dialectic of an organization's potential for change and its resistance to change.

The themes in part 4 are applicable across organizations. The authors come from different sectors of chaplaincy and spiritual care education: the army, a graduate theological seminary, and a CPE center located within a graduate theological seminary. Chaplains in such different contexts as law enforcement, hospitals, and businesses and among the unhoused will find these themes ubiquitous in their work.

Traditionally, chaplains have not been trained in organizational competencies. Pastoral care courses in seminary tend to focus on individual and family care; some include consideration of the impact of racism, sexism, and classism on the spirits and bodies of care receivers. Each branch of the military develops curriculum for training its chaplains in keeping with its own unique mission and culture.

It is the rare seminary course or CPE unit that teaches chaplains to see and think systems-wise, especially as applied to organizational change. The role of advising the commander is well established in the military. In healthcare settings, if systems theory is taught, it is generally applied in the context of family systems or internal family systems. In the "Objectives and Outcomes" for students in CPE, Objective 8 is "*to develop students' capacity to use one's pastoral and prophetic perspectives* in preaching, teaching, *leadership*, management, pastoral care, and pastoral counseling" (emphasis added).[2] The outcomes to demonstrate this objective, however, do not address organizational change.

At the level of certified professional chaplaincy, among other competencies, the Common Standards for Professional Chaplaincy asks that a chaplain be able to "articulate conceptual understanding of group dynamics and organizational behavior" and "articulate an understanding of institutional culture and systems, and systemic relationships."[3] Noticeably absent is applying one's theories at the organizational level. The Canadian Association for Spiritual Care / Association canadienne de soins spirituels goes further, requiring that a certified professional (chaplain) "envision creative possibilities that inspire oneself and others to supportive and advocacy action with individuals and communities and within organizations."[4]

In the United States, it is only implicit at the level of training to be a CPE certified educator that the requisite competencies include holding a vision for and working toward a more just organization. The leadership and development competencies for ACPE certified educators include "demonstrat[ing] an understanding of the role of the CPE Certified Educator as an

Organizational Competencies

advocate on behalf of students and spiritual care within the organizational context and for the profession."[5] This competency does not clearly point to embodying leadership for institutional change. In practice, most chaplains and chaplain educators today have not been taught to understand how organizations function or how to contribute to their positive change.[6]

Fortunately, chaplain training is being widely reconsidered in the present moment. Hopeful signs are emerging. The U.S. Army is developing a graduate school focused on enhancing the professional development, training, and readiness of its Chaplain Corps in order to meet the diverse spiritual needs of a rapidly changing army. The ACPE in the United States is working with a new certification process for its educators, which requires some demonstration of how to function in a system. The Canadian CPE organization now requires transformative organizational leadership skills in its certified professionals (chaplains), as noted above. Pastoral theologians are considering chaplains' roles in the broad context of the whole human web. This part of the volume reflects its authors' conviction that educating effective chaplains does require teaching organizational competencies. Training chaplains in how organizations function would help establish them as change agents and guides in the organizations they serve and with which they collaborate.

Chaplains, whether lay or ordained, tend to have a strong felt sense of calling to their work. Most would include "healing" in the aspirations for their work, starting with the spiritual/emotional healing of the persons directly served. The circles of healing move outward from there to include the organization's staff, the local community, the wider community, and so on. It is because of chaplains' grounding in religious/spiritual/existential tradition that the range of their moral concern reaches beyond the parameters of one institution to include, ultimately, this much wider perspective. The spirituality of chaplaincy includes a sense of the Holy/Ultimate being present in their human-to-human encounters, to be sure. It continues expanding outward, the vision of a healed world serving as ballast in challenging circumstances. Inspired by their religious/spiritual/existential traditions, chaplains are sustained by a spirituality of moving through and a spirituality of motivation to create a more just, compassionate, and flourishing world. Chaplaincy is justice work.

Chaplains, then, must be leaders. Some are managers, with responsibility to supervise and coordinate other chaplains. Others are line staff. All, however, are called to leadership. As understood by organizational leadership theorists Lee Bolman and Terence Deal, "leadership is **situational** (dependent on organizational, environmental, and/or historical context), **relational** (a relationship between leader and followers), and **distinct from position** (not synonymous with authority or high position). It is a subtle process of mutual influence that fuses thought, feeling, and action to produce cooperative effort in the service of the purposes and values of *both* the leader and followers."[7] Chaplains' ultimate vision and values are grounded in their religious/spiritual/existential tradition. Yet their leadership is not about conversion of people in the organization to the beliefs and practices of their tradition but about holding forth a moral vision larger than any single organization.

Chaplains are in a unique position to leverage such organizational change. They are in the organization (hired by or volunteering in it) but not of it (belonging instead to a religious/spiritual/existential tradition). Their moral perspective is larger than the organization's. This is in some traditions known as the chaplain's prophetic role—the commission to speak truth to power. Chaplains carry great symbolic power in being a religious leader. Persons in the organization respond to this power in different ways, with transference impacting how the chaplain's role is understood. Some will assume chaplains are deferential, kind, and naive. Some will react to chaplains' power negatively, their transference serving as a block in finding collaboration between them. Others will grant extra moral authority to chaplains, drawing on positive transference and trusting them. Chaplains' clarity about their role in the organization helps them manage these different perceptions in service of the greater goal of working toward positive change.

The three chapters in part 4 share three themes. First, the authors agree that the scope of care of a faithful and effective chaplain is beyond one-on-one chaplaincy relationships. Second, essential to the role of the chaplain is organizational leadership and concern for ethics. And consequently, third, the chaplain needs to be knowledgeable and skilled in creating change in organizations in the direction, ultimately, of global flourishing. Rev. Dr. Nathan H. White's chapter offers a broad view of the purposes of organizations and applies this to chaplaincy's moral advisory role in the military. Rev. Dr. Laurie Garrett-Cobbina demonstrates the impact that the white supremacy patterns embedded in an organization have on employees and those served by the organization. She calls for chaplains to draw on their spiritual roots to work toward greater justice at all levels within and beyond the institution. Dr. Su Yon Pak introduces the reader to Bolman and Deal's **four-frames approach** for organizational leadership and to the white supremacist culture characteristics developed by Tema Okun and Kenneth Jones and uses them to analyze the part's case study.

The case study in part 4 provides opportunities for important integration of the theoretical material in each chapter. It follows the work of a chaplain creating momentum in her organization for serving survivors of intimate partner violence (IPV) and advocating for the eradication of cultural dynamics and practices contributing to IPV. Part authors shine light on the case study from their own perspectives.

Equally important, the case study offers important learning about what a chaplain sees and doesn't see. The three authors work from viewpoints that would require additional information to be included in the case study to be fully congruent with their own organizational perspectives. Missing or "deleted" data bespeak the implicit biases and blind spots of the case writer, who might benefit from having the perspectives of the part 4 authors in his or her chaplain's leadership toolkit. All chaplains should continue to expand organizational competencies over their career, understanding with greater nuance how organizations work, being able to analyze what is at work and not at work in a particular situation, and expanding the range of what they see going on in an organization.

It will be most helpful to read the case study before turning to this part's chapters. Reading all three offers the potential to maximize one's learning, as each chapter is written in trialogue with the others. Most persons are drawn to chaplaincy out of love for the interpersonal or meaning-making competencies of the field, as addressed in parts 2 and 3 of this book. We hope that learning about chaplaincy's organizational competencies will pique your interest in chaplaincy as healing justice work. Skilled chaplains know how to leverage their interpersonal and meaning-making competencies to change an organization. Supporting spiritual well-being and meaning making for all connected with an organization ripples out to influence each successive entity of the greater world toward social change and healing.

PART 4 CASE STUDY

The setting is a large organization (a hospital, military base, school, prison, or something similar) in an ethnically diverse city in which a traditional religious designation is the largest religious identity and "none" is the second largest.

A white woman, well-dressed and perhaps in her early forties, knocks hesitantly on the director of spiritual care's (DSC) door early one afternoon. The chaplain welcomes her into the office and invites her to share what brought her to this moment. The woman is married to a man, with whom she has three school-age children. Her husband has always wanted her home with the children, so she has not developed the promising career she began newly out of school. She volunteers teaching religious education for children in her home congregation and deeply values her faith. Step by cautious step, she gets to her question for the chaplain: The clergyperson from her Christian denomination in a different town—she confesses she hasn't dared consult with her own pastor—has told her that thinking about leaving her marriage is selfish, a breach of her marriage vows and the laws of God, and a sign of lack of faith. Does the chaplain agree?

The chaplain wonders to herself whether interpersonal violence, or the threat of it, or other dynamics of power and control might be part of the woman's context. She says gently that she can only imagine how painful it is to be having to consider this option and that she—the chaplain—believes that leaving a marriage can sometimes be a faithful thing to do. She invites the woman to share whatever she is ready to share of what has brought her to explore whether leaving her marriage can be congruent with her Christian faith.

Every few months over the next several years the woman checks in with the chaplain, telling a bit more each time about the dynamics in her marriage and the outbursts of violence she tries to hide from others, how she worries about their impact on her children, how she could support herself if she left, and whether she might lose in a custody battle for her children. Always, she worries about whether leaving can be congruent with her faith and the vows she made before God on her wedding day.

The chaplain knows she cannot make the woman's decision for her or guarantee a safe outcome for her and her children, whatever the woman decides. Some years into her career now, the chaplain has seen how sexism, classism, and racism are often at work in the very institutions purporting to protect the vulnerable: religion, medicine, psychiatry, education, law, the police, politics, the economy, the insurance industry, and so on. She is particularly pained by how constrained the woman perceives herself to be by the organizational power structures of her religious tradition.

The DSC decides she must connect her one-on-one chaplaincy with advocacy for organizational and systemic change from within her organizational context. With limited staffing, the director of spiritual care chooses intimate partner violence as the primary issue she will champion for the department's internal and community outreach and advocacy. She wants her organization and those it serves to know that the Department of Spiritual Care offers survivors religious and spiritual support in keeping with their safety and well-being. She hires the local interfaith partnership against domestic violence to provide training to all the chaplains in the department in how to provide survivors with safe, appropriate, and religiously/spiritually supportive care.

The DSC speaks with her boss to get herself named to the interdisciplinary Intimate Partner Violence Task Force. The task force begins advocating with the organization's administration for funding for a specialized IPV program. Through the work of the task force, the DSC gets to know staff from other departments who are also invested in serving survivors well. The task force sponsors educational events for staff each year during Intimate Partner Violence Awareness Month. After several years the organization agrees to support an IPV program, space is allotted for the program, and several staff members with expertise in the field are hired.

The DSC reaches out to the new program staff to explain her vision of the unique contribution chaplains can make to the interdisciplinary support of survivors and to education of staff. She receives mixed responses. Several staff members make it clear that they would never refer their clients to a chaplain because of the religious trauma many survivors have already endured (or because the organization is not explicitly religious). One staff person is cautiously open to the DSC. As the program staff begin planning an organization-wide frontline staff education program, the DSC offers to research and provide for the curriculum survivor-supportive resources from the major religious traditions represented in the organization and wider community. She makes connections with the national Faith Trust Institute, the local interfaith partnership against domestic violence, and individual clergy from several religious traditions not represented in the spiritual care department who are willing to consult with chaplains or with IPV survivors with religious/spiritual concerns. She engages the IPV program staff to provide additional education for the chaplains, including on the topic of how best to protect survivors' confidentiality and safety in the way they document a spiritual care visit in which IPV is disclosed.

The staff education program is rolled out for frontline caregivers throughout the organization, raising awareness of IPV, introducing the best practice of screening all people for IPV, and describing the organization's resources available to IPV survivors. Cards with contact information for the organization's IPV program, the Department of Spiritual Care, police and security, and the national IPV hotline are placed in all public restrooms in the organization's building(s). Survivors begin to seek out chaplains in greater numbers, and referrals from the IPV program begin to come in as well. The DSC purchases cartons of *Keeping the Faith: Guidance for Christian Women Facing Abuse* by Marie Fortune for free distribution, as appropriate, by chaplains and by staff of the IPV program, since many or even most of the organization's members come from Christian traditions. The Department of Spiritual Care makes financial donations each year to one local and one national advocacy organization.

The DSC decides to use her unique role in the institution to coordinate and sponsor an organization-wide memorial service each year in honor of those persons from their state who died as a result of IPV in the previous twelve months. Her planning includes volunteers from many areas of the community who play a role in serving IPV survivors: administration, the IPV program, social work, police and security, spiritual care, community relations, communications, and the emergency department. The local interfaith partnership against domestic violence participates in the service, as do some local clergy. Sometimes persons served by the organization's IPV program take part as well. The service includes components that are interfaith as well as secular, in languages representative of the community. It is noteworthy for the ringing of a large gong at the reading of each name from a list that is always too long. The spiritual care budget provides for live musicians, for kosher and halal box lunches—so that staff who attend the service during their lunch hour do not have to forgo their meal—and for the gong.

Each year attendance at the organization's IPV memorial service increases, as the culture of the organization shifts toward public advocacy for IPV survivors, publicity about the service has wider reach, and word of mouth encourages colleagues' attendance. When the DSC moves on to another job, the memorial service has enough institutional momentum to continue without her leadership. She does not get to know whether the woman who first knocked on her door those years ago ever left her husband.

· ·

CHAPTER NINE

Facilitating Resilience: Chaplaincy as a Catalyst for Organizational Well-Being

· ·

NATHAN H. WHITE

ABSTRACT *Organizations possess great potential for good and for ill. On the one hand, they serve a necessary function within human society in the promotion of great good, such as preserving cultural memory and enabling positive collaborative efforts. On the other hand, organizations tend to resist change, acting as monolithic powers that can silence dissenting voices and exploit those without power. Yet no matter their most obvious effects, organizations are dynamic rather than static entities, and organizational change is possible. Those within organizations are responsible to shape them for their betterment, using the inherent power and stability of the organization to help and protect, rather than to marginalize or exploit vulnerable and diverse populations. Chaplains can and should play a vital role in this effort by becoming catalysts for beneficial change. Such transformation will not occur, however, without deliberate effort to facilitate competencies of organizational understanding and assessment, effective collaboration within and across organizations, and advisement of organizational leadership.*

Chaplains[1] play an increasingly important role in the spiritual and religious landscape of organizations.[2] Chaplains provide religious and spiritual (R/S) care to individuals in settings as diverse as healthcare, industry, prisons, education, and the military. They are often one of the only religious ministry professionals with whom many individuals come into contact in an era of declining religious service attendance.[3] In fact, 2017 marked the first time more clergy worked outside of parish contexts (53 percent) than in religious organizations.[4] A growing body of research indicates that interactions with chaplains are generally positive and lead to outcomes such as greater patient well-being, increased patient satisfaction, and more beneficial health outcomes in primary care healthcare settings.[5] This mirrors broader findings regarding the positive effects of religion/spirituality upon health[6] and resilience outcomes.[7]

Despite these encouraging trends for chaplaincy as a profession, there are also reasons for concern. Although many chaplaincy training programs exist, there is little standardization of training for chaplains across sectors.[8] Further, within organizations themselves there are often few mechanisms for the proper management of chaplains or their integration into broader organizational structures.

These difficulties, I argue, are inherent to the nature of chaplaincy itself, but they also provide unique opportunities for chaplaincy. A chaplain, by definition, usually works within a "secular" (that is, not explicitly religious) organization while maintaining R/S core foundational commitments and competencies. In essence, a chaplain occupies a liminal space,[9] as a representative of both an organization and an R/S body. Specific educational and leadership-formational needs arise because chaplains occupy a position that is both inherently liminal (between religious and secular) and organizational (employed by the military, by prisons, by universities, and the like). Chaplains require specific competencies to navigate organizational dynamics successfully. These fundamental competencies include understanding and assessing organizational culture, the capacity to work together with professionals, and the ability to advise leadership.

Greater attention needs to be paid to the organizational systems in which chaplains operate and, to an extent, for whose benefit chaplains work. To understand the distinct challenges and opportunities within a chaplaincy context, it is necessary to assess the purpose and nature of an organization itself as well as how these affect chaplains. This skill supports the chaplain competency of understanding and assessing organizational culture.

THE NATURE OF ORGANIZATIONS

What is the purpose of an organization? This question, to one extent or another, has been asked for millennia. In the early Greek philosopher Aristotle's thought, for instance, the purpose of human beings is inextricably linked to our communal nature, wherein human beings come together in organized societies to seek mutual flourishing. Here, the telos (goal/purpose) of the sociopolitical establishment is to facilitate development "for the sake of the good life [*eudaimonia*]."[10] Aristotle viewed organizations of various kinds—from family units to political bodies—as vital to individual and communal human flourishing.

Today, organizations are both informal (such as book clubs or Little League baseball teams) and extremely formalized (such as corporations and governments); their purposes range from providing opportunities for socialization to making money. Each organization, in its own way, enacts its vision of "the good life," if not for an entire society, at least for its members. Potential difficulties appear when one organization's efforts come in conflict with those of another organization or group, especially if that group uses its power to exploit or disempower individuals, inside or outside of the organization.

The existence of chaplains within an organization inevitably raises significant questions regarding the organization's vision of flourishing, especially in relation to morality: Is the moral status of the chaplain, as a religious leader, tied to the moral status of the organization? In what ways is a chaplain implicated in the broader dynamics of an organization (including its moral component)? Is the fact of an organization's existence "value-neutral," or do organizations have inherent moral valuation? Finally, what responsibilities and opportunities does a chaplain possess to influence an organization's values? Many different answers to these questions are possible.

One view holds that an organization's purpose and goals give it its moral value; for example, the military exists to defend a nation and therefore could be understood as promoting the flourishing of its citizens. Certainly, an organization's vision of "the good life" and its goals in relation to this vision are decidedly moral considerations. Yet these purposes and actions may possess different moral value (as arguments between pacifists versus just-war theorists show).[11] The moral status of a chaplain in a military context, for instance, could be questioned because of the implicit tension between commitments to the organization and to the chaplain's faith. Could an organization be immoral in its entirety?[12] Many would suggest so, as in the case of a drug cartel or human trafficking ring, but one has trouble imagining a chaplain in these contexts.

Another view holds that the actions of individuals in an organization specifically give it moral value; for example, those in the military kill enemy combatants who threaten a nation—a potentially morally problematic action. Thus, although organizations themselves possess different moral cultures (some more positive and others more negative), this model emphasizes not the organization itself as imbued with moral weight but rather the individuals within that organization who have particular attitudes and make decisions that establish and nurture a specific moral orientation. These actions may be linked to the overall purpose of the organization (such as soldiers in the military), but here the moral value of individuals' decisions is preeminent when determining moral valuation. Further discussion of the differences between these models is beyond the scope of the current chapter, but it is nonetheless clear that the dynamic interplay of organizational purpose and decisions by individuals has significant moral bearing. The chaplain helps set proper conditions for the moral orientation of an organization.

The values of an organization are important to its identity. I think about this in terms of organizational "culture," which describes the internal world and "personality" of an organization, including its moral orientation, goals, and purpose.[13] An organization's values or "culture" not only describes the organization but also prescribes—sets the expectations for and fosters growth toward—what an organization believes is necessary for its ongoing success and well-being: "That's the way we do things around here," as some like to say, which is another description of organizational culture.[14]

Implicit organizational culture is so powerful that it is difficult to change, even when many factors work against it. An organization's culture protects its values over time by being slow and difficult to change. Organizational culture influences members of an organization to act in ways they would normally not (either for good or for ill) outside of the organizational context. In short, organizational values and culture support organizational "preservation" (or degradation) and even its "resilience" (that is, its ability to bounce back after a challenge).

Organizational Competencies

Very practical outcomes arise out of organizational culture, including its moral aspects. Enron and Abu Ghraib prison are vivid negative examples of how organizations exist in cultures that support immoral practices. Members then act out or exhibit organizational culture. Although individuals may reflect the culture of an organization (and live it out by engaging in well-established practices), organizations can also exhibit the moral codes of the people who lead and influence them. Thus, chaplains can and should actively shape a positive moral culture in their organizations. Yet pressures—both from within and from outside an organization—complicate this effort. "Organizational fallibility" is real, which is to say that all organizations are flawed, just like the individuals who compose them.[15]

FALLIBLE ORGANIZATIONS

Organizations are a necessary, though fallible, human construct. We cannot live without them, so it behooves us to influence them by seeking the flourishing of their members, those they serve, and, in some measure, the betterment of the organization itself. Given the optimism of Aristotle and other thinkers, is it possible that organizations in our own day can improve the world and seek the good of all? If so, how could this come to be, given that so many are driven by values and goals that are limited and often negative in their focus?

Despite my optimism that organizations can act as a vital part of human and societal flourishing, too often organizations serve the status quo of injustice and discrimination. Organizations often do not improve the lives of people and in fact perpetuate evils such as racist and misogynist perspectives and practices. Resonances of this fact can be seen in the case study provided for part 4, where, in the background, as it were, organizational cultures that may perpetuate negative outcomes are apparent. Engagement with the chaplain, however, elicits different possibilities. These realities are due to a dual problem/opportunity regarding the nature of organizations themselves.

Organizations, at their center, are made up of and controlled by human beings. The same fallibilities that are present in people—selfishness, abuse of power—are present in organizational settings and are amplified through organizational systemic structures. A person in leadership who holds racist views, for instance, may enact (unknowingly, even) organizational policies and procedures that affect many individuals beyond the leader's personal sphere of influence, and this influence can enter into the organization's culture. Change, however, is possible not only through the sway of a single leader but also through the solidarity of members. These dynamics are described by theorists as diverse as social theorist Michel Foucault[16] (who describes power dynamics as underlying all human relationships) and Christian theologian Alistair McFadyen[17] (who identifies a connection between structural sin and personal sin). Organizations can misuse their power to create structures that themselves become evil (or sinful) inasmuch as they reinforce and perpetuate systems of abuse, neglect, and exclusion. Even so, organizations may use their implicit power for great benefit—a hope also elicited by the case study, where the chaplain creates and utilizes organizational systems to help a vulnerable population. While there is always potential for evil, systems can also preserve and maintain freedoms, justice, and morality. An organization's resilience and resistance to change can become a site of stable promotion of good—influencing individuals away from negative patterns toward flourishing. This suggests that the innate nature of an organization qua organization may not be good or evil but is contextual.

ORGANIZATIONAL RESILIENCE

Organizations do not only perpetuate evil. Points of failure can become points of growth—opportunities for organizational resilience. Resilience is the process of rebounding from adversity. Resilience presupposes the possibility of failure (another way to describe fallibility). If we (and the organizations of which we are a part) never make mistakes, then resilience would be unnecessary. Although an organization's resistance to change can perpetuate the negative aspects of that organization's culture, it can also be described positively in terms of "organizational resilience." Resilience is illustrated by a tree sapling—the wind blows against it, but it bends with the wind rather than breaks under its power. The tree rebounds from the stressor, perhaps changed by it but not destroyed by it. This capacity to bend is not a rigid and brittle strength but rather a flexible, enduring strength. For an organization to be successful in the long term, it weathers any number of storms, many of which are unanticipated and present novel challenges. To survive this, organizations must be resilient—embodying an almost paradoxical mix of openness to change and commitment to established successful norms and practices. They remain stable, if also changed.

Because organizations necessarily must change over time (as internal members and external partners change), the question is, What type of change will occur? Will the organization adapt in positive ways, or will it further entrench itself in unhelpful and immoral patterns? The chaplain has a significant role in this process, yet it is clear that an organization's fallibility and flexibility are necessary prerequisites for organization resilience.

An organization's change over time is not a fixed (or static) commodity. In one sense, organizations do change over time (think of their flourishing or foundering and the innovation or lack of innovation that goes along with it); in another sense, organizations retain a particular identity—inasmuch as a fast-food chain does not suddenly become a motorcycle manufacturer. These two parts of organizational identity (change and constancy) are related to each other in a mutually interdependent relationship that philosophers call a dialectic.[18] Neither aspect can be divorced from the other, but in terms of organizational identity, constancy of identity often trumps change due to the strength of organizational culture.

A significant characteristic of organizations is their resistance to change, which, in practice, gives organizations much power. An organization's lifespan may go well beyond that of a human being, and by definition it is a conglomerate of individuals, all working together for a purpose larger than themselves. Each organization develops unique practices, traditions, and values, with a culture transcending any one person. An individual organization's culture has its own "center of gravity," or fundamental purpose that enables the organization to achieve its mission—whether that is to heal patients, make money, or protect a nation. Each organization creates its own set of rules, regulations, and policies that enable its members to fulfill the mission. These (collectively, the organizational culture) may be consciously shaped but more often are implicitly "felt," learned, and carried on by those who are members of the organization. Hence, some may talk of "toxic work environments" or of an organizational team so unified it feels like "family." Both of these descriptions name the "felt" culture, embodying the values, goals, and practices of the organization.

FACILITATING ORGANIZATIONAL CHANGE

How does an organization get from "here" to "there"—from being an organization that perpetuates a negative culture to possessing a healthy, even life-giving culture? Further, what role can chaplains play in this endeavor?

Beyond gaining competency in understanding organizational culture, a chaplain changes negative culture through collaborating across organizations. This is where chaplains, as those already implicitly residing in a liminal moral space (both insiders and outsiders at the same time, as described above), can have profound effect. Input from "outside" the organization is often needed to achieve its goals, and this input often must address deeply held values such as culture and ethics.

Getting "Unstuck"

Organizations must change from within and without in response to challenges. Leadership expert Edgar Schein submits that "it is a paradox of evolution or development that the more we learn how to do things and to stabilize what we have learned, the more unwilling or unable we become to adapt, change, and grow into new patterns, even when our changing environment demands such new patterns."[19] It is indeed a paradox to suggest (as I have) that one of an organization's greatest strengths is its ability to remain constant, while also arguing that this same organization must change to remain effective; yet this paradox is at the heart of resilience. To this end, Schein says, "The inevitable dilemma for any group, then, is how to avoid becoming so stable in its approach to its environment that it loses its ability to adapt, innovate, and grow."[20]

How does an organization remain both stable and open to change? Schein suggests that creating an organizational culture centered on a mindset of constant learning is inherently "learning oriented, adaptive, and flexible."[21] Such an organization, paradoxically, has a constant desire to learn and change.

It is the responsibility of organizational leaders, with the help of others in the organization, to foster cultural change. Formal organizational leaders need others within the organization to provide a variety of viewpoints, while also leveraging relationships with external stakeholders to diagnose problems, develop solutions, and to effect organizational change. This is challenging (particularly when one wants to change an organization's culture) but necessary to ensure the continuing health of the organization. Here chaplains play an important role, because they already exist within a liminal space, having commitments and influence both inside and outside the organization as well as roles and responsibilities that cut across traditionally distinct domains. Such influence was evident in the aftermath of the Abu Ghraib scandal, when a military chaplain utilized organizational

Organizational Competencies

influence to advise leaders and individuals, empowering a connection between leaders and their shared values and commitments as professionals and human beings to address potential abuses of humans. In concert with one another, the influence of the chaplain and effective leadership ensured that the dignity and respect of all individuals were affirmed.

Creating Change

Responsibility for organizational success, including improving an organization's culture, lies primarily with formal organizational leadership. This is as true of the "bottom line" of the organization (which, for many organizations, is the financial bottom line) as it is with the "ethical culture" of an organization. Schein says that "senior leadership represents an important component of an organization's ethical culture, as integrity (or the lack of it) flows from the top down and employees take their cues from the messages sent by those in formal leadership roles."[22]

Because of these responsibilities, leaders (both formal and not) in organizations must ask questions like, "What kind of organization do we want to be?" To a certain extent, this is a question regarding the purpose and viability of an organization—and of course most leaders want to create a lasting organization that is "successful" according to some rubric. But mere existence and viability is a rather low bar to achieve. The much more difficult questions to answer are, "What does it mean to be successful?" and "How will we define success?"

Financial considerations are one measure, but this can be shortsighted. Any organization that achieves "success" off of the exploitation of others would not, in the end, be a "success," when understood ethically. Financial gains do not outweigh injustice against the most vulnerable in any organization. The chaplain can be a leader, even if not designated as a formal one, by aiding organizational leadership to properly answer fundamental questions about success and by being part of consultation involving multiple parties within the organization.[23]

Yet in most organizations there is little understanding of these important considerations, especially among those involved in senior, formal leadership.[24] In most cases, this is not the fault of the leaders themselves: business and leadership education usually has very little in the way of curriculum on ethics. Given the importance of ethical and just decision-making for the well-being and success of an organization, however, more attention should be paid to these kinds of considerations. But leaders must also rely on their staff, including chaplains, to provide expert advice on ethical and moral matters. This is why the chaplain competency of leader advisement is crucial.

A growing number of organizations find it useful to include chaplains in numerous aspects of their operations. Chaplains have a unique role to play in creating organizational change for good. Organizations such as hospitals, prisons, the military, and even corporate entities employ chaplains as a vital part of organizational operations. For some organizations, the incorporation of chaplains is a new development (for example, in corporate settings), while for others, chaplains have long been an essential part of organizational operations and identity (such as the U.S. Army, which has had a Chaplain Corps since 1775).

Chaplains do the important work of providing frontline R/S care to individuals from all walks of life in diverse and often difficult settings. However, I argue that the role of the chaplain can and should extend beyond this. For chaplaincy to effect organizational change, deeper integration into organizational structures is needed. The issues that our society faces today require broader, deeper efforts than one-on-one interaction, no matter how effective such efforts have been.

Chaplains play a role at an organizational level. They are ideally situated to facilitate the kind of moral and ethical change that organizations need. But adjustments must be made to how chaplains are trained to take full advantage of this opportunity. For instance, if chaplains were to exert influence at an organizational level, how might training for this role differ from training for primary care intervention? How can chaplains speak to issues of morality and directly affect organizational outcomes? How can chaplains collaborate with other partners to improve the culture of an organization? These are questions that have not often been considered, perhaps due to particular understandings of chaplaincy, or perhaps due to some of the inherent difficulties surrounding the moral nature of organizations. Nevertheless, it is important that chaplains begin to see this organizational work as part of their responsibility. The part 4 case study illustrates the interplay between the chaplain's role in working with individuals and her role in working within the organization. Beyond providing personal solace to the woman in need, the chaplain leverages organizational resources through collaborating with internal and external organizational leaders to change policies and programs, ultimately creating cultural change to support vulnerable populations. In this way, through the chaplain's influence, the organization itself becomes a positive witness to the possibility of change as well as a means of achieving that change.

Organizational Competencies

Chaplains influence organizations and individuals within those organizations (both staff and careseekers) in a number of ways. Chaplaincy has largely focused on one-on-one spiritual care and has found great success in these efforts. While there are a host of other possible avenues for chaplains to benefit organizations, I highlight three related to the chaplain competencies identified above:

1. organizational assessment and leadership
2. collaboration within and outside organizations
3. advising formal organizational leadership

These efforts may seem foreign to some chaplains and contexts, but they are powerful tools, especially within settings that already have well-defined roles for chaplains that give them "organizational capital."[25]

Chaplain Leadership

Including chaplains in an organization does not guarantee that they will benefit the organization. There are a variety of reasons for this, but a primary one is resistance to the work of a chaplain. Others may include inadequate training for the chaplain, mismanagement (or lack of management) of chaplains, and chaplain burnout. To facilitate effectiveness, chaplains need to be trained to understand their role from both interpersonal and organizational perspectives. Chaplaincy work is distinct from R/S leadership in a congregational setting and so requires specialized training, both within graduate theological contexts and in the course of "on the job" training, prior to and throughout service as a chaplain.

Because of its inherent hierarchical structure, military chaplaincy models organizational structure and mentoring for chaplains. Yet, even in the military context, until recently (in the U.S. Army, at least) there have been few concerted efforts to define clear professional competencies for chaplains' work, nor have professional development efforts been informed by definite goals or benchmarks. This leads to haphazard or uneven applications of mentoring, leadership, and development. If this is true even in an organization like the military that has implicit management structures and a clear federal mandate to include chaplains at all levels of organizational hierarchy, how much more difficult might this be in less-defined organizational settings? Too little emphasis has been placed on leading, managing, and developing chaplains to be able to do their job in an increasingly complex and difficult (though promising) environment.

These contentions raise issues: How does one develop a chaplain professionally? What are the standards of care to which a chaplain should be held? Without answering these fundamental questions, training for the complex roles of chaplaincy is often incohesive, nonstrategic, and reactive to the challenge of the moment. But questions about how to train chaplains are best answered by an organization or community of chaplains. Because chaplains exist to serve an organization, organizations that hire chaplains and organizations that send them (for example, ACPE training sites, theological schools) must cooperatively develop unified standards. Students should be aware of the variety of chaplaincy contexts, understand strengths and weaknesses of each context, and seek opportunities for diverse training and experiences in preparation for work in these settings.

Collaboration within and outside Organizations

Chaplains operate in unique ideological and practical contexts where they simultaneously have responsibilities to, relationships with, and interest in multiple entities. As employees (or official volunteers) of an organization, chaplains represent the organization both to those for whom they care and to those who have employed them. But chaplains represent their particular religious/faith tradition as well, and they are representatives of "faith," "spirituality," "religion," "morality," or even "God" more broadly. In a military context, a soldier may seek out a chaplain for spiritual counsel without any knowledge of the chaplain or her or his specific tradition but simply out of a deep-felt need for spiritual assistance. These are opportunities to meet significant needs for individuals who do not normally seek out a religious leader. But such situations can lead to tensions. The actions of chaplains may be perceived in a variety of ways, both positive and negative, based on beliefs and past experiences.

Yet differing commitments and perceptions of chaplains and their work can benefit those to whom chaplains minister. For example, in the part 4 case study, the chaplain was immediately credible to the patient even though there was no previous relationship. Because the chaplain had a formal and religious role in the organization, she could gain the trust of the patient quickly and intervene in positive ways in a difficult situation.[26] The chaplain was not solely responsible to heal the patient, but her position allowed her to effect quality patient care, bringing organizational resources to address personal, individual concerns. Because of the relationship the chaplain had already developed with healthcare staff, as well as with outside organizations such as sexual assault response programs, she was able to marshal the organization's strengths while offering personal spiritual care.

Providing care through, to, and with organizations and individuals requires that the chaplain be skilled in the collaborative work of relationship building, which includes, at a minimum, understanding the culture, values, and expectations of one's own organization as well as those of potential partners. It also involves a willingness to understand other points of view and the ability, at times, to compromise to accomplish the greater good. This also means, though, that some individuals or organizations are unwilling (or perhaps unable) to cooperate and collaborate with chaplains. Working across differences, both interpersonally and inter-organizationally, and building coalitions are critical elements of a chaplain's work, but sometimes it is just as important to know what not to do and what boundaries should not be crossed. In the military, advisement of leaders is a fundamental competency for chaplains.[27]

Advising Organizational Leadership

The immediate spiritual care of individuals is chaplaincy's legacy and is typical of most chaplaincy approaches. However, this focus can obscure the other roles that spiritual leaders play in organizational life, such as training staff (including chaplains) or providing guidance to leaders. Chaplains should consult on matters of organizational policy that have moral, ethical, or spiritual ramifications. Take, for instance, the considerations involved in decisions to lay off employees—who, when, why, and to what effect? Could implicit moral and ethical judgments be at play in these decisions, reinforcing structural evils?

This level of involvement fulfills a "prophetic" role wherein a chaplain "speaks truth to power"—a task undertaken to ensure that those with great power and responsibility are held accountable to moral and ethical standards. This is possible because chaplains are employed by an organization and likely already have "organizational capital" in the form of relationships with senior leaders and an understanding of organizational culture. Chaplains become a part of organizations by being formed by organizational culture itself (for example, its language and rituals). This enables the chaplain both to better understand the situation and to more effectively engage multiple constituencies. Yet the chaplain's ties to an organization may constrain a "prophetic" role, and the tension between cultures and commitments is evident here. This is precisely why the liminal space that chaplains occupy (between two realms) matters—it is a place of creative synthesis. Chaplains' R/S grounding in and commitment to a religious or spiritual community outside the organization means that they do not hold ultimate allegiance to the organization and that they draw on their traditions to illuminate situations within the organization. The chaplain can speak truth to leaders as both an "insider" and an "outsider" by virtue of insight into specific situations and cultural dynamics within the organization as well as by drawing on deeply formed relationships. Both sides of this dialectic relationship in the work of the chaplain are necessary to create an opportunity for a fusion of spiritual insight and organizational need.

CASE STUDY

The benefits of chaplains' engagement in systems and organizations become clearer when further considered in relation to the case study provided in part 4. I explore the case study from my military context because of some special considerations this highlights.

First, it would be easy to skip over one of the most important factors in this case study—the presence of a chaplain. We may take for granted that the chaplain is there, on location in a large organization—here, a military base. But this is not a given. Without the chaplain having a place in the organization, including a physical office with access to individuals in the organization, the entire situation described in the case study would not be possible and the woman could not receive the help that she did. Note also that the chaplain is present over a long period. The stability of the organization and of the chaplain's place in that organization means that the woman in the case study had opportunity to reengage the chaplain at multiple points along her journey, even after being out of touch for long periods.

Chaplains serve as an "entry point" for individuals who need support but may not know where else to go. Because of the established nature of chaplaincy within Western culture, especially in the military, most people know that they can go to a chaplain to receive help. On this same day, the chaplain in the case study may have also counseled a soldier dealing with separation anxiety, provided religious instruction, counseled a family with financial issues, and performed religious ministrations. In each situation, the chaplain provides care and comfort as well as connects individuals with other organizations, including specialists who may be able to help in other ways. Chaplains are often seen as safe people to disclose one's troubles to, who will provide immediate care, and who can serve as referral sources.

In this case study, the chaplain hopes to connect the woman with experienced professionals who can support her as she deals with intimate partner violence (IPV). The military has created particular organizations to address this situation, such as the U.S. Army's Sexual Harassment/Assault Response and Prevention program[28] or its Family Advocacy Program.[29] A military chaplain in this situation would be able to refer the woman to representatives of these programs as well as to a Unit Victim Advocate or Sexual Assault Response Coordinator. The military has recognized the need to create institutional support structures to address problems like IPV and to help those who are affected by it. Chaplains play a vital role in this effort and have unique legal privileges, such as protected confidentiality in privileged communication, that enable appropriate, professional interventions.

The chaplain in the case study decides to do more than a onetime intervention and leverages organizational capital and resources to create system-wide programs designed to aid other individuals affected by IPV. Because such programs are tied to an organizational structure, they often grow beyond the work of a single chaplain and become a part of shaping organizational culture, rituals, and rhythms. Sometimes the organization even changes its structure, such as by hiring additional personnel to perpetuate the changes started by the chaplain. The chaplain's legacy is built into the structure of the organization itself. In the case study, the chaplain was familiar enough with organizations to realize that the efficacy of her work could be either hindered or helped by implicit organizational systems. Rather than working against these systems, she chose to utilize them for the benefit of the vulnerable in her organization by helping shape organizational culture and systems to protect, rather than exploit, these individuals.

As with much change, however, the chaplain often faces setbacks and opposition. Not everyone understands the work of a chaplain or the reasons an organization employs one, so a staff education program can be beneficial since it raises awareness of the role of chaplaincy and allows helpful dialogue to take place. It sets expectations that chaplains not only will be involved in providing spiritual care to people but also will engage significant organizational issues from their vital perspective.

The chaplain in this case study has begun to utilize some of the broader chaplain competencies identified in this chapter: She assesses organizational culture. She collaborates with a number of other organizations (both internal and external to her own) on behalf of her careseekers. She advises

leaders in the broader institution and changes many of the existing perspectives and practices. The chaplain brought about positive organizational
change. However, there are other opportunities to explore as well. For instance, could her labors be further integrated and aligned with the broader
efforts and goals of her organization as a whole?

CONCLUSION: CHAPLAINS AS
CATALYSTS FOR RESILIENCE

Individual Resilience

Much research suggests the importance of religion/spirituality in the promotion of individual and communal resilience.[30] The chaplain, both as a
representative of an R/S tradition and as an employee of an organization, interacts with individuals whom many R/S leaders in congregational contexts
would not. The chaplain has unrivaled opportunity to care for individuals
during times of distress and thereby to become a catalyst for resilience by
supporting positive R/S coping and being a source of connection to community and resources.

Organizational Resilience

To be successful, especially in the long term, organizations need to be concerned about the well-being of their employees and of their customers or
clients. If trends continue, chaplains will increasingly participate in this
effort. In fact, the influence of chaplains is growing even in a culture where
the influence of congregation-based R/S leadership is waning.

The positive impact of chaplains on organizations happens when chaplains and organizations are intentional about shaping the direction of this
relationship in the future. More needs to be done to train and manage
chaplains effectively, and chaplains need to be better integrated into organizational planning as advisors as well as included in collaboration with
outside organizations.

Discernment is required in these efforts since any organization has inherent flaws; a chaplain should not unquestionably support or be used
to support unethical or immoral organizational policies or goals. Yet the
flaws of organizations are also exactly why chaplains are needed within
them—beyond simply providing primary care R/S support, chaplains can
and should seek to change systemic organizational issues that have broad

negative effects on many. Indeed, if the chaplain does not play this role, who will? No one else within an organization has the cultural knowledge and capital as well as the grounding within an external moral tradition to effectively facilitate organizational change. To do so, chaplains must assess their organization's culture, leverage relationships across domains, and advise the organization's leadership. Chaplains have the ability not only to create change but also to facilitate continuing development. Chaplains can harness the existing strength and resilience of organizations but also prophetically sharpen, clarify, and redirect their potential.

Chaplains exist in an in-between place, at a nexus between realms— the religious/spiritual and the secular/organizational. This means that the chaplain has commitments and responsibilities to both domains that, at times, can lead to tension. However, I argue that this is also a position of possibility where the fusion of worlds creates new opportunities. While there is certainly still room for new developments in personal chaplaincy care, I argue that one of the most significant opportunities for improvements in the future of chaplaincy is in arming chaplains with organizational competencies such as cultural assessment, collaboration, and advisement. Taking advantage of these opportunities strengthens the role of chaplains in organizations and ultimately creates more just, resilient, and accountable organizations.

REFLECTION QUESTIONS

1. Why should chaplains be concerned with organizational change as well as one-on-one spiritual care?
2. How can an organization change for the better?
3. Why are organizations often so resistant to change?
4. What role(s) could you play in helping an organization change?
5. How could chaplains be better trained to prepare for their role in organizations? Could a chaplain's organizational usefulness be at odds with the chaplain's R/S identity?
6. What are the key competencies that chaplains need in order to be effective in organizations? How and where are they developed in training?

RECOMMENDED READINGS

Kelly, Ewan, and John Swinton, eds. *Chaplaincy and the Soul of Health and Social Care: Fostering Spiritual Wellbeing in Emerging Paradigms of Care.* Philadelphia: Jessica Kingsley, 2020.

Kotter, John P., and James L. Heskett. *Corporate Culture and Performance.* New York: Free Press, 1992.

Lencioni, Patrick. *The Advantage: Why Organizational Health Trumps Everything Else in Business.* San Francisco: Jossey-Bass, 2012.

Schein, Edgar H. *Organizational Culture and Leadership.* 5th ed. Hoboken: Wiley, 2017.

Schneider, Benjamin, and Karen M. Barbera, eds. *The Oxford Handbook of Organizational Climate and Culture.* Oxford: Oxford University Press, 2014.

CHAPTER TEN

Through a Multi-frame Lens: Surviving, Thriving, and Leading Organizations

SU YON PAK

ABSTRACT *Organizations are complex. We live much of our personal and professional lives in relation to organizations. It is hard to know what is really going on, harder to know how to make sense of what is going on, and hardest to know how to work for cultural change in organizations most effectively. Understanding how "frames" operate in organizations, spiritual care providers can cultivate good diagnostic habits to develop a more comprehensive and complex view of how organizations function. This competency positions chaplains to focus their energies on ways most likely to impact organizations in the direction of human flourishing. The four-frames approach (structural, human resource, political, and symbolic) to organizations developed by Lee Bolman and Terrence Deal is one such analytical tool. This chapter uses this tool, along with interrogations of the "white racial frame," to assess the white supremacist culture characteristics operating in organizations and to position chaplains to be effective agents of change toward an even fuller vision of just organizational life.*

INTRODUCTION

We live much of our lives in relation to organizations. Whether the context is where we work, study, purchase goods, or receive healthcare, organizations touch our lives in both conspicuous and inconspicuous ways. While organizations are made up of people, they are also composed of structures, cultures, practices/rituals, and interpersonal and intra-organizational dynamics. We often note that something is "baked into the DNA of an organization" as if the organization is a living and breathing organism. This chapter, and indeed this part, contends that organizations *are* living, breathing organisms and offers ways to understand and interact with them in life-giving ways.

As an Asian American queer cisgender woman working in predominantly white institutional contexts, analyzing organizations through multiple frames and counter-frames that interrogate the white supremacy culture helps me navigate the confounding terrains of these contexts. It is my hope that these tools are resources for chaplains surviving, thriving, and leading organizations. In short, chaplains need competencies in seeing the frames in operation, analyzing the frames in order to understand what is happening, and acting in strategic and effective ways.

To begin, it is important to understand that organizations are complex. There are many factors and variables (for example, people's behaviors, departments with different functions and perspectives, technologies, and goals) that interact in organizations that themselves are embedded in changing and erratic environments. Second, organizations are unpredictable. It is difficult to predict outcomes; in fact, sometimes past solutions create problems for the future. Third, organizations can be deceptive, at times disguising and covering up mistakes and failures. And because of these three characteristics, organizations are ambiguous. It is hard to know what is really going on and harder to know how to make sense of what is going on.[1]

Organizational life can include a variety of functions. For example, organizations structure how work gets accomplished; balance human potential with organizational needs; decide how finite resources will be allocated; discern where and how power will be located in its structure; have patterns of dealing with inevitable conflicts that arise; and draw on the symbols and stories of their history and habits in order to communicate their values and vision. As chaplains who work in and with organizations, whether in a leadership position or in a midlevel position, it is essential to understand

Organizational Competencies

how organizations function in all their complexity in order not only to be effective but perhaps more importantly to survive and thrive.[2]

REFRAMING ORGANIZATIONS AS
AN ANALYTIC APPROACH

While there are many different approaches to and theories of organizations—social psychology, anthropology, sociology, and management science, for example—Lee Bolman and Terrence Deal integrate these various approaches into four distinct frames: structural, human resource, political, and symbolic.[3] The goal of this chapter is to help chaplains, both seasoned and aspiring, "read" organizations through these four possible frames and let those frames help them strategize their engagement with—and possible interventions in—organizational life. Throughout the chapter, I use the terms "leader" and "chaplain" interchangeably, recognizing that chaplains lead organizations through their influence whether or not they have a formal structural leadership role.

Reframing an event or an issue—that is, seeing it from multiple frames—exposes the biases and assumptions built into each of the frames, which can help chaplains better understand an issue without oversimplifying. The language of the frames—structural, human resource, political, and symbolic—is a heuristic tool that can be empowering, especially in the midst of organizational confusion or anxiety. As a diagnostic tool, these four frames expand options by generating four different analyses with corresponding implications and responses.[4]

Additionally, as we recognize that all organizations are embedded in the systemic structures and cultures of inequalities in our Western society, or the "white racial frame,"[5] it is important to filter these four frames through anti-oppressive and antiracist lenses as well, thus effectively adding a fifth frame. The white racial frame is a centuries-old racial worldview constructed by white Americans that has "long legitimated, rationalized, motivated, and shaped racial oppression."[6] And because culture (including organizational culture) is ubiquitous, like the air we breathe, it is not easy to see these white supremacist characteristics in operation.[7] Culture is made up of the assumed organizational norms of what "competency" looks like, or what a "good" organization should strive for, or how the work is designed, prioritized, resourced, assigned, and implemented. By naming these characteristics and examining organizational practices alongside the four-frames analysis, we can better understand the complexity of organizations that are also funded by systemic inequalities. We can, then, consider some "antidotes" that mitigate these assumed norms by offering a "counter-frame," addressing the ways centuries of white supremacy have influenced the ways we understand organizational challenges. We will delve more deeply into this later in the chapter, but first, we will explore the four-frames approach.

WHAT IS A "FRAME"?

Our ideas, assumptions, and biases deeply inform how we see and understand the world. Familial and kinship networks, formal and informal education, societal pressures, history, and our own experiences shape our ideas, assumptions, and biases. It is what we learn in books as well as what we learn through the experiences, relationships, and contexts of our own lives that "frame" our worldview. Frames are "mental maps" that give us the lay of the land and help us to navigate the terrain; frames are what inform our perspectives on what we see, hear, read, and experience. Frames can also help organize vast and disparate bits of information into a coherent pattern that enables a "rapid recognition"[8] that is nonconscious and results in judgments that integrate thinking and feeling.[9]

Frames, like looking through a window, allow us to see some things but block other things outside the window from view. And those things that we do not see may be important in providing us with a fuller and more complex picture of what is going on. Frames drive the questions we ask and answers we seek. Breaking, shifting, or adding to the frame (or "reframing") can expose things that were hidden from view and invites different questions. Bolman and Deal demonstrate the power of the right question to break the frame through this example: "'What is the sum of 5 plus 5?' The only right answer is '10.' Ask a different way, 'What two numbers add up to ten?' Now the number of solutions is infinite (once you include fractions and negative numbers)."[10] Chaplains and spiritual care providers in all kinds of organizational contexts recognize easily the power of a good question that can break open a patient's/careseeker's resistance and create opportunities for sacred conversations. While chaplains are typically trained to do this with individual persons, the skill of reframing needs to be developed in relation to organizations as well. Understanding the benefits and limitations of the frames—structural, human resource, political, and symbolic—and learning how to use them better equips our efforts to assess what is at stake and how

Organizational Competencies

we might respond. Being a multi-frame professional means stepping back to imagine how different maps may draw the terrain differently and present a way to reach the destination differently. It is a competency that requires both an analytic and creative mind and one that chaplains will find very useful.

THE STRUCTURAL FRAME

The structural frame focuses on the architecture of work, how an organization structures work. Organizations design units and subunits, rules and roles, goals and policies. They address two essential issues: how to differentiate and assign work and how to coordinate and integrate these allocated responsibilities.[11] The structural frame seeks to align structure with goals and environment, and as such these assumptions undergird the frame: The purpose of organizations is to achieve their goals; specialization and division of labor are efficient processes to achieve these goals; therefore, all working units need coordination. Rational processes achieve the goals more efficiently than personal agendas or outside pressures; the organizational structure must align with the dynamics of the current context; and, when an organization fails to meet goals, restructuring is employed to correct the problem. Simply put, the essential task of the structural frame is structuring how an organization divides and coordinates the work to effectively achieve its goals.

Organizational Structures

There is no ideal structure that will work for every organization. Each organization needs to respond to a series of its own internal and external parameters, such as the organization's size, age, core process, outcome goals, environment/context, strategies, information technology processes, and workforce demographics.[12] The organization will need to consider these parameters to create an optimal structure. No structure is perfect or even optimal for very long, since organizations are constantly changing.

There will always be factors that will require structural change. When structures no longer align with the goals and environment of the organization, problems arise. Factors like environmental/context shifts, technological changes, organizational growth, and leadership changes may bring about structural misalignment that can be remedied with restructuring. Those who utilize a structural frame will see this as an opportunity and imperative to restructure toward a new optimal structure.

A leader/chaplain who operates out of the structural frame sees the essential tasks as clarifying goals, ensuring that structure aligns with environment, and developing defined roles and responsibilities appropriate to the work that needs to be done. For structural leaders, problems with staff are typically understood to stem from structural flaws, not personal flaws. Thus, as they design and implement processes that fit the situation,[13] leaders focused on structural issues depend on task allocation, facts, and logic rather than on engaging the different personalities and emotions among the members.

While a structural lens offers a distinctive perspective that has real benefits, there are also risks of overusing this lens. The structural frame tends to over-rely on the rational sphere of tasks, procedures, policies, and organization charts. It neglects the human, political, and cultural elements of an organization. It overestimates authority as a source of power and underestimates other sources of power and can often miss the "human" or people side of challenges. Here, the human resource frame can be a good corrective.[14]

THE HUMAN RESOURCE FRAME

The human resource frame is about people, "the human side of organizations."[15] In this approach, people's skills, attitudes, energy, and commitment are indispensable resources for an organization.[16] Thus, understanding people's strengths and shortcomings, their reasoning capacities and emotions, including their desires and fears, is a key feature of the human resource frame. In addition, people's needs and the organization's needs must align for an organization and the people within it to flourish. This frame concerns how people "fit" with the organization and how they and the organization mutually benefit when the fit is good. The following assumptions undergird the human resource frame: The purpose of an organization is "to serve human needs";[17] the relationship between organization and people is synergistic, each needing the other to achieve goals; therefore, the fit between the organization and the individual is paramount for an optimal working relationship. Good fit benefits both; poor fit harms both parties. As such, in this frame, an organization's main quest is to find the people with the "right" skills and attitudes and then to retain and develop them. For individuals, the main quest is to see how well the organization will fit for them. This question of "fit" has three components: an organization's response to individuals' desires for meaningful work; opportunities for individuals to communicate their sense of self and develop and demonstrate their skills; and fulfillment of individual careers and financial and lifestyle goals.[18]

Organizations that operate out of a human resource frame employ strategies that involve significant engagement of managers with employees. These strategies begin with developing a clear management philosophy that is then implemented to management practices. These include hiring the right people who bring appropriate skills and cultural fit, working to keep employees once hired, investing in employee development and motivating them to stay, and empowering employees with information and support.[19] Finally, promoting diversity is another important strategy for human resource management. Promoting diversity does not end with hiring a diverse workforce. Rather, it is built into day-to-day management and institutional practices of inclusion. It is an ongoing commitment that strives to examine the dominant culture of the organization and identify harmful assumptions and standards, to diversify the board, and to purchase from minority vendors, for example.[20] Creating a genuinely diverse organization means full inclusion of underrepresented persons and groups at all levels of the organization. This practice can disrupt the normalized assumptions of the appropriate "fit" between employees and an organization.

Human Resource Leaders/Chaplains

A chaplain/leader who operates out of the human resource frame believes that people are at the heart of the organization, and therefore it needs to respond to people's needs and goals. In turn, people will be committed to the organization. A human resource leader's key tasks are to support people by showing concern and listening to their aspirations and to empower people through participation and openness by providing resources and autonomy to do their jobs.[21]

There are risks associated with the human resource lens. It can adhere to an overly romanticized view of human nature that assumes that everyone desires growth, commitment, and collaboration with and within an organization. This optimism can be at best naive and at worst detrimental in high-risk situations of conflict and scarcity.[22] The political frame can be a good alternative that will take into account the power at play and the ways that power is used toward an organization's goals.

THE POLITICAL FRAME

The political frame centers power as an essential component in any organization.[23] Organizations make decisions and allocate finite resources in a context of competing and divergent interests. Power dynamics play a central role, and therefore politics is at the heart of all decision-making. The political frame assumes the following: "Organizations are coalitions of different individuals and interest groups";[24] and "coalition members have enduring differences in values, beliefs, information, interests, and perceptions of reality."[25] The most important task is the allocation of limited resources; therefore, conflict is inevitable and central in organizational dynamics. The power relationship undergirds bargaining and negotiation, out of which goals and decisions emerge.[26] Alliances and interest groups form to consolidate power in order to accomplish their aims. Allocating scarce resources becomes the key function of the political frame.

As such, it is essential to understand where power is located in an organization. While the structural frame might understand power in terms of authority, and the human resource frame might de-emphasize power and emphasize empowerment that enhances mutuality and collaboration, in the political frame, authority is but one locus among many loci of power. Consider the following forms of power that operate in an organization: positional power or authority; control of rewards; collective power (for example, the ability to strike or to sit-in); the power of information and expertise; the power of one's or a group's reputation; alliances and networks; the power to access and control agendas; the ability to control the meaning and symbols; and one's personal power.[27] I would add to this list the power of ideologies and structures such as racism, sexism, classism, ableism, and heterosexism that infuse the organization, functioning to keep some people in dominant positions while marginalizing others.

In the political frame, conflict is inevitable, even necessary. The political frame assumes that the battle over power in all its forms is part of organizational collective life. Consequently, the political frame does not seek to eliminate conflict. Rather, it emphasizes strategy and tactics to manage conflict. Conflict can create change, creativity, and innovation by encouraging new ideas and approaches to problems, and poorly managed conflict can lead to destructive power struggles. In the political frame, goals, structure, and policies emerge from ongoing processes of bargaining and negotiating among the coalitions.[28]

Organizational Competencies

Chaplains who operate out of the political frame recognize the political nature of organizations and skillfully handle conflict. Identifying major constituencies, developing connections throughout the organization, building a power base, and managing conflict all require that a chaplain use power carefully. No group will get everything it wants, but a chaplain/leader can create opportunities for negotiation and compromise to happen. Indeed, while conflict is inevitable, too much internal conflict can take the organization off course, making it ineffective. A chaplain's role is to find common interest and articulate it in order to bring cohesion to disparate groups.[29]

As with other frames, the political frame has its risks if misused. Preoccupation with political realities can heighten conflict and mistrust, creating a cynical view of the organization. Political strategies can be seen as "amoral, scheming, and oblivious to the common good"[30] and can miss opportunities for the rational discourse and collaboration found in the previous two frames. The political frame, due to the central use of power as its core process, requires an ethical framework to ground all action. Hence, ethical considerations should be the basis of any power analysis and actions. Some key ethical questions might include these: Who benefits from this decision, and who has the most to lose? Who is not at the table in discussions and in decision-making? Such analysis can concretize and operationalize moral values that can often appear intangible and elusive. For chaplains, grounded in their faith and ethical traditions, such considerations are primary and fundamental to their vocation. All chaplains need to develop the competence and capacity to articulate their ethical commitments clearly in the context of organizations.

THE SYMBOLIC FRAME

Stories and symbols help humans make meaning and create a cohesive sense of the world they live in.[31] The symbolic frame centers meaning-making and culture-making practices for organizations. Life is not linear, certain, or rational. For this reason, the symbolic frame explores the realms of the "serendipitous," "allegorical," and "mystical."[32] Since chaplains are trained and work in attending to the symbolic sphere, they are often comfortable with this frame. While Bolman and Deal approach the symbolic frame from the perspective of organizational theory, it is important to note that chaplains as trained religious professionals have much to bring to this frame. The symbolic frame operates with these assumptions: What matters is not what happens but "how it is interpreted" or "believed to mean"; the connection between activity and meaning can be fluid and therefore can have multiple interpretations; people create symbols to "resolve confusion, find direction, and anchor their hope and faith";[33] what processes signify are more important than their outcomes, and thus stories, rituals, and ceremonies are used to help people find purpose; and culture, tradition, and established patterns form the basic organizational glue that unites and inspires people.[34]

Culture is communicated through the use of symbols. Symbols may take different forms, however, and it is important to recognize how they are embodied in an organization's story about itself. Such symbols might include myths, values, and vision;[35] exemplary people to emulate;[36] stories that communicate the organization's culture;[37] and ritual and ceremonies.[38] Finally, metaphor, humor, and play open up the imagination to the "as if" or "what if" quality of symbols.[39] As such, these practices help create flexibility, creativity, and innovation.

Symbolic Leaders/Chaplains

A main task of a chaplain operating in the symbolic frame is to provide inspiration. By giving members of an organization a way to create meaning, a sense of belonging, and a clear and compelling vision, a symbolic leader uses the symbolic forms discussed above to communicate passion and to build cohesive culture. Drawing on the best of the organization's tradition and values, they articulate a vision that communicates the unique qualities and mission of the organization.[40]

While symbols are powerful and effective tools that can benefit an organization, they can at times be elusive and can be employed to camouflage or manipulate situations. Symbols are as effective as the artistry of the leader who employs them. Unskilled use of symbols can be ineffective, empty, or even dangerous, leading to confusion and misrepresentation. At the hands of an authentic and effective leader, however, symbols can bring inspiration and cohesion to an organization.

Organizational Competencies

FOUR FRAMES IN ACTION: A CASE STUDY

Each of the frames—structural, human resource, political, and symbolic—has its unique assumptions, goals, and processes. Each frame has benefits as well as risks. To see a situation through multiple frames—namely, to reframe one's perspective rather than relying on just one frame—is to understand the situation more fully, in all its complexity. A particular frame can mitigate the risks of another frame. For example, the question of "fit" central to the human resource frame can be interrogated by examining the power dynamics (the political frame) present in assumptions of "fit" in that organization. The four-frames map not only can help us to navigate this ambiguous terrain but also can offer correctives for the risks of each of the frames.

Using a portion of the case study found in the introduction to this part, this section will examine how the four frames operate in a large urban hospital. The case has been coded with brief explanations of the frames present in the text. For the purpose of coding the case study below, note the abbreviations: STR for structural, HR for human resource, POL for political, and SYM for symbolic. I encourage readers to consider the case it in its entirety, carefully, identifying their perspective on the frames that are operating. Seeing all of the frames operating at once in any situation can help chaplains figure out where and how to leverage their own positional role and power to effect positive change, both for their careseekers and for the organization they serve.

A CASE STUDY IN INTERSECTING FRAMES

The setting is a large hospital in an ethnically diverse city in which a traditional religious designation is the largest religious identity and "none" is the second largest. [POL: differing constituencies, coalitions to serve.]

The director of spiritual care (DSC) speaks with her boss to get herself named to the interdisciplinary Intimate Partner Violence Task Force. [POL: recognize the task force as a useful coalition; STR: distribute work through task force; SYM: chaplain lends certain symbolic legitimacy.] The task force begins advocating with the organization's administration for funding for a specialized IPV program. [POL: distribute scarce resources, build partnerships.]

The DSC reaches out to the new program staff to explain her vision of the unique contribution that chaplains can make to the interdisciplinary support of survivors and to education of staff. [SYM: offer vision for unique contribution.] She receives mixed responses. Several staff members make it clear that they would never refer their clients to a chaplain because of the religious trauma many survivors have already endured (or because the organization is not explicitly religious). [SYM: chaplain/clergy as representative of oppressive religion, organizational culture of the way "things are done"; STR: clarify the role of chaplain in a secular organization; POL: resistant to giving up power to make changes.] One staff person is cautiously open to the DSC. [POL: opportunity for coalition building.] As the program staff begin planning an organization-wide frontline staff education program [HR: develop staff; STR: coordinate work; POL: build coalitions], the DSC offers to research and provide for the curriculum survivor-supportive resources from the major religious traditions represented in the organization and wider community. [HR: respond to need of the group; SYM and POL: religious resources as power to shape meaning and inclusion of major religious traditions to build coalition.]

* *

The DSC decides to use her unique role in the institution to coordinate and sponsor an organization-wide memorial service each year in honor of those persons from their state who died as a result of IPV in the previous twelve months. [POL, STR, and SYM: use structural, symbolic political power as chaplain; STR: coordinate various departments; SYM: provide ritual to name, remember, and grieve.] Her planning includes volunteers from many areas of the community who play a role in serving IPV survivors: administration, the IPV program, social work, police and security, spiritual care, community relations, communications, and the emergency department. [STR: coordinate various departments; POL: build coalitions of interest; SYM: coalitions as symbols of involvement with IPV prevention.] The local interfaith partnership against domestic violence participates in the service, as do some local clergy. [SYM: change perception and culture through clergy participation; POL: build alliances and partnerships.] Sometimes persons served by the organization's IPV program take part as well. [HR: empower people.] The service includes components that are interfaith as well as secular, in languages representative of the community. [HR: meet needs of people; SYM: include religious and secular traditions and languages.] It is noteworthy for the ringing of a large gong at the reading of each name from a list that is always too long. [SYM: ritual.] The spiritual care budget provides for live musicians, for kosher and halal box lunches—so that staff who attend the service during their lunch hour do not have to forgo their meal—and for the gong. [HR: meet people's needs; POL: allocate resources; SYM: create culture through meals.]

REFRAMING: A DISCUSSION

Having identified the frames that are operational in this case study, we now turn to some themes, patterns, and questions that the four-frames analysis highlights. The agility to move between frames and the acumen to employ specific frames for a particular time and context are essential skills for a leader.

This case study takes place in a hospital setting. In my experience, hospitals, in general, are highly structured institutions. They have a clear division of labor with a formal structure that coordinates the work. Authority is defined in structural roles. Policies and procedures guide the practices of hospitals. Chaplains working in a military, business, or prison context experience similarly highly structured institutions.

Hospitals are also high political-frame institutions. The limited resources and competing needs and interests vie for power to get the agenda set and met. Not only do various units serve, as in the structural frame, to divide labor, but they also function as coalitions of differing interests in the political frame. Policies and procedures of organizations may be a result of coalitions negotiating and bargaining their interests rather than a structural strategy of coordination and control.

Chaplains, on the other hand, tend to be most comfortable in the human resource and symbolic frames. Chaplains-in-training are drawn to human needs, which likely has attracted them to the work. They care about people's desires and life goals. They want to alleviate suffering and injustice. They support, encourage, and empower people they minister to. And, in the symbolic frame, chaplains offer ways to make meaning of confusion or chaos. They draw on traditions—religious and secular—to narrate a life. They inspire and cultivate belonging through use of symbols, sermons, and rituals. For example, organization-wide memorial services honoring those who died in the previous year bring staff together to mourn and to recommit to shared teamwork on behalf of patients and families.

Chaplains who favor human resource and symbolic frames while working in organizational contexts that operate out of structural and political frames may feel frustrated, misunderstood, or unable to navigate the complexity of the system to get things done. However, in the case study, the director of spiritual care skillfully moves through the organization to get her agenda set and implemented. She chooses IPV as an issue for the department's internal and community outreach. She has very limited funding. This means she will need partnership, coalition, and a compelling story or vision to carry this out. Over a period of time, she moves from "get[ting] herself named to the interdisciplinary Intimate Partner Violence Task Force" to institutionalizing a hospital-wide IPV memorial service. At least intuitively, she understands the building of coalitions of support and resource management of the political frame and the building of trust and culture through the symbolic frame.

It is important to note that good strategies often include multiple-frame perspectives, not simply those of a chaplain's most comfortable and intuitive frame(s). For example, when the DSC receives a less than enthusiastic response from the new program staff about her vision of chaplains playing a unique role in IPV prevention and support, she remains undeterred and develops a multi-framed strategy. The DSC provides religious resources from traditions represented in the hospital community by connecting with national and local organizations as well as with local clergy not represented in the spiritual care department. This is a human resource response that seeks to meet the need of the program staff members who are planning the education curriculum. It is also a political response that recognizes the coalition of various religious traditions present in the hospital community. And finally, a symbolic frame promotes "exemplary" clergy to counter the negative reputation of clergy for those who have experienced religious harm.

Fundamentally, this case study is a study in organizational change. The DSC artfully creates change, not only in the programs but in the ethos and culture of the hospital. Considering this case through the lens of change and how each frame manages change offers us a valuable lesson. Each of the frames brings a set of distinct questions to bear on change in organizations. In the structural frame, for example, the DSC might ask, What change is desired? What structure needs to be implemented (reporting line, roles and responsibilities, coordination, and the like) in order for the change to be successful? In a human resource frame, the DSC might ask, Whose needs will be met with this new program? Whose potential will be enlivened? What new needs might emerge as a result of this new program? In a political frame, the DSC might ask, Who will gain and who will lose? What coalitions of support and opposition to change are there? Is compromise or mutual gain a possibility? And in a symbolic frame, the DSC might ask, What new meaning will be created, and how will people

Organizational Competencies

interpret it? Is it aligned with the current culture? Does it strengthen or weaken the culture? The goal, of course, is to consider all these questions as the DSC manages change.

COUNTERING THE WHITE RACIAL
FRAME IN ORGANIZATIONS

While the four-frames model offers us a substantial tool and a lens through which to understand an organization, it needs to be coupled with another frame that questions and critiques the normativity of the dominant group's values and practices that are taken for granted in the society.[41] Understanding the persistent power of a white racial frame that is embedded in the "micro (interpersonal), meso (small-group), and macro (institutional) levels in the society"[42] is key to recognizing how this frame shapes, validates, and protects the racialized hierarchy of power. Because the white racial frame is more a "comprehensive racialized worldview" that requires commitment and conformity to "narratives, norms, and emotions" than a way of "interpreting the world," it becomes a "way of life."[43] It is imperative to critique the analysis of the four-frames model with a lens that examines the ideologies of power present in the frames. Regarding the case study, I suggest several questions as a "counter-frame" that would aid in its analysis. To offer a counter-frame is to first realize that our society has taken the culture of one dominant group, the white community, and made that the norm and the standard by which everyone else is judged.[44] It is to counter the white supremacy culture that believes that "white people and the ideas, thoughts, beliefs, and actions of white people are superior to People of Color and their ideas, thoughts, beliefs, and actions."[45] The white supremacy culture is reproduced in all institutions, including the media, education, and policies. This ideology, like the air we breathe, impacts us all, but it is hard to identify. Workers are hired, developed, evaluated, promoted, or fired according to the standards of white supremacy, whether or not those who hold these standards are conscious or unconscious of them. It is important to recognize this dynamic, to name it, and to find antidotes that disrupt this culture with different organizational practices. Chaplains' organizational competency requires it.

Here are some questions to consider as an assessment tool to identify characteristics of white supremacy culture that may be operating in an organization.[46] For clarity, I grouped them into three interlocking categories: values, organizational processes, and relational processes.

Values:

- Is there a tendency for perfectionism, which points out inadequacies with little appreciation of the work people are doing?
- Are decisions made through paternalistic expressions of power? Are those without power clear about the decision-making process, especially when it impacts them most? Do people in power act as if they know what is best for the "minoritized" groups when providing service?
- Is there a culture of individualism in the organization that values the ability to do it alone? Is there a culture of isolation and competition rather than cooperation? Is there an ability to delegate?
- Does the organization value logical thinking to the diminishment of other ways of thinking? Belief in objectivity distrusts emotions as destructive and irrational, thus granting them no place in the decision-making process. How well does the organization value multiple worldviews?

Organizational processes:

- Does a sense of urgency dominate the organization, making inclusive, democratic, long-term thinking and decision-making difficult?
- Does the organization prioritize producing measurable goals, thus valuing quantity over quality?
- Is the written word the dominant way of communicating and documenting, to the exclusion of other forms?
- Is there only one right way to do things in the organization? Does it assume that others will see the "light" and join the "right" way?
- Does the organization exhibit either/or thinking, tending to simplify complex realities and creating a sense of urgency as if there is no time to consider alternatives?
- Is there a belief in the organization that there is limited power to go around and therefore power must be hoarded? Do those with power feel threatened when changes are suggested?

Relational processes:

- Do people exhibit defensiveness and expend energy in trying to protect power rather than clarify who has the power and how it is best used?

Organizational Competencies

- Do people in the organization have a fear of open conflict? Do those in power either ignore the conflict or run away from it?
- Who claims the right to emotional and psychological comfort? Who is scapegoated as the ones who cause discomfort?

This set of questions as organizational inventory needs to be layered on top of the four-frames analysis. For example, the human resource frame emphasizes "fit." "Fit" has been used to prevent people of color and others with structural inequalities from being hired, retained, and promoted. Questions to ask here: Who defines fit? Fit to whose standards and norms? The human resource frame also emphasizes meeting the needs of the people in the organization. From this perspective we might ask, Are all people's needs valued equally? Do some people have more "right to comfort" than others, and at whose cost? From a political frame, a chaplain might investigate how conflict plays out in her organization: Are certain expressions of conflict legitimate and acceptable but others not? How does the organization handle open conflict? How does the political frame understand the flow of power? Does it need to be hoarded in order to achieve the goal? How does the assumption of scarcity create a sense of urgency that deters deliberate and democratic processes of decision-making?

Going back to the case study with this additional lens in mind, more questions surface. The hospital is located in an ethnically diverse community. How is the diversity represented in the careseeker base and among staff, doctors, administrators, and others with formal power? How are decisions made to provide services to the diversity of ethnic groups present? Who is consulted for how to make important changes? Is there a culture of openness and learning from mistakes, or do some persons "become mistakes"? How does the quest for perfectionism impact the way the department provides spiritual care and introduces new programs?

Other than the DSC and the careseeker, who are gender-identified in the case study, there is no further context indicating the social locations of any other players in it. In the reality of white supremacy and in the absence of explicit contextual identifiers, our reading defaults to dominant norms. For example, it is difficult to evaluate the effectiveness of the DSC's initiatives without contextualized information regarding her and others' race, gender, sexuality, class, and ability. Furthermore, there are additional elisions in the case study that raise certain questions. Was there any open conflict during this process of change? If so, how was it handled? How is success defined?

What are other measures of success of the hospital-wide IPV memorial service than the number of attendees?

These characteristics of white supremacy infect organizations. People within the organization are also likely to be infected by the assumptions and perspectives of the white dominant group. Undoing these patterns of thinking and behavior will take commitment and daily practice. It is not enough to provide a onetime training; changes at this level will require a continuous examination of the ways in which we act both individually and collectively.

CONCLUSION

I have been teaching the four-frames approach at my seminary for over a decade. And every year, I have my students take the Leadership Orientation Self-Assessment, which identifies students' preferred frame(s).[47] For some, the results are no surprise. It is a confirmation of their inclinations, strengths, desires, and preferences. For others, the results are quite illuminating. These students thought they were oriented toward the practices of one frame, but their results show another. They puzzle through and reflect on the disconnect, which is an opportunity for deep learning. What this exercise achieves is to get students to identify the frames they tend to operate out of and then to practice reframing. The purpose is not to label oneself as a "structural leader" or a "symbolic leader," thereby rigidly defining ourselves in terms of the frames. Rather, the goal is to learn to work with our nondominant hand, to engage, even if awkwardly, with frames that do not feel natural to us. Similarly, working with the white supremacist culture characteristics is doing this liberative work of learning, trying, failing, but trying again to undo oppressive ideologies that operate in our organizations. It requires patience and practice. It requires humility and forbearance. But if we are serious about this work of organizational accountability and justice, we need to commit to this daily practice.

In summary, organizational competencies for chaplains require three competencies—seeing the frames in operation, analyzing the frames in order to understand what is happening, and acting in strategic and effective ways—that grow out of two important orientations. The four-frames lens provides multiple perspectives to understand organizations in their complexities and expansive leadership strategies. The second orientation is an essential critique of the norm of white supremacy culture that exists in organizations. Current chaplaincy education excels at training to provide care on an individual basis. And rightly so. Future chaplaincy education will locate the work of a chaplain within an organizational matrix and consciously counter white supremacy culture. This will not only increase effectiveness of chaplains but provide capacity for broader, life-enhancing impact within the organization.

REFLECTION QUESTIONS

1. Consider your organization. How do you see the four frames operating there? What are the dominant frames?
2. Complete the Leadership Orientation Self-Assessment. What is your frame preference? Is there more than one? Reflect on your strengths and challenges. What do you need to learn in order for you to survive and thrive in chaplaincy and be an effective change agent in your organization?
3. Consider the white supremacy culture characteristics. In what ways do you see the white supremacy culture operating in your organization?
4. In what ways do you see the white supremacy culture characteristics operating in yourself? What work do you need to do?
5. Choose a challenge you are currently facing in your organization. Use the four-frames approach and white supremacy culture characteristics to analyze it, and with increased clarity consider how to leverage your own position in the organization to effect positive change.

RECOMMENDED READINGS

Bolman, Lee G., and Terrence E. Deal. *Reframing Organizations: Artistry, Choice, and Leadership*. 6th ed. San Francisco: John Wiley and Sons, 2017.

D'Angelo, Robin. *White Fragility: Why It's So Hard for White People to Talk about Racism*. Boston: Beacon Press, 2018.

Dismantling Racism Works (dRworks). "Dismantling Racism Works Web Workbook." https://www.dismantlingracism.org/.

Feagin, Joe R. *The White Racial Frame: Centuries of Racial Framing and Counter-Framing*. 3rd ed. New York: Routledge, 2020.

Menakem, Resmaa. *My Grandmother's Hands: Racialized Trauma and the Pathway to Mending Our Hearts and Bodies*. Las Vegas: Central Recovery Press, 2017.

Steele, Claude M. *Whistling Vivaldi: How Stereotypes Affect Us and What We Can Do.* New York: W. W. Norton, 2011.

Okun, Tema. White Supremacy Culture (website). 2021. https://www .whitesupremacyculture.info/.

CHAPTER ELEVEN

The Emotional Undercurrents of Organizations

LAURIE GARRETT-COBBINA

ABSTRACT *Being able to imagine what it looks like for an organization to be dedicated to justice, equality, and moral integrity in practice and procedure is vital. Offering a race-relevant, gender-conscious, and class-aware understanding of organizations will aid in recognizing what is really happening within organizations and why it is happening to the people within them. It is important to bring critical consciousness to how racism, sexism, and classism influence organizational practices and limit their efficacy. Chaplains can play a vital role in supporting the emergence of a sociocultural, political, and spiritual ethos that transforms and humanizes organizations.*

INTRODUCTION

As an African American clergywoman, professor of pastoral care, clinical pastoral educator, and congregational pastor, I daily negotiate intersecting and complex institutions. This means that every day I must be equipped to enter into organizational life with the clarity of identity and the authority to hold a positive sense of myself as I navigate the troubled waters of racist, sexist, and classist insults and invalidations that I encounter. Every day I am conscious of the injurious emotional disturbances embedded in my organizational relationships and interactions. As a competitive swimmer and swimming instructor, I am aware of turbulent undercurrents that churn beneath the surface and either impede or assist movement. "Undercurrents" is the metaphor I use to describe the mechanics, feelings, and behaviors that either impede or assist the destructive force that racism, sexism, and classism exert on organizations. Understanding how undercurrents function to maintain affluent white male, heteronormative privilege empowers me daily to use my spiritual care activism for the well-being of others, myself, and organizations. Consider this scenario:

I scheduled a meeting with two senior vice presidents of the seminary where I teach, a white cisgender women and a retired but reactivated white cisgender man. We were meeting to discuss an opportunity to establish a mutually beneficial relationship with a local hospital: the seminary's CPE program would contract to provide spiritual care to the hospital. This relationship would also allow the CPE program to place students at this site as part of their contextual education experience. I explained the enterprise to the VPs and reviewed the terms of the contract I was developing. The contract was financially advantageous to our institution as a whole as well as to the CPE program in particular. After I shared my thinking about the opportunity for the institution and the CPE program, the VP of finance said, "I think it's a bad idea." (Microinsult.) I asked about her concerns. She said, "I just don't like it." (Contempt.) "What is your concern?" I asked again. "It is too risky." (Defensiveness.) Since she was the financial expert, I thought she might know risks I was unaware of. "Risky in what way?" I asked, genuinely curious. "You were hired for a program nobody wanted because someone gave a donor gift. We have more important concerns." (Racism. Withdrawal. Inertia.) The VP of advancement took up the conversation. "Ahhh, when I worked with a hospital foundation my chaplains were so sweet. I don't think you understand what's involved here." (Microinvalidation. Microinsult. Sexism. Classism.)

It is important to be aware that similar conversations in organizational contexts carry emotional undercurrents of racism, sexism, and classism (isms). The **microaggressions** that accompany isms in interactions like this one corrupt organizations in predictable ways. Microaggressions are indignities and demeaning messages that become habitual and patterned in organizational relationships. Microaggressions are subtle behaviors—verbal or nonverbal, conscious or unconscious—that have harmful effects.[1] Microaggressions have three main manifestations: micro-assaults, micro-insults, and micro-invalidations.[2]

Organizational Competencies

The consequence of an organizational culture permissive of microaggression is, of course, grief, distress, and anxiety.[3] Patterns of interaction marred by isms carry microaggressions and sabotage operational practices throughout an organization. It is not only those who are disadvantaged by microaggressions that live with grief and angst within an organization; those who are privileged show maladjustment patterns too. Beneficiaries of ism treatment must compete in a cutthroat way for more favored positions and more class status and seek self-esteem from those they subjugate along the way.[4] All of this is done with growing empathy deprivation, bitterness, and self-destructive ways of finding happiness.

Maintaining a false superiority causes angst for those working to legitimize and franchise their imposter identity. The emotional energy needed to maintain an idealized false superiority leads to fear of failure and heightened survival anxiety. When "selves" become disassociated from reality-based feelings and knowledge, such as the ideal that some bodies are superior to other bodies, they collectively become "people of the lie."[5] As an organizational collective, "people of the lie" become immoral. With decreased moral parameters and emotional awareness, organizations inevitably lose their way. Organizations collectively functioning as "people of the lie" develop interconnected systems of operation that lead to interpersonal maltreatment. Maintaining the lie can become more important than organizational solvency. The implicit license to relate through microaggressive behavior is an organizational malady best addressed through spiritual care as a complex and invasive intervention for soul-sickness.[6]

Assisting "people of the lie" to move toward becoming imperfect yet tenacious people of the truth is a beneficial therapy for organizational soul-sickness. People of the truth develop the wherewithal to seek authentic life within organizations with their accompanying complexities, pleasures, pains, and stressors. While all people experience stress in institutional life, not all experience stress on the same scale or of the same kind—not even close. Consider this: isms deny relational complexity and cultivate an unequal distribution of pleasure and pain. An organizational collective of truth equally distributes the pleasure and pain of corporate life. No one is overloaded, and no one is under-burdened. Isms function to overburden, overstress, over-police, and over-penalize some organizational members more than others. Isms also adversely affect alignment and commitment to organizational purpose.

As a **counternarrative** to isms culture, I have found that there is no bureaucracy, structure of oppression, or hegemonic power that stops anyone from using their authority to act ethically and with empathy.[7] This means that despite the deprivation of empathy endemic to isms, generosity of spirit can be used to persevere toward organizational goals.[8] Given this, I want to extend several learning invitations to chaplains.

Learning Invitation 1: Meet the impulse toward microaggression with the authority of truth, empathy, and moral integrity.

This process would allow for the re-narration of a corporate identity that includes using moral courage to inspire organizational transformation. Chaplains do this kind of work any time they initiate an empathic and truth-bearing encounter within the institution. Chaplains can use the skill set applicable for assisting others to bear truth with compassion and courage to detect and destabilize organizational isms. The very act of bearing truth destabilizes isms' distortion and perversion of truth. Chaplains engage the reorganization phase of grief care to assist others and groups in the creation of new patterns for living. Likewise, chaplains can assist organizations in the constancy of reorganizational change, creating new patterns of interacting that recover our collective humanity as interconnected people of the truth.

This chapter suggests ways to identify and disrupt the emotional attachments and patterned behaviors endemic to isms that get in the way of a corporate culture of care. In it I explore ways to maximize the emergence of a sociocultural, political, and spiritual grounding that has the potential to inform and transform organizational relationships. In complex organizational systems there are no straight lines; rather, there are intoxicating paths through existing socio-emotional structures of racism, sexism, and classism. If you benefit from the isms operating in your organization, this chapter may be difficult for you to read and understand. The intellectual, social, financial, and spiritual assaults of isms are largely obscured and obfuscated to their beneficiaries, layered beneath microaggressions for organizational maleficiaries. For this reason, I hope you will keep reading, wrestling with the ideas, doing the internal spiritual work, and developing a professional chaplain's capacity to inspire the abolishment of racism, sexism, and classism from hearts, beliefs, and organizational life.

ORGANIZATIONAL COUNTERNARRATIVES

Counternarrative can be used to disrupt systems of isms that contribute to empathy deprivation and ethical offense in organizations. At their core, organizations are an arrangement of people with related purposes. However, organizational purpose is full of incongruities because isms corrupt purpose. The moral bankruptcy of isms undermines efforts to build the kind of interdisciplinary cooperation that motivates innovative thinking on behalf of the organization. To truly understand organizations, it is important to identify and analyze the deep and pervasive emotional attachments to race, gender, and class hierarchy. Offering a race-relevant, gender-conscious, and class-aware counternarrative may help disrupt organizational attachment to isms and illumine what is really happening and why. Counter-narrating stigmatized biases may also generate ontological good—that is, access to the intrinsic beauty and balance that exist in caring relationships. Vital in the examination of organizations is imagining what it looks like to be dedicated to justice, equality, and competency in practice and procedure. Resisting isms sparks the imagination to envision such an organizational reality.

Learning Invitation 2: Engage others as if empathy, compassion, and moral integrity are organizational norms. As a counternarrative to isms, this is effective only when what chaplains say is congruent with what they do and how they implement acts of just care.

Shifting organizational dynamics from what is often called unconscious incompetence to conscious incompetence, with the hope of achieving conscious competence, means making learning a key component of corporate culture.[9] When the dynamic of not knowing that you do not know is denied by beneficiaries of isms, the pressure to learn and make known what is unknown and to develop persons and organizations beyond their incompetence is generally placed on the shoulders of those in the organization most negatively affected by isms. This presents a challenge to creating a shared path to organizational purpose shaped by a future without isms.

Learning Invitation 3: Be aware that beneficiaries of isms are largely unconscious of them; therefore, presenting care opportunities in ways that appeal to other organizational stakeholders is a strategic approach to making isms known while at the same time disrupting them.

Chaplains who are conscious of isms can often identify the markers of racism, sexism, and classism in the undercurrents of their organization. There are usually a variety of different undercurrents in organizations, including emotional ones that undermine the care of souls. Defensiveness, criticism, lack of empathy, bitterness, hostility, delays, frequent complaints paired with aggressive demeanor, and dishonesty are all markers of the emotional and structural undercurrents of isms. These undercurrents are indicative of conscious and unconscious thoughts, feelings, and actions that prevent the organization from just and competent pursuit of goals. Chaplains must harness their capabilities to meet isms with awareness, relational expertise, and spiritual care resources.

A question often posed to me by chaplains who are bringing their ism-blindness to critical consciousness regards what resources they might access to sustain their motivation to divest from the organizational isms that benefit them. The first step to committing to transformative spirituality is understanding that when we speak of isms, not only are we speaking of concepts or creeds or contexts, but we are talking about things that happen to the minds, bodies, and spirits of people. When chaplains remain unconscious to the assaults that isms make on the body, brain, and spirit, they act as collaborators to the lies, illusions, and insinuations that a privileged utopia exists and is valid, even desirous. When chaplains are motivated to recover their own inner being, blessed body, impeccable mind, and spiritual integrity, the commitment to disrupt inequalities within organizations can be sustained. Nevertheless, for chaplains advantaged by the conflagration of isms, motivation and commitment can be easily suppressed by the many conscious and unconscious comforts of privilege.

Learning Invitation 4: Provide competent care to all persons within the organization as you navigate the complex effect of isms while at the same time transforming these organizations into more ethical, empathic, and just entities through the care you provide.

When chaplains identify and evaluate patterns of behaviors in organizational relationships, they can correlate seemingly unrelated behaviors that increase and reinforce ism beliefs, practices, and policies. This is a distinctive assessment competency of chaplains and a uniquely vital expertise they can offer to organizations. Chaplains must have the capacity to learn how to move isms-awareness from unconscious incompetence to critical consciousness so that patterns inherent to the insidious intersection of racism, sexism, and classism become knowledge.

Learning Invitation 5: Look for patterns of behavior that seem to have little or no connection but that you suspect are in deeply connected.

At their core, racism, sexism, and classism are complex, interconnected systems that function as ubiquitous forces of the heart that support the maintenance of primarily affluent white male, heteronormative power structures. Therefore, they persist as psycho-socio-emotional constructs—not because they are logical (they are completely illogical) but because they are emotional forces of the heart that shape responses in the brain and body. Isms are the result, in part, of emotional attachment to their underlying hierarchy. Affluent white male heteronormativity has a covenantal reverence that feels like an existential threat when challenged—it quite literally feels like dying for a person of privilege when attachment to the precepts and practices on which isms are built, and on which they depend, are dismantled.[10]

To maintain isms without psychic trauma for those who benefit from racial, gender, or class privilege, organizational life hides, normalizes, and mystifies the way certain people are advantaged by the oppression of others. Systems are so efficiently racist, sexist, and classist in the way some are advantaged and others are disadvantaged that biases happen whether persons within the organization will them or not. Race, gender, and class preconceptions regulate the psyche so effectively that isms are made to feel normal.

This normalization process shields those who are advantaged by isms from the sociopathic shock of becoming conscious of inflicting injury on such a pervasive scale. The normalization process is reinforced by the disconnection from one's feelings and the loss of the capacity for empathy. Isms embed injustice into the emotional web of organizations. If at this moment you feel yourself wanting to deny or withdraw from this analysis of organizational reality, then the conscious and unconscious decrees of isms are functioning within your psyche just as intended.

Understand that whatever you may feel right now is not shared by your affiliate organization(s). But while organizations do not feel, they do transmit what may be experienced as good feeling to its members through the symbolic power of their meta-narratives.[11] Certain grand narratives have the power "to impose meaning and conceal the power relations which are the basis of its force."[12] For example, to give legitimacy to the good feeling of symbolic power, dominant persons/departments are assigned spacious offices in desirable locations in the primary building. Office space and location become the measure of worth, merit, or good feeling in the organizational meta-narrative and signal the symbolic power of those persons/departments. Symbolic power can give way to symbolic violence, which is the imposition of ideology onto subordinated groups that makes the position of the dominant group feel natural. Emotions such as guilt, anger, shame, and fear are essential to an organization's ability to use symbolic violence to impose the ideology of the dominant class onto the psychic, social, and operational mindscape of its members.[13]

Learning Invitation 6: Support the process of dismantling organizational isms through practices of empathy and truth-telling in every care encounter, meeting, and interprofessional conversation/collaboration.

In addition to empathy and truth-telling, chaplains' work includes the art of inspirational dialogue and use of prophetic voice. Empathy, truth, and inspirational and prophetic communication are the counternarratives to the status quo empathy deprivation of isms. Warning: do not mistake the aggressive expression of feelings stemming from hostility, bitterness, or rage as anything other than a sign of isms at work. Hostility, bitterness, and rage are the emotional glue that holds isms together, and as such, their expression is given permissiveness within organizations.

Learning Invitation 7: Develop your confidence that compassionate emotional labor is a powerful caregiving competence that counters prescribed organizational norms that elevate practices of emotional deprivation.

Chaplains often engage complex institutional relationships that view spirituality and emotion with suspicion.[14] Spirituality and emotion are embedded with suspicion because they have cathartic healing power beyond what dominant groups can fully control. Efforts to transform organizations into empathic, just, and moral entities are rooted in a pastoral identity that hinges on more than what we think, feel, or believe. Chaplains are called to act out of a spiritual care competence that assesses vulnerability, expresses empathy, and intervenes on behalf of those who suffer. This empathic identity is related to an identity and vocation inspired by connection with the holy. The development of a spiritual care identity is powerful because it can disrupt the human experience of abandonment, loneliness, trauma, and grief. The capacity to care in the reality of suffering lets us know we, human beings having human experiences, are not alone—and that is central to the formation process of chaplains' identity.

Chaplains' ability to understand and leverage different forms of power and authority for the purpose of ethical and caring practice is a vital competence that can be employed at any level of any organization. Developing this expertise is crucial if one wants to bring emotional-relational patterns into clearer focus and begin the work of dismantling toxic hierarchies. Chaplains can use their skills and knowledge to untether organizational systems from socio-emotional isms that limit the rich resource of human resiliency.

It may seem as if isms in organizations are inevitable. With our current social constructs, isms *are* inevitable. However, race is not real in a biological sense.[15] Race is a social, legal, economic, and emotional construct for obtaining and maintaining white privilege. Gender is influenced by how dominant powers define and enforce it. Class is a social, contextual, and historical construct. Class is not only about the money we make, the schools we attend, the clothes we wear, or where we live but about how we think, feel, and act. Race, gender, and class, although false, constructed, and always in flux, are fundamental features of every decision we make. The fact that these isms are not actual, though they have actual effects, means that chaplains have many opportunities every day to disrupt their power and performance.

Chaplains can help build something new that allows for the uniqueness of persons to be valued rather than falling back on the emotional deprivation needed to animate stigmas and stereotypes. For example, studies have found that people who feel judged by negative stereotypes related to race, gender, or class report poorer health in general. Both patients and healthcare workers are more likely to mistrust organizational leaders when they feel vulnerable to prejudice because of the stigmas projected onto them. As a result, both careseekers and care providers operate under a "healthcare stereotype threat."[16] Chaplains have many opportunities to break down ism stereotypes and help careseekers and care providers feel understood, heard, and cared for as they mutually engage in the very purpose of the healthcare organization.

THE SPIRITUALITY OF ORGANIZATIONAL MECHANICS

Mechanics is the science concerned with the motion of things. For example, mechanics study dynamics of movement or inertia when force is applied. The science of mechanics can provide helpful principles for charting organizational undercurrents caused by the influence of stubborn ism inertia. Organizational movement can stagnate when denial and numbing of emotions influence interpersonal interactions. Moreover, a careful examination of organizational mechanics reveals that meritocracy, the belief that people advance in organizations based on merit, is generally not true. Certain people advance through organizations because of the emotional infrastructure that supports the ideology of isms, often regardless of a person's merit. The infrastructure, by which I mean the established patterns of relating, policies, and procedures, allows persons who benefit from social stratifications to be promoted and remain unconscious of how emotional relationships influence choices, practices, and advancement, and prevents those in nondominant groups from advancing.

No matter a chaplain's context, awareness of organizational mechanics is helpful for assessing and understanding when an organization is motivated to change. Being able to see readiness to change is a caregiving competency. I learned to anticipate readiness to change as a swimming teacher. I could present numerous but varied opportunities to tackle a new skill, such as entering the deep end of the pool. There was an expression on the face, a quivering of the body, and subtle movement of arms and legs that indicated readiness to jump into deep water. I have noticed its similarity with spiritual readiness to change. When presented varied opportunities to transform or transcend a current practice, organizations exhibit "body language" and mental/emotional exertion that precede the change.

However, reading organizational mechanics is difficult when the organization's idealized identity is presented as reality. The idealized reality of organizations is not the lived reality. It is important for chaplains to be able to see and name the lived reality within organizations. A chaplain can give the organization many opportunities to learn, challenge, and change practices and ideas that are normalized through emotional attachment to ism constructs yet are not true. Chaplains must always come back to the central source of their identity and authority, that is, the transformative power of spiritual care. Chaplains can offer compassionate spiritual care to persons and groups that elicits and honors vulnerability. They can create and enact rituals, practices, and grand round–style events that support cathartic experiences and cultivate wholeness.

Empathy deprivation ultimately sabotages organizations' ability to realize their mission. However, even when function or production or service is compromised, organizations tend not to change in response to emotional appeals, which might be chaplains' first attempt, since many of us are skilled and comfortable working with emotions. Organizations change only when force is applied, as the science of mechanics suggests.

Chaplains are uniquely positioned in institutions to apply force. We are positioned and tasked, in part, to attend to moral quagmires that interfere with developing empathic patterns of interaction in organizations. Some chaplains may not agree that organizational empathy or having concern with principled practices is what they are hired to do. The designated role of chaplains differs from context to context. I am proposing that chaplains use their pastoral authority to study the patterned ways emotions are used against subjugated persons and groups and to consider what force can be applied to perceptions and practices to motivate organizations to become more equitable and just.[17]

Learning Invitation 8: Notice where force can be applied to create the conditions and contexts that encourage organizations to strengthen their practices of empathy, equity, and integrity as a characteristic of corporate culture.

In order to strategically observe patterns of system bias in organizations, chaplains must view them as if standing on high ground.[18] From this perspective, chaplains can notice many places of organizational stagnation. Inertia is a sign of stress and can highlight places where an organization may be experiencing chronic anxiety, inflexible compliance, or unresolved conflict that affects the spiritual wellspring of an organization. With perspective and ism awareness, a chaplain can identify systemic emotional attachments to entitlement and superiority for some and disadvantage and inferiority for others. These attachments appear as shared delusions that have concrete effects on organizational movement toward justice and empathy in policy, practice, and procedure. These shared delusions may be thought of as a perception disorder that causes distress and impairment in work and everyday life.

Organizational patterns guiding emotional and relational interactions that are entrenched in isms consciously and unconsciously create what they stigmatize. After a stigma is created, those identified through their stigma(s) are penalized for it. For example, the dominant power of "maleness" stigmatizes "femaleness" as something different and inferior from the normalized standard of "male." As a dominant power, "men" control the narrative that normalizes the subordination of "women." Penalties are then imposed on the stigmatized "female" mind, body, and spirit and on any other persons who do not meet the "female" ideal of affluent, straight white "men." Examples of penalties include lower wages for performing work identical to male counterparts; sexual harassment; healthcare insecurity; appearance pressures; and expectation to complete assignments without access to mentors.[19]

With the aid of policies, practices, and beliefs, misogynist expectations exert a hegemonic influence that both men and women normalize. In this example, maleness traffics femaleness—that is, it defines, stigmatizes, markets, invents, and invests in what it decides is female and feminine. Regardless of level of reflexivity chaplains have concerning their own ism awareness, recognizing how identities are constructed and normalized by dominant power can foster empathic interactions and support more just and ethical organizational practices.[20]

Applying force to organizations that motivates them to move toward equity means, as a starting point, opening opportunities for all to contribute to organizational purpose without the de facto limitations that isms imposed. When organizations are resource-equitable and all people have opportunity to contribute as human resources for the organization, then the emotional numbing practices of isms can be radically disrupted.

CORPORATE GRIEF CYCLE

Understanding the complex relational patterns of organizations from a spiritual care perspective means acknowledging the cycle of grief that isms activate within them. Grief refers to the many different emotional, spiritual, and social processes of sorrowfulness. Systemic racism, sexism, and classism are toxic by design and sorrow-inducing by intention. For example, a woman might be called "ambitious" as a belittling trope meant to cause grief, which delegitimizes her work by intention, further diminishing her opportunities of advancement, corporate contribution, and higher wages. Thus, the cycle of grief is reinforced and the cycle of sorrow is expanded into intersecting institutions, such as government, education, economy, and religion. Even though women may successfully navigate the microaggressions aimed at limiting their positive self-regard and movement through organizations, the microaggressions are still grief-producing.[21]

Organizational life is steeped in grief as isms infiltrate beliefs, politics, practices, emotions, and relationships that reproduce the status quo that sustains them. The ability of organizations to transmit psycho-socio-emotional wellness is fraught with experiences of grief. Chaplains who are conscious of and able to assess isms at work in organizations can counter some of isms' antisocial determinants and resulting grief. Acknowledging, analyzing, and engaging grief on a macro, micro, and meta level will ultimately allow chaplains to better diagnose and challenge the durable structural challenge of carrying out spiritual care on all of these levels.

Increasing conscious competence is critical for chaplains who are themselves steeped in relationships guided by isms. I recognize that the struggle with isms is multilayered and chronic. Chaplains must become aware of the ways their own complicity with isms renders them "common sense" and obscures their effects.[22] Nonetheless, isms produce toxic stress, grief, and inappropriate behavior in the workplace and other organizational contexts. Unacknowledged grief helps sustain organizational conditions that distress workers. Recognizing reactions that are expressions of grief, such as anger, fear, sadness, blame, guilt, hostile outbursts, denial, numbness, anxiety, and disorganization, has the potential to help chaplains remain non-defensive when members of their organization are resistant to new spiritual care initiatives that generate practices of empathy and equity.

Additional signs of grief include difficulty focusing on goals, impaired corporate memory, slowed cognitive processing, magical thinking, vindictiveness, despair, and loneliness. The history, magnitude, and frequency of prior griefs affect the ability to cope with and recover from organizational distress.[23] Grieving organizations are filled with anxiety-ridden people. Chaplains' capacity to care is a valuable resource to lower anxiety, which in turn has the potential to allow something potentially life-enhancing to emerge in organizational relationships and practices.

Let me give an example using loneliness as an outgrowth of ism-related grief. Organizational loneliness arises out of interpersonal or departmental isolation.[24] Loneliness, also known as social pain, develops as a biosocial prompt for people to move toward others.[25] Loneliness is especially dysfunctional when internalized isms discourage bonding or relationship building. Lonely people within organizations often fear for their own professional survival, which becomes emotionally and physically exhausting over time. A particular risk of loneliness is losing the creative, connective, and generative potential that moving toward others offers. The constant cycling of grief in organizations is insidious when a symptom such as loneliness receives no caring human response.

At its heart, grief is a crisis of meaning where what one expects of the world is disrupted. Because isms are highly emotional and trauma-inducing by design, the corporate cycle of grief felt when undoing ism injustice is particularly intense. However, the grief process is an opportunity to acquire meaningful knowledge that chaplains can use to influence organizational culture.

Culture refers to a set of mostly intangible aspects of organizational life that consists of inherited values, beliefs, systems of language and communication, food sources, geography and topography, material goods, and practices.[26] Culture is simply whatever we say it is. For example, it is common for healthcare systems to include some version of a culture where "we recognize the value of every person." Educational institutions promote some version of the cultural intention "to develop students' intellectual, moral, civic, and creative capacities." The military presents a culture "to protect and defend." The United States affirms itself as a culture where "all people are created equal."[27]

These statements are public declarations of aspirational culture. When those serving within these organizations have experiences contrary to aspirational culture, grief results—and not just personal grief but corporate grief. Distinguishing between personal and corporate grief is important. As an example, Africans Americans experience personal/communal grief from the historical and contemporary laws, policies, politics, and attitudes of systemic racism, which also cause moral injury, considering the United States' aspirational culture. The United States experiences corporate grief and existential crisis when those advantaged by white privilege begin to accept their complicity with racist practices or, alternatively, further entrench in racist rhetoric and practices that violate the nation's meta-narrative of being democratic and just. These are two distinct but connected experiences of grief.

Learning Invitation 9: Identify the signs and symptoms of grief and trauma and create contexts to invite and facilitate human bonding in response to them.

Nurturing a supportive community, seeking empathic responses, and drawing closer in proximity to reliable others is a way for chaplains to assess and respond to corporate grief. Chaplains can see the stressors that activate grief as opportunities to awaken the organization from complacency and complicity with status quo structures of injustice. Chaplains can also influence movement of the organization toward meaning-making processes that are healing, moral, and committed to the struggle for corporate integrity that will benefit all people, including fair wages, equal opportunities, self-esteem, environmental care, opportunities to exercise voice, and more. These shifts will also make it more difficult for people who are doing wrong to continue inflicting moral injury, because a corporate consciousness of integrity means more accountability and transparency.

Moral injury is the betrayal of what is right or the transgression of ethical parameters by those who exercise authority.[28] Immoral conduct desensitizes those carrying out injurious practices such that transgressors lose touch with their capacities for empathy. Given the horrors effectuated by isms that have been institutionalized, the grief process has an essential role in making people conscious of isms and in transforming grief into knowledge and practices that nurture resiliency, creativity, and care. Grief can be understood as a good gift from God, and grief guru is an essential role for chaplains.

Grief gurus can gather data about where people within the organization are hurting and ascertain what hurts, when it hurts, why it hurts, who is doing the hurting, and what remedy is being pressed. Mapping responses to these questions can help chaplains identify where organizational grief exists. Mapping grief to identify where force may be applied as a catalyst

Organizational Competencies

for organizational change and noticing where there is a lack of energy for changing into a more caring culture should be a fundamental competency for chaplains.

Resistance to identifying and addressing grief can be seen in formal and informal rules against providing time and space to express or even acknowledge grief. For example, Western institutional culture is not supportive of emotional displays at work. We receive strong cultural messages to rationalize isms, deny feelings, remain unconscious to injustice, and "get over" a moral injury. When these norms are not adhered to in the workplace, some type of punitive action usually follows.

Yet, the very reason it is important to assess cycles of organizational grief is to bring the feeling of pain to the fore and engage it. Spirituality is not meant to anesthetize pain. Spirituality is meant to increase human capacity to cope with pain while at the same time creating a less distressing human condition. The dual ability to cope with pain and alleviate its root causes positions chaplains to help organizations create structures that generate less stress and distress, establish more ethical standards, and develop more diverse relational networks. This grief process cannot be compartmentalized outside work environments because it *is* the work environment. Grief is the critical consciousness of organizational feelings, function, and transformation.[29]

ORGANIZATIONAL TRANSFORMATION

Members of an organization often consciously and unconsciously resonate with its aspirational identity, culture, story, and mystique. For example, the Declaration of Independence states that it is self-evident "that all men are created equal." Yet, for nearly four centuries the U.S. government kidnapped, enslaved, and brutalized an estimated 15 million people of African descent, sparking perennial racial struggle, gender oppression, and ever-growing class gaps, education gaps, healthcare gaps, and technology gaps that extend into organizations today.[30] Yet, people advantaged by isms are still blinded to the vastly different experiences and struggles that people disadvantaged by isms have in organizations. The American mystique has an astonishing anesthetizing effect on organizational transformation.

Organizations that operate with isms often require people to suspend critical thinking, a common form of avoidance. Members of organizations frequently feel they must set aside principles of equality, empathy, and ethics and their own values, commitments, and thinking to survive within them.

They are often unaware of how they seek the comfort of spiritual care while delegitimizing spiritual care precepts and practices. For example, you may have an executive leader who demands love, respect, and admiration, all the while bullying and humiliating subordinates. Such a leader seeks the comfort of spiritual care while delegitimizing care for others in policy and practice.

Organizations want to maintain their standard operating procedures, so they resist change.[31] Organizational resistance to change is entrenched in the preexisting hierarchical patterns of isms. Recognizing this complexity is the key to understanding, leveraging, and transforming organizations. Failure to seek clarity and truth, failure to identify who is stigmatized and normalized, and failure to challenge the status quo are quite simply mistakes that those in organizations often make. A standard competence that chaplains must develop is the ability to normalize difficult emotional processes and conversations and identify where and why change is happening or needs to happen.

Learning Invitation 10: Assert yourself as a care activist so that compassion becomes a strategic influencer for creating a critically conscious organization more responsive to pressure to change.

Chaplains routinely perform assessments to evaluate where growth is happening or needs to happen with individuals and small groups. Change rarely happens without pain or loss. The expertise that chaplains bring to organizations includes knowing how to work with growth and change, and the grief they engender, so that bitterness over shifts away from status quo isms does not overwhelm or undercut the change process. Bitterness is characterized by general negativity. Bitterness, as an unresolved form of grief, is the refusal to let loss or disappointment be transformed into acceptance and even contentment. It is a feeling state that those who benefit from isms use to maintain the status quo and results in aggressive resentment toward those who challenge it. Chaplains' own spiritual vitality is an important source of their power and resiliency. The power to carry out practices of care can "unfix" bitterness and dislodge other grief-sustaining patterns of interaction. Chaplains can help increase the spiritual vitality of organizations and the persons within them.

Learning Invitation 11: Develop policies, procedures, and practices—such as pathways for non-retaliatory complaints; diversity, equity, and inclusion; and

Organizational Competencies

restorative justice processes—that help organizations manage their production of inappropriate behaviors rooted in isms.

This is where spiritual care can be essential to organizational structure. Chaplains can bring their interpersonal skills to bear on corporate processes that help manage emotional relationships and their unconscious patterns of grief-inducing interactions and structures. They might ask, Does my organization have a process for reconciliation and reconnection post-conflict? Is there explicit time and effort dedicated to cultivating non-anxious relationships where isolation, abandonment, and fear do not pervade culture? Do people within the organization have the resources they need to cope with changes in leadership and the reality of impermanence for all persons in the workforce?[32] Are equitable streams of professional development in place? Are chaplains advocates for building fair and equitable organizational policies and practices? These practices are not difficult to implement. However, organizations often act as if they are because of embedded ism assumptions and practices and commitment to the ways dominant groups benefit from them.

As organizations stop accepting the fabricated ideal that there are people who count and people who do not count and reject inequality as norm, they gain insight into solving problems that heretofore were framed as unsolvable. There is emotional wisdom to leverage and creativity that is cultivated when everyone has a voice. There is inspiration to harness when the tasks of corporate mechanics are understood as aligned with processes of care. The more acceptance there is for empathy and conscious awareness, the more fluidly and rhythmically each member of the organization responds to shifts, changes, and challenges to isms.

CREATING EMOTIONALLY COMPETENT ORGANIZATIONS

It is my hope that chaplains as individuals and as a collective will develop the professional capacities and the spiritual will to support members of organizations through uncomfortable conversations, realities, feelings, and practices. The liminal geographic location and hierarchical placement of chaplains, often in the middle mass of organizations, is a useful place from which to initiate change. From this location, chaplains can and do act as bridges between careseekers and staff, lower-wage workers and management, community members and upper management. Chaplains then have the responsibility to apply the art of caring to engage the grief process as the organization changes and certain people and groups lose harmful advantage. Chaplains can help heal emotional and spiritual injuries and advocate for justice in organizational operations and relationships. This is part of the prophetic duty of chaplains to identify and name what is actual and call out what is possible.

Undoing the relational and structural systems that reinforce isms and create terrible disparity is the ongoing work of chaplains and organization members. Every interaction, every relationship in organizational life is embedded in a system of hierarchies in which there are winners and losers. Denying this fact, rationalizing it, avoiding it, or maligning the subjugated persons and groups who speak of it will not change the reality that there are invisible and grievous inequalities that are the major determinants of organizational life. The remedies for creating a shared vision of equality and compassion are spiritually based. They must be spiritually based because equality and compassion are spiritual forces.

Let me make clear that developing more just organizations is not a best practice–based critique, although listening, assessing, and empathic engagement are spiritual care best practices. It is not fundamentally a material-based argument, although well-being of material bodies is on the line. It is not a utopian-based ambition, although empathy and equality have the potential to reduce suffering and build restorative community. What is presented here is a spiritually grounded argument that focuses on disrupting the many interrelated systems of race, gender, and class suffering in organizations. Such spiritual care work must be engaged as a collective struggle for organizational wellness—indeed, for its foundational fitness and likelihood of surviving. Disrupting so many interrelated systems of oppression may seem like an undoable task in corporate life. However, creating just, ethical, and emotionally competent organizations is completely within our power and capacity to accomplish. We construct isms; therefore, it is within our power to abolish them.

REFLECTION QUESTIONS

1. Have you lied to survive in your workplace/educational setting?
2. Are you afraid an upset authority person will set off vindictive punishments?
3. Are you emotionally, physically, spiritually, and intellectually safe at work/school?

4. Do you often feel anxiety or sorrow at work/school?
5. Do you often mistrust your feelings and the feelings expressed by others?
6. Are you allowed adequate time and resources for recreation, meditation, rest, healthcare, holidays, and basic living needs?

RECOMMENDED READINGS

Kendi, Ibram X. *How to Be an Antiracist.* New York: Penguin Random House, 2019.

Levchak, Charisse. *Microaggression and Modern Racism.* New Britain, Conn.: Palgrave, 2018.

Mills, Charles W. *The Racial Contract.* Ithaca, N.Y.: Cornell University Press, 1997.

CONCLUSION

. . . .

A Commissioning

. . . .

TRACE HAYTHORN *and* JASON CALLAHAN

The field of chaplaincy is defined by its paradoxical nature. It is centuries old, and yet it is only beginning to grow into its potential. It is historically tied to religious communities, traditions, and practices, but best practices today are embodied by those who serve people regardless of faith tradition or source of meaning. Much of this work is done in private moments of pain and grief, yet chaplaincy's public role is rarely understood. It has often been an area that administrators struggle to fund, and yet in the wake of pandemics it has never seemed more essential.

These circumstances are not necessarily conflicts to be resolved but the creative tensions that give chaplaincy its vibrancy and value. As noted in this text, there are no uniform standards for the education of chaplains, largely due to the traditions, contexts, legal issues (that is, church-state issues), and interpersonal nature of formation for this work. At the same time, this variability has made it much more difficult for chaplains to move between sectors, even as it has been difficult for the general public to understand what chaplains do. Like many professional arts, creativity, imagination, and contextual adaptation can find themselves in tension with the public need to understand, appreciate, and fund chaplaincy positions. If people do not understand the work and the need for it, how can they know to ask for it?

We want to conclude with less of a "final word" and more of a commissioning to those who sense the preceding chapters speaking to them, encouraging them in their own work and exploration. The work of chaplaincy is both a science and an art. As such, it has both rules and freedom, boundaries and explorations. There are best practices and experts of the craft, and there are ways for those with very little training to demonstrate the kinds of compassionate care one can expect from a chaplain. As a science, it is increasingly centered on evidence-based understandings of effective spiritual care, guided and informed by an emerging body of research. As an art, it is always and already being refined, reimagined, and challenged, even as its history is recognized for its important grounding and shaping of the field.

During the onset of COVID-19, chaplains suddenly found themselves banned from rooms of the patients they were called to serve. The families of those patients were also banned from the hospitals caring for their loved ones. In these moments, the chaplains did not wait for direction from an organizing entity; they did not need new orders to do their work. They began to improvise. Chaplains gave nurses baby monitors to place in patients' rooms while they coordinated with family members on ways to connect with their loved ones. Similarly, they encouraged nurses to put patients' phones or tablets in plastic bags, reducing the possibility of passing the virus to others while allowing them to FaceTime family members. Were these ideal? Of course not. But they made communication possible in seemingly impossible conditions.

In 1975, jazz pianist Keith Jarrett was invited to perform at the Cologne Opera House in Germany. When he arrived to prepare for the concert, he discovered that there had been a mix-up with the pianos, leaving him with a broken upright rehearsal instrument. Another piano could not be found, and only minor repairs were done to the piano. Jarrett sat at the keyboard, took note of what worked and what didn't, and proceeded to play. To date, the recording of that concert has sold more than any other jazz piano recording in history. Jarrett agreed to go ahead and play because he wanted a recording of what he expected to be a disaster to prevent it from ever happening again. But Jarrett is an artist, and he made something beautiful out of incredibly difficult circumstances.[1]

In some ways, that is precisely what effective chaplains do every time they visit with someone who is vulnerable, in pain, or suffering. They bring what they know into the moment, and then, like a great jazz musician, they begin to play. When COVID-19 struck, many chaplains who had always believed digital/virtual forms of spiritual care were suspect quickly adapted to use whatever medium was available. They refined their practices to meet the needs of the people and contexts they served. Along the way, they began to share their stories with colleagues, and ultimately they advanced the profession, helping create new ways of serving more people in an even wider variety of contexts and circumstances. Newspapers and magazines across the country printed their stories for people desperate for answers but no sense of where to turn. Chaplaincy was experiencing a moment of emergence from the margins.

To be clear, the arts require practice and are stronger if informed by science. One does not simply learn to do certain tasks that become the routines of their profession. Keith Jarrett never would have been able to adapt so quickly had he not practiced his art. Chaplaincy and professional spiritual care require ongoing learning, a commitment to professional development, and an awareness that each of us has room to learn and grow. Chaplains acquire evidence-based practices that have been crafted through careful scientific research. Seasoned chaplains develop spiritual care "muscles," strengths and capacities to stand in what Parker Palmer calls "the tragic gap," that is, "the gap between the hard realities around us and what we *know* is possible—not because we wish it were so, but because we've seen it with our own eyes."[2]

Make no mistake: while many characterize this as deeply compassionate and beautiful work, it is also very difficult. Spiritual care professionals are wise to have peer support, regular professional emotional and spiritual support (for example, therapy, spiritual direction), and relationships that provide accountability (such as professional associations, communities of practice, or regular peer reviews). If we have learned anything about spiritual care during the pandemic and cultural upheavals of 2020, we have seen the kinds of exhaustion under which many chaplains have functioned. They have been pushed to creatively adapt their practices to the realities of the unfolding conditions, to work hours well beyond their normal routines, to face significant increases in death and grief, to see professional colleagues freighted with emotional burdens that compelled some to leave their work, and to persist in contexts where their relevance and role were often questioned. Even amid such conditions, the role of chaplains has been elevated (and celebrated) by the media to unprecedented levels, meaning chaplains have also been pushed to show up at their best even on the days when they, too, were struggling to hang on.

So where does the profession go from here? What are the key areas for growth, development, and maturity for this old yet young enterprise known as spiritual care? We will conclude with outlining key areas that we believe will require significant attention and strategic engagement for chaplaincy to reach its full potential.

In 2015, Wendy Cadge (Brandeis University) and George Fitchett (Rush University) received a grant from the John Templeton Foundation that launched Transforming Chaplaincy, an initiative that "aims to better equip healthcare chaplains to use research to guide, evaluate, and advocate for the daily spiritual care they provide patients, family members and colleagues."[3] While Cadge and Fitchett have been among several important researchers in the field for many years, this grant helped move spiritual care research to a new level of professionalism. Eighteen chaplaincy fellows earned master's degrees in research-related fields to bring research into their own settings, multiple educational programs expanded to include research, and hundreds of chaplains completed free research literacy training. The increase in publications and changes in practice is but one measure of the effectiveness of this initiative.[4]

At the same time, this work is almost exclusively in healthcare, and the need for spiritual care and chaplaincy research in other domains is critical. For the foreseeable future, collaborative initiatives from organizations like the Chaplaincy Innovation Lab have the potential to broaden knowledge and evidence-based care practices in places like prisons, colleges, and the military. Chaplaincy continues to rely too heavily on anecdote and borrows heavily from psychotherapeutic models. Seminaries and divinity schools have been eliminating positions in pastoral theology, and the professional society for those educators, the Society for Pastoral Theology, has declined from over three hundred members in 2010 to just over one hundred members in 2018. While the military has engaged in some very important research, it is not in the public domain and thus does not influence the larger field. To come fully into its own, chaplaincy needs to continue to investigate and expand on the practices identified through research about healthcare-based spiritual care to other contexts.

COMMITMENT TO ANTIBIAS PRACTICE AND THEORY

Because of the positions that chaplains occupy, they are often ideally situated to address systemic racism, white privilege, and other forms of discrimination. It is incumbent upon the professional associations and educational organizations to advance research, theory, and pedagogies that equip professional spiritual care providers with the skills to engage this essential aspect of their work. Standing with a care recipient to assure just treatment within an institution; engaging colleagues within those institutions to raise awareness about biased practices and advocating for antibias alternatives; serving in the larger community in ways that confront and challenge discriminatory actions at both the individual and systemic level; and researching, writing, and contributing to the further development of antibias standards, competencies, and theory: each of these is more than an opportunity for chaplains. As a profession that has historically been marginalized and practiced by those who know multiple forms of discrimination, this work is integral to the ongoing development and coherence of spiritual care as a profession.

BUSINESS MODELS AND SUSTAINABILITY

In contexts where financial metrics and results-based accounting models have defined personnel structures, support for chaplaincy has been difficult. How does one make a financial argument for spiritual care when it is often seen as a "soft" service? Considering the level of education for chaplains that many contexts expect, what is a reasonable salary? Should there be some consistency across contexts upon which administrators can establish hiring credentials, salaries, and benefits?

In many ways these questions are directly related to the research questions above. Evidenced-based data is needed to support not only those currently practicing spiritual care but also those seeking to develop new models among new constituencies. Many programs have found initial financing through grants, usually tied to the specific services they seek to back. Those funds, however, are time-limited and cannot underwrite ongoing chaplaincy past the initial grants. Theological schools are rapidly developing degrees, certificates, and concentrations in chaplaincy, but they aren't communicating with each other, resulting in a hodgepodge of requirements, competencies, and skills. Few foundations provide ongoing support for chaplaincy, and most chaplaincy programs have concerns about developing "fee for service" models (that is, structures that charge individuals or organizations per chaplain visit).

In 2020, the E. Rhodes and Leona B. Carpenter Foundation provided funds for a team of spiritual care researchers to explore how healthcare executives make decisions about chaplaincy in their institutions. Most leaders recognized that while chaplaincy is not a revenue-generating function of their hospital, the services provided are critical to the health and well-being of patients, families, and staff. As chaplains facilitate Critical Incident Stress

Management processes (for addressing trauma shared by a staff group) and Code Lavenders (a crisis intervention tool for staff support) and organize annual memorial services and informal spiritual care offerings, executives see chaplains as important members of their healthcare teams.[5] This is the first evidenced-based study of decision makers, and much more is needed across the contexts in which chaplains serve.[6]

Not only did 2020 shut down our traditional delivery methods, but we found ourselves relying more on the natural supports located within communities. When there are already people in the community who may come from backgrounds that share the core values of spiritual care, providing them with the pathways to pursue professional chaplaincy strengthens our ability to reach individuals who may not have benefited from a chaplain's care in the past. This also opens the door for more entrepreneurial forms of chaplaincy. Although it does not solve the issue of funding, those who already have created their own pathways to income will be able to practice as a professional chaplain, while those in the profession itself will benefit from learning from them and can enhance our ability to develop better financial models collectively.

Significant work is needed to develop demand-based models for spiritual care that do not place the onus of fundraising on the backs of chaplains, that do not default to scarcity-based funding models, and that are informed by data that have been developed through meaningful and substantive research. Funding for professional spiritual care ordinarily falls into the general overhead costs of institutions. There is no support from insurance, and chaplaincy is not seen as "revenue-generating." As such, chaplains and their departments live in constant fear of the next round of cost-cutting measures within their organizations.

CARE FOR THE CHAPLAIN

While some chaplains have the privilege of working on teams with spiritual care colleagues, many serve as the only spiritual care professional in their setting. Either way, chaplains shoulder far too much to go it alone. As witnesses to some of the most vulnerable and painful moments in people's lives, chaplains must commit to the kind of self-care that allows them to faithfully serve for years to come. Chaplains carry the stories of those they serve, of the family members of those who suffer, and of the staff alongside whom they serve. The weight of so much grief and pain is simply too great for anyone to bear without ongoing emotional and spiritual support.

This group of chaplains and researchers gathered at Boston University in 2019 as part of the Educating Effective Chaplains Project to discuss the future of chaplaincy and bring resources, such as this book, to fruition. *Photo credit: Dan Aguirre.*

Many chaplains learn versions of Bowen family systems theory as a part of their training. A key theoretical concept from this perspective is that of differentiation of self. While it is vital for those who engage in conflict, it is also a key dimension of individuals' ability to offer care to others, making sure they are meeting care recipients' needs instead of imposing the providers' frame of meaning on them.[7] In addition, healthy chaplains need space to process what they experience, to not let the grief and pain of others come to define them. Such support also helps avoid the kind of loneliness that can have long-term health effects on those who live with such stories and hold them confidentially.

THE CHANGING LANDSCAPE OF
AMERICAN RELIGIOUS LIFE

All of this is taking place within a rapidly changing sociocultural moment. Since the 1960s, mainline Protestantism has seen a rapid decline in both membership and leadership. Those trends are now beginning to appear in other religious traditions. Over the last decade, we have seen a marked rise in those who identify as "spiritual but not religious," a group that often has strong convictions but has become disaffected with religious organizations. Even as chaplaincy has seen steady growth over the same time periods, the general population does not understand what chaplains are or what they do. Professional spiritual care may be diversifying into more and more areas, but the profession as a whole needs the equivalent of a marketing and branding campaign to raise awareness about the work, its need, and the availability of those called to serve.

Although professional chaplains will respond to the needs of all regardless of beliefs, the need for more tribal connections and the care associated with being a part of that tribe is a dynamic that enhances one's quality of care. The word "chaplain" itself may in fact be a deterrent to those who would benefit greatly from our care. Although not all organizations may be swift to adopt new titles, there is room to articulate what the profession is today in a way that enhances the utilization of its services. As the profession grows more integrated in the nonreligious world, titles of meaning will continue to show up within communities that utilize the role. More important than the name itself, however, will be the promotion of the supports provided.

In addition to a name change and advertising campaign to advocate for chaplaincy, the profession itself is becoming more humanized in practice and representation and breaking down barriers to entry that once stood to those who did not follow traditional paths to chaplaincy or represent the perspectives and images that have historically represented the idea of chaplaincy. An example of this is the fact that those who are endorsed as humanists may become board certified chaplains. Humanism itself is a life stance rather than a religion, guided by reason, inspired by compassion, and informed by experience.[8] In essence, the life stance tries to enhance human flourishing by focusing on the inherent capacity of each human being to be good, without the existence of the supernatural or a divine being.[9]

In addition to a more humanized profession, the field of chaplaincy and its certification bodies are opening up more to people who want to be chaplains yet do not come from the traditional educational backgrounds that chaplaincy has historically drawn from. Due to the nature of professional chaplaincy and the developmental process that goes into becoming a chaplain, educational barriers continue to keep talented individuals out. Opportunities are increasing, however, for those holding a more diverse group of master's degrees. The profession is now seeking ways to include more people with master's degrees in philosophy, psychology, and social work. This is making a way for more people to enter the field and incorporate more diverse skill sets and research, as well as use more evidence-based skills and interventions to enhance practice.

In this text, the contributors have provided an introduction to the interpersonal, organizational, and systemic competencies for effective practice of chaplaincy in a variety of contexts. We have presented case studies to help ground discussions and explorations in situations that chaplains are likely to encounter. This is just a beginning, and yet it is built on a rich and complex history.

ACKNOWLEDGMENTS

This book emerged from a collaborative conversation about the training and education of chaplains. Through a generous grant from the Henry Luce Foundation, we were able to gather a group of theological school faculty, clinical educators, social scientists, and other chaplaincy leaders to consider how to strengthen the preparation of chaplains for the rapidly shifting landscape of spiritual care in North America. We want to thank our Luce program officer, Jonathan Van Antwerpen, for making this collaboration possible.

We first gathered in Boston in July 2019. We discovered educators, not only well-positioned to forecast changes to existing programs but invigorated by the opportunity to connect and network. The palpable energy and visionary thinking over three days spawned subsequent collaborations. The generativity of this group is evidenced in multiple projects beyond this book: the creation of online chaplaincy case studies (led by Lars Mackenzie and Liz Aeschlimann); a yearlong faculty course redesign initiative supported through the Wabash Center at Boston University, including the composition of the Competency Checklist found in the appendix (led by Shelly Rambo, Trace Haythorn, and Celene Ibrahim); the development of materials for bolstering chaplaincy programs within theological school (led by Su Yon Pak, Mychal Springer, and Zachary Moon); and collaborations on a journal issue (led by Shelly Rambo and Cheryl Giles). These products can be traced to aha moments, collective brainstorming sessions, and the development of collegial friendships. It required moving out of our comfort zones and disciplinary silos and, in some cases, adjusting our styles of writing and relating.

While the pandemic foreclosed the possibility of travel, it also brought new intensity to our collective work due to the heightened visibility of chaplains responding to multiple challenges in care provision. The events of 2020 surfaced other challenges—of anti-Black and anti-Asian racism, white Christian nationalism—leading our authors and participants to pivot and underscore ongoing disparities in spiritual care education and delivery.

We want to thank the members of the group for contributing their time and energy, especially during a year when demands from their institutions were increasing: Brenda Bennefield, Duane Bidwell, Wendy Cadge, Leticia Campbell, Carol Damm, Carrie Doehring, David Fleenor, Victor Gabriel, Kathy Gallivan, Laurie Garrett-Cobbina, Cheryl Giles, Elisa Goldberg, David Grafton, Dagmar Grefe, Danielle Tumminio Hansen, Trace Haythorn, Celene Ibrahim, Allison Kestenbaum, Dennis LoRusso, Pamela McCarroll, Barbara McClure, Jan McCormack, Zachary Moon, Mary O'Neill, Su Yon Pak, Glenn Palmer, Bill Payne, Shelly Rambo, Rochelle Robins, John Schmalzbauer, Judith Schwanz, Munir Shaikh, Michael Skaggs, Mychal Springer, Ronit Stahl, Tiffany Steinwert, Mary Martha Thiel, and Taylor Winfield.

Special thanks go to Rachel Payne, who administratively supported all of these projects while finishing her master of divinity degree at Boston University School of Theology. Claire Wolf took over for Rachel in the last six months of the project, for which we are grateful. Our institutions, Brandeis University and Boston University School of Theology, also helped in the development of the book. Special thanks are due to former dean Mary Elizabeth Moore for recognizing the impact of this collaboration and contributing additional institutional resources to support it. Thanks, as well, go to Michael Skaggs, Darra Sweetser, Aja Antoine, and other colleagues at the Chaplaincy Innovation Lab who helped with details large and small from the beginning to the end of this project.

We are grateful for our editor, Elaine Maisner at the University of North Carolina Press, for believing in our vision for chaplaincy education and to Andreina Fernandez for her editing assistance. Special thanks go to Kristen Redford Hydinger for editing multiple drafts, prodding authors, and making this all feel seamless. The aim of the book is to lift up the work. For all of those providing spiritual care—we hope this supports you.

Competency Checklist: Assessing the Effectiveness of Chaplaincy Programs

We believe these three broad areas of competency are required for chaplains regardless of the setting in which they work. Consider how your program contributes to the development of these competencies. We encourage you to use this appendix as a checklist for examining the strengths and weaknesses of your program. This list is also attentive to what we call the "demand side" of chaplaincy. As chaplains enter the workforce, this list provides a way to explain the work of spiritual care and chaplaincy to employers who may speak a very different language.

MEANING-MAKING COMPETENCIES

Developing a public voice: How does the program prepare students to be spiritual leaders? This includes attention to the following:

- drawing from wisdom traditions (texts and practices) to respond to contemporary situations
- developing skills in oral and written communication for diverse public audiences
- developing ethical and moral leadership amid climates of social chaos, deception, violence, gaslighting, moral crises, and the like
- creating and leading rituals

Offering culturally relevant care or religious literacy: How does the program prepare students to provide care that is culturally informed and attends to those from various religious communities and spiritual orientations? This includes attention to the following:

- translating between the language of religious traditions and the language of workplace institutions
- shifting from highly specialized fields of religious knowledge to insights offered in spiritual care
- facilitating and promoting religious understanding
- developing tools for spiritual care for nonreligious persons
- fostering basic religious literacy training for caregivers of different traditions

INTERPERSONAL COMPETENCIES

Interpersonal work: How does the program prepare individuals to do the interpersonal work with the individuals and groups chaplains serve? This includes attention to the following:

- reflective listening
- making space for another's experience
- basic skills in counseling
- understanding family systems and theories of human development
- interpreting trauma

Inner work: How does the program help students do the internal/psychological work that will enable them to be more effective caregivers? This includes attention to the following:

- interrogating bias
- working through past experiences of trauma
- developing character
- setting boundaries
- caring for self through embodied practices

ORGANIZATIONAL COMPETENCIES

Understanding and navigating organizations: How does the program help students understand, interpret, and effect change within the organizations where they work? This includes attention to the following:

- understanding the chaplain's position within the organization's bureaucracy
- articulating the significance of spiritual care within the organization
- identifying and marshaling resources of the organization
- knowing how to move through and work with staff in different positions in the organization
- knowing how to connect with staff and other care partners

Advocacy and justice-based care: How does the program prepare students to advocate for care recipients and for just practices within institutions? This includes attention to the following:

- skills in collaborating with other care partners in making systemic-level changes
- tools that are spiritually informed and intersectionally robust
- ability to work with conflict
- ability to respond to collective system-level disruptions (pandemic, economic uncertainty, widespread environmental devastation, endemic corruption, ongoing and blatant bigotry, and so on)

GLOSSARY

attunement Listening to words and body language, to content as well as delivery

boundary situations Transitional moments in life demarcated by particular events that often require the rearticulating or redefining of meaning and purpose

code-switching The ability to understand and use the practices and language of careseekers from diverse backgrounds

competency The knowledge and skills required to do the work of chaplaincy and spiritual care in the settings where work is conducted

corporate grief cycle The chronic and systemic incorporation of isms in an organization

counternarrative Alternative approaches to understanding and interacting with and within organizations that disrupt systems of isms and can generate ontological good

countertransference All the unfinished business, triggers, and personal experiences that may arise within chaplains during conversations with careseekers that is displaced onto those careseekers

distinct from position leadership An approach to leading that is not synonymous with authority or high position

empathy An ability to "feel with" the careseeker through a therapeutic encounter

the four-frames approach A diagnostic tool of four theoretical perspectives—structural, human resource, political, and symbolic—with respective implications and responses for each perspective

grounding A practice by which chaplains prepare their minds and bodies to be present with a careseeker or by which they rest their minds and bodies after an encounter

interpathy The process of entering into another's narrative, cultural, and symbolic world

interpersonal competence The knowledge of how power, social location, patriarchy, and systemic racism impact interactions between chaplains and other individuals

intersectionality Overlapping biases and power dynamics inherent in helping relationships

interventions Actions influenced by spiritual assessment that support careseekers' capacities for meaning making following crises

life transitions Expected or unexpected experiences that substantially change the day-to-day of a person's life

liminal spaces Points on the map of life that are in between normalcy as one has known it and what life will become

microaggressions Subtle verbal or nonverbal, conscious or unconscious behaviors that have harmful effects and that become habitual and patterned in organizational relationships

moral injury The betrayal of what is right or transgression of ethical parameters by those who exercise authority

neutralizing Using broader spiritual language and practices that build upon commonalities rather than differences

non-anxious presence A common expectation of chaplains that involves the ability to remain calm and attentive to others experiencing emotional flooding

normalizing Providing a wider perspective that helps careseekers feel less alone and more connected with others who have also gone through similar experiences

plan of care Action steps toward healing or meaning making developed in dialogue with careseekers that works with their needs and rhythms

presence A mindfulness to the sacred within the details of life that establishes important ground in the task of meaning making

rapport A trust-filled relationship established through repeated careseeker-centered and careseeker-directed interactions

reflective listening A repetition of words or sentences the careseeker has expressed

relational leadership An approach to leading that requires rapport between leaders and followers

religious literacy The awareness of the basic beliefs, history, ethics, and practices of a variety of spiritual or religious traditions

representative role A designation often entrusted to chaplains by others, usually based on others' own experiences of spiritual or religious leadership within their own contexts

resonance The relational connection between chaplain and careseeker that occurs when the chaplain is attuned to the body language, voice, and nonverbal communication of the careseeker

rituals Communal events with the potential to facilitate connection and belonging

self-differentiation The process of managing relational boundaries, emotions, thoughts, and behaviors to maintain a healthy relationship between chaplain and careseeker

situational leadership An approach to leading that is dependent on organizational, environmental, or historical context

social location An individual marker that affords a particular level of power based on the general way it is recognized and treated in a given context

spiritual assessment An interpretive process by which chaplains listen both for the ways people construct meaning in their lives and for the practices and words that express their beliefs and values

the Spiritual Assessment and Intervention Model A conceptual framework focused on identifying a careseeker's primary unmet spiritual need, devising strategies for addressing this need through relationships, and evaluating the outcomes of a focused conversation

spiritual distress Crisis of identity, vocation, meaning and purpose, traumatic loss, moral distress and injury, bereavement, or recovery from catastrophic events that a careseeker's existing spiritual framework cannot resolve

unconditional positive regard The chaplain's stance of acceptance toward the careseeker as a person of worth and value

validating Confirming a careseeker's feelings without judgment or evaluation

NOTES

....

INTRODUCTION

1. Winnifred Fallers Sullivan, *A Ministry of Presence: Chaplaincy, Spiritual Care, and the Law* (Chicago: University of Chicago Press, 2014), ix–x.

2. Wendy Cadge, *Paging God: Religion in the Halls of Medicine* (Chicago: University of Chicago Press, 2012).

3. Francis A. Lonsway, "Profiles of Ministry: History and Present Research," *Theological Education* 41, no. 2 (2006): 111–25.

4. Wendy Cadge, George Fitchett, Trace Haythorn, Patricia K. Palmer, Shelly Rambo, Casey Clevenger, and Irene Elizabeth Stroud, "Training Healthcare Chaplains: Yesterday, Today and Tomorrow," *Journal of Pastoral Care and Counseling* 73, no. 4 (2019): 211–21.

5. Ronit Y. Stahl, *Enlisting Faith: How the Military Chaplaincy Shaped Religion and State in Modern America* (Cambridge, Mass.: Harvard University Press, 2017).

6. E. Brooks Holifield, *A History of Pastoral Care in America: From Salvation to Self-Realization* (Nashville: Abingdon, 1983); Cadge, *Paging God*.

7. Holifield, *History of Pastoral Care in America*; Lawrence E. Holst, *Hospital Ministry: The Role of the Chaplain Today* (New York: Crossroad, 1985); Charles Hall, *Head and Heart: The Story of the Clinical Pastoral Education Movement* (Decatur, Ga.: Journal of Pastoral Care Publications, 1992).

8. Holifield, *History of Pastoral Care in America*; R. Hunter, ed., *Dictionary of Pastoral Care and Counseling* (Nashville: Abingdon, 1990).

9. Bonnie J. Miller-McLemore, "The Living Human Web: Pastoral Theology at the Turn of the Century," in *Through the Eyes of Women: Insights for Pastoral Care*, ed. Jeanne Stevenson Moessner (Minneapolis: Fortress Press, 1996), 9–26; Nancy J. Ramsay, *Pastoral Care and Counseling: Redefining the Paradigms* (Nashville: Abingdon, 2004); Emmanuel Yartekwei Lartey, *Pastoral Theology in an Intercultural World* (Cleveland: Pilgrim Press, 2006); Carrie Doehring, *The Practice of Pastoral Care: A Postmodern Approach*, rev. and exp. ed. (Louisville: Westminster John Knox Press, 2015); Barbara McClure, *Moving beyond Individualism in Pastoral Care and Counseling: Reflections on Theory, Theology and Practice* (Cambridge: Lutterworth Press, 2011).

10. Nancy J. Ramsay, ed., *Pastoral Theology and Care: Critical Trajectories in Theory and Practice* (Chichester, UK: Wiley Blackwell, 2018); Ryan LaMothe, *Care of Souls, Care of Polis: Toward a Political Pastoral Theology* (Eugene, Ore.: Cascade Books, 2017); Sheryl

A. Kujawa-Holbrook and Karen B. Montagno, eds., *Injustice and the Care of Souls: Taking Oppression Seriously in Pastoral Care* (Minneapolis: Fortress Press, 2009).

11. Wendy Cadge and Michael Skaggs, "Chaplaincy? Spiritual Care? Innovation? A Case Statement," working paper, Department of Sociology, Brandeis University, 2018.

12. Cadge et al., "Training Healthcare Chaplains"; Wendy Cadge, Irene Elizabeth Stroud, Patricia K. Palmer, George Fitchett, Trace Haythorn, and Casey Clevenger, "Training Chaplains and Spiritual Caregivers: The Emergence and Growth of Chaplaincy Programs in Theological Education," *Pastoral Psychology* 69, no. 3 (2020): 187–208.

13. Shelly Rambo, *Spirit and Trauma: A Theology of Remaining* (Louisville: Westminster John Knox Press, 2010); Pamela R. McCarroll, *The End of Hope—the Beginning: Narratives of Hope in the Face of Death and Trauma* (Minneapolis: Fortress Press, 2014); Zachary Moon, *Warriors between Worlds: Moral Injury and Identities in Crisis* (Lanham, Md.: Lexington Books, 2019).

14. Dagmar Grefe, *Encounters for Change: Interreligious Cooperation in the Care of Individuals and Communities* (Eugene, Ore.: Wipf and Stock, 2011); Duane Bidwell, "Religious Diversity and Public Pastoral Theology: Is It Time for a Comparative Theological Paradigm?," *Journal of Pastoral Theology* 25, no. 3 (2015): 135–50; Lonsway, "Profiles of Ministry."

15. Wendy Cadge, Katherine Wang, and Mary Rowe, "Perspectives from the Edge: Chaplains in Greater Boston, 1945–2015," *Journal for the Scientific Study of Religion* 58, no. 1 (2019): 269–86; Cary Funk and Greg Smith, "'Nones' on the Rise: One-in-Five Adults Have No Religious Affiliation," Pew Research Center, October 9, 2012, https://www.pewresearch.org/wp-content/uploads/sites/7/2012/10/NonesOnThe Rise-full.pdf; "In U.S., Decline of Christianity Continues at Rapid Pace: An Update on America's Changing Religious Landscape," Pew Research Center, October 17, 2019, https://www.pewforum.org/2019/10/17/in-u-s-decline-of-christianity-continues -at-rapid-pace/; Cyrus Schleifer and Wendy Cadge, "Clergy Working Outside of Congregations, 1976–2016," *Review of Religious Research* 61 (2019): 411–29.

16. Wendy Cadge, Taylor Paige Winfield, and Michael Skaggs, "The Social Significance of Chaplains: Evidence from a National Survey," *Journal of Health Care Chaplaincy* 26, no. 1 (2020): 1–10.

17. George Fitchett, Kelsey B. White, and Kathryn Lyndes, eds., *Evidence-Based Healthcare Chaplaincy: A Research Reader* (Philadelphia: Jessica Kingsley, 2018); Allison Kestenbaum, Michele Shields, Jennifer James, Will Hocker, Stefana Morgan, Shweta Karve, Michael W. Rabow, and Laura B. Dunn, "What Impact Do Chaplains Have? A Pilot Study of Spiritual AIM for Advanced Cancer Patients in Outpatient Palliative Care," *Journal of Pain and Symptom Management* 54, no. 5 (2017): 707–14.

CHAPTER I

1. Godwin Kelly, "Flagler Hospital Chaplain Comforts Those Dealing with COVID-19 Pandemic," *Daytona Beach News Journal*, October 25, 2020, https://www.news -journalonline.com/story/news/local/flagler/2020/10/25/adventhealth-chaplain-ney -ramirez-covid-first-responder/3671034001/.

2. Press Release, "Pelosi Appoints Rear Admiral Margaret Grun Kibben First Woman to Serve as Chaplain of the U.S. House of Representatives," December 31, 2020, https://www.speaker.gov/newsroom/123120; Jack Jenkins, "How House Chaplain Calmed Tense Hours in Besieged Capitol with Prayers for 'God's Covering,'" Religion News Service, January 9, 2021, https://religionnews.com/2021/01/09/house-chaplain-siege/.

3. "Crimping at Newport News," *Sailors' Magazine and Seamen's Friend* 80, no. 7 (July 1908): 197.

4. James Angell, quoted in Margaret M. Grubiak, "The Danforth Chapel Program on the Public American Campus," *Buildings and Landscapes* 19, no. 2 (Fall 2012): 79.

5. Winnifred Fallers Sullivan, *A Ministry of Presence: Chaplaincy, Spiritual Care, and the Law* (Chicago: University of Chicago Press, 2014), x.

6. Marsh v. Chambers, 463 U.S. 783 (1983).

7. On the history of the legislative chaplaincy, see Andy G. Olree, "James Madison and Legislative Chaplains," *Northwestern University Law Review* 102, no. 1 (2008): 146–222; Christopher C. Lund, "The Congressional Chaplaincies," *William & Mary Bill of Rights Journal* 17, no. 4 (2009): 1171–214; S. Spencer Wells, "'For Conscience Sake': Quaker Campaigns against Legislative Chaplaincies, 1789–1797," *Quaker History* 107, no. 2 (2018): 1–18; Kevin J. Dellape, *America's First Chaplain: The Life and Times of the Reverend Jacob Duché* (Bethlehem, Pa.: Lehigh University Press, 2013); and Spencer W. McBride, *Pulpit and Nation: Clergymen and the Politics of Revolutionary America* (New York: Oxford University Press, 2017), 38–67.

8. Spencer McBride, "Firing the House Chaplain Politicized One of the Last Apolitical Parts of Congress," *Washington Post*, April 28, 2018, https://www.washingtonpost.com/news/made-by-history/wp/2018/04/28/firing-the-house-chaplain-politicized-one-of-the-last-apolitical-parts-of-congress/.

9. John Leland, *The Writings of the Late Elder John Leland: Including Some Events in His Life* (New York: G. W. Wood, 1845), 119.

10. On the religious composition of the congressional chaplaincy, see Mildred Amer, "House and Senate Chaplains," CRS Report for Congress, 2006, 1, https://www.everycrsreport.com/files/20061027_RS20427_07fd2e6f859b2b418aac306341d5d6ocbbd9cc22.pdf.

11. Earl Stover, *Up from Handymen: The United States Army Chaplaincy, 1865–1920* (Washington, D.C.: Government Printing Office, 1977). On the development of religious diversity in the military chaplaincy, see Ronit Y. Stahl, *Enlisting Faith: How the Military Chaplaincy Shaped Religion and State in Modern America* (Cambridge, Mass.: Harvard University Press, 2017). The military originally categorized LDS, Christian Science, and Eastern Orthodox chaplains as "Protestant" chaplains. On the organizational development of the military chaplaincy, see Richard M. Budd, *Serving Two Masters: The Development of the American Military Chaplaincy, 1860–1920* (Lincoln: University of Nebraska Press, 2002).

12. Rebecca McLennan, *The Crisis of Imprisonment: Protest, Politics, and the Making of the American Penal State, 1776–1941* (New York: Cambridge University Press, 2008), 3.

13. Jennifer Graber, *The Furnace of Affliction: Prisons and Religion in Antebellum America* (Chapel Hill: University of North Carolina Press, 2011), 44–45, 48.

14. Quoted in W. Ralph Graham and Bryn A. Carlson, "The American Protestant Correctional Chaplains Association, Inc.," *Journal of Pastoral Care and Counseling* 42, no. 3 (1988): 220.

15. Andrew Skotnicki, *Religion and the Development of the American Penal System* (Lanham, Md.: University Press of America, 2000).

16. Jody L. Sundt and Francis T. Cullen, "The Role of the Contemporary Prison Chaplain," *Prison Journal* 78, no. 3 (1988): 272–73.

17. Quoted in Wendy Cadge and Michael Skaggs, "Serving Seafarers in the Boston Harbor: Local Adaptation to Global Economic Change, 1820–2015," *International Journal of Maritime History* 30, no. 2 (2018): 255.

18. Harold Kelley, "The Early History of the Church's Work for Seamen in the United States," *Historical Magazine of the Protestant Episcopal Church* 9, no. 4 (1940): 350–56.

19. Tony Cawthon and Camilla Jones, "A Description of Traditional and Contemporary Campus Ministries," *College Student Affairs Journal* 32, no. 2 (2004): 158. On the long history of religiously affiliated higher education, see Frederick Rudolph, *The American College and University: A History* (1968; repr., Athens: University of Georgia Press, 1991); George Marsden, *The Soul of the American University: From Protestantism to Established Nonbelief* (New York: Oxford University Press, 1994); and Julie Reuben, *The Making of the Modern University: Intellectual Transformation and the Marginalization of Morality* (Chicago: University of Chicago Press, 1996).

20. Grubiak, "Danforth Chapel Program," 79.

21. Grubiak, 79.

22. Cawthon and Jones, "Traditional and Contemporary Campus Ministries," 159–63.

23. Rodney Stokoe, "Clinical Pastoral Education," *Nova Scotia Medical Bulletin* (February 1974): 26; Wendy Cadge, George Fitchett, Trace Haythorn, Patricia K. Palmer, Shelly Rambo, Casey Clevenger, and Irene Elizabeth Stroud, "Training Healthcare Chaplains: Yesterday, Today, and Tomorrow," *Journal of Pastoral Care and Counseling* 73, no. 4 (2019): 213; Wendy Cadge, "Healthcare Chaplaincy as a Companion Profession: Historical Developments," *Journal of Health Care Chaplaincy* 25, no. 2 (2019): 47.

24. "History : A Brief History of the Association of Professional Chaplains," Association of Professional Chaplains, accessed 2021, https://www.professionalchaplains.org/content.asp?pl=24&sl=31&contentid=31.

25. Cadge et al., "Training Healthcare Chaplains," 213; Cadge, "Healthcare Chaplaincy," 48–51.

26. Quoted in Cadge, "Healthcare Chaplaincy," 53.

27. George Fitchett, Kelsey B. White, and Kathryn Lyndes, eds., *Evidence-Based Healthcare Chaplaincy: A Research Reader* (Philadelphia: Jessica Kingsley, 2018).

28. Chad E. Seales, "Corporate Chaplaincy and the American Workplace," *Religious Compass* 6, no. 3 (2012): 197–99.

29. Quoted in Sarah Hammond, *God's Businessmen: Entrepreneurial Evangelicals in Depression and War*, ed. Darren Dochuk (Chicago: University of Chicago Press, 2017), 161, 164.

30. Seales, "Corporate Chaplaincy and the American Workplace," 195.

31. Wendy Cadge, "The Evolution of American Airport Chapels: Local Negotiations in Religiously Pluralistic Contexts," *Religion and American Culture* 28, no. 1 (2018): 135–65; Courtney Bender, "Idlewild/John F. Kennedy International Airport 'Tri-Faith Plaza,'" *Reverberations: New Directions in the Study of Prayer*, August 4, 2014, http://forums .ssrc.org/ndsp/2014/08/04/idlewildjohn-f-kennedy-international-airport-tri-faith -plaza/.

32. On the Clergy and Laity Concerned about Vietnam (CALCAV), see Mitchell Hall, *Because of Their Faith: CALCAV and Religious Opposition to the Vietnam War* (New York: Columbia University Press, 1990).

33. Jack Jenkins, "'Protest Chaplains' Shepherd Movement's Spiritual Side," Religious News Service, October 10, 2011, https://religionnews.com/2011/10/10/protest -chaplains-shepherd-movements-spiritual-side/.

34. Quoted in Cecil Bradfield, Mary Lou Wylie, and Lennis G. Echterling, "After the Flood: The Response of Ministers to a Natural Disaster," *Sociological Analysis* 49, no. 4 (1989): 406.

35. Storm Swain, "The T. Mort. Chaplaincy at Ground Zero: Presence and Privilege on Holy Ground," *Journal of Religion and Health* 50, no. 3 (2011): 482.

36. Swain, 491.

37. Valerie Gouse, "An Investigation of an Expanded Police Chaplaincy Model: Police Chaplains' Communication with Local Citizens in Crisis," *Journal of Pastoral Care and Counseling* 70, no. 3 (2016): 195–202.

38. Wendy Cadge, Irene Elizabeth Stroud, Patricia K. Palmer, George Fitchett, Trace Haythorn, and Casey Clevenger, "Training Chaplains and Spiritual Caregivers: The Emergence and Growth of Chaplaincy Programs in Theological Education," *Pastoral Psychology* 69, no. 4 (2020): 187–208.

CHAPTER 2

1. Wendy Cadge, "God on the Fly? The Professional Mandates of Airport Chaplains," *Sociology of Religion* 78, no. 4 (2018): 437–55; Wendy Cadge and Michael Skaggs, "Humanizing Agents of Modern Capitalism? The Daily Work of Port Chaplains," *Sociology of Religion* 80, no. 1 (2019): 83–106; Wendy Cadge, *Paging God: Religion in the Halls of Medicine* (Chicago: University of Chicago Press, 2012); Joshua Dubler, *Down in the Chapel: Religious Life in an American Prison* (New York: Farrar, Straus and Giroux, 2013); Kim Philip Hansen, *Military Chaplains and Religious Diversity* (New York: Palgrave Macmillan, 2012); Lake Lambert III, *Spirituality, Inc.: Religion in the American Workplace* (New York: New York University Press, 2009); John Arnold Schmalzbauer and Kathleen A. Mahoney, *The Resilience of Religion in American Higher Education* (Waco, Tex.: Baylor University Press, 2018).

2. U.S. Const. amend. I.

3. Abington School District. v. Schempp, 374 U.S. 203 (1963).

4. Marsh v. Chambers, 463 U.S. 783 (1983).

5. Katcoff v. Marsh, 755 F. 2d 223 (Court of Appeals, 2nd Circuit 1984).

6. Theriault v. Silber, 547 F. 2d 1279 (Court of Appeals, 5th Circuit 1977).

7. Wendy Cadge, Taylor Paige Winfield, and Michael Skaggs, "The Social

Significance of Chaplains: Evidence from a National Survey," *Journal of Health Care Chaplaincy* 26, no. 1 (2020): 1–10.

8. Winnifred Fallers Sullivan, *A Ministry of Presence: Chaplaincy, Spiritual Care, and the Law* (Chicago: University of Chicago Press, 2014), 6.

9. U.S. Congress, "United States Code: Chaplains, 10 U.S.C. §§ 231–240," 1952, https://www.loc.gov/item/uscode1952-001010013/.

10. Hansen, *Military Chaplains and Religious Diversity*, 3.

11. Parker v. Levy, 417 U.S. 733 (1974).

12. Hansen, *Military Chaplains and Religious Diversity*.

13. Mark Faram, "No 'Atheist' Chaplains, Lawmakers Tell Navy," *Navy Times*, March 26, 2018, https://www.navytimes.com/news/your-navy/2018/03/26/no-atheistchaplains-lawmakers-tell-navy/.

14. *Holistic Health and Fitness (FM 7–22)*, Department of the Army, 2020; *Strategic Plan for Religious Ministry*, Department of the Navy, 2020.

15. Hansen, *Military Chaplains and Religious Diversity*.

16. Larsen v. U.S. Navy, 525 F. 3d 1 (Court of Appeals, Dist. of Columbia Circuit 2008); Chaplaincy of Full Gospel Churches v. England, 454 F. 3d 290 (Court of Appeals, Dist. of Columbia Circuit 2006); Neela Banerjee, "Proposal on Military Chaplains and Prayer Holds Up Bill," *New York Times*, September 19, 2006, https://www.nytimes.com/2006/09/19/washington/19chaplains.html; Heather Cook, "Service before Self? Evangelicals Flying High at the U.S. Air Force Academy," *Journal of Law and Education* 36, no. 1 (2007): 1, https://www.questia.com/library/journal/1P3-1191262401/service-before-self-evangelicals-flying-high-at-the; Alan Cooperman, "Military Wrestles with Disharmony among Chaplains," *Washington Post*, August 30, 2005, https://www.washingtonpost.com/archive/politics/2005/08/30/military-wrestles-with-disharmony-among-chaplains/fdb782ad-bcbb-42ed-be2f-38cf56cbfdef/; Laurie Goodstein, "Evangelicals Are a Growing Force in the Military Chaplain Corps," *New York Times*, July 12, 2005, sec. U.S., https://www.nytimes.com/2005/07/12/us/evangelicals-are-a-growing-force-in-the-military-chaplain-corps.html.

17. Veitch v. England, 471 F. 3d 124 (Court of Appeals, Dist. of Columbia Circuit 2006); Weinstein v. U.S. Air Force, 468 F. Supp. 2d 1366 (Dist. Court 2006).

18. *Religious Liberty in the Military Services (DOD Instruction 1300.17)*, Department of Defense, 2020.

19. Goldman v. Weinberger, 475 U.S. 503 (1986).

20. "Army Directive 2017-03 (Policy for Brigade-Level Approval of Certain Requests for Religious Accommodation)," memo, Department of the Army, 2017.

21. "Armed Forces Chaplain Board," Office of the Under Secretary for Personnel and Readiness, U.S. Department of Defense, accessed January 21, 2021, https://prhome.defense.gov/M-RA/Inside-M-RA/MPP/AFCB/.

22. *VHA Directive 1111*, Department of Veterans Affairs, 2020.

23. Conservative Baptist Assn. of America v. Shinseki, 42 F. Supp. 3d 125 (Dist. Court 2014).

24. "Chaplain," Federal Bureau of Prisons, accessed January 21, 2021, https://www.bop.gov/jobs/positions/index.jsp?p=Chaplain.

25. *Religious Beliefs and Practices (5360.09, CN-1)*, Federal Bureau of Prisons, 2015, 7.

26. *Religious Beliefs and Practices (5360.09, CN-1)*.

27. Cooper v. Pate, 378 U.S. 546 (1964).

28. Cruz v. Beto, 405 U.S. 319 (1972).

29. O'Lone v. Estate of Shabazz, 482 U.S. 342 (1987); Turner v. Safley, 482 U.S. 78 (1987).

30. Religious Freedom Restoration Act, Pub. L. No. 141, 42 U.S.C. § 2000bb (1993).

31. City of Boerne v. Flores, 521 U.S. 507 (1997).

32. O'Bryan v. Bureau of Prisons, 349 F. 3d 399 (Court of Appeals, 7th Circuit 2003).

33. *Religious Beliefs and Practices (5360.09, CN-1)*, 1.

34. *Religious Beliefs and Practices (5360.09, CN-1)*, 4.

35. "5.7 Religious Practices," *Family Residential Standards 2020*, U.S. Immigration and Customs Enforcement, 2020; "5.5 Religious Practices," *Operations Manual*, U.S. Immigration and Customs Enforcement, 2011, https://www.ice.gov/doclib/detention -standards/2011/5-5.pdf.

36. "Religion in Prisons," Pew Forum on Religious and Public Life, Pew Research Center, 2012, https://www.pewforum.org/2012/03/22/prison-chaplains-exec/.

37. *Standards for Adult Correctional Institutions*, 4th ed. (Lanham, Md.: American Correctional Association, 2003).

38. "Religion in Prisons."

39. Dubler, *Down in the Chapel*; Mumina Kowalski and Wendy Becker, "A Developing Profession: Muslim Chaplains in American Public Life," *Contemporary Islam* 9 (2014): 17–44.

40. Cadge, Winfield, and Skaggs, "Social Significance of Chaplains."

41. Cadge, *Paging God*.

42. Joint Commission on Accreditation of Healthcare Organizations, "Evaluating Your Spiritual Assessment Process," *The Source* 3 (2005): 6–7, https://www.professional chaplains.org/files/resources/reading_room/evaluating_your_spiritual_assessment _process.pdf; Wendy Cadge, George Fitchett, Trace Haythorn, Patricia K. Palmer, Shelly Rambo, Casey Clevenger, and Irene Elizabeth Stroud, "Training Healthcare Chaplains: Yesterday, Today and Tomorrow," *Journal of Pastoral Care and Counseling* 73, no. 4 (2019): 211–21.

43. *State Operations Manual*, Centers for Medicare and Medicaid Services, 2020.

44. Wendy Cadge, Jeremy Freese, and Nicholas A. Christakis, "The Provision of Hospital Chaplaincy in the United States: A National Overview," *Southern Medical Journal* 101, no. 6 (2008): 626–30.

45. Cadge et al., "Training Healthcare Chaplains."

46. Cadge, *Paging God*.

47. George Fitchett, Kelsey B. White, and Kathryn Lyndes, eds., *Evidence-Based Healthcare Chaplaincy: A Research Reader* (Philadelphia: Jessica Kingsley, 2018).

48. Wendy Cadge, "Healthcare Chaplaincy as a Companion Profession: Historical Developments," *Journal of Health Care Chaplaincy* 25, no. 2 (2019): 45–60.

49. Deborah B. Marin, Vanshdeep Sharma, Eugene Sosunov, Natalia Egorova, Rafael Goldstein, and George F. Handzo, "Relationship between Chaplain Visits and Patient Satisfaction," *Journal of Health Care Chaplaincy* 21 (2015): 14–24; Jeffrey R. Johnson, Ruth A. Engelberg, Elizabeth L. Nielsen, Erin K. Kross, Nicholas L. Smith, Julie C. Hanada, Sean K. Doll O'Mahoney, and J. Randall Curtis, "The Association of Spiritual Care Providers' Activities with Family Members' Satisfaction with Care after a Death in the ICU," *Critical Care Medicine* 42, no. 9 (2014): 1991–2000; Paul S. Bay, Daniel Beckman, James Trippi, Richard Gunderman, and Colin Terry, "The Effect of Pastoral Care Services on Anxiety, Depression, Hope, Religious Coping, and Religious Problem Solving Styles: A Randomized Controlled Study," *Journal of Religion and Health* 47, no. 1 (2008): 57–69.

50. "Objectives and Outcomes for Level I/Level II CPE," ACPE, 2020, https://www .manula.com/manuals/acpe/acpe-manuals/2016/en/topic/objectives-and-outcomes -for-level-i-level-ii-cpe.

51. "Chaplaincy Intro: What Enforcement Chaplains Do," International Conference of Police Chaplains website, accessed January 18, 2021, http://www.icpc4cops .org/chaplaincy-intro/chaplains-work.html.

52. "FBI Chaplains: Bringing the Light in the Darkest Hours," Federal Bureau of Investigation, March 5, 2018, https://www.fbi.gov/news/stories/fbi-chaplains.

53. The Federation of Fire Chaplains, *The Federation of Fire Chaplains Brochure*, 2010, https://ffc.wildapricot.org/resources/Documents/FFC%20brochure-2020.pdf; Federation of Fire Chaplains website, accessed January 21, 2021, https://ffc.wildapricot.org/.

54. "Disaster Relief Chaplaincy," Baptist Convention of New England, accessed January 19, 2021, https://www.bcne.net/chaplain; "Become a Chaplain," Billy Graham Rapid Response Team, accessed January 19, 2021, https://rrt.billygraham.org /become-a-chaplain/; "Meeting Emotional and Spiritual Needs," American Red Cross, 2017, https://www.redcross.org/local/oregon/about-us/news-and-events /news/Meeting-Emotional-and-Spiritual-Needs.html.

55. *Disaster Spiritual Care Standards and Procedures*, American Red Cross, November 2015, https://crisisplumbline.files.wordpress.com/2013/02/dsc-standardsand procedures.pdf.

56. *Disaster Spiritual Care Standards and Procedures*; "Meeting Emotional and Spiritual Needs."

57. Cadge, "God on the Fly?"; Wendy Cadge and Michael Skaggs, "Serving Seafarers in the Boston Harbor: Local Adaptation to Global Economic Change, 1820–2015," *International Journal of Maritime History* 30, no. 2 (2018): 252–65.

58. Cadge, "God on the Fly?"

59. Cadge and Skaggs, "Serving Seafarers in the Boston Harbor."

60. Jeff Finley, "The Truckers' Chaplain," *Light and Life Magazine*, 2013, https:// lightandlifemagazine.com/the-truckers-chaplain/; "TFC Global," Transport for Christ, accessed November 30, 2020, https://tfcglobal.org/; Truckstop Ministries website, accessed November 30, 2020, https://www.truckstopministries.org/; Jessica Wei, "Truckin' on a Prayer: Trucker Chaplains Spread Their Faith on the Highway," *The Guardian*, July 2, 2015, http://www.theguardian.com/world/2015/jul/02 /transport-for-christ-trucker-chaplains.

61. Chad E. Seales, "Corporate Chaplaincy and the American Workplace," *Religion Compass* 6, no. 3 (2012): 195–203.

62. David Miller, Faith Ngunjiri, and James Lorusso, "Human Resources Perceptions of Corporate Chaplains: Enhancing Positive Organizational Culture," *Journal of Management, Spirituality and Religion* 14 (2016): 1–20; Lambert, *Spirituality, Inc.*

63. Miller, Ngunjiri, and Lorusso, "Human Resources Perceptions of Corporate Chaplains."

64. Cadge and Skaggs, "Humanizing Agents of Modern Capitalism?"

65. *Employee Wellness: Mental Health and Workplace Chaplaincy*, Marketplace Chaplains, September 24, 2020, http://1w49192fjz98s4pjl44rqa8u-wpengine .netdna-ssl.com/wp-content/uploads/2020/09/Marketplace-Chaplains-Mental -Health-and-Workplace-Chaplaincy-White-Paper-online.pdf.

66. Miller, Ngunjiri, and Lorusso, "Human Resources Perceptions of Corporate Chaplains."

67. John Schmalzbauer, "Campus Religious Life in America: Revitalization and Renewal," *Society* 50, no. 2 (2013): 115–31.

68. Rebecca Barton, Wendy Cadge, and Elena G. van Stee, "Caring for the Whole Student: How Do Chaplains Contribute to Campus Life?," *Journal of College and Character* 21, no. 2 (2020): 67–85; Elena G. van Stee et al., "Assessing Student Engagement with Campus Chaplains: A Pilot Study From a Residential Liberal Arts College," *Journal of College and Character* 22, no. 3 (2021): 215–238; Schmalzbauer and Mahoney, *Resilience of Religion in American Higher Education*.

69. Barton, Cadge, and van Stee, "Caring for the Whole Student"; Victor Kazanjian, "Spiritual Practices on College and University Campuses: Understanding the Concepts—Broadening the Context," *Journal of College and Character* 14 (2013): 97–104; John Schmalzbauer, "Campus Prophets, Spiritual Guides, or Interfaith Traffic Directors? The Many Lives of College and University Chaplains" (2018); Schmalzbauer and Mahoney, *Resilience of Religion in American Higher Education*; van Stee et al., "Assessing Student Engagement."

70. Seymour A. Smith, *The American College Chaplaincy* (New York: Association Press, 1954); Phillip E. Hammond, *The Campus Clergyman* (New York: Basic Books, 1966).

71. Sophie Gilliat-Ray, *Understanding Muslim Chaplaincy*, Ashgate AHRC/ESRC Religion and Society Series (Burlington, Vt.: Ashgate, 2013); Kowalski and Becker, "Developing Profession"; John Schmalzbauer, "The Evolving Role of the College and University Chaplaincy: Findings from a National Study," 2014, https://www.academia .edu/12868135/The_Evolving_Role_of_the_College_and_University_Chaplaincy_ Findings_from_a_National_Study; van Stee et al., "Assessing Student Engagement."

72. Gilliat-Ray, *Understanding Muslim Chaplaincy*; Shenila Khoja-Moolji, "An Emerging Model of Muslim Leadership: Chaplaincy on University Campuses," 2011, https://www.academia.edu/985836/An_Emerging_Model_of_Muslim_Leadership _Chaplaincy_on_University_Campuses; Kowalski and Becker, "Developing Profession."

73. Barton, Cadge, and van Stee, "Caring for the Whole Student"; Schmalzbauer and Mahoney, *Resilience of Religion in American Higher Education*.

74. van Stee et al., "Assessing Student Engagement."

75. Schmalzbauer, "Evolving Role of the College and University Chaplaincy."

76. Wendy Cadge, Irene Elizabeth Stroud, Patricia K. Palmer, George Fitchett, Trace Haythorn, and Casey Clevenger, "Training Chaplains and Spiritual Caregivers: The Emergence and Growth of Chaplaincy Programs in Theological Education," *Pastoral Psychology* 69, no. 4 (2020): 187–208.

77. *Chaplains' Employment, Responsibilities, and Endorsements*, Program Statement 3939.07, Federal Bureau of Prisons, U.S. Department of Justice, 2001, https://www .bop.gov/policy/progstat/3939_007.pdf; *The Appointment and Service of Chaplains*, Instruction 1304.28, U.S. Department of Defense, May 12, 2021, https://www.esd .whs.mil/Portals/54/Documents/DD/issuances/dodi/130428p.pdf.

78. "Clinical Training Organizations," Chaplaincy Innovation Lab, accessed January 19, 2021, https://chaplaincyinnovation.org/training-credentials /clinical-training-organizations.

79. Gordon J. Hilsman, *How to Get the Most Out of Clinical Pastoral Education: A CPE Primer* (Philadelphia: Jessica Kingsley, 2018).

80. Cadge et al., "Training Healthcare Chaplains."

81. *VA Handbook 5005/135* (Washington, D.C.: Department of Veterans Affairs, 2020).

82. Cadge, "Healthcare Chaplaincy as a Companion Profession."

83. "Certification," Veterans Affairs National Black Chaplains Association, April 20, 2017, https://vablackchaplains.org/certification/; "Application for NAVAC Board Certified Chaplain," NAVAC: The National Association of Veterans Affairs Chaplains, accessed January 18, 2021, https://www.navac.net/board-certified-chaplain; "Objectives and Outcomes for Level I/Level II CPE"; International Conference of Police Chaplains website; "Standards of Practice for Professional Chaplains," Association of Professional Chaplains, 2015, https://www.professionalchaplains.org /content.asp?pl=200&sl=198&contentid=514; "Requirements for Military Specialty Certification," Board of Chaplaincy Certification Inc., accessed January 21, 2021, https://033012b.membershipsoftware.org/content.asp?pl=72&sl=42&contentid=74; "Certification," The American Correctional Chaplains Association, accessed January 21, 2021, https://www.correctionalchaplains.org/certification.htm#BECOMING; Federation of Fire Chaplains, "FFC Training Institute," accessed January 28, 2021, https://ffc.wildapricot.org/Institute.

84. Bilal Ansari, "'Whispers' of Black Exclusion in the ACPE Pacific Region GTU Archives," Medium, November 23, 2018, https://medium.com/@bilalansari/whispers -of-black-exclusion-in-the-acpe-pacific-region-gtu-archives-a41f42a666a3; Gilliat-Ray, *Understanding Muslim Chaplaincy*; Barbara Pesut et al., "Hospitable Hospitals in a Diverse Society: From Chaplains to Spiritual Care Providers," *Journal of Religion and Health* 51, no. 3 (2012): 825–36; Rabbi Bonita E. Taylor and Rabbi David J. Zucker, "Nearly Everything We Wish Our Non-Jewish Supervisors Had Known about Us as Jewish Supervisees," *Journal of Pastoral Care and Counseling* 56, no. 4 (2002): 327–38.

1. Ronald B. Miller, *Facing Human Suffering: Psychology and Psychotherapy as Moral Engagement* (Washington, D.C.: American Psychological Association Press, 2004), 153.

2. D. Musser and Joseph Price, eds., *A New Handbook of Christian Theology* (Nashville: Abingdon, 1992), 219.

3. Miller, *Facing Human Suffering*, 10.

4. Viktor Frankl, *Man's Search for Meaning* (Boston: Beacon Press, 2006), 99.

5. Irvin D. Yalom, *Existential Psychotherapy* (New York: Basic Books, 1980), 8–9.

6. Wendy Cadge and Emily Sigalow, "Negotiating Religious Differences: The Strategies of Interfaith Chaplains in Healthcare," *Journal for the Scientific Study of Religion* 52, no. 1 (2013): 146–58.

7. Regarding the continuum of interreligious care, see Dagmar Grefe, *Encounters for Change: Interreligious Cooperation in the Care of Individuals and Communities* (Eugene, Ore.: Wipf and Stock, 2011), 121–43.

8. Chaplaincy training is beginning to move beyond a focus on only human suffering and flourishing to include a focus on nature's suffering and flourishing, with humans as part of that. See Andy S. Calder and Jan E. Morgan, "'Out of the Whirlwind': Clinical Pastoral Education and Climate Change," *Journal of Pastoral Care and Counseling* 70, no. 1 (2016): 16–25.

CHAPTER 3

1. In this chapter, the term "chaplain" is used rather than "spiritual care provider," and the term "careseeker" is used to reflect not only those who seek care but also care recipients and the like.

2. The case is a composite based loosely on experiences of chaplains in different settings.

3. Kenneth I. Pargament, *Spiritually Integrated Psychotherapy: Understanding and Addressing the Sacred* (New York: Guilford Press, 2011).

4. This idea is similar to a Muslim's awareness of individual responsibilities (*fard al 'ein*) and communal responsibilities (*fard al kifaya*). See Umar F. Abd-Allah, "Living Islam with Purpose," 14, accessed October 23, 2020, https://static1.squarespace.com/static/54eb86afe4b0b896afa4080a/t/58dc25766a4963e5f5beoc50/1490822557426/Living+Islam+with+Purpose.pdf.

5. Shari Geller, *A Practical Guide to Cultivating Therapeutic Presence* (Washington, D.C.: APA, 2017), 31–41.

6. Carl Rogers, *Client-Centered Therapy*, 3rd ed. (Boston: Houghton-Mifflin, 1956).

7. James Hillman, *Insearch: Psychology and Religion*, 2nd rev. ed. (Woodstock, Conn.: Spring Publications, 1996), 31.

8. Thich Nhất Hanh, *The Heart of the Buddha's Teaching: Transforming Suffering into Peace, Joy and Liberation; the Four Noble Truths, the Noble Eightfold Path, and Other Basic Buddhist Teachings* (New York: Harmony, 1999).

9. Gabriel Fackre, "Ministry as Presence," in *Dictionary of Pastoral Care and*

Counseling, ed. R. Hunter (Nashville: Abingdon, 1990), 950–51; Matthew 25:35–36 and Philippians 2:6–11.

10. Hans Wehr and J. Milton Cowan, *Arabic-English Dictionary: The Hans Wehr Dictionary of Modern Written Arabic* (Ithaca: Spoken Language Services, 1976), 214–16.

11. Rabbi Dayle A. Friedman, ed., *Jewish Pastoral Care: A Practical Handbook from Traditional and Contemporary Sources* (Woodstock, Vt.: Jewish Lights, 2001), 56–60.

12. Wehr and Cowan, *Arabic-English Dictionary*, 588–89.

13. Daniel Goleman, *Social Intelligence* (New York: Bantam, 2006); Daniel Goleman, *Emotional Intelligence* (New York: Bantam, 1995).

14. Geller, *Practical Guide to Cultivating Therapeutic Presence.* Many of her insights are applicable to spiritual care and are utilized for this chapter.

15. Edwin Friedman, *Generation to Generation* (New York: Guilford Press, 2011).

16. Geller, *Practical Guide to Cultivating Therapeutic Presence*, 50, 58.

17. In Muslim practice, *niyyah* emphasizes the priority of the intention of one's heart for right action. Buddhism similarly prioritizes the importance of intention for right action.

18. Abu Hamid Al-Ghazali, *Al-Ghazali on Disciplining the Soul and on Breaking the Two Desires: Books XXII and XXIII of the Revival of the Religious Sciences (Ihya' 'ulum al-Din)*, trans. T. J. Winter, 2nd ed. (Cambridge: Islamic Texts Society, 2016).

19. Sherman Jackson, *Sufism for Non-Sufis: Ibn 'Atā' Allāh al-Sakandarî's Tâj al-'arûs* (New York: Oxford University Press, 2012), 45, 113.

20. Froma Walsh, ed., *Spiritual Resources in Family Therapy*, 2nd ed. (New York: Guilford Press, 2009), 100.

21. Herschel Knapp, *Therapeutic Communication*, 2nd ed. (London, UK: Sage, 2015).

22. Mattson illustrates this summarizing practice as a scriptural example of validating and normalizing marginalized voices. Ingrid Mattson, *The Story of the Qur'an: Its History and Place in Muslim Life*, 2nd ed. (West Sussex, UK: Wiley-Blackwell, 2013), 2–3.

23. An Islamic scriptural example of directive communication as an intervention for marginalized voices experiencing deep emotional duress can be found in Mattson, 2.

24. Eboo Patel, *Interfaith Leadership* (Boston: Beacon Press, 2016), 36.

25. Anton T. Boisen, *The Exploration of the Inner World: A Study of Mental Disorder and Religious Experience* (New York: Harper and Brothers, 1936), 185.

26. See Ursula Riedel-Pfaefflin and Julia Strecker, *Fluegel Trotz Allem: Feministische Seelsorge und Beratung, Konzeption, Methoden, Biographien*, 2nd ed. (Guetersloh: Guetersloher, 1999); and Elsie Jones-Smith, *Strength-Based Therapy* (New York: Sage, 2014).

27. Emmanuel Yartekwei Lartey, *In Living Color: An Intercultural Approach to Pastoral Care and Counseling*, 2nd ed. (London: Jessica Kingsley, 2003).

28. Wendy Cadge and Emily Sigalow, "Negotiating Religious Differences: The Strategies of Interfaith Chaplains in Healthcare," *Journal for the Scientific Study of Religion* 52, no. 1 (2013): 146–58.

29. Maurianne Adams and Khyati Y. Joshi, "Religious Oppression," in *Teaching for Diversity and Social Justice*, ed. Maurianne Adams and Lee Anne Bell (New York: Routledge, 2016), 257.

30. Pargament, *Spiritually Integrated Psychotherapy*; Kenneth Pargament, Margaret Feuille, and Donna Burdzy, "The Brief RCOPE: Current Psychometric Status of a Short Measure of Religious Coping," *Religions* 2, no. 1 (2011), 51–76.

31. Frankl, *Man's Search for Meaning*.

32. Pargament, Feuille, and Burdzy, "Brief RCOPE."

33. Stefanie M. Monod, Eteinne Rochat, Christophe J. Büla, Guy Jobin, Estelle Martin, and Brenda Spencer, "The Spiritual Distress Assessment Tool: An Instrument to Assess Spiritual Distress in Hospitalised Elderly Persons," *BMC Geriatrics* 10, no. 1 (2010): 88.

34. Julie Taylor, "Spiritual First Aid," in *Disaster Spiritual Care*, ed. Willard Ashley and Stephen Roberts (Nashville: Skylight, 2008): 128–141.

CHAPTER 4

1. This clinical anecdote was adapted from Duane R. Bidwell, "Toward an Adequate 'Pneumatraumatology': Understanding the Spiritual Impact of Traumatic Injury," *Journal of Pastoral Care and Counseling* 52, no. 2 (2002): 135–43. Like all clinical anecdotes in this chapter, the person's name and identifying details have been changed to protect privacy.

2. Simon Lasair, "A Narrative Approach to Spirituality and Spiritual Care in Health Care," *Journal of Religion and Health* 59, no. 3 (2020): 1524–40, 1525.

3. Steven. J. Sandage, David Rupert, George S. Stavros, and Nancy G. Devor, *Relational Spirituality in Psychotherapy: Healing Suffering and Promoting Growth* (Washington, D.C.: American Psychological Association, 2020), 150.

4. See Duane R. Bidwell, *When One Religion Isn't Enough: The Lives of Spiritually Fluid People* (Boston: Beacon Press, 2018).

5. Daniel S. Schipani, "Pastoral and Spiritual Care in Multifaith Contexts," in *Teaching for a Multifaith World*, ed. Eleazar S. Fernandez (Eugene, Ore.: Pickwick, 2017), 127, 132.

6. John J. Thatamanil, *Circling the Elephant: A Comparative Theology of Religious Diversity* (New York: Fordham University Press, 2020), 156–59.

7. Thatamanil, *Circling the Elephant*, 170–80.

8. Cecilia chose her own pseudonym and gave permission to share her story. Some details are changed to better protect her identity.

9. Lasair, "Narrative Approach to Spirituality and Spiritual Care," 1524–40.

10. Jonathan Morgan and Steven J. Sandage, "A Developmental Model of Interreligious Competence: A Conceptual Framework," *Archive for the Psychology of Religion* 38, no. 2 (2016): 129–58.

11. See Kenneth I. Pargament, *Spiritually Integrated Psychotherapy: Understanding and Addressing the Sacred* (New York: Guilford Press, 2011).

12. See Mary M. Solberg, *Compelling Knowledge: A Feminist Proposal for an Epistemology of the Cross* (Albany: State University of New York Press, 1997), 125–38.

13. Elizabeth Liebert, "The Role of Practice in the Study of Christian Spirituality," *Spiritus: A Journal of Christian Spirituality* 2, no. 1 (2002): 30–49.

14. Sandage, Rupert, Stavros, and Devor, *Relational Spirituality in Psychotherapy*, 131.

15. Duane R. Bidwell, *Short-Term Spiritual Guidance* (Minneapolis: Fortress Press, 2004), 13–25.

16. Sandage, Rupert, Stavros, and Devor, *Relational Spirituality in Psychotherapy*, 148.

17. Sandage, Rupert, Stavros, and Devor, 148.

18. Code of Ethics of Professional Chaplains, accessed May 28, 2021, https://www.professionalchaplains.org/Files/professional_standards/professional_ethics/apc_code_of_ethics.pdf.

19. Sandage, Rupert, Stavros, and Devor, *Relational Spirituality in Psychotherapy*, 129.

20. Kathleen J. Greider, "Soul Care amid Religious Plurality: Excavating an Emerging Dimension of Multicultural Challenge and Competence," in *Women Out of Order: Risking Change and Creating Care in a Multicultural World*, ed. Jeanne Stevenson-Moessner and Teresa Snorton (Minneapolis: Fortress Press, 2010), 310–13.

21. Greider, 303–11.

22. Greider, 309–10.

23. Sandage, Rupert, Stavros, and Devor, *Relational Spirituality in Psychotherapy*, 149–50.

CHAPTER 5

1. Sexual assaults on the campuses of elite boarding schools in the Northeast in particular have garnered public attention since 2015, when news broke of a possible sexual assault at St. Paul's School in New Hampshire. The resulting trial of Owen Labrie received intense news coverage; following his conviction, Chessy Prout, the victim in the case, came forward publicly and published a book about her experiences. Several years later, Lacy Crawford also published a memoir about St. Paul's, documenting her experience not just of sexual assault but also of a systemic coverup by the school administration. Crawford's and Prout's experiences echo those of many others, as documented most extensively in the *Boston Globe*'s "Private Schools, Painful Secrets" report, which interviewed over two hundred victims at various elite boarding schools throughout the United States. See Chessy Prout and Jenn Abelson, *I Have a Right To: A High School Survivor's Story of Sexual Assault, Justice, and Hope* (New York: Margaret K. McElderry Books, 2018); Lacy Crawford, *Notes on a Silencing* (New York: Little Brown, 2020); and Spotlight Report, "Private Schools, Painful Secrets," *Boston Globe*, May 6, 2016, https://www.bostonglobe.com/metro/2016/05/06/private-schools-painful-secrets/OaRI9PFpRnCTJxCzko5hkN/story.html.

2. International Women's Day website, accessed March 15, 2020, https://www.internationalwomensday.com/.

3. For a more expansive consideration of liminal experiences in individuals, groups, and societies over varying periods of time, see the work of Victor Turner, particularly *Ritual Process: Structure and Anti-structure* (New York: Routledge, 2017). See also Bjørn Thomassen, "The Uses and Meanings of Liminality," *International Political Anthropology* 2, no. 1 (2009): 16–28.

4. For a book-length Christian theological consideration of liminality in relation to

the space between life and death and the liturgical time known as Holy Saturday, see Shelly Rambo, *Spirit and Trauma: A Theology of Remaining* (Louisville: Westminster John Knox Press, 2010).

5. For a book-length exploration on the effects of trauma on the self, see Susan J. Brison, *Aftermath* (Princeton: Princeton University Press, 2003).

6. For a consideration of how the origins of a culture can result in collective trauma that affects the trajectory of the country as well as the perception of one's belonging in it, see Susan Abraham's case study of the origins of modern-day India in "Traumas of Belonging: Imagined Communities of Nation, Religion, and Gender in Modernity," in *Post-traumatic Public Theology*, ed. Stephanie N. Arel and Shelly Rambo (Cham, Switz.: Palgrave Macmillan, 2016), 267–90.

7. For a selection of articles on chaplaincy at Ground Zero, see the research of Storm Swain, in particular *Trauma and Transformation at Ground Zero: A Pastoral Theology* (Minneapolis: Fortress Press, 2011) and "The T. Mort. Chaplaincy at Ground Zero: Presence and Privilege on Holy Ground," *Journal of Religion and Health* 50, no. 3 (2011): 481–98.

8. For a selection of articles profiling chaplaincy during COVID-19, see Emma Goldberg, "Hospital Chaplains Try to Keep the Faith during Coronavirus Pandemic," *New York Times*, April 11, 2020, https://www.nytimes.com/2020/04/11 /health/coronavirus-chaplains-hospitals.html; Bari Weiss, "The Men and Women Who Run toward the Dying," *New York Times*, April 3, 2020, https://www.nytimes .com/2020/04/03/opinion/coronavirus-hospitals-chaplains.html; and Wendy Cadge, "The Rise of the Chaplains," *The Atlantic*, May 17, 2020, https://www.theatlantic.com /ideas/archive/2020/05/why-americans-are-turning-chaplains-during-pandemic /611767/.

9. Less socially complicated and traumatic situations may be painful on the local or personal level but possess minimal concern from the perspective of social stigma and care practices. The spiritual care response to these circumstances may still address complexities in grief, loss, and trauma but do not require the chaplain to navigate the social aspects of ill will and the suffering caused by it.

10. John Swinton writes more extensively about the value of lament as a constructive way to address suffering, particularly relying on the psalms as a biblical source of solidarity in lament, in *Raging with Compassion: Pastoral Responses to the Problem of Evil* (Grand Rapids, Mich.: Eerdmans, 2007).

11. The term "careseeker" is being used here instead of the word "patient." The term "careseeker" is more active, more central, and less objectified, as being only the receiver is to be compliant or noncompliant with a medical or professional team.

12. These rituals can function as "a leveling process [that] brings about the dissolution of structure, the absence of social distinctions, a homogenization of roles, the disappearance of political allegiance, the breakdown of regular borders and barriers. With the suspension of status distinctions, human beings recognize the core humanity they share. Relationships are immediate and spontaneous, of Buber's 'I-Thou' type. Communitas strives for release from daily obligations and requirements, and seeks universalism and openness." See Jeffrey Rubenstein, "Purim, Liminality, and Communitas," *AJS Review* 17, no. 2 (1992): 251.

13. *Tzaraat*, a Jewish concept that reflects an in-between state of affliction, is relevant here and will be discussed in depth later in this chapter.

14. Rochelle Robins, "Tzaraat: A Case for Support of Opposition," Academy for Jewish Religion of California, March 28, 2014, https://ajrca.edu/parsha/parshat-tazria-2/.

15. Samson Raphael Hirsch, *The Chumash Trumath Tzvi: The Torah with a Timeless Commentary* (New York: Judaica/J Levine Millennium, 2012). Direct quote extracted from Robins, "Tzaraat." Tamara Eskenzi wrote, "This means that the ordination of the priest and purification of the formerly infected individual share some fundamental and unique features. Such parallels express a profound statement about the rehabilitation of the person who had been excluded." See "Reading the Bible as a Healing Text," in *Healing and the Jewish Imagination: Spiritual and Practical Perspectives on Judaism and Health*, ed. William Cutter (Woodstock, Vt.: Jewish Lights, 2007), 86.

16. Yael Danieli and Kathleen Nader, "Respecting Cultural, Religious and Ethnic Differences in the Prevention and Treatment of Psychological Sequelae," in *Group Approaches to Terrorist Disasters*, ed. Leon Schein, Henry I. Spitz, Gary Burlingame, and Phillip R. Muskin (New York: Haworth Press, 2006), 203–34.

17. Mary Douglas, *Purity and Danger: An Analysis of the Concepts of Pollution and Taboo* (New York: Routledge Classics, 2002).

18. Rabbi Stacey Peterson quoted in in Alissa Wilkinson, "Why Christians Keep Appropriating Jewish Ritual Symbols: The Difference between Religious Exchange and Appropriation, according to a Rabbi," Vox, January 15, 2021, https://www.vox .com/22229063/judaism-christian-evangelical-shofar-jericho-seder.

INTRODUCTION TO INTERPERSONAL COMPETENCIES

1. Allison L. Baier, Alexander C. Kline, and Norah C. Feeny, "Therapeutic Alliance as a Mediator of Change: A Systematic Review and Evaluation of Research," *Clinical Psychology Review* 82, no. 12 (2020): 1–14.

2. Winnifred Fallers Sullivan, *A Ministry of Presence: Chaplaincy, Spiritual Care, and the Law* (Chicago: University of Chicago Press, 2014).

3. As described in the first two chapters, chaplains are also active in educational contexts that may include religiously sponsored K–12 schools, state and local police and fire departments, government contexts (for example, the U.S. Senate chaplain), disaster relief (Red Cross and FEMA), homeless shelters, ports and airports, sports teams, and many other religiously diverse contexts.

4. *CASC/ACSS Policy and Procedure Manual*, Canadian Association for Spiritual Care, 2016, https://spiritualcare.ca/members/manual-2/.

CHAPTER 6

1. Doehring draws upon trauma research to describe the role of spiritual practices in searching for meanings, illustrating how listening to sacred music revealed meanings as she grieved the death by suicide of her second son, in Carrie Doehring, "Searching for Wholeness amidst Traumatic Grief: The Role of Spiritual Practices

That Reveal Compassion in Embodied, Relational, and Transcendent Ways," *Pastoral Psychology* 68, no. 3 (2019): 241–59.

2. Hisham Abu-Raiya, Kenneth I. Pargament, and Julie J. Exline, "Understanding and Addressing Religious and Spiritual Struggles in Health Care," *Health and Social Work* 40, no. 4 (2015): 126–34.

3. The case study is adapted from course materials created by Duane R. Bidwell, PhD, Claremont School of Theology at Willamette University.

4. Kenneth Pargament, Kavita M. Desai, and Kelly M. McConnell, "Spirituality: A Pathway to Posttraumatic Growth or Decline?," in *Handbook of Posttraumatic Growth: Research and Practice*, ed. Lawrence G. Calhoun and Richard G. Tedeschi (Mahwah, N.J.: Erlbaum, 2006), 130.

5. Murray Bowen, *Family Therapy in Clinical Practice* (New York: Jason Aronson, 1978).

6. David Schnarch and Susan Regas, "The Crucible Differentiation Scale: Assessing Differentiation in Human Relationships," *Journal of Marital and Family Therapy* 38, no. 4 (2012): 639. Their scale measures these components of self-differentiation: Solid Self, Connectedness, Anxiety Regulation through Self-Soothing, Anxiety Regulation through Accommodation, Reactivity through Avoidance, Reactivity through Arguments, and Tolerating Discomfort for Growth.

7. Schnarch and Regas, 642.

8. Schnarch and Regas, 641. The quotes in the rest of this paragraph are from this page.

9. When academic degree programs do not include courses in comparative studies of religion supporting interreligious practices, students and religious leaders may perpetuate spiritual harm through interreligious naïveté. For an introduction to how comparative studies shape interreligious dialogue, see Paul Hedges, *Controversies in Interreligious Dialogue and the Theology of Religions* (London: SCM Press, 2010).

10. Building on developmental assessments of intercultural competency, Morgan and Sandage have proposed a theoretical model of interreligious competency (IRC) where people have a greater capacity for spiritual empathy and "complexity in understanding (a) one's own religiosity, and (b) other religious perspectives." Jonathan Morgan and Steven J. Sandage, "A Developmental Model of Interreligious Competence," *Archiv für Religionspsychologie / Archive for the Psychology of Religion* 38, no. 2 (2016): 144.

11. Marianne Moyaert, "Recent Developments in the Theology of Interreligious Dialogue: From Soteriological Openness to Hermeneutical Openness," *Modern Theology* 28, no. 1 (2012): 25–52; Hedges, *Controversies in Interreligious Dialogue*.

12. Stephen Prothero, *God Is Not One: The Eight Rival Religions That Run the World and Why Their Differences Matter* (New York: HarperOne, 2010).

13. See Linda S. Golding and Walter Dixon, *Spiritual Care for Non-communicative Patients: A Guidebook* (London: Jessica Kingsley, 2019).

14. Thatamanil describes how religions provide "interpretive schemes" for understanding suffering and "therapeutic regimens" for spiritual practices and rituals that help people experience a transcendent sense of trust. He describes interreligious learning as a process of cocreating meanings in an ongoing process of interreligious

learning. John J. Thatamanil, *Circling the Elephant: A Comparative Theology of Religious Diversity* (New York: Fordham University Press, 2020). The relevance of Thatamanil's scholarship is explored further in chapter 4.

15. Doehring uses process theologies to define and describe agential and receptive power in spiritual care relationships. See chapter 2 in Carrie Doehring, *The Practice of Pastoral Care: A Postmodern Approach*, rev. and exp. ed. (Louisville: Westminster John Knox Press, 2015), 45.

16. For a complete description of communication styles and skills, see chapter 3 in Doehring, *Practice of Pastoral Care.*

17. Jean Decety, "Dissecting the Neural Mechanisms Mediating Empathy," *Emotion Review* 3, no. 1 (2011): 92–108.

18. Elizabeth A. Segal, Karen E. Gerdes, Cynthia A. Lietz, M. Alex Wagaman, and Jennifer M. Geiger, eds., *Assessing Empathy* (New York: Columbia University Press, 2017), 12.

19. Doehring has used the term "theological empathy" to describe imagining another's lived theology or theological orientation to a particular stressor. See Carrie Doehring, "Teaching Theological Empathy to Distance Learners of Intercultural Spiritual Care," *Pastoral Psychology* 67, no. 5 (2018): 461–74.

20. Intersectional theory was first defined and elaborated by Kimberlé Crenshaw, "Mapping the Margins: Intersectionality, Identity Politics, and Violence against Women of Color," *Stanford Law Review* 43, no. 6 (1991): 1241–99.

21. Chanequa Walker-Barnes, *I Bring the Voices of My People: A Womanist Vision for Racial Reconciliation* (Grand Rapids, Mich.: Eerdmans, 2019); Phillis I. Sheppard, "Building Communities of Embodied Beauty," in *Black Practical Theology*, ed. Dale P. Andrews and Robert London Smith Jr. (Waco, Tex.: Baylor University Press, 2015), 97–111.

22. See, for example, Phillis I. Sheppard, "Mourning the Loss of Cultural Selfobjects: Black Embodiment and Religious Experience after Trauma," *Practical Theology* 1, no. 2 (2008): 233–57.

23. Lizardy-Hajbi uses the term "'post/decolonial' in order to acknowledge both the separate contextual and theoretical streams from which challenges to coloniality have arisen in the literature, as well as to highlight their common foundational aims as critiques to colonial being-thinking-acting." Kristina I. Lizardy-Hajbi, "Frameworks toward Post/Decolonial Pastoral Leaderships," *Journal of Religious Leadership* 19, no. 2 (2020): 98–128.

24. Lizardy-Hajbi, "Frameworks toward Post/Decolonial Pastoral Leaderships," 99.

25. "Settler colonialism, on the other hand, often involves the movement of large numbers of people from the colonizing country to the colony, imposing the colonizers' military, economic, and administrative patterns on the colony." Lizardy-Hajbi, 101.

26. Lizardy-Hajbi, 102.

27. Larry Kent Graham, *Moral Injury: Restoring Wounded Souls* (Nashville: Abingdon, 2017), 139, 44.

28. Kathleen J. Greider, "Religious Location and Counseling: Engaging Diversity

and Difference in Views of Religion," in *Understanding Pastoral Counseling*, ed. Elizabeth A. Maynard and Jill L. Snodgrass (New York: Spring, 2015), 235–56.

29. See Graham, *Moral Injury*; Melinda McGarrah Sharp, *Creating Resistances: Pastoral Care in a Postcolonial World* (Boston: Brill, 2019); Richard Coble, *The Chaplain's Presence and Medical Power: Rethinking Loss in the Hospital System* (Lanham, Md.: Lexington Books, 2018); Nancy J. Ramsay, ed., *Pastoral Theology and Care: Critical Trajectories in Theory and Practice* (Chichester, UK: Wiley Blackwell, 2018); and Emmanuel Lartey, "Postcolonializing Pastoral Theology: Enhancing the Intercultural Paradigm," in Ramsay, *Pastoral Theology and Care*, 79–97.

30. Greider, "Religious Location and Counseling," 248.

31. Greider, 249.

32. Kenneth Pargament, Serena Wong, and Julie Exline, "Wholeness and Holiness: The Spiritual Dimension of Eudaimonics," in *The Handbook of Eudaimonic Wellbeing*, ed. J. Vitterso (Tromsø, Nor.: Springer, 2016), 379–94.

33. Michele Shields, Allison Kestenbaum, and Laura B. Dunn, "Spiritual AIM and the Work of the Chaplain: A Model for Assessing Spiritual Needs and Outcomes in Relationship," *Palliative and Supportive Care* 13, no. 1 (2015): 78.

34. George Fitchett, Anna Lee Hisey Pierson, Christine Hoffmeyer, Dirk Labuschagne, Aoife Lee, Stacie Lavine, Sean O'Mahony, Karen Pugliese, and Nancy Waite, "Development of the PC-7, a Quantifiable Assessment of Spiritual Concerns of Patients Receiving Palliative Care Near the End of Life," *Journal of Palliative Medicine* 23, no. 2 (2020): 248–53.

CHAPTER 7

1. Peter VanKatwyk, *Spiritual Care and Therapy: Integrative Perspectives* (Waterloo, Ont.: WLU Press, 2003).

2. College of Registered Psychotherapists of Ontario (CRPO), *CRPO Competency Profile* (Toronto, Ont.: CRPO, 2015). For more on a definition of competency in spiritual care, especially the role of interpersonal skills, see Thomas St. James O'Connor and Sylvia Davis, "Roll of the Dice and Running the Gauntlet: Critical Examination of the Praxis of the CAPPE National Certification Appearance," *Pastoral Sciences*, Fall 1999, 91–100.

3. CRPO, *CRPO Competency Profile*; also see Erin Snyder, Ayse Erenay, Thomas St. James O'Connor, Colleen Dotzert, Stephanie Hong, Ruth Smith, Lisa Dolson, and Michael P. Foulger, "Evidence-Based Spiritual Care Practice in the Canadian Context: Twenty Years Later," *Journal of Pastoral Care and Counseling* 73, no. 2 (2019): 88–95.

4. Carrie Doehring, *The Practice of Pastoral Care: A Postmodern Approach*, rev. and exp. ed. (Louisville: Westminster John Knox Press, 2015).

5. Doehring, *Practice of Pastoral Care*.

6. Emmanuel Yartekwei Lartey, *In Living Color: Intercultural Approach to Pastoral Care and Counseling* (Philadelphia: Jessica Kingsley, 2003).

7. Thomas St. James O'Connor and Elizabeth Meakes, "Hope in the Midst of Challenge: Evidence-Based Pastoral Care," *Journal of Pastoral Care and Counseling* 52, no. 4 (Winter 1998): 359–68.

8. VanKatwyk, *Spiritual Care and Therapy*.

9. Thomas St. James O'Connor, Elizabeth Meakes, Marlene Bourdeau, Pam Mc-Carroll-Butler, and Maria Papp, "Diversity in the Pastoral Relationship: An Evaluation of the Helping Styles Inventory," *Journal of Pastoral Care and Counseling* 49, no. 4 (Winter 1995): 365–375.

10. This composite case study is loosely based on a spiritual care relationship between chaplain residents and patients in a CPE residency with coauthor Michelle Kirby as the educator.

11. Alex is a derivative of Alejandro, his Latino name. In the military, and by extension in the VA, many service members choose to anglicize their names.

12. See Lynne Mikulak, "Spirituality Groups," in *Professional Spiritual and Pastoral Care: A Practical Clergy and Chaplain's Handbook*, ed. Stephen B. Roberts (Woodstock, Vt.: SkyLight Paths, 2012), 193–208.

13. See Richard Roukema, *Counseling for the Soul in Distress: What Every Religious Counselor Should Know about Emotional and Mental Illness* (New York: Psychology Press, 2003).

14. For more information on the Columbia-Suicide Severity Rating Scale, see https://cssrs.columbia.edu/.

15. Stephen Stratton, "Mindfulness Contemplation: Secular Religious Traditions in Western Context," *Counseling and Values* 60, no. 1 (April 2015): 100–118.

16. Dana D. Colgan, Helané Wahbeh, Mollie Pleet, Kristen Besler, and Michael Christopher, "A Qualitative Study of Mindfulness among Veterans with Posttraumatic Stress Disorder: Practices Differentially Affect Symptoms, Aspects of Well-Being, and Potential Mechanisms of Action," *Journal of Evidenced-Based Complementary and Alternative Medicine* 22, no. 3 (July 2017): 482–93.

17. Benjamin Hall, Jon R. Webb, and Jameson K. Hirsch, "Spirituality and Suicidal Behavior: The Mediating Role of Self-Forgiveness and Psychache," *Psychology of Religion and Spirituality* 12, no. 1 (February 2020): 36–44.

18. Hall, Webb, and Hirsch, 36.

19. National Institute for Mental Health Database, 2020, https://www.nimh.nih .gov/.

20. GC InfoBase, Government of Canada, 2020, https://www.tbs-sct.gc.ca/ems -sgd/edb-bdd/index-eng.html.

21. Jennifer Buchman-Schmidt, Austin J. Gallyer, and Carol Chui, "Military Suicide Research Consortium Common Data Elements: Bifactor Analysis and Longitudinal Predictive Ability of Suicidal Ideation and Suicide Attempts within a Clinical Sample," *Psychological Assessment* 32, no. 7 (Jul 2020): 609–21.

22. Hall, Webb, and Hirsch, "Spirituality and Suicidal Behavior."

23. Renee Bazley and Kenneth Packenham, "Perspectives on Suicide and Suicide Prevention among Members of Christian Faith-Based Organizations," *Spirituality in Clinical Practice* 6, no. 1 (2019): 5–14.

24. Paul Tillich, *The Courage to Be* (New Haven: Yale University Press, 1952).

25. Susan L. Nelson, "Facing Evil: Evil's Many Faces: Five Paradigms for Understanding Evil," *Interpretation* 57, no. 4 (2003): 403.

26. Nelson, 407.

27. Viktor Frankl, *Man's Search for Meaning* (Boston: Beacon Press, 1992).

28. John O'Donohue, *Anam Cara (Soul Friend): Book on Celtic Wisdom* (New York: Random House, 1998).

29. Pam McCarroll and Helen Cheung, "Re-imaging Hope in the Care of Souls: Literature Review Redefining Hope," in *Psychotherapy: Cure of the Soul*, ed. Thomas St. James O'Connor, Kristine Lund, and Patricia Berendsen (Waterloo, Ont.: Waterloo Lutheran Seminary, 2014), 97–108.

30. McCarroll and Cheung, "Re-imaging Hope."

31. Harold G. Koenig, Donna Ames, Nagy A. Youssef, John P. Oliver, Fred Volk, Ellen J. Teng, Kerry Haynes, Zachary D. Erikson, Irina Arnold, Keisha O'Garo, and Michelle Pearce, "The Moral Injury Symptom Scale–Military Version," *Journal of Religion and Health* 57, no. 1 (2018): 249–65.

32. Michele Shields, Allison Kestenbaum, and Laura B. Dunn, "Spiritual AIM and the Work of the Chaplain: A Model for Assessing Spiritual Needs and Outcomes in Relationship," *Palliative and Supportive Care* 13, no. 1 (2015): 75–89.

33. Alan Wolfelt, *Reframing PTSD as Traumatic Grief: How Caregivers Can Companion Traumatized Grievers through Catch-Up Mourning* (Fort Collins, Colo.: Companion Press, 2014).

34. Karen McClintock, *Sexual Shame: An Urgent Call to Healing* (Minneapolis: Fortress Press, 2001).

35. For VA resources on military sexual trauma, see https://www.mentalhealth.va.gov/mentalhealth/msthome/index.asp.

36. Sonia Waters, *Addiction and Pastoral Care* (Grand Rapids, Mich.: Eerdmans, 2019).

37. Larry Kent Graham, *Moral Injury: Restoring Wounded Souls* (Nashville: Abingdon, 2017).

38. "The Twelve Steps of Alcoholics Anonymous," Alcoholics Anonymous (AA), accessed October 31, 2020, http://aa.org/assests/en.US/smf-121.en.pdf.

39. Michelle Clearly and Sandra Thomas, "Addiction and Mental Health across the Lifespan: An Overview of Some Contemporary Issues," *Issues in Mental Health Nursing* 38, no. 1 (2018): 2–8.

40. Gabor Mate, *In the Realm of Hungry Ghosts: Encounters with Addiction* (Toronto: Random House, 2018).

41. The steps quoted here are published by Alcoholics Anonymous. While many individual members of twelve-step organizations object to the male-identifying and theistic God language of the steps, the organization has chosen to retain the original wording. See "The Twelve Steps of Alcoholics Anonymous."

42. J. Scott Tonigan, Elizabeth McCallion, Tessa Frohe, and Matthew Pearson, "Lifetime Alcoholics Anonymous Attendance as a Predictor of Spiritual Gains in the Relapse Replication and Extension Project (RREP)," *Psychology of Addictive Behaviors* 31, no. 1 (2017): 54–60.

43. Patricia Erickson, Jennifer Butters, and Krystina Walko, "CAMH and Harm Reduction: A Background Paper on Its Meaning and Application for Substance Abuse Issues," Addiction, Pain and Public Health, 2005, http://www.doctordeluca.com. For background on definitions of addictions, see David Smith, "Editor's Note: The

Process Addictions and the New ASAM Definition of Addiction," *Journal of Psychoactive Drugs* 44, no. 1 (2012): 1–4.

44. Mate, *In the Realm of Hungry Ghosts*.

45. Megan E. Laffey, Jeffery P. Bjorck, and Joseph M. Currier, "Coping and Quality of Life in Veterans with Chronic Posttraumatic Stress Disorder," *Traumatology* 26, no. 2 (June 2020): 215–226.

26. Also see Whiney S. Livingston, Jeffery D. Fargo, Adi V. Gundlapali, Emily Brignone, and Rebecca K. Blais, "Comorbid PTSD and Depression Diagnoses Mediate the Association of Military Sexual Trauma and Suicide and Intentional Self-Inflicted Injury in VHA-Enrolled Iraq/Afghanistan Veterans, 2004–2014," *Journal of Affective Disorders* 274 (2020): 1184–90.

46. Patricia Berendsen, "Supporting the Integration of the Body into Psychotherapy and Trauma Treatment," in *Psychotherapy: Cure of the Soul*, ed. Thomas O'Connor, Kristine Lund, and Patricia Berendsen (Waterloo, Ont.: Waterloo Lutheran Seminary, 2014), 121.

47. Peter A. Levine, *Healing Trauma: A Pioneering Program for Restoring the Wisdom of Your Body* (Boulder, Colo.: Sounds True, 2008). Also see B. van der Kolk, *The Body Keeps the Score: Brain, Mind and Body in the Healing of Trauma* (New York: Viking, 2014).

48. Shelly Rambo, *Resurrecting Wounds: Living in the Afterlife of Trauma* (Waco, Tex.: Baylor University Press, 2017). Also see Alida van Dijk and Dan Brister, "Thriving after Trauma: How a Past Trauma Can Be Transformed into a Hopeful Future," in *Thriving on the Edge: Integrating Spiritual Practice, Theory and Research,* ed. Angela Schmidt, Thomas O'Connor, Michael Chow, and Patricia Berendsen (Oakville, Ont.: CASC, 2016), 243–53.

49. Carrie Doehring, "Searching for Wholeness amidst Traumatic Grief: The Role of Spiritual Practices That Reveal Compassion in Embodied, Relational, and Transcendent Ways," *Pastoral Psychology* 68, no. 3 (2019): 241–59. Also see Berendsen, "Supporting the Integration of the Body."

50. See Berendsen, "Supporting the Integration of the Body"; and Levine, *Healing Trauma*.

51. Peter VanKatwyk believes that Carl Rogers's three attributes of unconditional positive regard, empathy, and congruence are foundational for a spiritual care relationship and for the Helping Styles Inventory. VanKatwyk, *Spiritual Care and Therapy*. Rogers also believes that these skills and attitudes are crucial to healthy relationships and persons. See Rogers, *On Becoming a Person* (Boston: Houghton Mifflin, 1961).

52. Carrie Doehring, "Military Moral Injury: Evidence-Based and Intercultural Approach to Spiritual Care," *Pastoral Psychology* 67, no. 1 (2018): 15–30.

53. Murray Bowen, *Family Therapy in Clinical Practice* (Lanham, Md.: Rowman and Littlefield, 1978). Also see Edwin Freidman, *Generation to Generation* (New York: Guilford Press, 2011).

54. Berendsen, "Supporting the Integration of the Body."

55. Nafsin Nizum, Rosanra Yoon, Laura Ferreira-Legere, Nancy Poole, and Zainab Lulat, "Nursing Interventions for Adults Following a Mental Health Crisis: Systematic

Review Guided by Trauma-Informed Principles," *International Journal of Mental Health Nursing* 29, no. 3 (June 2020): 348–73.

56. Christine A. Courtois, "First, Do No More Harm: Ethics of Attending to Spiritual Issues in Trauma Treatment," in *Spiritually Oriented Psychotherapy for Trauma*, ed. Donald F. Walker, Christine A. Courtois, and Jamie D. Aten (Washington, D.C.: American Psychological Association, 2015), 55–75.

57. Steve de Shazer, *Putting Difference to Work* (New York: W. W. Norton, 1991). For another strengths-based approach, see Michael White and David Epston, *Narrative Means to Therapeutic Ends* (New York: Guilford Press, 1987).

58. Amy S. Ellis, Vanessa Simola, Margaret-Anne Mackintosh, Victoria A. Schlaudt, and Joan Cook, "Perceived Helpfulness and Engagement in Mental Health Treatment: Study of Male Survivors of Sexual Abuse," *Psychology of Men and Masculinities* 21, no. 4 (2020): 632–42.

59. Nancy Ramsay and Carrie Doehring, eds., *Military Moral Injury and Spiritual Care: Resources for Religious and Professional Leaders* (Nashville: Chalice Press, 2019).

60. Carrie Doehring, "Resilience as the Relational Ability to Spiritually Integrate Moral Stress," *Pastoral Psychology* 64 (2015): 635–49.

61. Doehring, 636.

62. Doehring, 637.

CHAPTER 8

1. "Objectives and Outcomes for Level I/Level II CPE," ACPE, 2020, https://www.manula.com/manuals/acpe/acpe-manuals/2016/en/topic/objectives-and-outcomes-for-level-i-level-ii-cpe.

2. "Objectives and Outcomes for Level I/Level II CPE."

3. See "Common Qualifications and Competencies," Association of Professional Chaplains, accessed October 8, 2021, https://www.professionalchaplains.org/content.asp?pl=198&sl=254&contentid=254.

4. Carrie Doehring, *The Practice of Pastoral Care: A Postmodern Approach*, rev. and exp. ed. (Louisville: Westminster John Knox Press, 2015), 44–45.

5. "Kimberlé Crenshaw on Intersectionality, More Than Two Decades Later," Columbia Law School, June 8, 2017, https://www.law.columbia.edu/news/archive/kimberle-crenshaw-intersectionality-more-two-decades-later.

6. In fact, as queer theorists such as Judith Butler and Anne Fausto-Sterling have pointed out, the very binary of only two genders, man and woman, understood as being rooted in biological sex characteristics, is a patriarchal construct that obscures identities such as those who identify as transgender, gender-queer, and intersex, among others. For an overview of the social construction of the gender binary and its use by patriarchal systems, see Judith Butler, *Gender Trouble: Feminism and the Subversion of Identity* (New York: Routledge, 1990); and Anne Fausto-Sterling, *Sexing the Body: Gender Politics and the Construction of Sexuality* (New York: Basic Books, 2000).

7. Nikki Graf, Anna Brown, and Eileen Patten, "The Narrowing, but Persistent, Gender Gap in Pay," Pew Research Center, March 22, 2019, https://www.pewresearch.org/fact-tank/2019/03/22/gender-pay-gap-facts/.

8. Taken from a longer list by Judith Warner, Nora Ellmann, and Diana Boesch, "The Women's Leadership Gap," Center for American Progress, last modified November 20, 2018, https://www.americanprogress.org/issues/women /reports/2018/11/20/461273/womens-leadership-gap-2/.

9. See Pamela Braboy Jackson and David R. Williams, "The Intersection of Race, Gender, and SES: Health Paradoxes," in *Gender, Race, Class and Health: Intersectional Approaches*, ed. Amy J. Schulz and Leith Mullings (San Francisco: Jossey-Bass, 2006), 136.

10. bell hooks, *Feminist Theory: From Margin to Center*, 2nd ed. (Cambridge, Mass.: South End Press, 2000), 37.

11. Some critical race theorists such as Layla F. Saad and Tema Okun term widespread systemic racism "white supremacy" or "white supremacy culture" in order to denote the systemic and cultural advantage of white-identifying people. In Saad's words, "White supremacy is far from fringe. In white-centered societies and communities, it is the dominant paradigm that forms the foundation from which norms, rules, and laws are created. . . . White supremacy is an ideology, a paradigm, an institutional system, and a worldview. . . . I am talking about the historic and modern legislating, societal conditioning, and systemic institutionalizing of the construction of whiteness as inherently superior to people of other races." Layla F. Saad, *Me and White Supremacy: Combat Racism, Change the World, and Become a Good Ancestor* (Naperville, Ill.: Sourcebooks, 2020), 13. See also Tema Okun, "White Supremacy Culture," Dismantling Racism, https://www.dismantlingracism.org/uploads/4/3/5/7/43579015 /okun_-_white_sup_culture.pdf. However, we have chosen to employ the term "systemic racism" because it better describes the institutionalization of racist trends and bias as they are systematized in the institutions where chaplains work.

12. As Ibram X. Kendi traces exhaustively in his work *Stamped from the Beginning: The Definitive History of Racist Ideas in America* (New York: Nation Books, 2016), current iterations of systemic racism have historical roots in Western colonialism and the slave trade. Kendi further points out that the structural oppression of Western colonialism preceded racist understandings and ideas. The latter serve as an ideological basis to substantiate the violence of colonialism. As pointed out above, this continues in the institutions in which chaplains operate today. Racist ideas serve as a rationale for systemic oppression and inequality. For a thorough overview of how religious leaders can bring a post/de-colonial lens to their leadership in faith communities, see Kristina I. Lizardy-Hajbi, "Frameworks toward Post/Decolonial Pastoral Leaderships," *Journal of Religious Leadership* 19, no. 2 (2020): 98–128.

13. Linda Villarosa, "Myths about Physical Racial Differences Were Used to Justify Slavery—and Are Still Believed by Doctors Today," *New York Times Magazine*, August 14, 2019, https://nyti.ms/38RE95Y.

14. Donald A. Barr, *Health Disparities in the United States: Social Class, Race, Ethnicity, and Health*, 2nd ed. (Baltimore: Johns Hopkins University Press, 2014), 39–44.

15. See Nancy J. Ramsay, "A Time of Ferment and Redefinition," in *Pastoral Care and Counseling: Redefining the Paradigms*, ed. Nancy J. Ramsay (Nashville: Abingdon, 2004), 1–43.

16. Anton Boisen, *Out of the Depths: An Autobiographical Study of Mental Disorder and Religious Experience* (New York: Harper, 1960), 187.

17. Rodney Hunter and James Patton, "The Therapeutic Tradition in Pastoral Care and Counseling," in *Pastoral Care and Social Conflict: Essays in Honor of Charles V. Gerkin*, ed. Rodney Hunter and Pamela Couture (Nashville: Abingdon, 1999), 36–38. Note: these are direct quotes from Hunter and Patton.

18. See Richard Coble, *The Chaplain's Presence and Medical Power: Rethinking Loss in the Hospital System* (Lanham, Md.: Lexington Books, 2018), 23–30.

19. Chaplaincy itself is often referred to as a ministry of presence, a definition that emphases the empathic and relational rather than functional work of the chaplain. Recently, scholar Winnifred Fallers Sullivan has noted that presence itself, however, by emphasizing relationship, is resistant to instrumentalist or systemic dehumanizing of care receivers: "Presence also works as a place of resistance to instrumentalist approaches to religion and spirituality. The ministry of presence refuses interpretation and explanation. . . . Presence can refuse to be made part of a system—to be measured and quantified and offered as a means to an end. It is the end." *A Ministry of Presence: Chaplaincy, Spiritual Care, and the Law* (Chicago: University of Chicago Press, 2014), 177.

20. Bonnie J. Miller-McLemore, "The Human Web: Reflections on the State of Pastoral Theology," *Christian Century* 110, no. 11 (1993), 366–69, expanded in "The Living Human Web: Pastoral Theology at the Turn of the Century," in *Through the Eyes of Women: Insights for Pastoral Care*, ed. Jeanne Stevenson Moessner (Minneapolis: Fortress Press, 1996), 9–26.

21. Richard Coble, "From Web to Cyborg: Tracing Power in Care," *Journal of Pastoral Theology* 26, no. 1 (2016): 6. Coble quotes Bonnie J. Miller-McLemore, "Feminist Theory in Pastoral Theology," in *Feminist and Womanist Pastoral Theology*, ed. Bonnie J. Miller-McLemore and Brita L. Gill-Austern (Nashville: Abingdon, 1999), 90.

22. Miller-McLemore, "Living Human Web," 20.

23. Emmanuel Yartekwei Lartey, *In Living Color: An Intercultural Approach to Pastoral Care and Counseling*, 2nd ed. (Philadelphia: Jessica Kingsley, 2003), 34.

24. Edward P. Wimberly, *African American Pastoral Care: Revised Edition* (Nashville: Abingdon, 2008), 7.

25. Evelyn L. Parker, "Womanist Theory," in *The Wiley-Blackwell Companion to Practical Theology*, ed. Bonnie J. Miller-McLemore (Malden, Mass.: Blackwell, 2012), 206.

26. Carroll A. Watkins Ali, *Survival and Liberation: Pastoral Theology in African American Context* (St. Louis: Chalice Press, 1999), 123.

27. Teresa E. Snorton, "What About All Those Angry Black Women?," in *Women Out of Order: Risking Change and Creating Care in a Multicultural World*, ed. Jeanne Stevenson-Moessner and Teresa Snorton (Minneapolis: Fortress Press, 2010), 217.

28. Jacqueline Kelley, "Womanist Pastoral Care Using Narrative Therapy," in *Women Out of Order: Risking Change and Creating Care in a Multicultural World*, ed. Jeanne Stevenson-Moessner and Teresa Snorton (Minneapolis: Fortress Press, 2010), 141.

29. For an introduction and outline of this form of prayer, see Anita Diamant, "Viddui: The Deathbed Confession—Traditional and Liberal Possibilities for this Little-Known Practice," My Jewish Learning, accessed October 5, 2021, https://www.myjewishlearning.com/article/viddui-the-deathbed-confession/.

30. H. Russell Searight and Jennifer Gafford, "Cultural Diversity at the End of Life: Issues and Guidelines for Family Physicians," *American Family Physician* 71, no. 3 (2005): 519.

31. Ezra Gabbay and Joseph Fins, "Go in Peace: Brain Death, Reasonable Accommodation and Jewish Mourning Rituals," *Journal of Religion and Health* 58, no. 5 (2019): 1675. While this article explores brain death specifically, the contentiousness over brain death also extends to full codes for patients who decline to sign DNRs. Full codes include medication such as pressors, chest compressions, electrical shock, and mechanical ventilation for patients when their hearts stop.

32. Andrew M. Cuomo, Howard A. Zucker, and Sally Dreslin, "Health Advisory: COVID-19 Guidance for Hospital Operators Regarding Visitation," New York State Department of Health, March 18, 2020, https://coronavirus.health.ny.gov/system/files/documents/2020/03/covid19-hospital-visitation-guidance-3.18.20.pdf. These guidelines were updated March 27, April 10, and May 20, 2020, and following.

33. Andrew Schumann, "Logical Cornerstones of Judaic Argumentation Theory," *Argumentation* 27, no. 1 (2013), 305–26.

34. Andrew M. Cuomo, Howard A. Zucker, and Sally Dreslin, "Health Advisory: COVID-19 Updated Guidance for Hospital Operators Regarding Visitation," New York State Department of Health, April 10, 2020, https://coronavirus.health.ny.gov/system/files/documents/2020/04/doh_covid19_hospitalvisitation_041020-002.pdf.

35. See Ersilia M. DeFilippis, Lauren S. Ranard, and David D. Berg, "Cardiopulmonary Resuscitation during the COVID-19 Pandemic: A View from Trainees on the Front Line," *Circulation* 141, no. 23 (2020), 1833–35; and Lina Ya'Qoub, "CardioPulmonary Resuscitation (CPR) in the Time of COVID-19," American Heart Association, July 17, 2020, https://earlycareervoice.professional.heart.org/cardiopulmonary-resuscitation-cpr-in-the-time-of-covid-19/.

36. See Ravina Kullar, Jasmine R. Marcelin, Talia H. Swartz, Damani A. Piggott, Raul Macias Gil, Trini A. Mathew, and Tina Tan, "Racial Disparity of Coronavirus Disease 2019 in African American Communities," *Journal of Infectious Diseases* 222, no. 6 (2020), 890–93.

37. Gabbay and Fins, "Go in Peace," 1682.

38. Katherine Fischkoff, Gerald Neuberg, Joyeeta Dastidar, Erin P. Williams, Kenneth Prager, and Lydia Dugdale, "Clinical Ethics Consultations during the COVID-19 Pandemic Surge at a New York City Medical Center," *Journal of Clinical Ethics* 31, no. 3 (Fall 2020): 212–18.

1. Miroslav Volf, *Flourishing: Why We Need Religion in a Globalized World* (New Haven: Yale University Press, 2015).

2. "Objectives and Outcomes for Level I/Level II CPE," ACPE, 2020, https://www.manula.com/manuals/acpe/acpe-manuals/2016/en/topic/objectives-and-outcomes-for-level-i-level-ii-cpe.

3. Council on Collaboration, Common Standards for Professional Chaplaincy, 2004, https://www.professionalchaplains.org/files/professional_standards/common_standards/common_standards_professional_chaplaincy.pdf. See TPC5 and PRO3.

4. Canadian Association for Spiritual Care / Association canadienne de soins spirituels, Competencies of CASC/ACSS Certified Professionals, 2019, https://spiritualcare.ca/explore-spiritual-care/cascacss_competencies/.

5. ACPE: The Standard for Spiritual Care and Education, Certified Educator Competencies Assessment Form, End of Phase I Assessment, New Certification Process Manual 2020.

6. Most chaplains today understand themselves as change agents as they engage with individuals and (for some) with interpersonal relationships, as in a family or team. We do not perceive that most chaplains currently understand themselves to be change agents in the organizations in which they work.

7. Joan V. Gallos, *Using Bolman and Deal's Reframing Organization: An Instructor's Guide to Effective Teaching*, 5th ed. (San Francisco: John Wiley and Sons, 2013), 194.

CHAPTER 9

1. The views expressed are the author's alone and do not necessarily represent the views of the U.S. Army, the U.S. Army Chaplain Corps, or the Graduate School for Army Chaplain Corps Professional Development.

2. See this volume's introduction.

3. Robert P. Jones and Daniel Cox, *America's Changing Religious Identity: Findings from the 2016 American Values Atlas*, Public Religion Research Institute, Pew, 2017, https://www.prri.org/wp-content/uploads/2017/09/PRRI-Religion-Report.pdf.

4. Bureau of Labor Statistics, U.S. Department of Labor, *Occupational Employment Statistics-Clergy*, U.S. Government, May 2017, https://www.bls.gov/oes/2017/may/oes212011.htm.

5. Peter Kevern and Lisa Hill, "'Chaplains for Well-Being' in Primary Care: Analysis of the Results of a Retrospective Study," *Primary Health Care Research and Development* 16 (January 2015): 87–99; Barbara Pesut, Shane Sinclair, George Fitchett, Madeleine Greig, and Sarah E. Koss, "Health Care Chaplaincy: A Scoping Review of the Evidence 2009–2014," *Journal of Health Care Chaplaincy* 22 (April 2016): 67–84; Austyn Snowden and Iain Telfer, "Patient Reported Outcome Measure of Spiritual Care as Delivered by Chaplains," *Journal of Health Care Chaplaincy* 23 (October 2017): 131–55; Deborah B. Marin, Vanshdeep Sharma, Eugene Sosunov, Natalia Egorova, Rafael Goldstein, and George F. Handzo, "Relationship between Chaplain Visits and Patient Satisfaction," *Journal of Health Care Chaplaincy* 21 (January 2015): 14–24;

Katherine R. B. Jankowski, George F. Handzo, and Kevin J. Flannelly, "Testing the Efficacy of Chaplaincy Care," *Journal of Health Care Chaplaincy* 17 (July 2011): 100–125; Fiona Timmins, Sílvia Caldeira, Maryanne Murphy, Nicolas Pujol, Greg Sheaf, Elizabeth Weathers, Jacqueline Whelan, and Bernadette Flanagan, "The Role of the Healthcare Chaplain: A Literature Review," *Journal of Health Care Chaplaincy* 24 (July 2018): 87–106; Kevin J. Flannelly, Linda L. Emanuel, George F. Handzo, Kathleen Galek, Nava R. Silton, and Melissa Carlson, "A National Study of Chaplaincy Services and End-of-Life Outcomes," *BMC Palliative Care* 11 (December 2012): 10; A. Edwards, N. Pang , V. Shiu, and C. Chan, "Review: The Understanding of Spirituality and the Potential Role of Spiritual Care in End-of-Life and Palliative Care: A Meta-Study of Qualitative Research," *Palliative Medicine* 24 (December 2010): 753–70.

6. Harold G. Koenig, Dana E. King, and Verna B. Carson, *Handbook of Religion and Health*, 2nd ed. (New York: Oxford University Press, 2012).

7. Christopher C. H. Cook and Nathan H. White, "Resilience and the Role of Spirituality," in *The Oxford Textbook of Public Mental Health*, ed. Dinesh Bhugra, Kamaldeep Bhui, Stephen E. Gilman, Samuel Yeung, and Shan Wong (Oxford: Oxford University Press, 2018), 513–20.

8. See this volume's introduction.

9. "Liminal" has the connotation of a "doorway"—a place of transition between one defined area and another. Thus, a "liminal space" is both a place "in between" unlike areas and a place of possible change due to its synthesis of these "worlds." See chapter 5 in this volume.

10. Aristotle, *Politics* I.2, 1252b30. Quotations are from *The Complete Works of Aristotle: The Revised Translation*, ed. Jonathan Barnes, 2 vols., Bollingen Series no. 71, part 2 (Princeton: Princeton University Press, 1984). While Aristotle's comments are insightful, we must also acknowledge that they come from a framework that considered only the rights of Greek citizens, thereby excluding foreigners, slaves, and women and denying the value and insights of these persons.

11. Generally speaking, pacifists maintain that the act of killing a human being is wrong in any context, while a just-war theorist may suggest the taking of human life is sometimes morally justified, such as to prevent a greater evil like genocide.

12. See Reinhold Niebuhr, *Moral Man and Immoral Society: A Study in Ethics and Politics*, 2nd ed. (Louisville: Westminster John Knox Press, 2013).

13. Linda K. Treviño and Katherine A. Nelson, *Managing Business Ethics: Straight Talk about How to Do It Right*, 5th ed. (Hoboken: John Wiley and Sons, 2010), 151.

14. This is closely connected to the "symbolic frame" that Su Yon Pak describes in chapter 10.

15. These realities are clearly demonstrated in chapters 6, 8, and 11 in this volume.

16. Michel Foucault and Colin Gordon, *Power/Knowledge: Selected Interviews and Other Writings, 1972–1977*, 1st American ed. (New York: Pantheon Books, 1980).

17. Alistair McFadyen, *Bound to Sin: Abuse, Holocaust and the Christian Doctrine of Sin* (Cambridge: Cambridge University Press, 2000).

18. Paul Ricoeur's description of human identity in terms of a dialectic relationship between constancy and change over time could analogously be applied to

organizational identity. Compare Paul Ricoeur, *Oneself as Another*, trans. Kathleen Blamey (Chicago: University of Chicago Press, 1992).

19. Edgar H. Schein, *Organizational Culture and Leadership*, 3rd ed. (San Francisco: Jossey-Bass, 2004), 84; compare Schein, *Organizational Culture and Leadership*, 5th ed. (Hoboken: Wiley, 2017), 343.

20. Edgar H. Schein, *Organizational Culture and Leadership*, 4th ed. (San Francisco: Jossey-Bass, 2010), 218.

21. Schein, 365.

22. Schein, 365.

23. Recent history indicates that these considerations—financial and ethical—are more connected than once might have been assumed. Ethical missteps by organizations can result in negative financial repercussions and diminish the organization's success (for example, Black Lives Matter protests, Enron, Deepwater Horizon oil spill). Ethical considerations should not be analyzed simply for utilitarian purposes, but nonetheless ethical considerations have very practical outcomes, even in purely monetary metrics.

24. These ethical concerns have been central to religious traditions for millennia, and R/S leaders continue to speak powerfully on these topics. More recently, neoliberal critiques of capitalism highlight significant concerns for ways ethical considerations may be subsumed by financial matters, even using seemingly positive constructs like "resilience" toward this end. See Sara Holiday Nelson, "Resilience and the Neoliberal Counter-Revolution: From Ecologies of Control to Production of the Common," *Resilience* 2 (January 2014): 1–17.

25. "Organizational capital" is a metaphor for implicit influence within an organization, drawing upon the image of monetary riches.

26. Significantly, this credibility was largely due to identification with organizational credibility. The personal credibility of a chaplain builds toward organizational credibility, but the immediate trust of patients was gained by the hard work of many chaplains who went before.

27. U.S. Army, Army Regulation 165–1, *Army Chaplain Corps Activities* (June 23, 2015), 2–3b.

28. U.S. Army, "Sexual Harassment/Assault Response & Prevention (SHARP)," accessed September 17, 2021, https://www.armyresilience.army.mil/sharp/.

29. U.S. Army, "The Family Advocacy Program," accessed September 17, 2021, https://www.militaryonesource.mil/family-relationships/family-life/preventing-abuse-neglect/the-family-advocacy-program.

30. Cook and White, "Resilience and the Role of Spirituality."

CHAPTER 10

1. Lee G. Bolman and Terrence E. Deal, *Reframing Organizations, 6th Edition: Artistry, Choice, and Leadership* (San Francisco: John Wiley and Sons, 2017), 31–32. For a fuller consideration, refer to Nathan White's chapter.

2. Refer to the notion of individual and organizational resilience addressed in Nathan White's chapter for a fuller treatment.

3. Bolman and Deal, *Reframing Organizations,* 15–18.

4. Joan V. Gallos, *Using Bolman and Deal's Reframing Organization: An Instructor's Guide to Effective Teaching,* 4th ed. (San Francisco: John Wiley and Sons, 2008), 11–12.

5. Joe R. Feagin, *The White Racial Frame: Centuries of Racial Framing and Counter-Framing,* 3rd ed. (New York: Routledge, 2020).

6. Feagin, 4.

7. See the Dismantling Racism Works (dRWorks) website, accessed September 19, 2021, https://www.dismantlingracism.org/white-supremacy-culture.html. See also the (divorcing) White Supremacy Culture website, accessed September 19, 2021, https://www.whitesupremacyculture.info/.

8. Bolman and Deal, *Reframing Organizations,* 12. They mention this "rapid recognition" as examined by Malcolm Gladwell in his book *Blink: Power of Thinking without Thinking* (New York: Little, Brown, 2005).

9. Bolman and Deal, *Reframing Organizations,* 12.

10. Bolman and Deal, 13.

11. Bolman and Deal, 53.

12. Bolman and Deal, 64–68.

13. Bolman and Deal, 315.

14. Bolman and Deal, 314–15.

15. Bolman and Deal, 117.

16. Bolman and Deal, 117–18.

17. Bolman and Deal, 18.

18. Bolman and Deal, 18.

19. Bolman and Deal, 138–52.

20. Bolman and Deal, 152–54.

21. Bolman and Deal, 317.

22. Bolman and Deal, 317.

23. Refer to Laurie Garrett-Cobbina's chapter in this book for an excellent treatment of power.

24. Bolman and Deal, *Reframing Organizations,* 184.

25. Bolman and Deal, 184.

26. Bolman and Deal, 184.

27. Bolman and Deal, 193.

28. Bolman and Deal, 196–97.

29. Bolman and Deal, 206–13.

30. Bolman and Deal, 323.

31. Laurie Garrett-Cobbina's chapter in this part on corporate grief and understanding grief as a crisis of meaning adds a powerful dimension to the discussion of the symbolic frame.

32. Bolman and Deal, *Reframing Organizations,* 242.

33. Bolman and Deal, 242.

34. Bolman and Deal, 242.

35. Bolman and Deal, 242–45.

36. Bolman and Deal, 245–47.

37. Bolman and Deal, 247–50.

38. Bolman and Deal, 250–56.

39. Bolman and Deal, 256–57.

40. Bolman and Deal, 320.

41. There are many resonances with Laurie Garrett-Cobbina's chapter in this part. In particular, see her treatment on "organizational counter narrative."

42. Feagin, *White Racial Frame*, 5.

43. Feagin, 25.

44. Tema Okun and Kenneth Jones worked together for many years in anti-oppression, antiracism efforts within organizations. This piece is a product of many years of study and grassroots training. See the complete paper at the (divorcing) White Supremacy Culture website, accessed September 19, 2021, https://www.whitesupremacy culture.info/uploads/4/3/5/7/43579015/okun_-_white_sup_culture_2020.pdf.

45. "White Supremacy Culture," (divorcing) White Supremacy Culture website, accessed September 19, 2021, https://www.whitesupremacyculture.info/uploads /4/3/5/7/43579015/okun_-_white_sup_culture_2020.pdf.

46. These questions are based on the work of Tema Okun, Kenneth Jones, Daniel Buford, and other collaborators and their work, "White Supremacy Culture," (divorcing) White Supremacy Culture website, accessed September 19, 2021, https:// www.whitesupremacyculture.info/uploads/4/3/5/7/43579015/okun_-_white_sup _culture_2020.pdf. They also suggest antidote practices as a way to counter these harmful characteristics. See also Nathan White's chapter for a discussion of "fallible organizations."

47. Leadership Orientation Self-Assessment is a quick guide for the students' frame preference. Lee Bolman: Author, Educator website, accessed September 19, 2021, http://www.leebolman.com/frames_selfrating_scale.htm.

CHAPTER II

1. Daniel Solorzano et al., "Critical Race Theory, Racial Microaggressions, and Campus Racial Climate: The Experiences of African American College Students," *Journal of Negro Education* 69, nos. 1/2 (Winter/Spring 2000): 60–73.

2. Chris Antal and Kathy Winings, "Moral Injury, Soul Repair, and Creating a Place for Grace," *Religious Education* 110, no. 4 (2014): 382–94.

3. Solorzano et al., "Critical Race Theory."

4. See chapter 10.

5. Scott Peck, *People of the Lie* (New York: Touchstone, 1983), 232.

6. Rita Nakashima-Brock and Gabriella Lettini, *Soul Repair: Recovering from Moral Injury after War* (Boston: Beacon Press, 2013), 51.

7. Miebaka Dagogo Tamunomiebi and Iyioriobhe Ezekiel Ehior, "Diversity and Ethical Issues in the Organizations," *International Journal of Academic Research in Business and Social Sciences* 9, no. 2 (2019): 839–64. Ethical grounding is most effective when practical and actionable.

8. Generosity of spirit is a worldview and a spiritual disposition that is nurtured through radical reflexivity, understanding how your actions affect others, taking responsibility for your words and actions, and commitment to service-learning. Service-learning is premised on reciprocal learning, mutual caring, and providing care that meets actual needs. See Jeffrey Howard, ed., *Praxis I: A Faculty Casebook on Community Service Learning* (Ann Arbor: Office of Community Service-Learning Press, University of Michigan, 1993).

9. David Flinders and P. Bruce Uhrmacher, eds., *Curriculum and Teaching Dialogue* (Charlotte, N.C.: Information Age Publishing, 2011), chap. 3, p. 13, no. 1; Benjamin S. Bloom, Max D. Engelhart, Edward J. Furst, Walker H. Hill, and David R. Krathwohl, *Taxonomy of Educational Objectives* (New York: David McKay, 1964). The four stages of learning competence based on Bloom's taxonomy are (1) unconscious incompetence, (2) conscious incompetence, (3) conscious competence, and (4) unconscious competence.

10. John Bowlby, *The Making and Breaking of Affectional Bonds* (New York: Routledge, 1979), 67–70. Attachment theory emphasizes that bonding happens at a preconscious, emotional, biological level. Bonding is a social behavior given meaning through the biological and emotional impulse for survival. Survival anxiety is activated when attachment is threatened or broken. This includes the preconscious, emotional, biological attachment to racism, sexism, and classism. Bowlby's theory provides a frame for explicating attachment to ideas, habits, and practices.

11. Pierre Bourdieu, *Outline of a Theory of Practice* (Cambridge: Cambridge University Press, 1977); Bourdieu, *Distinction: A Social Critique of the Judgment of Taste* (Cambridge, Mass.: Harvard University Press, 1984); Bourdieu and Jean-Claude Passeron, *Reproduction in Education, Society and Culture* (Thousand Oaks, Calif.: SAGE, 1990), 31–32, 54–55; Ulwyn Pierre, *The Myth of Black Corporate Mobility* (New York: Routledge, 1998), 4–9. Bourdieu's concept of symbolic power accounts for the tacit, unconscious modes of sociocultural domination occurring within the everyday social habits of people. Symbolic power is used against another to confirm that person's subjugated placement in the social hierarchy of systems and organizations.

12. Bourdieu and Passeron, *Reproduction in Education, Society and Culture*, 4–11.

13. Sara Ahmed, *The Cultural Politics of Emotion* (New York: Routledge, 2012), 2–3, 10–11. "'Emotion' is viewed as 'beneath' the facilities of thought and reason."

14. Charles W. Mills, *The Racial Contract* (Ithaca: Cornell University Press, 1997), 1–3.

15. Zeus Leonardo, "Ideology, Race and Science: A Love/Hate Relationship," in *Race, Whiteness and Education* (New York: Routledge, 2009), 29–33. "A scientific discrediting of race is insufficient because the racial mind is hardly scientific: it is ideological. This means that a theory of ideology is necessary," 30. Ian Haney Lopez, *White by Law* (New York: New York University Press, 1996). Critical race theorists have shown that race is socially, legally, and emotionally constructed. On one level, race is clearly a social construct. There is no such thing as a Negro or a Caucasian race. There are people who share some characteristics in geographic locations consistent with latitudes north or south of the earth's equator.

16. University of Southern California, "Healthcare: How Stereotypes Hurt: Stereo-

types in Health Care Environment Can Mean Poorer Health Outcomes," ScienceDaily, October 20, 2015, http://www.sciencedaily.com/releases/2015/10/151020091344.htm.

17. Ibram X. Kendi, *How to Be an Antiracist* (New York: Penguin Random House, 2019).

18. Ronald Heifetz, *Leadership without Easy Answers* (Cambridge, Mass.: Harvard University Press, 1998).

19. Workplace Fairness website, October 2020, https://www.workplacefairness .org/sexual-gender-discrimination.

20. Martin Luther King Jr., *Where Do We Go from Here: Chaos or Community?* (Boston: Beacon Press, 1968); Toni Morrison, *The Origin of Others* (Cambridge, Mass.: Harvard University Press, 2017).

21. Charisse Levchak, *Microaggression and Modern Racism* (New Britain, Conn.: Palgrave, 2018), 105–212.

22. Leonardo, *Race, Whiteness and Education.*

23. Bowlby, *Making and Breaking of Affectional Bonds,* 67–70.

24. Mario Mikulincer and Phillip R. Shaver, "An Attachment Perspective on Loneliness," in *The Handbook of Solitude: Psychological Perspectives on Social Isolation, Social Withdrawal, and Being Alone,* ed. Robert Coplan and Julie Bowker (Malden, Mass.: John Wiley and Sons, 2014), 34–50.

25. John Cacioppo and William Patrick, *Loneliness* (New York: Norton, 2008), 7.

26. Nicki Lisa Cole, "So What Is Culture, Exactly?," ThoughtCo, August 2, 2019, thoughtco.com/culture-definition-4135409.

27. This phrase is based on the writings of John Locke. In chapter 7, section 87 of *Two Treatises of Government* (1689), Locke expressed that "no one ought to harm another in their life, health, liberty, or possessions."

28. Jonathan Shay, "Moral Injury," *Intertexts* 16, no. 1 (2012): 58.

29. Erika Doss, *Memorial Mania: Public Feeling in America* (Chicago: University of Chicago Press, 2010), 59.

30. Henry Gates Jr., "How Many Africans Were Really Taken to the U.S. during the Slave Trade?," America's Black Holocaust Museum, January 6, 2014, https://www .abhmuseum.org/how-many-africans-were-really-taken-to-the-u-s-during-the-slave -trade/.

31. See chapter 9.

32. Ruby Payne, Philip DeVol, and Terie Dreussi Smith, *Bridges Out of Poverty: Strategies for Professional and Communities* (Highlands, Tex.: aha! Process, 2001).

CONCLUSION

1. Tim Harford, "How Can Chaos Lead to Creative Breakthroughs?," *TED Radio Hour,* NPR, May 10, 2019, https://www.npr.org/transcripts/719557642.

2. Parker Palmer, "The Tragic Gap," Center for Courage and Renewal, accessed February 23, 2021, http://www.couragerenewal.org/the-tragic-gap/.

3. "Transforming Chaplaincy," Transforming Chaplaincy | Promoting Research Literacy for Improved Patient Outcomes, November 1, 2017, https://www.transform chaplaincy.org/projects/transforming-chaplaincy/.

4. "TC Final Report," Transforming Chaplaincy | Promoting Research Literacy for Improved Patient Outcomes, June 17, 2019, https://www.transformchaplaincy.org/2019/06/17/transforming-chaplaincy-final-report/.

5. Aja Antoine, George Fitchett, Deborah Marin, Vanshdeep Sharma, Andrew Garman, Trace Haythorn, Kelsey White, Amy Green, and Wendy Cadge, "What Organizational and Business Models Underlie the Provision of Spiritual Care in Healthcare Organizations? An Initial Description and Analysis," *Journal of Health Care Chaplaincy* (2020), https://doi.org/10.1080/08854726.2020.1861535.

6. Aja Antoine et al., "How do Healthcare Executives Understand and Make Decisions about Spiritual Care Provision?," *Southern Medical Journal* 114, no. 4 (April 2021): 207–12.

7. "Learn about Bowen Theory," The Bowen Center for the Study of the Family, accessed February 23, 2021, https://www.thebowencenter.org/core-concepts-diagrams.

8. "Humanism and Its Aspirations: Humanist Manifesto III, a Successor to the Humanist Manifesto of 1933," American Humanist Association, accessed February 23, 2021, https://americanhumanist.org/what-is-humanism/manifesto3/.

9. *Humanism and Its Aspirations: Humanist Manifesto III, a Successor to the Humanist Manifesto of 1933*, American Humanist Association, February 23, 2021, https://americanhumanist.org/what-is-humanism/manifesto3/.

CONTRIBUTORS

Imam **Dr. Bilal Ansari** is the vice president for Campus Engagement at Williams College. He is also an associate faculty member, codirector of the MA in chaplaincy, and codirector of the Islamic Chaplaincy Program at Hartford Seminary. His professional chaplaincy work has been on college campuses, on military bases, and in prisons.

Rev. Dr. Duane R. Bidwell is a professor of practical theology, spiritual care, and counseling at Claremont School of Theology. He specializes in comparative approaches to spirituality and mental health and in Buddhist-Christian studies. A minister of the Presbyterian Church (USA), his most recent book is *When One Religion Isn't Enough: The Lives of Spiritually Fluid People.*

Dr. Wendy Cadge is the dean of the Graduate School of Arts and Sciences at Brandeis University and is an expert in contemporary American religion, especially related to religion in public institutions, religious diversity, religious and moral aspects of healthcare, and religion and immigration. She is the author of *Paging God: Religion in the Halls of Medicine.*

Jason Callahan serves as an instructor in the Department of Patient Counseling, College of Health Professions, Virginia Commonwealth University, and as a chaplain endorsed by the Humanist Society for the Thomas Palliative Care Unit in VCU Massey Cancer Center.

Rev. Dr. Richard Coble is an associate pastor at Grace Covenant Presbyterian Church (USA) in Asheville, North Carolina, and an adjunct professor of pastoral care and counseling at Lexington Theological Seminary. He is the author of *The Chaplain's Presence and Medical Power: Rethinking Loss in the Hospital System.*

Rev. Dr. Carrie Doehring is the Clifford Baldridge Professor of Pastoral Care and Counseling at Iliff School of Theology in Denver. She is also a licensed psychologist in Massachusetts and Colorado, a diplomat in the American Association of Pastoral Counselors, and an ordained minister in the Presbyterian Church of Canada and the Presbyterian Church (USA). She is the author of *The Practice of Pastoral Care: A Postmodern Approach.*

Dr. Victor Gabriel is the master of divinity program coordinator and an assistant professor of Buddhist chaplaincy at the University of the West in Rosemead, California. He works with the Chaplaincy Innovation Lab on the Educating Effective Chaplains project, identifying the key competencies and teaching methods for training the next generation of chaplains. Gabriel is a Buddhist lay minister.

Rev. Dr. Laurie Garrett-Cobbina is the Shaw Family Associate Professor of Pastoral Care and Education at the University of Redlands in California and oversees the clinical pastoral education program at the school. She is an ordained minister in the Presbyterian Church (USA) and received the Helen Flanders Dunbar Award by the ACPE for pioneering contributions to the CPE movement.

Rev. Dr. Dagmar Grefe is the manager of spiritual care and clinical pastoral education at Children's Hospital Los Angeles and an ACPE certified educator. She is an ordained minister in the United Church of Christ and author of *Encounters for Change: Interreligious Cooperation in the Care of Individuals and Communities.*

Dr. Trace Haythorn is executive director of the Association for Clinical Pastoral Education. With George Fitchett and Wendy Cadge he was co-investigator of the Henry Luce Foundation–funded project Assessing + Reimagining Chaplaincy Education.

Allison Kestenbaum is the supervisor of Spiritual Care Services and the CPE program supervisor at UC San Diego Health, where she also serves as a palliative care chaplain for the Howell Palliative Care Service. She is an ACPE certified educator and board certified chaplain through Neshama: Association of Jewish Chaplains and the Association for Professional Chaplains and is a Cambia Health Foundation Sojourns Scholar.

Rev. Michelle Kirby is the director of the San Diego VA-DoD CPE Center, serving the VA San Diego Healthcare System and the Navy Medicine Readiness and Training Command, San Diego. She is a chaplain endorsed by the Metropolitan Community Church and board certified with the National Association of VA Chaplains. She specializes in mental health chaplaincy and LGBTQ care and has a case study published in *Chaplains as Partners in Medical Decision-Making*, edited by Jeanne Wirpsa and Karen Pugliese.

Rev. Dr. Pamela McCarroll is an associate professor of practical theology at Emmanuel College, a member college of the Toronto School of Theology. She is a registered psychotherapist in the College of Registered Psychotherapists of Ontario, a certified supervisor-educator through the Canadian Association for Spiritual Care, and an ordained minister with the Presbyterian Church in Canada. She has published widely in spiritual care and practical theology, including *The End of Hope—the Beginning: Narratives of Hope in the Face of Death and Trauma.*

Dr. Barbara McClure is an associate professor of practical theology and practice at Brite Divinity School at Texas Christian University in Fort Worth. She explores the assumptions that ground religious practices—especially those relating to care and healing—and asks whether they are adequate to the complexity of a deeply social theological anthropology. She is the author of *Emotions: Problems and Promise for Human Flourishing.*

Dr. Thomas St. James O'Connor is an emeritus professor of Martin Luther University College (formerly Waterloo Lutheran Seminary). He is still writing, even in retirement, with a focus on competency in spiritual care and psychotherapy. He is a coeditor of *Psychotherapy: Cure of the Soul.*

Dr. Su Yon Pak is a senior director and associate professor of integrative and field-based education at Union Theological Seminary in New York City. Her life and research passions include chaplaincy education, spiritual formation, contemplative practices, criminal justice, the elderly and spirituality, Asian American / Pacific Islander and women's leadership, and integrative and critical pedagogies. Most recently, she coedited with Mychal Springer *Sisters in Mourning: Daughters Reflecting on Care, Loss, and Meaning.*

Dr. Shelly Rambo is an associate professor of theology at Boston University's School of Theology. She locates her work at the intersections of Christian theology, literature, and postmodern thought. Her most recent book is *Resurrecting Wounds: Living in the Afterlife of Trauma.*

Rabbi Rochelle Robins is a vice president and dean of the Chaplaincy School and director of clinical pastoral education at the Academy for Jewish Religion/CA in Los Angeles. Her chapter in *Navigating Religious Difference in Spiritual Care and Counseling (Essays in Honor of Kathleen J. Greider)* explores ways in which chaplaincy educators can confront issues and incidents of antisemitism and raise awareness about them.

Rabbi Mychal Springer, an ACPE certified educator, oversees the multi-faith clinical pastoral education program at NewYork-Presbyterian Hospital. She was the founding director of the Center for Pastoral Education at the Jewish Theological Seminary. She is coeditor, with Su Yon Pak, of *Sisters in Mourning: Daughters Reflecting on Care, Loss, and Meaning.*

Dr. Ronit Y. Stahl is an associate professor of modern U.S. history at UC Berkeley, and her work focuses on how politics, law, and religion interact in institutional spaces such as the military and medicine. She is the author of *Enlisting Faith: How the Military Chaplaincy Shaped Religion and State in Modern America.*

Rev. Mary Martha Thiel is the director of clinical pastoral education at Hebrew SeniorLife in Boston and an ACPE certified educator. Ordained by the United Church of Christ, she is a board certified chaplain in the Association of Professional Chaplains. Thiel has authored multiple journal articles and book chapters and conducted webinars on spiritual care. Her areas of interest include older adults, end of life, LGBTQ+ elders, and those who are not religious.

Rev. Dr. Danielle Tumminio Hansen is an assistant professor of practical theology and spiritual care at Candler School of Theology in Atlanta. She is a public theologian, Episcopal priest, and author of *Conceiving Family: A Practical Theology of Surrogacy and Self.*

Rev. Dr. Nathan H. White is associate dean of the graduate school at the U.S. Army Institute for Religious Leadership in Columbia, South Carolina, where he implements and oversees professional development, education, and certification programs for U.S. Army chaplains and Religious Affairs Specialists. He is also a U.S. Army Reserve chaplain and is coeditor with Christopher Cook of *Biblical and Theological Visions of Resilience: Pastoral and Clinical Insights.*

Taylor Paige Winfield is a PhD candidate in the Department of Sociology at Princeton University. Her research focuses on the intersection of culture, institutions, cumulative inequalities, and innovations in justice and trauma-informed research methodologies. Her work has been published in multiple peer-reviewed journals, including the *Journal of Contemporary Ethnography* and the *Journal of the American Academy of Religion.* Outside of academia, she is a spiritual care provider with experience in correctional, healthcare, and online settings.

INDEX

ACPE (formerly Association for Clinical Pastoral Education), 12, 195

addiction, 158, 161, 163–164, 168; and twelve-step programs, 164, 166, 168–70, 297n41

advocacy, 85

agency, 65, 78, 84, 91–92, 107, 123

airport chaplaincy, 27, 45

alterity virtues, 103

Association for Clinical Pastoral Education (ACPE), 12, 195

Association of Theological Schools, 12

atheism, 130, 140, 165

attachment theory, 85, 308n10

attunement, 73

behavior, aligning with values, 92

bereavement, 85

bias. *See* discrimination

bitterness, 254

Boisen, Anton, 25, 178–79

Bowen family systems, 138, 264

Buddhism, 69–70, 107, 119–20, 122, 288n17; Buddhist chaplains, 12–13, 23, 30, 39, 94, 98, 100, 104, 107, 120, 122

capacities, 96

Center for Spiritual Care and Pastoral Education, 49

certification, 11, 54

chaplaincy: barriers to entering the field, 54, 265–66; emerging areas, 14; models of spiritual care pro-

vision, 23, 24, 25, 27, 29, 31, 38, 262–63

chaplains: as agents of organizational change, 210; and authority, 8, 13, 246, 248; defined, 2, 3, 20, 55, 202, 258, 265, 301n19; as leaders, 221; legal status of, 48; media attention on, 260; prophetic role of, 196, 215, 246, 258; as "spiritual care providers," 13, 54, 287n1 (chap. 3); value to institutions, 24, 42, 46, 48

chronic illness, 85

classism, 239, 308n10

clinical pastoral education. *See* CPE

Clinical Pastoral Education International, 49

Code Lavender, 263

code-switching, 64, 80

College of Pastoral Supervision and Psychotherapy, 49

colonialism, 131, 140, 147, 156, 294n23, 300n12

community chaplaincy, 14

competencies, 5; empathy, 7, 123, 135, 179, 298n51; intercultural humility, 102, 139, 293n10; interpersonal, 7, 295n2; interreligious and multireligious literacy, 5, 7, 92, 103, 293n10; meaning-making, 5, 95; navigating organizations, 7–8

congruence, 167, 298n51

Constitution of the United States, 2, 22, 31, 33, 35, 38, 55. *See also* First Amendment consultation, 104, 107

counseling, spiritual, 85–86

counternarrative, 241–42

countertransference, 75

COVID-19 pandemic, 3, 6, 56, 115, 183, 259, 291n8

CPE (clinical pastoral education): defined, 9; history of, 25, 177–81; and organizational change, 194; as requirement in various sectors of chaplaincy, 49–54

crisis intervention, 84–85, 87

Critical Incident Stress Management, 263

critical race theory, 174, 179, 300n11, 308n15

culture, 251

death and dying: and meaning-making, 95, 136, 148–50; as a primary site of spiritual care, 4, 39, 46, 75; and ritual, 114–16; and specific religious needs, 183–88

demand-based model of chaplaincy, 31, 263

despair, 159–61, 168

dialectics, 209, 305n18

disaster chaplaincy, 14, 28, 44; American Red Cross, 29, 44; Boston Marathon bombing, 45; Billy Graham Rapid Response Team, 44; Hurricane Katrina, 45; 9/11, 29, 291n7; Orlando nightclub shooting, 45

discrimination, 131; and antibias practice and theory, 261–62; as cause of suffering, 64; as sexism, 111–14; and social oppression, 145; within organizations, 193–94, 198, 226

education of chaplains, 30, 49, 262; MDiv, 9, 12–13; standards, 258. See also CPE; training

empathy: and body language, 74; as a competency, 7, 131, 137, 148–50; and listening, 118, 123, 166; loss or lack of, 242, 243, 245, 252; in organizations, 246, 248, 249, 251, 253, 255; as a skill, 69; social empathy, 146–47, 180; in spiritual care, 166, 179, 256, 298n51; spiritual empathy, 145–46, 184, 293n10; theological empathy, 294n19

empowerment, 84

end-of-life care, 183–88

endorsement, 9, 54

ethics: and careseeker integrity, 65, 168; and careseeker self-determination, 102–3; as CPE competency, 172; ethical reasoning as chaplaincy skill, 8; in healthcare, 187; in organizations, 209–10, 213, 216, 242, 253, 305n23, 307n7; as social critique, 305n24; in Veterans Affairs, 38; in workplaces, 46

existentialism, 160

family systems, 85, 196

feminism, 146, 160, 179–81

First Amendment, 2, 20, 22, 33–34, 39. See also Constitution of the United States

forgiveness, 165

frames (Bolman-Deal): and counterframes, 233; defined, 222; human resource frame, 224–25; intersecting frames, 229–31; multiple-frame perspective, 232; and organizations, 221–22; political frame, 226; structural frame, 223–24; symbolic frame, 227–28, 304n14; and white supremacy culture, 233

gender: as constructed, 247, 299n6; and ethical mandates of spiritual care professionals, 131, 162; lack of diversity within chaplaincy profession, 54; as linked to social outcomes, 172, 235; and relationship to religion/spirituality, 93, 101. See also feminism; patriarchy; sexism; womanism

government chaplaincy, 21–22, 279n10
grief, 162, 291n9; corporate grief cycle, 250, 253; defined, 250–251
grounding, 74
group facilitation, 85

harm reduction, 165
healthcare, 25, 42–43, 261–262, 302n31
Helping Styles Inventory, 156–57, 167, 298n51
hermeneutics, 62
higher education, 24, 47–48, 67–73, 280n19; Baptist Student Union, 24; National Association of College and University Chaplains (NACUC), 24; Newman Center, 24; Hillel, 24; YMCA, 24
homelessness, 1, 65, 172, 292
hope, 161
hospice chaplaincy, 42
humanism, 265
humanist-existential therapy, 85

identity, 85, 92, 305n18; constructing identity, 92
inclusivity, 123, 140
industrial chaplaincy. *See* workplace chaplaincy
Institute for Clinical Pastoral Training, 49
integration, spiritual, 137–42
intercultural humility, 102, 139, 293n10
interreligious spiritual care, 7, 129–31, 139, 293n14. *See also* competencies: interreligious and multireligious literacy
interpersonal violence, 198–200, 215
intersectional analysis, 92, 103, 172
intersectional theory, 104, 146, 156, 172–77, 294n20
Islam: and intention for right action, 288n17; Muslim corrections chaplaincy, 10, 30, 39, 41; Muslim higher-education chaplaincy, 30, 70–73, 79; Muslim military chaplaincy, 23;

Muslim social movement chaplaincy, 28; Muslim transportation chaplaincy, 27; revising MDiv programs in light of Muslim perspectives, 12–3; and self-reflexivity (related to *muraqabah*), 75
isms: behavior and treatment, 241–56 passim; defined, 240; in organizations, 242–56. *See also* classism; racism; sexism

Judaism and Jewish spiritual care, 292nn13–15, 302n29; in development of logo-therapy, 160; and end-of-life care, 183–87; within growth of diversity in spiritual care, 30; in higher education, 24; and meaning-making, 61; in military, 22, 35; and self-emptying (*tsimtsum*), 69; in social movements, 28

leadership: CPE as preparation for, 178, 194–95; in group settings, 158; in organizational change, 111–14, 123, 201–2; in organizational resilience, 216–17; through ritual, 117
liberation psychology, 85
liminality, 114–16, 124, 202, 290nn3–4, 304n9
living human document, 178
living human web, 179
logo-therapy, 63, 160
loneliness, 251

MDiv, 9, 12–13
meaning making, 4, 95
meditation, 166
metanarrative, 245
microaggressions, 240–56
military, 22, 34–38, 211, 261, 279n11, 296n11; Armed Forces Chaplain Board, 38
mindfulness, 85, 160, 166
moral distress, 7, 85, 188. *See also* moral injury

moral injury, 13, 85, 132, 155, 164, 168–69, 252–53; and Moral Injury Symptom Scale, 162. *See also* moral distress
moral stress, 168, 186
multifaith settings for spiritual care, 13, 30
Muslim. *See* Islam

narrative therapy, 85
National Association of Evangelicals, 27
National Guard, 2, 37, 52. *See also* military
neutralizing, 64, 80
non-anxious presence, 74
normalization of discriminatory behavior, 245–54

ordination, 9, 49
organizations: behavior of, 194; change within, 208–10; culture of, 204, 251; mechanics of, 247–50; navigating, 8; purpose of, 203; transformation of, 253–55. *See also* empathy: in organizations; resilience: within organizations

paradigms of spiritual care, 177–81
pastoral care, 9–13, 22, 38, 178–81, 194
pastoral theology, 12, 146, 195, 261
patriarchy, 173, 175–76, 184, 240, 299n6. *See also* gender; sexism; womanism
person-centered therapy, 85
pluralism, 61, 63–65
police and fire chaplaincy, 29, 43–44; and FBI, 43; International Conference of Police Chaplains, 29
ports, 23, 24, 45; and International Transport Workers' Federation, 46; Young Men's Church and Missionary Society, 24
positive regard. *See* unconditional positive regard

post-traumatic stress disorder (PTSD), 162–64, 166–67
power: abuse of, in relationships, 174–77; agential and receptive, 142–43, 294n15, 308n11; dynamics in relationships, 206; in organizations, 226–27, 234; in societal structures, 244–46; systemic power dynamics in spiritual caregiving, 180
presence, 68–77
prison, 10, 23, 38; American Correctional Chaplains Association, 23; chaplaincy in non–federal government correctional facilities, 40
professional development for chaplains, 260, 263
prophetic role of chaplaincy. *See* chaplains
psychache, 159
psychology, 11, 85
psycho-spiritual distress, 101
psychotherapy, 103, 261
PTSD. *See* post-traumatic stress disorder

race, 181–82. *See also* racism
racism: and antibias practice, 261, 307n44; in culture of "isms," 64, 193–94 ; as "dis-ease" (*tzaraat*), 119; as experienced by careseekers, 6–7, 10–11, 173, 176–77; in organizations, 198, 205, 226, 239–56; and racial justice, 3; and religious abuse of power, 131; systemic, 146, 156, 176–77, 221, 300n12; unconscious, 308n10; and white supremacy culture, 220, 300n11, 307n44
reflection, 13, 98–107
reflective listening, 73–77
reflexivity, 97, 148–50, 156, 184, 308n8
relationality, 130
religion: careseekers with non-religious backgrounds, 33-34, 61; defined, 95, 293n14; rates of affiliation, 14, 31, 202, 264–66; serving religious

minorities, 183; "spiritual but not religious," 42, 61, 122, 124, 265
Religious Freedom Restoration Act of 1993, 39, 40, 43
religious literacy, 5
religious and spiritual coping, 81, 173
religious struggle, 159, 185
research on chaplaincy, 25, 42, 259, 261; and research literacy, 150
resilience, 202, 216; within organizations, 206, 216–17
rituals, 9, 62; addressing community tension, 111–14, 122–24; contexts of, 114–16; defined, 124; functions of, 116–17; development of 117–22. *See also* death and dying

schools, chaplaincy in, 66–89, 111–14, 194, 290n1
self-awareness, 73
self-care, spiritual, 135, 139
self-differentiation, spiritual, 135, 138–45, 149; Crucible Differentiation Scale, 293n6
self-emptying, 69
self-harm, 83
self-psychology, 85
sexism: in cultural of "isms," 64, 193; as "dis-ease" (*tzaraat*), 119; in educational settings, 111–14; and interpersonal violence, 197–200; in organizations, 239–41, 250; systemic, 131, 145–48, 176–77, 226; unconscious, 308n10. *See also* gender; patriarchy; womanism
sexual abuse, 161–68, 290n1
sexual orientation, 54, 131, 153, 162, 166, 299n6
skills: accessing and influencing worldview, 92, 105; adapting, 259; advocating, 86; attuning, 73; aligning behavior and values, 92; clarifying values, 92; constructing identity, 92; consulting, 104, 107; developing a plan of care, 83; developing

resonance, 73; developing self-awareness, 73; differentiating oneself, 264; empathizing, 7, 69, 123, 145–47, 156, 166–67, 179, 183; engaging in interpathy, 80; enhancing agency, 92, 123; facilitating groups, 86, 158; grounding, 74; intersectional analysis, 92, 103, 172; navigating organizations, 8; normalizing, 77, 85; practicing and facilitating reflexivity, 97, 148–50, 156, 184; practicing non-anxious presence, 74; providing spiritual first aid, 84; providing unconditional positive regard, 69, 167, 298n51; reflecting, 13, 97–107; reflective listening, 73–77; self-emptying, 69; validating, 77
social construction, 140
social justice, 129–31, 137, 147, 172–77, 182–88; socially just spiritual care, 137
social justice therapies, 85
social movements, 14; Occupy Wall Street, 28
somatic and arts-based modalities, 85
somatic therapy, 167
spiritual assessment, 103, 117, 123, 151, 155–56, 162, 166; Spiritual Assessment and Intervention Model (Spiritual AIM), 150–51
spiritual care: defined, 135; practice of, 85. *See also specific perspectives and therapies*
spiritual counseling, 85–86
spiritual distress, 78, 85
spiritual integration, 137–42
spirituality, 195; as area of expertise for chaplains, 120; chaplains as representatives of, 212; cultural assumptions about, 102, 106; impact on health and resilience, 202, 216; in institutions, 246; and intersectional theory, 104; and meaning making, 95; and pain, 253; socially transformative spirituality, 244; as source for

spirituality (*cont.*)
careseeker reflection, 92, 107; sources of, 82; and spiritual assessment, 150; and "spiritual first aid," 84; and suicide, 160
spiritual practices, 137
spiritual trust, 130, 136–38, 144, 160
Society of Pastoral Theology, 261
substance abuse. *See* addiction
suffering, 63, 291n10
suicide, 157–61, 168; Columbia-Suicide Severity Rating Scale, 158
supervision in professional practice, 162
symbols, 228
systems theory, 12

training, 9, 33. *See also* CPE; education of chaplains
transportation chaplaincy, 46
trauma, 291nn5–9, 292n1 (chap. 6); collective trauma, 291n6; and liminality, 114; religious trauma, 199; and spiritual counseling, 85; in theological education, 13; trauma-informed spiritual care, 84, 167; vicarious trauma, 167. *See also* post-traumatic stress disorder

unconditional positive regard, 69, 167, 298n51

values, clarifying, 92
Veterans Affairs, 38, 49. *See also* military
veterinary chaplaincy, 14
vocation, 85

war, 304n11. *See also* military
womanism, 146, 182. *See also* gender; patriarchy; sexism
workplace chaplaincy, 26, 46–47; Corporate Chaplains of America, 27; Marketplace Chaplains, 27
worldview, accessing and influencing, 92, 105

CHAPLAINCY
Innovation Lab

RESOURCES FOR CHAPLAINS AND SPIRITUAL CARE PROVIDERS

The Chaplaincy Innovation Lab brings together educators, chaplains, and spiritual care providers to learn, grow, and nurture ourselves and the communities we serve. All are welcome to access the research-driven teaching and learning resources at ChaplaincyInnovation.org.

Case studies: Four interactive case studies designed for use with this book are available for educators and students. These cover topics such as meaning making, navigating institutions, and more. Visit https://chaplaincyinnovation.org /training-credentials/case-studies.

Sample syllabi: Educators may review and draw from these syllabi for their own courses. Eight syllabi specifically constructed to innovate spiritual care education are also available.

Resources for chaplains of color: A series of resources is available for chaplains of color, including:

- An online reader
- A working paper on the history and present state of
  spiritual care providers of color
- A recorded lecture series
- Information on conversation circles as a model of professional support

Perspectives from employers: What do chaplaincy employers look for in successful applicants? Watch interviews with leaders in six key spiritual care sectors to find out.

Free ebooks: These include an introduction to clinical pastoral education and a beginner's guide to spiritual care.

Webinars: These include panels on course-level innovation, case studies, and employers' perspectives on hiring new chaplains. They can be used in the classroom, for internal institutional education, and more.

Field guide: The lab's *Field Guide for Aspiring Chaplains* offers prospective chaplains, whether students, individuals seeking a second career, or others, an informal overview of the basics of spiritual care.

Access these resources and more at https://chaplaincyinnovation.org/resources /backpack.

Made in the USA
Las Vegas, NV
30 November 2022

60785306R00194